Unmaking the Public University

Unmaking the
Public University

*The Forty-Year Assault
on the Middle Class*

Christopher Newfield

Harvard University Press

Cambridge, Massachusetts

London, England

2008

Library of Congress Cataloging-in-Publication Data

Newfield, Christopher.
Unmaking the public university : the forty-year assault
on the middle class / Christopher Newfield.
p.   cm.
Includes bibliographical references and index.
ISBN-13: 978-0-674-02817-3 (alk. paper)
1. Public universities and colleges—United States.   2. Middle class—United States.
3. Social mobility—United States.   I. Title.
LB2328.62.U6N49   2008
378'.050973—dc22   2007038305

To the many who have built—and fought for—
public higher education

Contents

Unmaking the Public University

Introduction

During the early 1990s, California's state government decided to solve its revenue shortfalls with program cuts, and as a result the state's four-year public universities lost about a fifth of their per-student public support in the space of three years. At the same time, the state's high-tech, white-collar industrial base—led by military aerospace—was looking as though it would never again be big enough to support California's famously affluent middle class. The Republican governor had angered his suburban supporters by raising taxes but had learned to use racial wedge issues to drive them back his way. As his campaigns against immigration and affirmative action heated up, and the economy faltered, the classic middle-class institution, the public university, took its biggest budget hits since the Great Depression. In the midst of what seemed to many like general institutional decline, University of California (UC) students on two campuses sought more resources for their Chicano Studies departments by staging hunger strikes.

The size of these protests was minute by comparison to the state's problems and to the scale of its everyday politics. The hunger strikers—at UC Los Angeles (UCLA) in 1993 and at UC Santa Barbara (UCSB) in 1994—were small in number, attracted little media attention, and had goals that most non-Latino students did not try to understand. From the outside the hunger strikes could be dismissed as typical examples of ethnic separatism fueled by political correctness, which was the kind of activity that conservatives said led to politicized campuses, biased classrooms, reduced learning, and the depreciation of a unified American culture rooted in European civilization. Even sympathizers doubted that the strikers had picked the best issue, or that their issue—more Chicano Studies faculty, a PhD program—merited a life-threatening strategy normally provoked by otherwise unopposable state oppression. In the

1

spring of 1994, the campaign for Proposition 187 was doing very well, and given that this proposition sought to deny public education to undocumented immigrants, some felt that the Chicano Studies department growth plan was a distraction from the larger battle. At UCSB the persistent small encampment in front of the administration building seemed too small to bother to remove, a remnant of an earlier time that any minute would fade away.

The truth was rather different. Many or most of the strike supporters were first-generation college students, themselves immigrants or the children of immigrants. They had worked to get into a public research university, and though their families were often from the factories and the fields—perhaps *because* their families were from there—these students were demanding resources for more academic research. Though the strike supporters were part of a generation that supposedly went to college only so they could earn more money, they wanted to help change the university to fit better with public need. The need they identified was for more research into cultural and social issues—for cultural, social, political, and economic knowledge that would not overlook or be biased against Latino communities.[1]

These small protests insisted on three principles that had been central to the rise of the public university as a dynamic institution in U.S. society. The first of these was a broad social egalitarianism, here expressed by the idea that Latino culture and social life should receive the same top level of study and training—to master's and doctoral degrees—that was available for the study of British or Spanish culture. The second was a new kind of meritocracy, in which accurate knowledge was compatible with, and often dependent on, direct action on institutions that created and applied knowledge. The third was that educational needs should dictate budgets and not the other way around—that educational development should not be determined by the long series of economic crises that the state's leaders had managed to produce. By the 1990s, these three principles were no longer central enough to university culture to insure a pre-strike resolution.

The term "middle class" in this book's subtitle is shorthand for "college-educated": as I explain in the chapters to come, it applies regardless of what social class the student comes from, or returns to. The middle class whose rollback is my subject is composed of Chicano hunger strikers, the children of blue-collar and service workers, of low-income shopkeepers—the full range of socioeconomic positions and family incomes who have had contact with higher education because of the public university system that was built throughout the twentieth century.

I do not use the term "middle class" in this broad way to support the American myth that the whole society is middle class. To the contrary, the middle class is being reduced in size, and is losing its non–college-educated members to stagnating or declining wages. I use "middle class" to refer to the numerical majority of the population whose contact with college was interwoven with the mainstream and politically powerful ideal that this majority was to have interesting work, economic security, and the ability to lead satisfying and insightful lives in which personal and collective social development advanced side by side. In common usage, "middle class" has been a metaphor for the white suburbs, but there has long been a deeper vision for which "middle class" served as the respectable, Protestant, politically palatable face. This vision was of a full political, economic, and cultural capability that would be in reach of more or less everyone through higher education and related public services.

This underlying vision has been under assault since the 1970s. The assault began in earnest just as the American middle class was starting to become multiracial, and as public universities were moving with increasing speed toward meaningful racial integration. This book tells the story of the assault, of its diverse strategies, and of the larger vision that the assault tried and yet finally failed to discredit.

American higher education is highly stratified: the wealthiest private universities can spend ten times as much per student as can a four-year public university. I discuss this inequality in some detail, but in the context of a distinctive type of public university that tried to overcome this stratification within the limits of the American social system. That type has been the public research university. In spite of its frequent ambivalence about inclusion, it sought to combine nearly universal access with the highest quality in teaching and research, and saw access and quality as not only compatible but, in a profound way, as mutually reinforcing. To achieve access in which the daughters of the artichoke fields and the sons of the auto body shops would study with Pulitzer-prize winners, these research universities had to become university systems and then move each of their campuses toward the synthesis of access and quality that had been at least provisionally achieved at their oldest flagships.

This vision was the product of the economic "golden age" that followed the global chaos and destruction of the Great Depression and World War II.

4   Introduction

It was defined by massive public works and publicly subsidized industrial development in North America, Japan, and Europe. It was propelled by widespread social activism and the various civil rights movements that sought universal access to its ideals of social development. This notion of development could not be reduced to growth or increased living standards, but was to be defined by a people in the active process of shaping their desires, dreams, interests, interpersonal relations, and collective goals. This vision of publicly funded social development resulted in the creation of the first mass middle class in the United States—a middle class that included blue-collar production workers, unionized service workers, public-sector employees, and members of construction trades, to name just a few of the groups that were enjoying the most egalitarian access to prosperity in recorded history.

In the economically more difficult decades that followed—the period that begins in the late 1970s and that I cover in this book—the working-class portions of the mass middle class suffered the first wave of deindustrialization. Their white-collar cousins did little to help them, and to the contrary used the college degree as a dividing line between those who would succeed in the new postindustrial economy and those who, lacking the appropriate college credentials, would and should fail.

Readers with a knowledge of history will point out that this is what the middle class always does to the working class. It uses the vast numbers of working people for political leverage against hostile elites, and yet as soon as it can bond with those elites, it dumps the working class. In the 1980s the college-educated middle class in the United States betrayed the social majority just as its predecessors had, to take one example, after the creation of the Second Republic in France in 1848, when the bourgeoisie turned against the national workshops and workers' movements that had made the new republic possible. Drawing class boundaries did not work this time around. In the 1990s and the first decade of the 2000s, large-scale layoffs spread from the blue-collar workforce to become routine among white-collar staffers and managers.

This trajectory shows why the public university has such great historical importance. The public university was the institution where blue- and white-collar, children of both workers and managers, citizens of every racial background were being invited into a unified majority. As these normally opposed classes came together, they might outnumber and outthink traditional elites. In so doing, they could take over the leadership of the society. Of course, this creation of a functional middle-and-working-class majority never quite happened. But it was a future repeatedly foretold and imagined, analyzed, and achieved here and there. Throughout this process, the public university was this new majority's principal workshop. No less importantly, the specter of this multiracial, worker-inclusive majority—formed not exclusively but influentially through higher education—motivated twenty-five years of conservative attacks on the university and its emerging, inclusive, hybrid middle class.

In the 1980s it seemed to many that economic decline would be limited to the blue-collar employees in the economic sectors like steel that were most vulnerable to international price competition. By the year 2000 this decline had spread to include the majority of the population: some estimates suggested that as much as four-fifths of the overall workforce had seen no increase in real wages since the late 1970s. One study found that between 1966 and 2001, "only the top 10 percent of the income distribution enjoyed [income growth] equal to or above the average rate of economy wide productivity growth." Although the United States was supposed to be a full-fledged "knowledge economy," it was increasingly "winner-take-all."[2] Even college-graduate incomes were starting to stagnate, and real income increases went to a tiny minority: "the top one-tenth of one percent of the income distribution earned as much of the real 1997–2001 gain in wage and salary income as the bottom 50 percent."[3] It has turned out that the increased emphasis on college education has coincided with the decline of middle-class as well as of blue-collar, working-class fortunes.

Most observers have been reluctant to blame middle-class economic stagnation on U.S. economic policy: they point to irreversible changes in the global economy and note that no American government has explicitly sought to lower middle-class living standards. But given the complexity of modern economies, no government would need to attack the middle class openly to downgrade and reduce it. More roundabout methods would work just as well—better, in fact, since they arouse less opposition. In this book, I argue that this is precisely what has happened. To oversimplify somewhat, conservative elites who had been threatened by the postwar rise of the college-educated economic majority have put that majority back in its place. Their roundabout weapon has been the culture wars on higher education in general, and on progressive cultural trends in the public universities that create and enfranchise the mass middle class.

In *Unmaking the Public University*, I show that the culture wars have co-incided with the majority's economic decline for the simple reason that these wars propelled the decline by reducing the public importance and economic claims of the American university and its graduates. While most commentators have seen the culture wars as a distraction from economics, I show that the culture wars were economic wars. They sought to reduce the economic claims of their target group—the growing college-educated majority—by discrediting the cultural framework that had been empowering that group. This target group was to provide the postindustrial economy and its descendant, the "New Economy," with the knowledge workers on which its productivity and adaptability depended. The culture wars discredited the cultural conditions of the political and economic ascent of these college-educated, middle-class workers. The culture-war strategy was a kind of intellectual neutron bomb, eroding the social and cultural foundations of a growing, politically powerful, economically entitled, and racially diversifying middle class, while leaving its technical capacities intact.

The early material in the present volume covers the period in which commentators were describing the country's shift from an industrial to a postindustrial economy, and it overlaps in time with the end of my previous volume on higher education, *Ivy and Industry*. That book described the meanings of the university to industrial society and traced a hundred years of efforts to identify the value of cultural knowledge—incarnated in various forms of humanism—in light of the superior authority of technological and managerial thinking. The focus of that volume was the set of *cultural capabilities* that the university instilled in the generations that it sent off into the world. One pivotal form of cultural capability in the industrial economy was the combination of procedures and sensibilities we call professionalism, which I analyzed as a type of craft labor that enabled both relative independence and large-scale organization. It is hard to overestimate the economic value of the kinds of professional and intellectual independence that came out of universities and that could maintain individual agency even in large organizations in conjunction with similar capabilities among blue-collar workers. This independence underwrote the many waves of knowledge economies that swept the United States and Europe throughout the twentieth century. Professional labor also managed to protect itself with good salaries, working conditions, benefits, and security that were not generally available to blue-collar workers, and these maintained the white-collar belief that capitalism could fulfill and develop at least some of its workers. The economic importance of professional craft labor also elevated the institution that created and groomed this labor—the university. *Ivy and Industry* explored the economic as well as the cultural frameworks that this university-made labor produced.

That story ended in the early 1980s, as the forces shaping today's university were gathering strength. Economic development—service to market share, profits, and growth—was looming larger in university decision making, and I discussed several ways in which the humanities fields lost confidence in the university mission they sponsored, most particularly in one major goal of undergraduate humanities instruction: to instill a capacity for individual agency that allowed for self-governed *human* development even within complex institutions. Such development went well beyond growth and technological improvement, involved active and collaborative processes of self-definition, and thus needed its own goals and standards. Yet these were either weakly advocated or eclipsed by simpler economic goals. The outcome was something like an agency crisis, a combination of a weak individualism and a weak socialization that made it harder to articulate objectives, desires, and activities other than those that adapted to direct economic pressures.

When the first long wave of thinking about postindustrial society arose in the 1950s and 1960s in the writings of economists and sociologists like David Riesman, Richard Nelson, Kenneth Arrow, Fritz Machlup, Clark Kerr, Gary Becker, John Kenneth Galbraith, Daniel Bell, and William Whyte, it drew on the period's concerns about the excessive other-directedness and conformity of the new "organization man." Partly in response to this, and partly floated by the great expectations for society in the period, the writers of the 1960s and early 1970s took for granted the persistence of majoritarian economics and the value of noneconomic forms of human development. These closely related ideas pervaded the culture of the time. California governor Edmund "Pat" Brown, in his 1963 inaugural address, declared, "Through the turmoil of change, and sometimes chaos, Californians have pressed on toward the good society—not for the few, not for the many, but for all." He continued, "We are here to prove that a civilization which can create a machine to fulfill a job can create a job to fulfill a man."[4] This sort of egalitarian humanism was common to the Keynesian growth policies that dominated American policy making in the period: economic development led to human development, and the latter should be available to everyone. Though the women's and civil rights movements were needed to provide correct definitions of "everyone," capitalist development was viewed as a means to a range of higher ends.

The research university's leaders had also combined economic and noneconomic goals, and having completed an analysis of the university's pre-1970 history, I asked at the end of *Ivy and Industry* whether in the post-1970s period the concept of human development would be able to compete with and influence economic development. Would the university's public mission remain distinct from, even as it contributed to, the private sector's pursuit of growth and profit, not to mention product monopolies and global dominance?

On the surface, it seemed that the university and its graduates were set to inherit the earth. After all, the term "postindustrial" and its successor the "New Economy" had no meaning outside of the knowledge economy. The contemporary period was an era in which, as Daniel Bell wrote, "information and knowledge" would replace the industrial economy's dependence on "capital and labor" as the "major structural features" and sources of value.[5] Services would now be more important than manufacturing, and knowledge would be the crucial source of new value and competitive success. Technological innovation would be the central driver of prosperity and change, and it would have to be rapid and continuous. Enormous amounts of financial capital were required, and capital markets were becoming increasingly sophisticated partners in creating the new products and new industries that technology made possible.

In this schema, information, technology, and financial capital depended in the end on human capital. The formation of the cutting-edge workforce of today and tomorrow was a matter of survival in a global economy. Practical education was the most—and for some, the only—valuable government-funded program. This education had to be technical, adaptable, and, perhaps most important, responsive to market pressures rather than to abstract intellectual goals. In a market context, professional standards could damage the most adaptive and functional forms of education just as government bureaucracy had, in this view, damaged the economy. Though liberals like Robert Reich wanted an orderly transition to the New Economy with many social supports, and conservatives like Gary Becker wanted faster transitions with no supports, nearly all agreed that the replacement of an industrial economy with a knowledge economy made intense and continuous education of central importance, and that it could not be held back by regulations, whether from legislators, administrators, or faculty, that delayed adaptation to the new conditions. The truth of this transition to a postindustrial economy and society seemed confirmed by the Clinton years, when slow growth in productivity and gross domestic product finally gave way to a boom based on information technology, bio-medicine, the Internet, advanced technical knowledge, and, it was said, the world's most savvy and risk-loving capital markets.

If the university's social importance grew through the 1980s and 1990s, it was largely as a postindustrial institution. It was relatively poor in financial capital but rich in human and knowledge capital. It created the new technology and the technocratic workforce to run and continuously reinvent the New Economy. It produced flexible, adaptable, innovative workers who could thrive in a rapidly changing market economy by constantly upgrading their skills and creating the new value that would give their companies the indispensable competitive edge. Students were to focus on developing the knowledge base for tomorrow's jobs. If they were constantly having to pay more and more for their education, this was not necessarily bad: they were buying a private good that would arm them to create the higher incomes for themselves that would also benefit society as a whole. Their rising incomes would allow them to repay their rising tuition.

And yet this vision of the university as a privatizable knowledge factory coincided with a decline in the vision of broadened access and egalitarian development that I tracked in *Ivy and Industry*. Even those who supported the "market-smart" and industry-friendly university recognized that the public university's democratizing mission was being eclipsed by financial concerns.[6] Other signs of change appeared. The university's administrators and much of its faculty became closer to industry. More research funding came from industry in leading-edge science and engineering fields. Public funding was sharply reduced during the downturns of the early 1990s and early 2000s, causing sharp tuition increases and intensified private fund-raising. Public universities were influenced by changing business practices, including the cash-flow evaluation of individual academic units and the outsourcing of many non-core services such as student dining, which had some striking effects, including the transformation of most student centers into midprice shopping malls. In general, universities became more important elements in various industries' attempts to control market share, sometimes through product tie-in agreements, and more centrally through efforts to own and market their employees' intellectual property to outside firms. Major new initiatives at public universities—building construction, laboratory facilities—were increasingly dependent on private funds. These flagship projects raised the university's prestige but could also cost it dearly: a $50 million research sponsorship over five years might require an equal amount from the university to build new facilities and hire new personnel. Administrators at times had to rob Peter's teaching budget to cover Paul's new research institute while hoping Mary would get a similar gift to stem the deficit later on. Resources were more likely to flow toward fields that were close enough to the market to provide a possible return on investment; funding for core functions and for their infrastructure was sometimes shorted, so that it became more common for older teaching buildings to look like they belonged on the other side of an iron curtain from the new laboratory center. This dependence on private funding fed the tendency to judge higher education less by its overall contribution to all the forms of development—personal, cultural, social, and economic—than by its ability to deliver new technology and a plug-in workforce to regional businesses.

An internally coherent logic drove this vision: since the New University would be judged by its economic contribution, and since private enterprise drove the creation of economic value, there was no reason not to privatize the university's core functions—that is, make them more responsive to market forces and business methods.

And yet questions persisted: What of the public university's traditional and distinctive mission of broad cultural and human development? What about research on fundamental scientific questions with no visible commercial potential? What about the pursuit of complex sociocultural knowledge to help a polarized world? The issue could be posed subtly, in the language of conference addresses to educational and industry leaders that expressed concern about the vagueness of the modern university's mission, or more starkly, as by the cardiologist Stanton A. Glantz when he told *Inside Higher Ed*, "The university is about the seeking and discovery of truth—and the protections of academic freedom are to protect that process. Academic freedom isn't about money. It's about free speech and free thought."[7] However it was expressed, the point remained that the university, though open to and serving a capitalist society, had to preserve methods and goals that distinguished it from society—at least from its financial measures and motives. And yet these distinctive university goals were harder and harder to define.

This brings us back to this book's core question: why would the university and its graduates, the supposed leaders of the knowledge society, have less cultural and economic latitude—to say nothing of influence—than they had had in the "industrial" society prior to 1980? My answer, which I lay out in the following pages, centers on the success of the Right in the culture wars. The Right's culture warriors did not openly attack the economic position of the middle class, but they did attack the university. In doing so, they created the conditions for repeated budget cuts to the core middle-class institution. More fundamentally, they discredited the *cultural* conditions of mass-middle-class development, downsized the influence of its leading institution, the university, and reduced the social and political impacts of knowledge workers overall.

This book is intended as an intellectual and institutional history, and it can be read sequentially. I include quite a bit of detailed argumentation about the topics I cover, since they have become distorted in the world of assertion, polemic, and spin that marks so much public debate on controversial topics. Readers are also invited to explore topics of special interest in greater depth, and I group chapters thematically to facilitate that kind of reading.

Part I of the book is called "The Meaning of a Majoritarian Society." It describes the vision of a knowledge society that presumed both general development and majority rule. I identify the threats that the college-educated middle class, blue- and white-collar alike, appeared to pose to traditional forms of economic and cultural governance. This period is often associated with 1960s forms of antiauthoritarianism and the success of the civil rights movement. Here I stress the related arrival of mass mainstream divergence from traditional business values among that half of the country's younger people that were at least starting college. The appearance of a majority that was economically and intellectually prepared to govern the whole society gave rise to the counterreaction of the "culture warriors." This term, which I always use to refer to the members of the conservative offensive against new academic and social forces, denotes a coalition on the American Right that linked economic and social conservatives, all of whom had reasons to sever knowledge workers from the cultural conditions that gave them authority and prominence.

That story of the counterrevolution begins in Part II, "Inventing PC: The War on Equality." This section analyzes the real meaning of the attacks on "political correctness." The culture wars took place through a range of issues—the "canon wars" about how much to enlarge the "great books" backbone of literary curricula, "politics" in the human sciences, and the place of feminist and lesbian and gay studies. But race relations emerged as the consistent setting for attacks on a central element of university-related "declarations of independence"—the possibility of a functional equality among traditionally stratified racial groups. I chronicle the ways conservatives defined race-conscious social policies as incompatible with market forces, democracy, political order, affirmative action, and economic efficiency. The racial politics of the Clinton administration overlap with the debates about racial policies in the university, and I show how culture warriors persuaded many mainstream liberals that economic success now depended on replacing (and not combining) racial equity with enlightened business practices. Professional standards became a major political football in the same period, and the culture wars all but destroyed the idea that these standards were fully compatible with racial equality. Finally, I show how "diversity" blocked the old hope that a multiracial college-educated population would avoid the stratification of older models. As a result, racial resegregation and economic stratification now enjoy a renewed sanction as obstacles to the broad-based social development that had been evolving during the postwar period of optimistic expansion.

Part III, "Market Substitutes for General Development," focuses directly on the economic dimension of the culture wars. I examine the commercialized or "corporate" university and the trend that has come to be called privatization. One chapter focuses on the withdrawal of public money from higher education on the grounds that it can be replaced by private money: I show that this view is wrong. Other chapters describe the expanded role of university-industry partnerships and of technology transfer and indicate that the culture wars distorted and curtailed the impact of technological fields in ways that their practitioners did not intend and did not sufficiently recognize. As a result of the pressure to find private funding sources for knowledge creation and distribution, public universities became more interested in donor priorities, financial interests loomed larger over academic planning, and relations between the university and the commercial world became more detached from social interests. The response of many faculties has been counterproductive, and I look at the pivotal humanities discipline of English literature as a case in point.

I also show in Part III how privatization has distorted the university's accounts, thus underestimating the contribution of cultural fields to the university and of the university to society. The culture wars twisted the framework through which we understood the public university's not-for-profit outputs to the nation and the world. Though most university supporters insisted that the university be allowed to engage in self-directed *non*commercial behavior, they increasingly kept the books as though basic research would lead to commercial benefits. They also kept the books incorrectly, which resulted in disfavoring the humanities and social sciences while obscuring the little-known fact that externally funded scientific and technological research requires subsidy from internal funds that are generated in large part by teaching enrollments in the human sciences. The misuse of market standards made it more difficult for the university to pursue its distinctive developmental missions.

Culture war and recovery are the subjects of Part IV, "The New War—and After." I focus on the attacks in the early 2000s on academic knowledge and personnel in the concocted debates about campuses' political bias. I show how this campaign has rested on poor data poorly interpreted by its gatherers, and that the concern about a subversive faculty was unfounded. Although by 2007 media interest in the campaign was beginning to fade, its mission had already been accomplished. The cultural framework of the rising middle and knowledge classes—including sociocultural equality, general development, professional independence, and not-for-profit knowledge creation—was assumed by much of the public to be intrusive, wishful, manipulative, and economically untenable.

The final chapter suggests possible modes of recovery, which depend on creating a new framework for higher education's nonmarket purposes. My concern is to identify the conditions that would allow the university to concretize its missions of full social inclusion, general development, cultural equality, and majoritarian economics. These missions must not only often operate independently of market signals, they also depend on the university acting like a noncapitalist domain, and imagining postcapitalist alternatives that would support human development more fully than has the current system in its period of relentless narrowing. The university's missions have been curtailed by the culture wars. A more equitable and effective future awaits us when these wars are done.

This book project is motivated by a quarter century spent in several quite different research universities, first as a graduate student and then as a faculty member of different ranks. My analysis of the university is a running attempt to understand the combination of centrality and fragility in the university's contribution to society. In this book I tell a tale that at times seems like a traditional American jeremiad of decline from a more noble and imaginative past. As in the earliest jeremiads, that past was perhaps more envisioned than actual, and more a tendency than a tradition. But the vision of general social development animated much of what was best about recent American history, from its unstoppable social movements to its superb academic research. This vision underlay the core justification for American wealth: that wealth would lead to a progress that would not sacrifice the goals and purposes of the whole society. This vision of universal benefit has been pushed aside. The absence of this vision has made the United States far less meaningful to the world, and far more dangerous.

The book is also motivated by my concern about the country's intellectual and imaginative decline. By the early 2000s, the American majority seemed to have lost its vision of a society devoted to the development and happiness of its members. Judging from media discourse, we had come to believe in economic growth and little else, more money and little else. Other aims, particularly coming from other cultures and countries, seemed increasingly mysterious and even threatening to us. Did we still have the cultural capability to understand, interact, and respond positively to a world of countless motives, one where sheer growth was no longer an environmental option? At the moment when we needed these capacities more than ever, public discourse had been polarized and dumbed down, both simplified and falsified, and we became accustomed to thinking about our affairs in terms that resembled propaganda: we thought about social policy for years in terms of "welfare queens" and about cultural difference through television features called "Hip-Hop: Art or Poison?" and we were being asked by some to think of foreign policy through the lens of "Islamofascism." The comfortable classes showed habituation, resentment, an obsession with maximum financial returns, and a fatalism that discouraged independent thinkers from finding and applying new models.

The university's cultural missions have declined at the same time as leaders in politics, economics, and the media have lost much of their capacity to understand the world in noneconomic terms, to understand cultural divergence as its own kind of enlightenment and as in any case a fact that will never submit to political or economic coercion. The elite private universities that supply most of the top leadership in the United States are more insulated from the larger society than they were in the days when civil rights and other social movements took place on their campuses, and the same tendency is apparent in the public university. The university's postwar insight and impact depended on full interaction with its base, which came to include, little-by-little, the country's multiracial working classes. This collaboration raised the prospect of a middle class that would rewrite the rules of capitalism in collaboration with the working class, and on the basis of college knowledge. The culture wars successfully severed the public university from this broader base, curtailing the social impact of both, and encouraging the middle class to replay its familiar historical role of abandoning noncollege working people to the economy's "new rules" in the hopes of saving itself. Although the top fraction of the professional and managerial classes have been doing very well, the abandonment of egalitarian and democratic impulses has destabilized U.S. culture, downgraded the mass middle class, and disoriented many people who thought the country stood—or at least could stand—for inclusive and inspiring progress.

This book is written for everyone who is still working on turning both cultural and scientific knowledge toward that end. It is for my colleagues past and present, for faculty and staff, for college and university students, for anyone who believes as I always do in the centrality of freedom of thought, the pleasure of discovery, the progress that is always part of knowledge, the intuition that things can be better than they are right now—that they must be better, and must be so for a far larger percentage of the population both at home and abroad. This book is for parents and students, teachers, administrators, and politicians who wrongly assume that it is best to ignore the effects of the cultural wars and get on with the job of market adaptation. The book says to them that society's well-being—with the exception of a small layer at the very top— lies in the opposite direction, with supporting the cultural foundations of general development as much as supporting its technological and economic foundations. Our ability to move the world forward depends on our cultural capacity. The way forward, I show here, starts with resubmitting the economy to the majoritarian cultural visions that this economy must one day serve again. This restoration will be far more likely if the public university can recover its base and reinvent its mission.

— I —

The Meaning of a
Majoritarian Society

— 1 —

The Three Crises and the
Mass Middle Class

By 2005 or so, it had become impossible to ignore the sense of crisis that hung over the American college and university. It had become hard to see higher education in terms other than crisis, and harder to capture its situation in other than crisis terms. Campuses had become habituated to worried talk about money, and the less money they had, the more they talked about it. Financial management and fund-raising had come to dominate the daily lives of academic administrators who used to spend more time on program development. Confirming the sense of crisis, the first-draft report of the Secretary of Education's Commission on the Future of Higher Education said, "Our year-long examination of the challenges facing higher education has brought us to the uneasy conclusion that the sector's past attainments have led it to unseemly complacency about the future."[1] There was in fact no complacency on campus, only pervasive concern.

The Eclipse of Development

Humanities faculties were particularly afflicted, and carried a list of problems in their heads. We now work in corporate universities, they said, not liberal arts ones. Science was for sale to the highest bidder, while humanities fields stayed poor for lack of something to sell. Enrollment in the liberal arts had never recovered from earlier drops, they knew, and they watched administrators make their colleges more like vocational schools. Academic departments were treated as cost centers, and winning sports coaches could make ten times the salaries of Nobel-prize winners. Even the term "liberal arts" was now a problem, since it was made up of two words, "liberal" and "arts," each of which was suspect in its own right.

Academia's labor policies deserved special mention. Academia had long used its educational status to pay non-star employees modest wages. Colleges and universities had generally opposed unionization, as the long campaigns against graduate-student unions attest. The university had increasingly differentiated salary scales for different faculty specialties, while a bidding system for star faculty increased salary spreads within fields.[2] As public funds were cut and costs continued to rise faster than the inflation rate, universities of all kinds increasingly used two-tiered employment systems in which the status, salaries, and working conditions of tenure-track faculty were of a different order than those of temporary instructors. Since 1970, the proportion of temporary instructors—most of whom were "permatemps" who worked for long periods on short-term contracts—to that of full-time instructors had doubled. In literary and cultural study, more than half of undergraduate instruction nationally was delivered by "temporary" instructors by the year 2000.[3] The university generally followed prevailing business methods toward reducing labor costs and did not take a leadership position on the principle of good work for all.

Many scholars noted that in recent decades humanistic knowledge had had to contend with a resurgent commercialism in every walk of American life. American commercialism was of course as old as America itself, and yet in the 1990s and its "New Economy," this commercialism seemed to reach into new areas of public and private life. The recession of the early 1990s intensified awareness of the university's dependence on public funds. The private-sector boom of the later 1990s encouraged the university to look to business for its growth opportunities. The boom also enhanced the prestige of business prescriptions for university ills, offered a stock-market cure for endowment anxieties, and encouraged everyone to see knowledge entrepreneurs as the key to future prosperity.

In the midst of powerful business solutions to educational problems, what role could the humanities play? As the overall culture got more commercial with every passing year, as the arts of interpretation seemed overwhelmed by broadcast media, as reading faded before viewing, as college-educated people seemed eager to give up their political power and their college administrations to market forces, in what areas could the humanities disciplines make deep and yet visible contributions?

One obvious area was that of "human enhancement," though that had become once again the province of the biosciences, including those associated with nanotechnology.[4] This was a transhumanist twist on a long-standing area of enormous interest we could call "human development," a field that covered the social, cultural, intellectual, and psychological factors that are required for any forward movement of society. We can think of human development as a central though largely undiscussed outcome of the liberal arts. Music, dance, theater, literature, sculpture, film, and other disciplines normally operated on two different levels. They produced enhanced, even Dionysian, states of cognitive capability that overcame at least for a time the limits of our ordinary condition. They allowed the imagination of a higher permanent state for both individual and humanity as a whole, one that would be more equitable, more peaceful, much smarter, and on a daily basis more ambitious and less defensive. These disciplines also operated on a second level: they produced *cultural knowledge* about the psychological, interpersonal, and cultural capabilities that allowed society to evolve. If the arts and letters produced states of pleasurable awareness that made human development seem possible and meaningful, they also produced literal forms of knowledge that could join the social and natural sciences in building the new architectures on which would rest new and better social worlds.

The postcolonial period intensified debates for and against development, which many analysts correctly saw as a proxy for economic forms of control reintroduced by the Western powers. The whole concept had at best a mixed reputation in the humanities and social sciences.[5] But development became increasingly important as the cold war wound down and as many of the social and economic payoffs of globalization were either slow in coming or absent altogether. One vivid expression of a broad notion of development came from the United Nations.

> Human development is about much more than the rise or fall of national incomes. It is about creating an environment in which people can develop their full potential and lead productive, creative lives in accord with their needs and interests. People are the real wealth of nations. Development is thus about expanding the choices people have to lead lives that they value. And it is thus about much more than economic growth, which is only a means—if a very important one—of enlarging people's choices.
>
> Fundamental to enlarging these choices is building human capabilities— the range of things that people can do or be in life. The most basic capabilities for human development are to lead long and healthy lives, to be knowledgeable, to have access to the resources needed for a decent stan-

dard of living and to be able to participate in the life of the community. Without these, many choices are simply not available, and many opportunities in life remain inaccessible.[6]

The passage goes on to cite Aristotle: "Wealth is evidently not the good we are seeking, for it is merely useful for the sake of something else." And it notes, "In seeking that something else, human development shares a common vision with human rights."

Human development has always struggled for attention, but since the end of the cold war in the 1990s, it has lost further ground to the economistic notion of world development called globalization. Economic development has in turn become increasingly identified with technological progress. When giving examples of twentieth-century progress, few would mention recent theories of international relations or the United Nations itself; a few more might cite modernist art or the civil rights movement; most would mention the automobile, radio, *Sputnik*, television, nuclear power, cell phones, and the Internet. Is this because science and technology produce nearly all progress and the arts and social practice virtually none? In fact there is nothing natural about this skew toward technology: *Cultural* capability is no less fundamental to human development. And yet this everyday interrelation between culture and technology now generally lies beyond the limits of both policy and felt experience.

In contrast, the centrality of culture to development was not lost on the mid-twentieth century, which remembered well the worldwide destruction of World War II and lived in the shadow of nuclear apocalypse. The period produced books like Ray Bradbury's *Martian Chronicles,* where, in another world represented by Mars, art and science had merged to produce an advanced civilization, where Mrs. K ate "the golden fruits that grew from the crystal walls" and cleaned her house "with handfuls of magnetic dust which, taking all the dirt with it, blew away on the hot wind," and where Mr. K read by moving his hands across the singing book. Interestingly for us, Bradbury described business as usual—murder and war, disrespect, ignorance, sorrow—as the result of a failure of *cultural* knowledge. The rockets had already gotten humanity to Mars, meaning that the big technological problems were already solved. There was easy travel to other planets, but then lethal cultural stupidity when we got there. The deeper problems turned out to be not scientific but cultural. In other words, if cultural knowledge was in crisis, then scientific knowledge was in crisis, too.

In the postwar period, there was an institution devoted to keeping cultural and scientific knowledge under one roof. That institution was the university.

The Three Crises

To understand the past and present of this problem of cultural knowledge, we need to see society, industry, and the university as tangled up together rather than polarized, and as experiencing three parallel crises. Each crisis characterized the post–World War II period, but became acute and unresolvable in the 1970s. The end of the Bretton Woods currency agreement in 1971, the Nixon resignation in 1974, and the withdrawal of U.S. troops from Saigon in 1975 signaled the end of the cold war political and economic order that had already been weakened by twenty years of attacks from civil rights, antiwar, and other social movements. But then something strange happened. Instead of the new political and economic order that might have resolved the social and cultural conflicts of the 1950s and 1960s, a previous leadership consensus was restored. We used to call this restored order "Reaganism"; Patrick Buchanan, the Republican speechwriter and media figure, called it the "Reagan counterreformation." The British called it "Thatcherism." Europeans and many in the global South called it "neoliberalism" or "the Washington consensus" or "neocolonialism." The French called it *la pensée unique*. Whatever it was called, it continued and intensified under the Bush II administration. Throughout this period that began in the late 1970s, three crises—economic, political, and cultural—remained unresolved. They were confined and contained on a national scale but continued to create division and hostility (see Table 1).

The political crisis emerged slowly with bus boycotts and lunch-counter sit-ins in the 1950s and grew to freedom rides and full-scale marches on the Pentagon in the 1960s. By the 1970s U.S. society was confronted with unrelenting claims for multilateral democracy within its borders. This was to

Table 1 The three crises

Domain	Epoch-making challenge
Politics	Multiracial mass democracy
Economy	Decline of profits, rise of knowledge-workers
Culture	Civil-rights "science"-movements rooted in qualitative, context-specific, cross-cultural knowledge

have meant power sharing among traditional white elites and communities of color all over the country. This potential dispersal or even democratization of power provoked the enormous improvement in Republican political organization after the defeat of Barry Goldwater in the presidential election of 1964; the effort culminated in the control of the three branches of the federal government and the escalation of executive authority in the early 2000s.[7] These strategies successfully delayed the imagined solution of cross-racial political parity. The crisis of American democracy continued, expressed by the sense after 2004 that the country had politically divided into "red" and "blue" halves.

The second crisis was the decline of American economic preeminence on which its golden-age affluence hinged. The devastated powers of Germany, Japan, and, to a lesser extent, France and England were back to full strength, cutting into the U.S. share of global markets. The erosion of position was marked by falling profits even in the best-positioned corporations. Income for four-fifths of the population stagnated between 1973 and 1996 and increased only slightly afterwards. Average annual gross domestic product (GDP) growth rates in the 1990s, even counting the vaunted New Economy boom, were about the same as those of the 1980s and well below the growth rates of the 1950s and 1960s. The first decade of the 2000s was worse. During the post-1980 period, the average annual work year increased in the United States by almost 20 percent, even as it fell in other wealthy countries.[8]

The core feature of this change has been what I call the *end of economic majoritarianism*. Progress continued for a minority who advanced at rates much higher than the growth of GDP in the top 10 percent as measured by wealth or income, and much higher than that in the top 1 percent and 0.1 percent. Income progress more or less ended after the mid-1970s for the bottom 80 percent. At the same time, anxiety about profitability and productivity increased, and policy makers gave executives a free hand in using mass layoffs as a routine business strategy.[9] Economic and management discourse overwhelmed discussion of broader social and cultural matters. Development was increasingly reduced to economic development, which was in turn narrowed to a few popular measures such as rates of GDP growth and the Dow Jones industrial average.

The third crisis was the eclipsing of qualitative knowledge about cultures and human relations. The areas that emerged from the classical trivium, and which Kant called the lower faculties—now including literature, language, philosophy, history, and the arts—faced renewed decline in the public eye. The humanities fields were said to produce no useful knowledge, only complications, ambiguities, multiple interpretations, and attacks on current social arrangements that arose from an irrational grudge against capitalist success. In politics, the humanities were linked to social movements and identities—Asian American, queer, the so-called underclass—that made new claims for recognition and resources. In the economic sphere, the humanities were associated with a restive middle class that in the 1960s had revolted against the iron law of productivism, and had come to demand job satisfaction, personal freedom, self-actualization, and plenty of mind-expanding leisure. While science and engineering fields were seen as producing profitable knowledge, the humanities were often cast as the source of nonknowledge or even a kind of *anti*knowledge, one that led to social division and economic costs.

Beneath the surface, this third crisis split qualitative from quantitative knowledge. C. P. Snow had called this the "two cultures" problem. A more contemporary formulation of this split was proposed by the communication scholar Sandra Braman, who defined it as a conflict between mathematical algorithms, associated with efficiency and control, and narrative creativity, associated with autonomy, desire, human relations, and human rights.[10] The same contrast, admittedly oversimplified, appeared in international relations, where a one-world model of capital and product markets presented itself as an enlightened, universal culture, and thus collided with the vision of professional cultural study, which had developed sophisticated understandings of context-specific and intertranslatable human communications that showed how meanings were both conditioned by their cultural contexts and yet negotiated across boundaries. This second, "narrative" view and its forms of complex cultural knowledge lost public credibility in the 1980s, as American majority nationalism was refounded in opposition to Soviet communism and the new Islamic Republic in Iran, and in the 1990s, as a security-minded economic nationalism stereotyped and repolarized the post–cold war world. Policy makers were obsessed with culture—recall the widespread interest in Samuel Huntington's *Clash of Civilizations*, written from within policy studies, or a book on religious culture called *Terror in the Mind of God*, written by a UCSB sociologist, or more recently Thomas Frank's bestselling *What's the Matter with Kansas?* But even as culture became central to mainstream analyses of domestic politics and international affairs, the standard version had little contact with culture as nonbinary and complicated as knowledge about life in actual communities around the world. Even as the Berlin Wall came down, many American policy makers intensified their attacks on domestic brands of multiculturalism and affirmative action and on international brands of economic diversity, though these practices were the foundation of a multilateral world.

The third crisis persisted in the mainstream policy and media misconception that culture was a source of economic regression, social disorder, and unruly pseudoknowledge. This mainstream failed to grasp or even acknowledge the sheer complexity and power of culture, which involves irreducible internal differences, constant change, and permanent negotiation; in short, which involves creative forces that cannot and should not be managed. The cultural knowledge required for sustaining human development in a multilateral world was disparaged or ignored.

The central mechanism by which the cultural knowledge was sidelined was the culture wars. The central site of this sidelining was the university. The university-focused culture wars blocked genuine solutions to the first two challenges of multiracial democratic politics and majoritarian economics by undermining the requisite cultural capabilities on which these solutions hinged.

The Middle Class Crucible

The restoration of traditional authority depended on blocking the three crises that had emerged within that system of authority. But why did these conservative countermovements need to spend so much energy attacking the university? Why did the attacks not only persist but intensify after the antiwar movements had left campus? Even as the culture wars were fought in rural congressional districts over issues like flag burning, abortion, and gay marriage, why were they fought just as bitterly in colleges and universities across the country? The reason was that changes in post–World War II American society had given the college-educated middle class a political, economic, and cultural weight that threatened the country's conservative elites with permanent marginalization.

The white middle class was of course not historically opposed to conservative rule. The nineteenth-century bourgeoisie of the United States had endorsed colonialism, exploitation, removal of Native Americans, and various other cruelties and crimes in the name of its superior virtue. By the middle of the twentieth century, however, the American middle classes seemed better positioned to justify a new direction. They had helped defeat fascism and end the Holocaust in Europe, and they did not actively support the maintenance of European colonialism. Though the middle classes had been dragged into the New Deal by labor and other liberal or left-wing social movements, they seemed finally to have come to endorse strong public services and collective provisioning. The middle classes also seemed to have shifted allegiances from laissez-faire capitalism to the social state. In 1945, big business was looking pretty bad and government was looking pretty good. Unregulated corporate capitalism had produced the Great Depression and had supported fascist regimes in Germany, Italy, Japan, Vichy France, and elsewhere. By contrast, big-government Keynesianism had gotten the majority back on its feet; big-government planning had, in the United States and the United Kingdom, just won World War II.[11] Veterans were returning from the European and Pacific theaters to expanded social subsidies for everything a white middle class could want—subsidized highways and hospitals, low-interest guaranteed government loans for building and buying the new suburbs, new forms of unemployment and disability insurance, and massively expanded higher education.[12] The trade union movement, once fought by private armies, shot by Pinkertons, and actually bombed in Kentucky by the embryonic army air force just after World War I, had been institutionalized and was now at the bargaining table in the country's largest and wealthiest firms.[13] The civil rights movement was gaining strength and was becoming a pillar of international diplomacy in the rivalry with the Soviets for the hearts and minds of the decolonizing global South.[14] Once again, but this time without a shot being fired, and in spite of McCarthyism and other forms of repressive anticommunism, the masses were making very large claims on the national treasure. And they were doing it from the inside, as members of the sacrosanct middle class.

Mass democracy was acquiring, for the first time in U.S. history, a material base in the form of mass prosperity.[15] The "affluent society" not only made the white population richer and, in many cases, elitist; it also created a new sense of *mass* entitlement and *mass* expectation.[16] There was something in the United States like the spread of an informal *mass right* to economic prosperity, which supported, fed, and was fed by the right to mass democracy, which was used to expand the right to prosperity beyond the white population.

The public university was at the center of this change. In the five years after World War II, California higher education enrollment tripled from

26,400 to 79,500; enrollment passed 300,000 by 1960. Nationally, higher education enrollment increased 78 percent in the 1940s, 31 percent in the 1950s, and 120 percent in the 1960s. Public institutions had about half of total higher education enrollment in 1950; by 1995 they had 80 percent.[17] These institutions depended utterly on the public coughing up unprecedented amounts of tax dollars, and cough up they did. Much of the funding came in the form of cold war defense spending, but most of it came from state taxpayers whose kids would be the first or second generation in the family to go to college. Though these universities were predominantly white—97 percent white in 1940; still 80 percent white in 1995—they were producing wave after wave of well-educated and potentially independent, intellectually active people who seemed to have lost their reflexive respect for authority. Political interests and advanced education formed an unsettling combination. The Right was already complaining bitterly about college campuses in the 1950s; Ronald Reagan launched his political career as governor of California in 1967 by having run not so much against his popular New Deal opponent, Pat Brown, as against the students and faculty of the University of California at Berkeley (UC Berkeley). The university had become a site of open dissent around civil rights and free speech, as well as a place of opposition to business and political leadership that had brought the country problems that ranged from racial inequality and air pollution to the Vietnam War.

To make matters worse, these college brats were being described as the center of a new kind of economy, a postindustrial economy.[18] At one time the loyal allies of elites had been the fairly small middle class—the clergy, tradesmen, and so on—who had been validated in the United States, from Jefferson to Emerson to Teddy Roosevelt, as a natural aristocracy. In the twentieth century this got a little trickier. Progressives and allies like Walter Lippmann described a class of technical experts who had organized themselves into professional societies: they had made themselves somewhat independent and more than a little indispensable.[19] In the early 1960s, UC president Clark Kerr, most famous for his opposition to the student radicals, had actually been placing college students at the center of the economic future. "The basic reality, for the university," he wrote, "is the widespread recognition that new knowledge is the most important factor in economic and social growth. We are just now perceiving that the university's invisible product, knowledge, may be the most powerful single element in our culture, affecting the rise and fall of professions and even of social classes, of regions and even of nations."[20] The moderate Kerr, running what was already a corporate university, was declaring the manifest destiny of the college-educated middle class. The destiny was to become the indispensable class within modern capitalism, to be the managers of capitalism, to be a class that might at some point wake up to its authority and rule capitalism.

Were this class to rule, what would its ruling values be? Three traditional values might have seemed pretty obvious. The class would be anticommunist, deeply wedded to home ownership, private cars, and everything else that consumer capitalism had to offer. They would be card-carrying members of the growth club, buying the view that sheer economic growth would solve social problems.[21] Second, they would be technocratic, meaning they would privilege scientific knowledge, narrowly defined, over cultural knowledge, which would be cast as secondary, and at times of potential social change, discarded as dangerous pseudo-knowledge.[22] The college-educated middle classes, in other words, would favor *expert rule over politics*, expertise over mass politics in which every last woman and man gets to have a say.[23] And third, they would be *racist*, continuing the tradition of either formal or informal segregation and super-exploited racialized labor (read: African Americans and Mexicans, Filipinos, Japanese, and Chinese immigrants, for starters).

We can expand Table 1 to see what this solidly conservative, antireform middle class might look like (see Table 2).

Or would the middle class be all these things? Many adhered to those values, which formed the core beliefs of the political Right. But many, and sometimes most, did not. These others—whites from the blue-collar as much as from the white-collar wing of the middle class—did not rise up in resistance or do much in the way of political dissent. But they did not oppose the civil rights movement and sometimes even helped it, only sort of

Table 2 The three crises and the middle-class bulwark

Domain	Epoch-making challenge	Middle-class bulwark
Politics	Multiracial mass democracy	Expert rule; no power sharing
Economy	Decline of profits, rise of knowledge-workers	Market-led growth, interpreted by financial interests
Culture	Civil-rights "science"-movements rooted in qualitative, context-specific, cross-cultural knowledge	White or "West" supremacism in the form of cultural hierarchy

supported the war in Vietnam and sometimes opposed it, and did not support unilateral business leadership and sometimes opposed it. The middle class not only covered a wide range of incomes and educational levels in the United States—at least three and perhaps as many as six classes according to the sociologist Erik Olin Wright—but was not really a class at all.[24] It was a "contradictory class position," both superior and subordinate, capitalist and noncapitalist; both rising up and falling down, looking up and looking down.[25] And as its college membership grew to be 20 percent, then 25 percent, then 35 percent of the voting population, the middle class was coming unglued from society's traditional leadership.

The 1960s meant many things, but one of its central meanings was this ungluing. Would traditional leaders maintain the loyalty of the college-educated middle class that their industrial economy required? Or would this middle class declare its independence? Would it declare some kind of republic of the economic majority? Would it try to replace the captains of cold war politics and industry as society's natural leaders?

There were in fact momentous questions. Traditional elites were getting a serious run for their money in the postwar period. Social movements were demanding egalitarian forms of human development, which if enacted would transform economic, race, and gender relations. Social movements were also getting unusual support from academic experts, whose research showed that the problems were real and that progressive solutions would work. Not only were universities producing new and potentially disruptive knowledge; by 1980 they were also producing nearly a million graduates a year. These graduates would bring their new technological *and* cultural learning to insider positions in the American economy. For conservative leaders, a quiet, continuous, slow, unrelenting, and internal revolution was a clear and present danger.

— 2 —

Declarations of Independence

In thinking about their place in postwar society, the middle classes faced a historically familiar choice. Put starkly, it was a choice to move forward *with* the large social majority or *without* it. Historically speaking, the middle classes of the Western countries tended to abandon their blue-collar or working-class allies once their large numbers were no longer needed. In the nineteenth century, the insurgent bourgeoisie "tail" of 1848 severed its artisanal and laboring "dog," transforming a renewed republic into a second empire ruled undemocratically by Louis Napoleon. In the United States, the northern middle class accepted the end of racial Reconstruction on both racial and economic grounds, and its abandonment of industrial workers to concentrated ownership and regimented work methods set the stage for decades of brutal labor struggles. During the 1930s, the middle classes were split and politically disoriented: much credit for the New Deal must go to the labor and radical political movements that saw the middle classes as part of the problem.

What would happen this time around? Would the college-educated middle classes side with African Americans and Chicanos around civil rights and racial equality? Would the college-educated side with the blue-collar workers when they started to suffer deindustrialization? The middle classes—finally experiencing the first stages of racial integration after the Eisenhower years—might remember the origins of most of its members in the working class, in trade union battles, and in civil rights. In economics, it might insist that sheer growth in production had always needed to be supplemented with a social infrastructure that broadened participation and widely distributed rewards. In politics, it might call for the expanding of the franchise, for a multiparty system, and for respecting the knowledge of "situated" communities as well as of experts. Around race and culture, it might embrace the civil rights struggle and throw its weight behind government-funded forms of social development for all communities, including poor and immigrant communities, and do this for the sake of equality and prosperity alike.

Or, on the other hand, the middle class could avoid all these things. It could move economics beyond politics, say the only thing society needs is a strong economy, affirm that all problems can be resolved by growth, that social leadership rightly belongs with business leaders, and that the function of the middle class is to provide the technical expertise that would ensure the dominance of American business. It could treat civil rights and labor struggles as drains on efficiency in an ever-changing economy, suggest that inequality is a natural part of economic growth and change, and seek its own place in an economic aristocracy it would define as natural.

Both tendencies were present in the growing college-educated proportion of the population, which steadily became more diverse socially, racially, and politically as time went on. But if one read some of the classics written across the ideological spectrum of this group as a whole—as many a conservative culture warrior would do—one could see the first and more democratic tendency gaining strength.

Political Alliances

At the end of the 1950s, whites in general and college grads in particular seemed unlikely supporters of cross-racial democracy. In 1962, James Baldwin had written that "there is simply no possibility of a real change in the Negro's situation without the most radical and far-reaching changes in the American political and social structure. And it is clear that white Americans are not simply unwilling to effect these changes; they are, in the main, so slothful have they become, unable even to envision them. It must be added that the Negro himself no longer believes in the good faith of white Americans—if, indeed, he ever could have."[1] Five years later, even after notable civil rights milestones had been achieved, Martin Luther King Jr. described Black Power as a "cry of disappointment." Writing in a book published by Boston's Beacon Press and destined for an audience of white liberals, King said that "for centuries the Negro has been caught in the tentacles of white power. Many Negroes have given up faith in the white majority because 'white power' with total control has left them empty-handed. So in reality the call for Black Power is a reaction to the failure of white power."[2] Even King, who had forged many successful alliances with liberal whites, had grave doubts about any general tendency among whites to fight for democratic racial politics. This included the first-generation middle class that had arrived in the suburbs largely thanks to expanded public services like higher education. The university seemed willing to accommodate a small African American presence, but to accommodate it on existing terms: the order of the day in college precincts seemed a traditional brand of assimiliationism.[3]

But cross-racial alliances had taken place and had advanced the civil rights movement. Many intellectuals in black freedom movements—including Malcolm X, Eldridge Cleaver, and Huey Newton—noted the importance of these alliances even when they did not lead to black-white agreement. Civil rights leaders always emphasized the need for historically powerless communities to become independent and self-sustaining.[4] But it was clear to all that some whites were willing to help the civil rights movement directly, many others sympathized, and still others had introduced civil rights concepts into their thinking and acting about their own issues. The unmistakable trend on college campuses and in college communities was toward increased self-organization of political activity. Some of the traditional ethnic barriers that had blocked alliances around common issues were becoming less important, suggesting that collaborative organization could spread. All of this was bad news for a traditional version of U.S. democracy in which everyday decision making remained in the hands of elites, where little power sharing took place, and where racial divisions made the social majority relatively disorganized and controllable. Many believed that a coalition had come into existence that included civil rights communities, antiwar protesters, and many university students and faculty as well. The effect, if this diverse coalition succeeded, was that democracy would become democratic.

Economics and Freedom I

The college-educated middle class had a love-hate relationship with the American business system. Though many of its members had carved out secure and well-paying jobs in the corporate world, they also bought many copies of 1950s books such as *The Lonely Crowd*, *Organization Man*, *The Man in the Gray Flannel Suit*, and *White Collar*, which meant that they were interested in demonstrations of their own conformism, inhibition, intellectual emptiness, political passivity, and spiritual demise. In the 1960s and

1970s, attempted cures of corporate-induced identity loss became the backbone of what we now call the "self-help" industry. If Tom Wolfe had been right to call the 1970s the "Me Decade," and Christopher Lasch to critique the "Culture of Narcissism," they were nonetheless defining compensatory stances—that is, stances that tried to make up for social, cultural, and emotional loss that had been induced by the American economy even at its best.

Much of the problem was quite simple: a large proportion of the population had never joined the affluent society. Michael Harrington's *The Other America* revealed the depth of poverty in a wealthy society. Martin Luther King Jr. noted that "there are, in fact, more poor whites Americans than there are Negro. Their need for a war on poverty is no less desperate than the Negro's."[5] King's "second phase" of the civil rights movement was the "Poor People's Campaign," which focused explicitly on economic injustice and deprivation. It was hard for worried conservatives to miss the connection between cross-racial democracy and the democratization of the economy.

One brutal intellectual blow was struck from very near the top of the economic establishment. This came from John Kenneth Galbraith, the prominent Keynesian economist who had served in various Democratic administrations and written about the limitations of consumer economies in *The Affluent Society*. His 1967 book about the new "technostructure" was widely attacked by economists and has since been dismissed by chroniclers of various New Economies as a relic of a bygone age. In fact this book, *The New Industrial State*, was a systematic and sometimes blistering attack on market assumptions and on existing economic elites. It was at the same time a sweeping defense of the rise of the educated middle classes to economic leadership.

Galbraith claimed that complex corporate economies had bypassed the effective control of owners and entrepreneurs. No one had made a political decision about this: the demands of modern production and distribution had created organizations that could not be intelligently handled by the traditional heroes of capitalism. The real agent of modern economic progress was the corporate ensemble, each member of which contributed "information to group decisions." Driving the point home, Galbraith continued, "This, not the narrow management group, is the guiding intelligence—the brain—of the enterprise. . . . I propose to call this organization the Technostructure." This technostructure was dominated by college grads, but it also included blue-collar expertise—focused knowledge of every description. It was impossible not to miss the implication that line-worker knowledge was as important as executive knowledge to the health of the firm, and probably more so.

Galbraith explicitly attacked the entrepreneur as out-of-date. "In the entrepreneurial corporation a visible line divided the bosses—those whose position depended on ownership or their ability to produce profits for the owners—from clerks, bookkeepers, timekeepers, secretaries, salesmen and others who were purely employees. In the mature corporation, this line disappears."[6] In reality, complex corporate operations were blurring the lines between those with property and those without, those with power and those without. It was in a preliminary sense democratizing the corporation from within. And it was doing this to improve the corporation's economic function by replacing narrow entrepreneurship with a general collaboration, one that harnessed the talent widely distributed in an educated workforce.

Galbraith claimed that the technostructure was linking economic activity to social goals. While shareholders sought maximum profits, employees looked for "a secure level of earnings and a maximum rate of growth."[7] Now that the entrepreneurial bottleneck was safely past, the corporation could aim at earnings and at the same time at "further goals"—"building a better community," "improved education," better health, and so on. In other words, the knowledge workers that made up the technostructure were running the economy for their own benefit and not for that of the owners. They were the majority of the firm, and they were redefining the firm's economic goals so that the results would serve majoritarian ends. Galbraith said that "what has been called the 'social corporation' is a logical manifestation of the mature corporation and the motivation of its members."[8] This was dramatic news: even as they continued to pursue economic gain, the college-educated cadres had redefined it to serve their own ways. "Corporate man" turned out to be majoritarian "social man." He would take care of the needs of production and then turn production to something else.

This "something else" preoccupied Galbraith in the later chapters of his book. He flatly rejected a claim that became a staple of conservative reformation discourse in the 1980s and 1990s, which was that "economic liberty" expressed itself in freedom of consumption. There was no freedom of consumption, he said, since it came from managed and even invented needs that were subject to elaborate care and guidance from the business system.[9] The more one thought about consumption, the more one realized that it was a veil over the deeper reality that "natural" man tended to "achieve contentment" in the material sense and to do something besides work. Contentment involved the pursuit of art, sport, education, spiritual development, or other simple enjoyment.[10] The corporate masses pursued economic growth to gain personal economic stability so that they could then consume more, but only up to a point, after which they sought economic stability so they could escape economic thought and turn their activity toward what the popular psychologist Abraham Maslow was calling "the higher needs."

One institution that allowed the new corporate middle classes to imagine and enact the noneconomic was the American university. Galbraith confirmed conservative fears that the academy had not been the historical friend of business: "A very large amount of legislation regarded as highly inimical by the entrepreneurial enterprise received its initial impetus from the academic community."[11] But this was only the beginning. Those whom the university had trained to run the planning system, and who now effectively controlled it, would spend much time and many resources outside the reach of that planning system. The technostructure—and not only student or civil rights protesters—would create the "mechanics of emancipation" in the name of the "neglected dimensions of life," which themselves had to resist "the powerful adaptive motivation of the planning system."[12] This would include "aesthetic experience," which encompassed the enjoyment of European cities of an "artistic interest" vastly greater than that of the newer industrial cities. All this envisioning of company man's love of art and freedom culminated in the chapter "Education and Emancipation." Here the university professor proved the necessary coexistence of production and the free exploration of undetermined experience. Galbraith's college graduate was rejecting the old elite alliance and favoring majority participation in a society in which economics served some larger notion of human progress.

Galbraith was a liberal Keynesian and no enemy of the American system overall. But his thinking posed a direct threat to traditional economic leaders and to their entrepreneurial hero presiding over every stage of economic progress. Marx had said that labor created value and that labor therefore deserved economic control. Now Galbraith, the Harvard professor, was saying that knowledge-labor created value and that it *did* have economic control. On top of this, the knowledge workers—working and middle class alike— would use their control to make economic development only one of society's purposes. Human development, "self actualization," and spiritual and creative welfare of various kinds were all equally important goals and would be pursued by the new builders of a majoritarian economy. The colleges and universities were fountainheads and proving grounds of "the values and goals of educated men—those who serve not the production of goods and associated planning but the intellectual and artistic development of man."[13]

Economics and Freedom II

Later liberals joined conservatives in rejecting Galbraith's image of the technostructure as too pyramidical and fixed. The kind of stability he imagined was largely dismantled over the next three decades; by the late 1990s, multiple careers, lifetime learning, "permatemps," and mass layoffs had all become familiar concepts and common practices. And yet Galbraith's principles were far more common than was the actual citation of Galbraith's texts. Many later writers took the decline of corporate stability as an opportunity for rather than as the defeat of the college-educated knowledge worker.

One popular account of this empowerment was Alvin Toffler's *Future Shock*, published in 1970. Toffler claimed that work hierarchies were gradually being extinguished not so much by left-wing social movements as by internal changes in modern economies: "As machines take over routine tasks and the accelerative thrust increases the amount of novelty in the environment, more and more of the energy of society (and its organizations) must turn toward the solution of non-routine problems. This requires a degree of imagination and creativity that bureaucracy, with its man-in-a-slot organization, its permanent structures, and its hierarchies, is not well equipped to provide. . . . In these frontier organizations a new system of human relations is springing up."[14]

Twenty years later, in *The Work of Nations*, Robert Reich recycled these ideas into another prophecy of the independence of the professional-managerial class (PMC). The high-value corporation has "no place for bureaucracy. . . . [Managers will be strategic brokers, and their job will be] to create settings in which problem-solvers and problem-identifiers can work together without undue interference. . . . Most coordination is horizontal rather than vertical. Because problems and solutions cannot be defined in advance, formal meetings and agendas won't reveal them. . . . [N]ew connections are being spun all the time."[15] I have never seen a discussion of the knowledge economy and knowledge workers that did not promise flattened layers and more self-management to its beneficiaries.

The culmination of this PMC empowerment liberalism occurred in the 1990s and came from the godfather of management gurus, Peter F. Drucker. The knowledge economy, he wrote, meant that society was not only post-industrial but also, surprisingly, postcapitalist.

The basic economic resource—"the means of production," to use the economist's term—is no longer capital, nor natural resources (the economist's "land"), nor "labor." *It is and will be knowledge.* . . . The leading social groups of the knowledge society will be "knowledge workers"—knowledge executives who know how to allocate knowledge to productive use, just as the capitalists knew how to allocate capital to productive use; knowledge professionals, knowledge employees. Practically all these knowledge people will be employed in organizations. Yet, unlike the employees under Capitalism, they will own both the "means of production" and the "tools of production."[16]

This was the core of the revolution: knowledge workers would not be working under capitalists because they were in fact replacing capitalists. Knowledge was the only real source of wealth, and the savings accumulated by knowledge workers would inevitably control the stock of the companies for which they worked. Knowledge workers as a group would control the economy and be society's leading citizens. Their fate would be sharply different from "the second class in post-capitalist society"—the "service workers" who "lack the necessary education to be knowledge workers." Like all the better prophets of the New Economy, Drucker admitted the potential for sharp social divisions between knowledge insiders and service outsiders. Like all of them, he was silent on the traditional racial pecking order that a knowledge economy pointed toward.[17] But he never wavered from his key point that the "intellectual capital" of knowledge insiders meant underlying ownership of the production process.

Nothing would be nicer for the knowledge worker with a good position. As the true owner of the production process, he or she would direct and manage his or her own work. Since knowledge production was unmanageable through traditional, external supervision, knowledge work would be, in this theory, post-*managerial* work. The age-old dream of labor would become a reality for the knowledge worker—for all relevant purposes, the knowledge worker managed him- or herself.[18]

In this view of the knowledge society, these two aspects—the centrality of knowledge and the power of its handlers—once again placed higher education on the commanding heights. Knowledge workers possessed the essential form of capital in the New Economy, and they were incubated in the universities: "Higher education became the live germ of a post-manufacturing production system with a competitive edge in imaginative ideas."[19] Economic leaders were always focused on getting a competitive edge and would fund and reward the creativity and originality of knowledge workers. The "vital ingredient in the discipline of originality" is the right of knowledge workers "to collectively self-manage their own work." Hence, by a kind of associative logic, the university would become a cooperative run by and for its real producers, who would make the major policy decisions while hiring others to help with the office work. The university, in this vision, would be well funded and left to govern itself. It would also serve as a model of a majoritarian economy run not by owners but by the new masses, the ones armed with college degrees.

The Cultural Dimension

This binding of knowledge to democratized power gave renewed importance to the concept of culture. It was the site at which social structures and individual experience existed in constant contact and reciprocal pressure. It was the site at which politics and economics overlapped with what Galbraith called the "further dimensions"—art and feeling and everyday life. Culture was the dimension in which the crucial ingredient of democratic politics *and* advanced economics was formed, and that element was reliable and imaginative personal agency.

One thinker who understood this perfectly well was Malcolm X, who in a speech at Harvard explained it in the following way:

> The social philosophy of Black Nationalism says that we must eliminate the vices and evils that exist in our society, and that we must stress the cultural roots of our forefathers, that will lend dignity and make the black man cease to be ashamed of himself. We have to teach our people something about our cultural roots. We have to teach them something of their glorious civilizations before they were kidnapped by your grandfathers and brought over to this country. Once our people are taught about the glorious civilization that existed on the African continent, they won't any longer be ashamed of who they are.[20]

Here Black Nationalist social philosophy is a cultural philosophy, one in which the presence of a culture that one sees as one's own becomes the psychological and intellectual basis of social action. Malcolm X was rejecting the cultural-deficiency thesis that was later reinvented as a central fixture in the culture wars. He assumed a basic equality among the various "glorious civilizations" of Africa, and between those civilizations and equality with the West. The effect of this knowledge of cultural tradition would be *cultural capability*, the capability of using knowledge of both past and present collaboratively to reconstruct black America. That reconstruction would be the result and the process of liberation, and would also form the continuing human development of black Americans as a group. The civil rights movement was itself a central component of this ongoing development process.

One surprising parallel to Malcolm X's is thought was that of Robert Pirsig, the previously unknown writer whose *Zen and the Art of Motorcycle Maintenance* became a huge best seller in 1974. Pirsig's subject was the country's depleted culture, its psychological effects, and possible cures. The book's protagonist was a white, middle-class, nonbourgeois everyman. He was from the Mid-west, lacked the slightest trace of the social connections one might acquire through an Ivy League education, and showed no interest in accumulating wealth. He decided to take his somewhat estranged son on a motorcycle vacation, to give him an "on the road" experience that required little money but might resuscitate their bond. Most nights father and son slept outdoors, while the father steadily consumed beer, cigarettes, coffee, diner food, and camp food. There was more than a hint of a dust bowl migration in the journey, and the protagonist's standard of living may have reminded his readers of a time when the white middle class was in fact working-class. The narrator certainly experienced no boundary between working- and middle-class activity. He had spent time in graduate school, had worked as a composition instructor, and, on the side, was a motorcycle mechanic. The rest of the time he read, thought, and wrote—living as an organic intellectual in a country that had few recognized intellectuals of any kind. The core theme of *Motorcycle Maintenance* was the seamless interconnection between technical labor and intellectual activity. The interconnection appeared in the narrator's status as a blue-collar middle-class intellectual who was trying always to inhabit the "further dimensions."

Motorcycle Maintenance had little interest in left-wing or racial or any other kind of politics. But it did start from the era's counterintelligence that the affluent society built on corporate capitalism was in a state of crisis. Watching some oncoming traffic, one of the narrator's friends remarked that the people in the first car looked so very sad. "And then the next one looked exactly the same way, and then the next one and the next one, they were all the same. . . . It's just that they looked so lost. . . . Like they were all dead. Like a funeral procession."[21] The narrator pointed out that they were just commuting to work, but this turned out to be the problem: middle-class work was a form of death, and the resurrection would not come from conventional politics. The essential symbol of American mobility, the personal car, had become a coffin. Psychological immobility followed suit in other realms.

The core problem for Pirsig was cultural. But for him, this did not mean a mainstream American belief system; it meant the mode through which Americans had experiential knowledge of their world. Culture appeared as the interpretative framework that created personal knowledge and allowed the individual to see the world as a place susceptible to human action. Pirsig might have engaged in complex analyses of the rich philosophical tradition that overturned Descartes' dualism of individual and world, subject and object, and might have written not only about the ancient Sophists, as he did, but also about Hegel, Husserl, Heidegger, and Sartre. Instead, Pirsig kept the narrative experiential. His narrator explained to a former colleague, "What's emerging from the pattern of my own life is the belief that the crisis is being caused by the inadequacy of existing forms of thought to cope with the situation. It can't be solved by rational means because the rationality itself is the source of the problem."[22] American culture had come to rely on a form of reason that could no longer describe reality, either psychological or social. Its culture or reason was misguided, and that culture had to change so that its members could again understand the actual lives of their fellow citizens, and their own lives as well.

Pirsig did not like American consumerism, but he located the country's cultural problem much farther back, in the crushing of antidualist Sophist philosophy by Socrates and Plato. The last section of the book is a suspenseful philosophical detective story, as the narrator's earlier self, Phaedrus, enrolled in a graduate program at the University of Chicago, gradually uncovers the epistemological culture of the Sophists that later figures persuaded history to forget. This had been a culture in which truth was not superior to the inquirer's way of life, but a part of that life, and always emerged from life as its subject-author explored and interpreted experience. The Good, or more accurately, excellence, or *arête*, was the precondition of truth and not the other way around. Truth was inseparable from the pursuit of excellence in various realms of life. Excellence was the awareness of experience and of how its parts fit together. Excellence was thus not a separable feature of experience, one that was part of some of our experiences but not others, or greater in some people's experience and much lower in others. Excellence was experience properly attended to—that is, experience not presided over by a preestablished law of reason.

Pirsig's antidualist philosophy was meant to describe a culture that supported a personal experience not alienated from its own understanding of the world. This culture was entirely compatible with science and technology, and the point of motorcycle maintenance was that it expressed a tie between observer and observed that allowed for both accurate knowledge and successful problem solving. The long chapter 26 described familiar obstacles to mechanical problem solving and how to overcome them. The solution was to avoid knowledge as a possession of the world in order to approach the world antidualistically, retaining an attitude of caring about the object and the problem, and reflecting on them from a position of interest and non-adversity, of patience and familiarity. This approach was confirmed by the period's more formal accounts of the creative process, which showed the value of various forms of unpressured pondering of alternative possibilities, the capturing of odd and straying impressions, the pursuit of the unauthorized idea that came from experience itself. This approach was also confirmed by the main philosophical currents of the time, from phenomenology and existentialism to the philosophy of language influenced by Ludwig Wittgenstein.

Pirsig's crucial insight was that real knowledge came from the relatively unalienated labor process of the ordinary mechanic. The appeal of his book was that it imagined an American culture that would value that kind of practice at least as much as it valued output and affluence. For a group like the American middle class to recover its power to make itself and remake its world, it would have to recover the craft labor that emerged from intimate contact with the inanimate world. This middle class would become much more aware of its real value, which lay not in having detachable knowledge or a greater power of consumption but in the world-changing experience of craft attention, including its craft on the job. The outcome was parallel to what Malcolm X imagined for black culture, though in a different political context. Pirsig's white America would also recover its culture. It would reconnect to a culture that had been actively suppressed by traditional elites. If the working and middle classes recovered their lost culture of craft practice, they would overcome their alienation from the world they had in fact made. If they reduced alienation, they would recover the agency to make personal *and* general development possible again.

Postmodernism and Cultural Knowledge

To complete our short sample list of declarations of independence, we can look to the fountainhead of postmodern darkness itself, Jean-François Lyotard's *The Postmodern Condition*, subtitled *A Report on Knowledge*.[23] Lyotard was writing in the context of what the critic John Guillory has called the "scientific monopoly on truth," about which Pirsig was equally concerned.[24] Though written in France, the book was widely circulated in American academia after its translation into English. Contrary to popular opinion, Lyotard's "postmodernism" did not advocate antirealist skepticism in itself, but a resubordination of economic production to cultural knowledge.[25]

In this book, Lyotard was trying to restore science to a relationship with cultural and other forms of knowledge.[26] Modern academic knowledge, Lyotard wrote, had been defined by two distinct narratives of knowledge. In the first narrative, "knowledge finds its validity not within itself, not in a subject that develops by actualizing its learning possibilities, but in a practical subject—humanity. The principle of the movement animating the people is not the self-legitimation of knowledge, but the self-grounding of freedom or, if preferred, its self-management."[27] The second narrative describes knowledge as self-legitimating. "The subject of knowledge is not the people, but the speculative spirit."[28] The first narrative has tied knowledge to human interests. The second narrative has separated them. The first narrative has associated knowledge with liberation. The second has associated it with truth as something quite distinct from liberation and humanity in general.

Lyotard's account was simplified: it omitted the coercion involved in instituting both "freedom" and "truth," and the varying definitions of both terms. But he was concentrating on a crucial historical feature of these two stories: freedom in the first narrative and truth in the second narrative were in fact not two separated and conflicting narratives but two versions of the same narrative of emancipation. In fact, Lyotard was arguing, people liberated themselves from tyranny in the same way in which knowledge freed itself from falsehood. Both movements depended on a cultural framework that understood their interconnection. The result would be, once again, a culturally based capability of self-management, one at least partially freed from external coercion. The source would be a recovered relation between scientific and cultural knowledge.

Lyotard recalled the centrality of the university to this relatively non-dualistic culture. Humboldt and other architects of the modern university sought to build an institution that would unite freedom of knowledge with the freedom of humanity: the university would allow "the nation-state itself to bring the people to expression . . . through the mediation of speculative knowledge."[29] The university would help the nation-state unite the liberation of the people with the freedom of knowledge. To do this, the university would need to establish ties among all the branches of knowledge and reveal their common ground in freedom.

This vision may now seem wishful or absurd, but this is in part because both versions of the emancipation narrative had been overwhelmed by a third narrative—the narrative of optimization.[30] Much of what Lyotard challenged in his 1979 report on knowledge became the truisms of today's knowledge society: the triumph of "post-Fordist" capitalism, continuous technological revolution, deregulated markets, democracy defined as the spread of technology, and lifestyle eclecticism ("one listens to reggae, watches a Western, eats McDonald's food for lunch and local cuisine for dinner, wears Paris perfume in Tokyo and 'retro' clothes in Hong Kong; knowledge is a matter for TV games").[31] Galbraith and Pirsig had both criticized the modern economic legitimation narrative, and Malcolm X had tied it to a racist model of modernization. It could also be found in Clark Kerr's work, and now, like Kerr, Lyotard was arguing that economic legitimation was not new, but that it had recently achieved an unprecedented power over the production of knowledge.[32]

The economy most directly influenced knowledge by encouraging researchers to focus on optimizing production. Lyotard located this influence in the logic of technology, which he defined as the language-game "pertaining not to the true, the just, or the beautiful, etc., but to efficiency: a technical 'move' is 'good' when it does better and/or expends less energy than another."[33] Technology either optimizes or fails; any adopted technology is an optimizing technology. Technology above all must optimize the economy, which it did by increasing "the surplus-value derived from this improved performance." Later New Economy discourse used different terms to say something similar—both profitability and survival depend on the continuous revolution of products and the organizations that produce them.[34]

Lyotard was not opposed to technology as such but to its reductive, economistic discourse about society. In this discourse, technology subordinated science to business's quest for unceasing optimization. Technology would then do little more than express a "generalized spirit of performativity." Lyotard's most basic point was not that knowledge lacked context-free foundations—the famous "postmodern" critique of realist epistemology—but that knowledge's defining context had become the drive to optimize. More than criticizing science or technology as such, Lyotard wanted to protect both from the master narrative of optimization. He read the relations between science and other disciplines through his sense that "even today, progress in knowledge is not totally subordinated to technological investment."[35] And he posed the question of how knowledge could continue to develop independently of its financial return.

Lyotard's answer lay within the optimization narrative itself. The narrative had triumphed not by promising sheer efficiency but by promising that efficiency would produce popular emancipation. This combination was an obvious feature of Internet discourse, which described a technology that was both a landmark of scientific research and a source of personal freedom. Similarly, the modern research university continued to support the development of both evolving economies and evolving selves. Business succeeded with the public not by abandoning freedom for technology or emancipation for truth but by claiming instead to have synthesized them. The university was still trying to retain its emancipation narrative even as it pitched its powers of optimization to the leaders of the economy. Freedom was still central to constructing a narrative of legitimation. Postmodernism did not *abandon* the older aspiration to furnish the union of freedom and truth but tried to give this aspiration a new cultural framework. It marked a moment in a century-long development in which the ground of the union of freedom and truth has shifted decisively from the humanities to technology.[36] Postmodernism was the condition in which freedom and truth *appeared* to be united through optimization; postmodern critique meant exposing this as a false solution.[37]

To be a postmodernist in Lyotard's sense meant therefore to critique rather than to advocate postmodernism. "Postmodern" cultural criticism objected to the optimization narrative that shaped *all* the domains of knowledge. It objected to optimization as the goal of knowledge creation. It objected to this narrative's claims to have preserved the freedom both of the people and of knowledge, and to measure these correctly by the standard of efficiency. Postmodern culture was confusing because it was the site both of the triumph of freedom-as-economic optimization *and* of a humanities discourse that rejected this.

This reading helps explain why "postmodernism" became so important in the academic humanities. It expressed a certain skeptical sophistication about "totalizing narratives," which in turn helped marginalized communities and cultures achieve greater academic and political visibility. At the same time, it expressed an antideterminism in philosophy that reinforced neighboring social movements. This was not simply the diminished language of a post-emancipation age, but the emancipation language of a post-revolutionary age, one in which human development remained the goal, and cultural knowledge would need to keep political and economic development on track.[38] This interconnection between social movements and professional knowledge, would have the university as its major experimental site.

King, Galbraith, Drucker, Toffler, Malcolm X, Pirsig, and Lyotard came from different generations, races, classes, and countries. But they were part of a broad, complex intellectual movement that sought to reconstitute a cultural framework in which the creative activity of individuals and groups would not be subordinated to economic production. For most of their postwar history, the academic humanities played a major role in this project. The humanities played this role because of their ties to movements and communities that had been largely excluded from the university, and were

Table 3 The middle class as an emerging anticonservative bloc

Domain	Challenge	Middle-class bulwark	Emerging nonconservative middle class
Politics	Multiracial mass democracy	Expert rule; no power sharing	Majoritarian democracy; antielitism
Economy	Decline of profits, labor conditions	Market, growth, consumption, deregulation	Planned mixed economy; mass affluence; human needs
Culture	Qualitative, context-specific, cross-cultural knowledge	White supremacism; "cultural deficiency" of other groups	Cultural and social equality; self-development; liberation

only now gradually finding the gates open to them. These fields provided huge advances in understanding sign systems, the effects of identity, collaborative invention culture as neither science nor religion, and in the truths that had been relegated to the margins. They articulated a vision for a future world—human development as the standard of market relations; art and labor as the standard for finance; race relations based on equality; international relations in the spirit of reciprocation. Those fields were constantly wracked with doubt. But they were part of a wide movement in society that was transforming the public university and its middle-class graduates from a conservative bulwark in a potentially volatile mixture of liberalism and radicalism.

I summarize the movement with a table that (like Tables 1 and 2 in chapter 1, "The Three Crises and the Mass Middle Class") artificially divides these declarations of independence into three domains (see Table 3).

The emergence of a nonconservative middle class was a pervasive and at times shocking threat to the business and political leadership that had thrived during the cold war. This new college-trained majority was the challenge that cultural warriors were learning to fight.

— II —

Inventing PC:
The War on Equality

— 3 —

The Discrediting of
Social Equality

Conservatives readily identified liberal and leftist heresy with colleges and universities, so the new wave of culture wars that began in the late 1980s had very little open water to cross, and little trouble finding its target. For many decades, however, the college system was relatively small, exclusive, and identified with old-line elite schools that were themselves bastions of the conservative establishment. The American Left was more visible in politics, labor, and the arts than it was in the American college or university. This all changed with the massive expansion of the public university after World War II.

The Dangerous University

The conservative politician who had made the most of the university threat was a product of the advertising and culture industries, the Hollywood anticommunist Ronald Reagan. In the 1950s, Reagan had closely followed developments in the California state legislature's Fact-Finding Committee on Un-American Activities (better known as the Burns committee), which, in June of 1951, had released a report claiming that the University of California had "wittingly or unwittingly . . . aided and abetted the international communist conspiracy in this country."[1] In 1960, five thousand people protested a San Francisco hearing conducted by the federal House Un-American Activities Committee (HUAC). A San Francisco–based FBI agent wrote to FBI director J. Edgar Hoover, "What is particularly significant, and undoubtedly of special interest to you, is the fact that much of the manpower for this riotous situation was provided by students of the University of California at Berkeley. Since Clark Kerr has become President, the situation on all campuses has deteriorated to the point where the so-called academic freedom has become academic license." This view found its way into the FBI's official report on the anti-HUAC protest, "Communist Target—Youth: Communist Infiltration and Agitation Tactics." This report caught the eye of Ronald Reagan, who called Hoover's office in August 1960 to offer to turn "Communist TargetYouth" into a film. Hoover declined, but Reagan stayed interested in the university as a symbol of social disorder.

Five years later, attacks on the University of California became a central, successful part of Reagan's gubernatorial campaign. At an appearance in early 1965, "Reagan said he approved of the arrests of the Free Speech Movement protesters. 'I'm sorry they did away with paddles in fraternities,' he quipped." When "Reagan formally entered the governor's race on Jan. 4, 1966, with his fireside chat, he made it clear that one of his major campaign issues would be the campus unrest at Berkeley. 'Will we allow a great university to be brought to its knees by a noisy, dissident minority? Will we meet their neurotic vulgarities with vacillation and weakness?' Reagan asked. 'Or will we tell those entrusted with administering the university we expect them to enforce a code based on decency, common sense and dedication to the high and noble purpose of the university?' "[2]

Helping to fan Reagan's fire, the Burns committee issued a long report in May 1966 that "accused [UC president Clark] Kerr of fostering an 'anything goes' atmosphere that had turned the university into a haven for protesters and sex deviants"; it also "blamed the litany of campus problems on Kerr's long-standing refusal to cooperate with the Burns committee's 'contact man' program to screen out 'subversive' faculty." At a large campaign rally at San Francisco's Cow Palace, Reagan said, "There is a leadership gap, and a morality and decency gap, in Sacramento. And there is no better illustration of that than what has been perpetrated . . . at the University of California at Berkeley, where a small minority of beatniks, radicals and filthy speech advocates have brought such shame to . . . a great university."[3] Reagan launched what became one of the most successful political careers of the twentieth century by depicting the University of California as a threat to social order and even national security, and by then tying the university around the neck of the incumbent governor. One of his first acts upon election as California governor was to fire UC president Clark Kerr.

If it was Reagan who best articulated the university's *political* threat, other conservatives had their eye on its economic implications. In August

1971, Lewis F. Powell, a Virginia corporate lawyer, wrote a long memo to the director of the U.S. Chamber of Commerce, called "Attack of American Free Enterprise System." Two months later, President Richard M. Nixon would nominate him to the U.S. Supreme Court, where he would become the author of major decisions affecting the university, which I discuss in chapter 6. Powell was concerned about the decline of business influence in U.S. politics—in spite of business's effective efforts to explain and extend its influence[4]—and he outlined a program for creating research and media institutions that is credited with inspiring the development of the Heritage Foundation, the Cato Institute, and other organizations that from the 1970s onward entirely renewed the intellectual foundations of conservative thought for the benefit of political and business leaders. These new conservative organizations were distinctive for their focus on research and education: they produced knowledge in the form of papers that had footnotes, numbers, and tables and in every way (except for their more accessible prose) looked like peer-reviewed academic research. "The Powell Manifesto" was one of the origins of the conservative think-tank system, a kind of shadow university that for the media in the 1990s and 2000s came to function as a source of credible information.[5]

Powell's most important insight was that the real threat to conservative views did not come from the "revolutionaries who would destroy the entire system" but from "perfectly respectable elements of society: from the college campus, the pulpit, the media, the intellectual and literary journals, the arts and sciences, and from politicians. In most of these groups the movement against the system is participated in only by minorities. Yet, these often are the most articulate, the most vocal, the most prolific in their writing and speaking."[6] Powell cited the favorable campus reception given to William Kunstler, a lawyer for the Chicago Eight, and to Charles Reich, author of the best seller *The Greening of America* and Yale professor, among others. Powell cannot be described as the father of the Right's media empire, but he did clearly understand that the university's educated middle-class cadres were more likely to change the U.S. business system in the short run than were more visible radicals.

A similar theme was taken up later in the 1970s by a figure who did become a major architect of the Right's new infrastructure of foundations, think tanks, publications, activist and journalist training centers, lobbying firms, and politicians—Irving Kristol.[7] Kristol argued that thanks to the university boom, "the traditions of the Left are being absorbed into the agenda of 'progressive reform,' and the structure of American society is being radically, if discreetly, altered."[8] Kristol recognized that the university was a problem for conservative views because of the independent insider that it was creating—because of the "critical thinker" that university leaders going back to Harvard's Charles Eliot had claimed to create for the top and middle ranks of the corporate world.

Conservatives recovered quickly from Republican presidential candidate Barry Goldwater's crushing defeat in the election of 1964, but in the 1970s it still looked as though American liberalism, now mixed with middle-class democratic progressivism, had taken over the country. Conservatives were correct to say that these views were nurtured by academic research and protected by academic freedom. Powell expressed dismay that "leaders in the system" of free enterprise were unable to control universities even though they ran university boards of trustees and funded universities with their tax dollars.[9] These nonconservative college-based middle-class assumptions became more salient as the troubles of Anglo-American capitalism intensified after the end of the Bretton Woods currency agreement in 1971 and the OPEC oil embargo in 1973. It looked to many like progressive positions, now implanted in an increasingly affluent, influential, and educated middle class, might succeed in modernizing, updating, defanging, enlightening, and even partially demilitarizing American capitalism at a time when solidly conservative political and business leadership was failing in visible ways. What if the 1970s were to turn into another 1930s, politically speaking, where a popular majority agreed that capitalist freedoms and affluence were damaged by the Right and helped by some version of Keynesian liberalism, a version that might, this time around, as Kennedy and Johnson yielded to a self-destructive Richard Nixon and a weak Gerald Ford, be more socialist than before? This was not a happy prospect for the Right, particularly its entrenched and economically faltering business leadership.

A Gradual Resurgence

The return of the Right to power during the Reagan presidency is a well-known story, and we should remember here that it was as profoundly cultural as it was economic. Reagan had launched his 1980 presidential campaign in Philadelphia, Mississippi, the site of the murders of four 1960s civil rights workers, and yoked racial to economic resentment with a facility that again made the combination a staple of American politics. Reagan's political movement successfully redefined deserving Americans as white, middle-class Christian conservatives without taint of conscious contact with the social state. The Right's attacks on academic culture rode on Reagan's coattails.

Reagan's rocky second administration witnessed many interrelated developments: the surprising popularity of Allan Bloom's dense, lengthy, and obsessional *The Closing of the American Mind* (1987), and its adoption as a manifesto by conservatives; the discrediting of post-structuralist theory via the posthumous discovery of World War II–era journalism by the eminent literary critic Paul de Man that included apparently anti-Semitic passages (1987); the public controversy surrounding Stanford University's attempt to replace its required Western Culture course, based on a canon of classical readings, with a course called Culture, Ideas and Values (CIV) that sought "to increase [students'] understanding of cultural diversity and the process of cultural interaction"[10] (1988); and an overblown *Newsweek* cover story on a new form of mind control known as political correctness that liberals and leftists were imposing on college campuses around the country (December 1990).

These early attacks targeted liberal and increasingly multicultural humanism, and renewed a tradition in which admonishments from policy makers and education officials became part of scholars' discussions of their field. But initially, the attacks demanded a limited compliance rather than a full-scale repudiation of academic liberalism. The first requests were restricted to rehabilitating teaching functions in the humanities while posing little danger to variegated research. Thus, William Bennett's relatively modest proposal, *To Reclaim a Legacy* (1984), had asked that the humanities "accept its vital role as conveyor of the accumulated wisdom of our civilization."[11] Lynne Cheney's 1988 National Endowment for the Humanities (NEH) report on the humanities in America, while sometimes criticized for its attack on academic specialization, had mostly focused on the need for improved public access to this accumulated wisdom. At the time, these documents seemed compatible with the continued expansion of humanities funding and with their broader dissemination.

The same could be said of books such as Bloom's *Closing of the American Mind* and Roger Kimball's *Tenured Radicals* (1990), which described the modern university's treatment of the humanities as a decline from an earlier, higher vision. They criticized alleged losses of canonical texts, the rise of trendy methodologies, the fragmentation of the knowledge base, and the teaching of material for reasons other than general quality or tradition. Rather than being exposed to time-honored Western values and ideas, 1980s students were said to be exposed to "nihilism, American style," to name a section of Bloom's book, or to "relativism," to cite Kimball's definition of the "New Sophistry." Such trends also expressed themselves in the increasing internationalization of English departments under the auspices of studies of post- or neocolonial culture—anything that suggested yet again, as race and gender studies had, that cultural thought could draw positively on political movements.

Cultural Nationalism from Above

The figure that presided over Roger Kimball's jeremiad was the nineteenth-century English poet, critic, and educator Matthew Arnold. Arnold is best known today for his essay "The Function of Criticism at the Present Time" (1865) and his book *Culture and Anarchy* (1869), but his overall oeuvre and his remarkable commitment to the social relevance of the arts and letters established him early on as a founder of both literary and cultural criticism. Arnold was the writer that most convincingly showed the Anglophone world that literary criticism *was* cultural criticism, that the analysis of poetry shaped the public world.

Yet Arnold held a very particular notion of criticism's public functions. A critic like Kimball could plausibly invoke an Arnold who "looked to criticism to provide a bulwark *against* ideology, against interpretations that are subordinated to essentially political interests."[12] Like other 1980s critics embraced by the political Right, Kimball demanded that the modern academy regard criticism in the same way: as a realm of "truth and virtue" that remains unaffected by partiality and conflict.[13]

Arnold had lived through various periods of social unrest in England, and most of them involved conflicts between different social groups over who would be included in parliamentary democracy. Would democratic sovereignty be expanded to the entire (male) population or not? In particular, would the laboring classes have the same vote as the upper classes, and because of their greater numbers, potentially outvote their educational superiors? Like the majority of his era's upper and educated classes, Arnold did not believe that the laboring classes were ready for self-rule: they allegedly lacked education, lacked culture, and thus lacked the sense of context and proportion that would enable an enlightened vote. Arnold's

originality lay not in his preference for a limited franchise but in his appli- ·
cation of *cultural* policy to the question of the political franchise—in seeking culture as a solution to the potentially disruptive implications of mass
democracy.

Arnold was quite insistent that the masses existed in conflict with civilization. Politics, he claimed, was the sphere where people think one should
be able to "do as one likes." Self-determination marked a crisis of authority:
"For a long time, . . . the strong feudal habits of subordination and deference continued to tell upon the working class. The modern spirit has now
almost entirely dissolved these habits, and the anarchical tendency of our
worship of freedom in and for itself . . . is becoming very evident."[14] The
state must of course exert itself to control the anarchical political will of the
working class—"force till right is ready," Arnold intoned. Cultural criticism
had to exert itself as well.

To see the pertinence of Arnold's thinking to the postwar United States,
we can make a rough analogy between Arnold's 1860s and the American
1960s. In the latter case, traditionally disenfranchised groups—African
Americans with legally impaired rights to public access and political power,
Asian immigrants denied citizenship status, Native American denied access
to their own cultures or control of their traditional lands, Latinos kept outside mainstream economic and political processes—had been demanding,
and gradually receiving, meaningful enfranchisement. The question for political and business leaders was how existing structures would be maintained with new forces and voices at work in society. The university played
an important role in this thinking, both as a treacherous element—the stage
for many disruptive demands—and as a solution—the site in which the
most socially appealing and economically valuable members of historically
marginalized groups would be acculturated, trained, and in some old-
fashioned sense civilized, given a taste for true excellence, made ready to
enter polite society, which was increasingly identified as the knowledge
economy. In short, Arnold supplied the *cultural* means whereby the
working classes would become civilized and therefore middle class. Once
they were middle class, they would be safely conservative.

By defining "culture" as timeless and universal human knowledge, Arnold
helped others see it as a mode of control in a time of democratization.[15]
Arnoldian culture was not the site of human creation, interests, innovation,
and collective interaction where values continuously *changed*. Culture was
an instructive eternity—"the best that has been known and thought in the

world." Cultural truths could be maintained only by being kept apart from the society that should regulate itself in accordance with them. The best way to destroy culture's power of governance was to connect it to a society that, instead of conforming to the rule of universal truth, governed itself with its own rules. Culture was useful (and beautiful) only to the extent that it offered a form of governance higher than democracy.

The distinctiveness of the Right's 1980s Arnoldians was the openness of their defense of a polarity of culture and politics to which many academic humanists more mutely adhered. And though the Arnold revival in the years 1986–1989 sold well and prompted many newspaper features, it did not create a wider stir. The books were not very radical, and the most learned of them, particularly Allan Bloom's, mixed their call for stricter cultural governance with a warm embrace of the liberal arts. In a profile in a national newspaper, Bloom talked about such things as how he "experienced in France the heritage of an intellectual life more organic than our own," and described Paris as a city of otherwise unglimpsed beauty, of "freedom and perspective."[16] Bloom's book might well have led students and members of the public back to the liberal arts, where they would have learned to move beyond his phobic misunderstanding of race consciousness and Black Power. Only a few critics felt the link between innovation in academic cultural studies and a threat to Reagan-era conservative rule. Critics pointed out the political footprints in the garden of the humanities, but, for a long time, no backup arrived.

The Invention of Political Correctness

Why, then, in 1991, did the media start to care about cultural politics on campus? The turning point was the media's discovery of "political correctness." "PC" had been a term used in left-wing circles in the 1980s to refer to fellow leftists who were excessively doctrinaire or inflexible when advocating their positions. The term was then adopted by conservatives as a term of abuse for most liberal-Left positions. Something was politically correct, in this right-wing usage, if it compromised free speech—or allegedly common-sense language—in order to avoid causing offense to a person or group. Much of the controversy focused on efforts to use gender-neutral language ("he or she" or "s/he" instead of "he") or non-racist language ("African-American" or "African American" instead of "Negro," certainly, but also instead of the earlier example of newly correct language, "Afro-

American," which many 1980s whites thought was still okay). Conservatives mocked efforts to replace terms such as "mentally retarded," which carried a historical stigma, with terms such as "intellectually challenged." Some of the fuss revolved around normal discomfort over changing social norms: it was no longer PC to tell the Polack jokes many grew up with, and it was obviously not acceptable for whites to call black folks "niggers," even as it became okay, cool, and even PC for black folks to call one another "niggas." People started writing and buying books with titles like *Politically Correct Bedtime Stories*, and perhaps top management at *Time* began to consider changing its Man of the Year to Person of the Year, which it did in 1999. A great deal of satirical fun was had by all.[17] But there was a more ominous element propelling the debate.

So-called PC terms and attitudes aimed at avoiding the harms that their predecessor terms and attitudes had enabled in the past and were in most cases continuing to enable. These harms were obvious in such terms as "moron," "faggot," and "nigger." But PC-bashing rapidly took on a tone of contempt for the claims of individuals or groups who had been damaged by such terms or attitudes and for their liberal sympathizers. Some of this contempt took the form of scorn for people who thought that changing words could lead to changing deeds. The art critic Robert Hughes asked sarcastically, "Does the cripple rise from his wheelchair, or feel better about being stuck in it, because someone back in the days of the Carter administration decided that, for official purposes, he was 'physically challenged'? Does the homosexual suppose others love him more or hate him less because he is called a 'gay?'"[18] The answer to these rhetorical questions was in fact yes: both terms marked a real interest in creating the conditions that would allow the full participation of both groups in society. Hughes's comment typified an increasing sense of entitlement to complain about attempts to reverse disenfranchisement rather than about the disenfranchisement itself. The terminology was more easily scorned than the policies themselves, since mainstream pundits like Hughes were not likely to attack programs that provided low-cost wheelchairs for injured Vietnam War vets. The vocabulary of enfranchisement rapidly became the primary target of anti-PC abuse.[19]

The media turning point came when *Newsweek* ended 1990 with a cover story on left-wing "thought police."[20] The article's meager data, written up by Jerry Adler, showed that the staff could find very little in the way of empirical referents for the PC movement; they cobbled the story together from a series of disparate campus incidents in which a racial or sexual minority rebelled against a routine slight coming from someone or some group for whom such back talk was "nontraditional." What to these students were often acts of disputation, remedy, reform, or clarified dialogue were described by Adler as insidiously totalitarian and part of a widespread popular front falling just short of conspiracy.

How did these incidents of redress or protest get translated as attacks on freedom? Adler concluded as follows: "There are in fact some who recognize the tyranny of PC, but see it only as a transitional phase, which will no longer be necessary once the virtues of tolerance are internalized. Does that sound familiar? It's the dictatorship of the proletariat, to be followed by the withering away of the state. These should be interesting years."[21] Adler's desperate attempt to show he had a story led him, even as the cold war was about to end, to adopt anticommunist descriptions of Soviet dictatorship to describe students preoccupied with antidefamation and civil rights issues. In reality, these students were largely opposing the everyday barriers to a media-sanctioned "common citizenship," and opposing these barriers with the help of already existing legislation. This made it still more bizarre that language previously used against an apparently expansionist, systematically anti-American nuclear superpower could be immediately redeployed against twenty-year-old members of traditionally powerless social groups whose grievances Adler accepted as valid. But these students were the reformist insiders that Lewis Powell had been concerned about twenty years before. They were being treated as the middle-class cultural wing of a far larger threat.

Adler's piece found many echoes, including one from the prominent columnist George F. Will. Also writing in *Newsweek*, Will claimed that the public had to start paying attention to "the many small skirmishes that rarely rise to public attention but cumulatively condition the nation's cultural, and then, political, life. In this low-visibility, high-intensity war, Lynne Cheney is secretary of domestic defense. The foreign adversaries her husband, Dick, must keep at bay are less dangerous, in the long run, than the domestic forces with which she must deal. Those forces are fighting against the conservation of the common culture that is the nation's social cement."[22] Will echoed McCarthy-era references to internal traitors against whom the nation must direct the forces of national security. He stopped short of calling on the NEH to give fellowships for organizing "common culture" citizens' councils, but he did declare war on insidious "domestic forces" for allegedly trying to start a new civil war at the very moment when Americanism was conquering the world. Arnold had called for "force till right is ready," and in

Will's vision a different Cheney would supervise each half of this marriage of light and power. The nation's our only defense against national fragmentation, he suggested, has been the unifying supervision of a common culture that was being challenged by the excessive self-assertion of college-based minority groups.

The Washington columnist Charles Krauthammer was more explicit about what would soon become a central theme. He too identified a renewed "Socialist" threat to American peace in similarities between political trends in foreign countries and in American universities. These menacing foreign trends were environmentalism and peace, which were bad enough in themselves, but were made worse through their international solidarity with a domestic mutation, the philosophy of deconstruction. Deconstruction was not just a decadent nihilism that the public had prudently ignored, but a Trojan horse for an "intellectually bankrupt 'civil-rights community.'" This civil-rights community, for Krauthammer, "poses a threat that no outside agent in this post-Soviet world can match": "the setting of one ethnic group against another, the fracturing not just of American society but of the American idea." PC was a new form of communism—however college-based and bourgeois—for one overriding reason: it allowed for ethnic differences that were *not* subsumed into a common culture.[23]

The Race Menace

Newspapers and magazines repeatedly suggested a blossoming anarchy, but the link between anarchy and racial difference was most explicit in Dinesh D'Souza's *Illiberal Education* and Arthur Schlesinger's *The Disuniting of America*, both published in 1991. Their books accelerated the evolution of the 1980s theme of "politics" threatening academic truth, virtue, and freedom into the 1990s theme of race consciousness threatening national security. D'Souza's book picked up the 1980s issues of censorship and "politicizing scholarship," but grounded these and other phenomena in the "minority victims' revolution on campus."[24] Readers should not have thought that this book was a brutal and silly mass of anecdotes simply because of the stuffy incompetence of D'Souza's paraphrasing of ideas or the boyish stupidity of his claim that no one feels impaired by "the effects of Western colonialism in the Third World, as well as race and gender discrimination in America."[25] The book's argument was in fact quite consistent: from coast to coast and north to south, the invasion of coercive left-wing politics was showing up in the "racial incidents" that were advancing the "victim's revolution" of those who sought remedies for their wrongly perceived subjugation by America.

D'Souza joined other journalists in seeing the race-based victim's revolution as a spillover from world communism: "One reason for this increasing radicalism is that, with the collapse of Marxism and socialism around the world, activist energies previously channeled into the championship of the proletariat are now 'coming home,' so to speak, and investing in the domestic liberation agenda. A good metaphor of this is that Angela Davis, former vice presidential candidate of the U.S. Communist party, is now professor of the politics of reproduction at San Francisco State University."[26] As D'Souza saw it, die-hard communists, having failed to dupe the workers of the world about production, then turned to reproduction, a topic on which women and minorities are apparently vulnerable to manipulation. "The real problem," he wrote, "is not reader-response theory or deconstructionism *per se*; rather it is the extent to which they serve the ends of a political movement that has propelled them to the forefront of the victim's revolution on campus."[27]

D'Souza's hodgepodge assimilation of disparate disciplines, groups, and intellectual traditions made sense only as moments in an overriding effort to identify civil rights with civil war. Any notion of civil rights based on a "consciousness of racial subordination and difference could lead to a revolution that was already in its first stage on college campuses."[28] Again and again, D'Souza and others denounced the alliance between antiracist social movements and their apparent middle-class university allies. The worst specter was of an outsider-insider alliance that would reconnect college grads to the world's laboring masses. The specter was worsened further by the academic rejection of the old Arnoldian solution. If universities were not going to assimilate the masses to elite culture, what was the point of the academic humanities or of mass higher education overall?

Readers who disliked D'Souza's right-wing diatribes could find a similar rejection of the core elements of the civil rights movement in an early 1990s work by the prominent liberal historian Arthur Schlesinger Jr. Schlesinger had been close to the Kennedy administration and might have been expected to carry a torch for the liberalism that had emerged from that period. Establishment racial liberalism had, at least for a time, endorsed race-conscious egalitarianism. In his famous commencement address at Howard University, President Lyndon Johnson had defined "the next and the more profound stage of the battle for civil rights. We seek not just freedom but opportunity. We seek not just legal equity but human ability, not just equality as a right and a theory but equality as a fact and equality as a result."[29] Equal racial outcomes were the second phase of the civil rights struggle: since no race was genetically or culturally inferior to others, existing gross inequalities of income, child mortality, personal health, were due to racial injustice. The removal of racial barriers would be indicated by relative equality of racial outcomes. This racial egalitarianism was precisely what Schlesinger attacked in his book *The Disuniting of America*.

Like most critics, Schlesinger acknowledged the reality of America's diverse "ethnic" cultures. He then systematically ignored ethnic disparities that could be traced to continuing economic and social injustice. He defined the antiracist agenda as a demand for "group rights"[30] and rejected it in the name of unity under an American Creed, America's answer to Arnold's cultural nationalism.[31]

Schlesinger's creed had three features. First, it required a return to George Washington's ideal of a "new race" forming "one people" in the New World. This now involved an end to "the attack on the common American identity" and renewed respect for "the assimilation process" that produces "an acceptance of the language, the institutions, and the political ideals that hold the nation together." To enable the assimilation process, the creed also required the elimination of race consciousness or color consciousness, on the ground that any group identity was in conflict with one's identity as an individual American. America diverged from more backward cultures through its rejection of racial or ethnic collectivism. These features of Schlesinger's creed directly repudiated two cornerstones of the civil rights movement, which were that Americans of different colors were in practice not treated as part of "one people," and that awareness of race-based wrong preceded corrective measures.

Schlesinger did not stop there. The creed's third element was cultural *inequality*. The unified nation must decisively reject any pretense that the different cultures of the mosaic are roughly comparable or equal to one another in their levels of achievement. "Whatever the particular crimes of Europe, that continent is also the source—the *unique* source—of those liberating ideas of individual liberty, political democracy, the rule of law. . . . There is surely no reason for Western civilization to have guilt trips laid on it by champions of cultures based on despotism, superstition, tribalism, and fanaticism." African and Asian cultures were the referents here. In short, cultural equality is bogus; the West is best. The same principle held true within the United States, in Schlesinger's account, where Euro-American culture need never apologize to, say, African American or Asian American culture for its innate superiorities.

The rise of Reagan had clearly diminished the country's sense that the civil rights movement had been one of the country's historical high points, and Schlesinger was not the only liberal who rejected its cultural and legal frame. The African Americanist Henry Louis Gates Jr. was not a conservative, and yet at the time he went out of his way to oppose what he called "cultural equity," which held that "as people enjoy equal standing under the law, so too must the cultural products of different groups be considered both as representative of those groups and as of at least equal value to those other groups."[32] Legal equality was good, but cultural equality was not. Due process should not lead to the presumption of parity in negotiations among distinct American cultures. Similar moves were made by still other centrists and leftists as the war on PC became part of media culture. The sixties leftist and media scholar Todd Gitlin singled out racial claims as the great enemy of general welfare in *The Twilight of Common Dreams* (1994).

The fact was that by this point in American history, mainstream integrationism—redefined via models like Schlesinger's creed—had rejected the racial egalitarianism of radical 1960s movements and leaders like Malcolm X, and had also rejected the race-conscious non-radicalism of activists like Martin Luther King Jr. Many white liberals joined conservatives in repudiating both the opponents of middle-class reformism *and* that middle-class reformism itself. Equality of opportunity would now end with the chance to apply and compete regardless of the material disadvantages and systematic disparities that influenced the outcome. The culture wars were creating the conditions in which liberals would help conservatives in denouncing the instruments of meaningful equal opportunity, that is, the kind that would have reduced racial disparity of *outcomes*. The language of "quotas" and "special preferences" became commonplace, as did the idea that affirmative action and similar programs penalized white citizens for racial crimes they did not commit. Conservatives portrayed every kind of social equality as a danger to economic efficiency, freedom, and meritocracy. In this deliberately polarized public climate, racial liberals were maneuvered into the position of linking racial progress to continued *in*equality. They generally felt bad about the effects of this inequality, but as the attacks on PC intensified, race consciousness became increasingly stigmatized and more liberals backed away.[33] This was fine with conservatives, for racial inequality was for them a natural part of national order.

The examples of Kimball and the others show that the early 1990s attacks on PC succeeded through their ability to associate PC with race consciousness, which they in turn described as an internal enemy that challenged national unity. The civil rights movement had yoked race consciousness to increased equality, and these were denounced interchangeably in culture-warrior attacks. Arnold-style invocations of a unified and universal national culture expressed a genuine nostalgia while running intellectual cover for a conceptual rollback. The attacks took advantage of a national culture in transition, one in which most of the American population seemed not to know what to do with an increasingly multiracial, culturally dispersed, and economically fragmented democracy, while their leaders seemed to know even less. American society needed new cultural capabilities, new powers of complex analysis and construction. The need was evident in the PC wars themselves, since the phony social crisis of a few ethnic studies courses and isolated campus incidents could have occurred only in a country that needed new bearings. What the country got, instead of new cultural knowledge about multiracial and egalitarian democracy, was the attack on PC. The attack tied racial equality to a communist-style threat to the nation, while making inequality the prerequisite to order.

Within a short time, the sidelines were jammed with pundits booing Team Ethnicity, and with Arnoldians like Kimball intoning, via Evelyn Waugh, that " 'once the prisons of the mind have been opened, the orgy is on.' "[34] The orgy that had finally gotten public attention in the late 1980s was the race orgy, where the top might be on the bottom, the bottom on top, where racial places might be traded—where, at the very least, there would be more sharing of power and real negotiation of new frameworks among relatively equal parties. The culture wars allowed the Red menace to be replaced by the rainbow menace,[35] which was equally dangerous to decent society.

The Triumph of Inequality

Through the attacks on political correctness, culture-war discourse cemented the Reagan-era loss of a key element of the country's cultural capability: to see racial equality as a benefit. Equality now appeared as a drain on efficiency, a handout to the undeserving, an injustice to American families, and an insult to all the whites who had not supported slavery or Jim Crow. This was a real decline in the intellectual ecosystem, much like the loss of a plant species that, by interacting with other plants and animals, had allowed the ensemble to thrive. One journalist defined the loss as "The End of Equality."[36] It was the end of equality as a core element of general social development.

The effects of this early 1990s conceptual decline were measurable and concrete. Racial gaps in college participation rates stopped closing around that time.[37] Racial gaps in test scores stopped closing around that time.[38] Overall college participation rates began to stagnate around that time and never recovered: internationally, by the early 2000s, the United States was regularly in last place among wealthy countries in gains in college participation rates.[39] Racial gaps in wealth, income, and health indicators, among many others, have shown little improvement since 1990 and in some cases have gotten worse. Poverty rates for African Americans fell dramatically during the 1960s' War on Poverty, fell again (though much less so) during the 1990s boom, and then, like Latino poverty rates, gave back their gains in the 2000s:[40] by the early 2000s, white families with children under eighteen had twice the income of their black and Latino counterparts, and a much higher multiple of wealth.[41] As racial gaps ceased to narrow, class gaps widened dramatically: since 1973, the top 5 percent of households have seen their wealth increase at about five times the rate of the middle 20 percent, and this trend accelerated markedly after 1990.[42]

While economic inequality increased, most traditional policy mitigations were cut. Here I mention only those involving higher education. Budget reductions and softening commitments to equality caused public universities to reduce their commitments to need-based financial aid. Aid to students from the most affluent families grew at five times the rate of aid to the poorest students. Wealthy colleges (those in the top quarter, ranked by expenditures per student) increased their expenditures per student at six times the rate of colleges in the bottom quarter.[43] The modes in which inequality has grown could form a lengthy list.

The PC wars did not single-handedly produce the backlash against equality. But the PC wars shattered the country's still incomplete cultural understanding of equality as a positive value. Prior to the culture wars, equality had survived Reaganism as a positive goal associated not only with justice but with effectiveness: much 1980s management literature, for example, documented a causal link between interpersonal fairness and higher corporate productivity.[44] By the time the PC wars were done, equality had become a synonym for mediocrity, failed government programs, and coddled incompetence. Equality came to be seen as the enemy of economic competitiveness, and the survival of American affluence came to depend on getting rid of it. Without the attacks on academic PC, there may well have arisen a national discussion about how to move our social structures beyond the stagnant government-market impasse. In the continued absence of this discussion, the United States would never learn how to build cross-racial systems of social development.

— 4 —

The Market Substitute
for Cultural Knowledge

The American college had never been a radical institution. Faculty were rightly famous for their ties to past traditions, for their attachment to peer-reviewed authority, for their slowness to change their minds. Before the boom of public universities after World War II, most colleges saw themselves as careful groomers of society leaders and professional elites. The administration of a university had to think about money day and night, and yet also about the quality and health of the academic community, since damage to that could never be repaired with money alone. This combination of complex financial calculations, deep involvement with government and industry, entrenched tenured faculty, and student concerns about institutional quality and prestige meant that major academic change was difficult and slow.

And yet higher education, by its very nature, challenged the conservative dogma that social and cultural practice had to submit to capitalist logic. In spite of the anti-PC attacks, colleges and universities were more in demand than ever, and these popular institutions saw cost as only one of many legitimate factors to consider. Cost had a secondary place in the thinking of faculty, students, and frontline staff, who were concerned primarily with the success of instruction and research, and then, just behind those, with public service. All of these involved the pursuit and dissemination of knowledge. This was also true of industry relations: in principle, the university side of the contract was only as good as its knowledge contribution. The pursuit and dissemination of knowledge were seen as nonmarket activities: sooner or later they would help the economy, but market mechanisms that included price signals and efficiency management were widely believed to interfere with the process of knowledge creation. Mainstream neoclassical economics had shown that basic research could never be justified by any one firm's rational calculations of returns on investment. Orthodox economists had called on society to bite the public funding bullet and pay for basic research.[1] This meant that from one side of campus to the other, from the dance studio to the IBM-funded scanning tunneling microscopy center, market factors had to compete with educational goals.

Thus even a conservative university was not conservative in the sense that mattered for PC warriors. What mattered to them was a unified and therefore highly manageable culture. The university, in contrast, had a divided culture, one in which economics had to share power with education—that is, with the complicated requirements of human development.

In the university, in short, there was really no way around a détente or partnership between economic and educational goals. Most of the relevant activities were expensively labor-intensive and risky. Most first drafts were mediocre. Most scientific experiments failed. Reliable profits can in general be made only from routinized production of already-completed inventions, while the processes of invention, creation, and learning are full of trial and terror and dubious but ultimately useful actions that, individually, do not pay off.

To make matters worse, the university was proud of its divided culture. It tried to be fiscally responsible, and if anything had been too conservative, too cautious, and too careful with its money. But it also trumpeted the process of creating both knowers and knowledge as unpredictable, mysterious, exciting, risk oriented, dangerous, exhilarating, magical, and unique. Although universities could be run prudently, their processes could not be rationalized. By their very nature, universities were a mild affront to market values. Simply by existing, they showed that markets could not encompass all human activity. In the moment in which the market claimed to transcend society, the university was still claiming, through its everyday operation, to transcend the market.

This is why the more advanced culture warriors held that cultural values had profound economic implications. We can see this in Dinesh D'Souza, who warned his readers that the minority revolutionaries sought "a fundamental restructuring of American society. [Their plan] involves basic changes in the way economic rewards are distributed, in the way cultural and political power are exercised, and also in privately held and publicly expressed opinions."[2] He entitled his attack on affirmative action "More Equal than Others" and called his exposé of victim-loving theorists "The Last Shall Be First." Both titles suggest that D'Souza saw academic thinking about race as a challenge to the economic and political hierarchies of American society, where the "first" should not have their places challenged. Similarly, his complaint about teaching the book *I, Rigoberta Menchú* in one of Stanford's eight Culture, Ideas, and Values classes was that the native Guatemalan activist and Nobel-prize winner Menchú regarded history as leading toward "the final emancipation of the proletariat."[3] For D'Souza, the ideals of racial and economic equality were continuously found together and posed a similar threat to the standing economic management on which social order was presumed to depend. The reduction of racial inequality of the kind that was in the offing after the 1950s threatened to reduce economic inequality—which was often assumed to mean reducing profitability for people and companies at the top. This was of particular concern from the mid-1970s on, when profit levels were falling, the rate of productivity increases was down, the gross domestic product was growing at its lowest rates since the Great Depression, and calls for better social programs and broader sharing of wealth were continuing to be heard. It was hardly surprising, in this context, that the culture wars had a simultaneous economic and racial agenda for those who waged them.

Culture warriors needed the kind of arguments that, in this post-1960s world, would block not only racial equality, but also the economic majoritarianism that was likely to follow. They needed arguments that would block the idea that wider distribution of wealth makes wealth-creation more efficient. What kinds of arguments would these be?

They would have to be arguments that did not stop with attacking the liberal intentions behind civil rights and its related economic broadening: the general principles of equal treatment and equal economic opportunity were more or less majority views, in principle if not in practice. Culture warriors would need to move beyond the base of anti-liberalism established by Reaganomics in the early 1980s, with its rejection of the economic value of government and its equation of economic self-interest with political liberty. Culture warriors would need to build beyond the University of Chicago's "Law and Economics" movement as well, though it had laid vital groundwork in the conservative revolution by claiming, as its leading light, Judge Richard Posner, did, in a case involving a university's regulation of a student journalist, that "market concerns should be weighed with the First Amendment rights of college journalists."[4]

In short, culture warriors would need arguments that could show why market forces could and should dominate race and other cultural factors in the management of economic institutions. We can see these arguments under development in two examples from the formative period of the late 1980s and early 1990s. An important Supreme Court decision on race in the workplace put market forces and their college-educated white-collar interpreters in a protected position. And a new president's abandonment of his nominee to a high position in his Justice Department again subjugated cultural knowledge to market thinking.

The Rehabilitation of Market Forces

American law had never been hostile to the consideration of market factors, but its highest levels embraced the market in a series of 1980s Supreme Court decisions involving race and employment. The most interesting of these was *Ward's Cove Packing Co. v. Atonio* (1989). In this case, Alaskan cannery workers had brought a suit against company management on the grounds that Asian and native Alaskan employees were far more likely to be found in unskilled line jobs than in better-paid managerial positions, where white employees predominated. The cannery workers' suit did not allege discriminatory intent but, instead, discriminatory effects. Their suit confronted the core issue of whether civil rights law, which aimed at racial equality, actually produced racial equality, here defined as some rough proportionality between the percentage of a racial group in the workforce and the percentage found at a given level of the organization. The stakes were familiar: Would civil rights change the racial structure of business organizations? Would the courts require forms of management that would both seek and achieve more proportionate racial representation at all levels of the organization? Or would "facially neutral" procedures continue to lead to traditional kinds of racial stratification?

Justice Byron White, writing the majority decision in favor of management's existing policy, acknowledged that the Court had interpreted Title VII of the Civil Rights Act of 1964 to prohibit not only discriminatory intentions but ostensibly unintended yet discriminatory outcomes.[5] He agreed that the "employer's selection mechanism" may not lead directly to a "percentage of selected applicants who are nonwhite [that is] significantly less than the percentage of qualified applicants who are nonwhite."[6] Nonetheless, White's opinion reaffirmed the capacity of managers to produce exactly such racial disparities as long as they did not use openly discriminatory language to do so.

White accomplished this by reasserting the rights of market factors over racial impacts and other sociocultural considerations. In important earlier cases, the Supreme Court had ruled that a determination of disparate impact would prevail over a management preference unless management could show business *necessity*.[7] This was not easy to do, since there was rarely only one best method to maintain profitability, and no theory had ever shown that the best method was an all-white executive suite. In practice, therefore, racial outcomes had been factored into labor-management relations along with the economic interests of employers. White's opinion undermined this precedent by reversing its priority: market outcomes had priority over racial ones. Unskilled cannery workers would now need to show that "any alternative practices which [they] offer up in this respect must be equally effective as petitioners' [management's] chosen hiring procedures in achieving petitioners' legitimate employment goals." Moreover, "[f]actors such as the cost or other burdens of proposed alternative selection devices are relevant in determining whether they would be equally as effective as the challenged practice in serving the employer's legitimate business goals."[8]

This passage marked a sea change in the relation between sociocultural factors and economics. By replacing business necessity with a mere business goal, White in effect said social discrimination need not be financially necessary, just financially desirable. Racism was neither financially desirable nor financially necessary, but White's decision shifted the burden of proof. Now employees would have to "persuade the factfinder that [their] alternative practices, which reduce the racially disparate impact of practices currently being used, would also serve the employers' legitimate interests." As Justice John Paul Stevens noted in his dissenting opinion, White had replaced the employer's obligation to prove a practice's "business necessity" with what was in effect merely management's reasonable preference.[9] In addition, though the employer must be willing to try to justify the preference, the employer need not actually succeed in persuading the affected persons or the courts.[10] This was a quiet but important blow to a negotiating framework in which the concerns of the less powerful party—whose lesser power, in this case, was directly tied to its racialization—could be set aside by market calculations as interpreted solely by management. It is worth noting that White assumed that unskilled employees would not understand economic and financial complexities, such that all financial decisions were rightly placed in the hands of college-grad managers.

White's decision was notable for sweeping aside the post-1960s assumption that progress toward racial justice required analyzing culture, law, politics, and economics in their interrelations. Racial integration had been thought to entail the conceptual integration of the various dimensions of social life. This view had both inspired and been inspired by major advances in academic cultural knowledge. One symptom had been the rise of cultural studies, in conjunction with ethnic studies and lesbian and gay studies, where economic, cultural, political, social, and organizational issues had come together. Cultural studies had arisen as a "fifth discipline," in Michael Denning's phrase, one that supplemented economics, political science, sociology, and anthropology by focusing on the new world of communications and noting the convergence of various disciplines around common problems.[11] The PC wars were attacking this kind of interdisciplinarity for being too left-wing, which in fact meant its refusal to allow economics and market dynamics to transcend other factors in social life. The implacable language of Supreme Court decisions inhabits a sphere far from that of anti-PC polemic. But these discourses worked in parallel and aided one another. The culture wars used a range of discourses to cut academic cultural knowledge down to size. Through *Ward's Cove* and related decisions, the Supreme Court formally subjected cultural knowledge to market factors as interpreted by management. The culture wars formed the context in which the joint dangers of racial and economic equality could be linked and contained through managerial authority.

Markets and Civil Rights

The election of Bill Clinton to the U.S. presidency in November 1992 at first seemed like the triumph of liberalism over conservatism and like a generational shift in power from the World War II generation to that of the 1960s. In fact it marked something starkly different: a series of liberal acceptances of new ground rules engineered in large part by culture-wars offenses.

Clinton's successful presidential campaign showed the symptoms early on. Three weeks before the New Hampshire primary, Governor Clinton returned to his home state of Arkansas to preside over the execution of Ricky Ray Rector, a mentally disabled black inmate who had been convicted of killing a white police officer. In June of that year, in the heat of the campaign, Clinton used a speech to the National Rainbow Coalition, Jesse

Jackson's organization, to denounce the black hip-hop artist Sister Souljah for some negative remarks she had made about whites.[12]

In setting himself up against stock figures in American racial politics—the black killer of whites and the black hater of whites—Clinton was adapting the racial symbolism deployed by his 1992 opponent George H. W. Bush in the latter's 1988 "Willie Horton" campaign. Bush's most famous attack ad had denounced the excessive racial leniency Governor Michael Dukakis had shown in supporting a weekend furlough program during which Horton, a convicted black murderer, had committed rape and armed robbery. Four years later, Clinton was moving against such figures before they could be moved against him.[13]

Those who expected Clinton to shift back to an outspoken pro–civil rights position after the election were slated for disappointment. Clinton instead replaced the campaign's racial symbolism with a more systematic but similar racial strategy. This involved a core element of Clinton's New Democrat vision, which had sought to move the party away from its post-1930s affiliations with labor and with black civil rights. Blue-collar and black Americans often collided politically, and yet in the emerging New Economy they were lumped together as economic losers, and socially expensive ones to boot. In the political sphere, the culture wars helped paint African Americans as lacking thē cultural values required to succeed in the post–cold war global environment. A related 1980s yuppie culture did the same to the blue-collar heartland, which in its Reagan-era reading was not being deliberately deindustrialized in order to reduce labor costs, increase short-term profits, and raise stock prices for the benefit of executives and shareholders, but was simply falling behind the global competition.[14] The culture wars reduced understanding of the sociocultural dimensions of economic development. They simultaneously discredited traditional hopes that increased profitability and economic growth would increase equality and lead to development for all. Though Clinton did strengthen some civil rights protections when he could do so quietly, and defended affirmative action when it was under attack in California, he shared this vision of an economic strategy that would reduce business's social costs today in exchange for assurances of a boom tomorrow.[15]

In theory, market forces are compatible with strong civil rights protections. In practice, civil rights raise the up-front social costs of doing business, in part by raising expectations for a better life through more inclusive, higher-quality social services and protections, which in turn support demands for decent wages. Though business overall gets this investment back in the form of a more productive workforce, lower health-care costs, and so on, it generally prefers that its economic interests, short-term especially, determine tax rates, labor protections, equal opportunity regulations, and related structures. Clinton's own culture war on, for example, black anger, became more systematic once he had taken office. It would thus be consistent with his prior commitments that he would reject a form of voting rights that, by requiring multilateral negotiations among distinct social interests, would have complicated the concentration of economic power that marked his time in office.

The Guinier Nomination

In April 1993, the Clinton administration announced the nomination of a University of Pennsylvania law professor named Lani Guinier to the position of assistant attorney general for civil rights. The post required Senate confirmation, and it slated her to become the leading figure for the enforcement of civil rights law. Guinier combined practical experience as a federal civil rights litigator with a substantial record of academic research. She had also been friends with the president and first lady for many years. The Clintons had attended Guinier's wedding in 1986, and she had socialized with them in the period after Clinton's inauguration. Although Guinier was part of a raft of Justice Department nominees who were expected to be confirmed as a "package deal," an editorial in the April 30 edition of the *Wall Street Journal* ended the routine nature of her confirmation by slamming her academic writings and labeling her a "quota queen." Guinier spent the next several weeks telling senators and other officials that she was in fact opposed to quotas, that her academic research sought alternatives to them, and that she believed in "one-man-one-vote" in spite of repeated press claims to the contrary. This self-defense and explication finally did not matter. After letting the debate go on throughout the month of May 1993, Clinton wound up pulling her nomination—over her public protests—before she had a chance to explain her ideas to the Senate's Judiciary Committee.

In terms of power politics, this retreat was a disaster for Clinton. It taught the Republican opposition that if they attacked one of his people hard and long enough—even a personal friend—he would back away. Clinton similarly retreated from his "gays in the military" campaign of that first year of his administration, and having taken a dive twice in his first year, Clinton politically doomed his already ambiguous health-care initiative in the following year. After Guinier, Clinton's victories consisted of those like the North American Free Trade Agreement (1994) and welfare reform (1996) that were desired by Republicans anyway. If the withdrawal of Guinier's nomination was a landmark blunder, why did one of the shrewdest politicians of his generation commit it?

The answer lies in the fact that Clinton was unwilling to buck the culture wars' racial consensus, and was most likely committed to it himself. Guinier had rejected this consensus's core elements: a preestablished unity that could regulate diversity; color blindness, and natural (now market-based) racial inequality, which meant that racial disparity would no longer be traced to discrimination. Although the Bush I administration's Glass Ceiling Commission had found that the American boardroom remained 95 percent white and male, it did not hold that such stratification required new forms of external monitoring or a change in legal rules.[16] The same logic was applied to politics: once a majority had been cobbled together through any legal process that worked, that majority had every right to pass rules that benefited itself at the expense of the minority. If a majority chose to better itself by making rules and following strategies that in effect cut opportunities, benefits, or services to a minority, this was not discrimination or unjust inequality; this was how majority rule worked.

In his announcement of the withdrawal of the Guinier nomination, Clinton went out of his way to reject her academically grounded ideas. Though this strategy forced him to admit that neither he nor, presumably, his staff had read Guinier's academic articles prior to nominating her, it allowed him to state that "they clearly lend themselves to interpretations that do not represent the views that I expressed on civil rights during my campaign, and views that I hold very dearly."[17] Pressed later to explain what he meant, Clinton said:

> I can give you an idea. In the *Michigan Law Review*, there was an article. Lani analyzed the weaknesses of the present remedies available under the Voting Rights Act, and many of her analyses I agree with, but seem to be arguing for principles of proportional representation and minority veto as general remedies that I think inappropriate as general remedies and antidemocratic, very difficult to defend.
>
> Now the Supreme Court has obviously changed the law on that. But the whole thrust of that kind of argument, it seems to me, is inconsistent with the arguments that I tried to make to members of all races all during my campaign.[18]

Clinton was clearly concerned that Guinier was more race conscious than the political mainstream, that she did not see the electorate as one whole, and above all, that she did not see majority rule as fair by definition.[19]

Guinier denied that she either favored quotas or sought increases in racial bloc voting, and there is nothing in her published work to suggest otherwise. She repeatedly claimed that she sought "an integrated legislature in which all of its members work together for the common good," but she believed that such integration was what American communities had yet to build together.[20] But on the charge of critiquing majoritarianism when it aggravates inequality, she pled guilty. Her academic writing focused on finding remedies for the familiar kinds of discrimination that emerge from the apparently neutral and in our terms market-based form of majority rule.

Guinier was particularly concerned with black-minority districts in which the historical fact of white bloc voting had prevented black representatives from holding power, sometimes for a hundred years.[21] In such cases, where the "totality of the evidence" suggested majority discrimination, Guinier proposed alternative voting schemes, such as cumulative voting.

Most discussants of Guinier's work appeared unable to give an accurate account of her contributions to legal thought, although the facts they describe had been central to American history. Clinton, though an unusually brilliant policy mind, made similar errors, describing, for example, voting schemes designed to improve coalition-building as fundamentally divisive. These kinds of systematic mistakes are signs of the impaired cultural capacity that blocks the appropriate synthesis of various social forces. They are signs of the culture wars at work.

The guiding principle in Guinier's research was the unradical but still-controversial concept of power sharing. Martin Luther King Jr. had advocated it, César Chávez had advocated it, any number of other civil rights leaders had advocated it, and Lani Guinier also advocated it.[22] The basic concept was simple and democratic. As Guinier put it, "The rules should reward those who win, but they must be acceptable to those who lose."[23] A situation in which the majority imposes rules that are unacceptable to the minority she called "the tyranny of the majority." The philosopher Jean-François Lyotard had called it "terror," in the sense of the coerced exclusion from a language game in this case, the language game of political negotiation.[24] In the context of U.S. racial history, with its white-power monopolies backed up by lynching and related terrorist practices, majority rule had in many cases functioned as a mechanism of impaired capacity in which many of the interests, perspectives, desires actually in play in a complex social system were ruled out of bounds. Power sharing, in contrast, replaced a hierarchy of winners and losers with enough equality for negotiation and inclusion.[25]

Although Clinton had continually called for reconciliation among different groups, he nonetheless accepted society's rules for turning the procedures of self-governance into a hierarchy of winners and losers. More to the point, he accepted mechanisms in which the winners could control the ground rules of the competition such that they would continue to win and then—once having won—exert unilateral power. On the other hand, Guinier's legal writings directly disputed the idea that it was either fair or necessary for the winners to be able to exclude the losers from power, resource sharing, or joint rule making. What was clearly more important to her than rewarding the winners was the functioning of the overall system. Was the voting process effective for everyone and *not only* for the winners? Was it fair for everyone and *not only* for the winners?

Where an individual or group loses again and again, and can be defined as a loser, Guinier saw a violation of democratic precept rather than an inevitable stratification of talent or initiative. She thus sought to replace winner take all with the "principle of taking turns." This simple process did indeed threaten to open the door to outcomes negotiated among all the parties in politics, including minority groups and electoral losers and the culturally marginalized. Voting would then not be a straightforward market competition between two competing brands, but a social process in which cultural factors—history, psychology, power relations, artistic output— would play a role in deciding how all the parties would treat one another.

There was a further, unspoken implication of Guinier's thinking: if politics was not a market but a process of negotiated intervention, might the same be said for the economy itself? Criticisms of Guinier implied that they saw her voting mechanisms as the political equivalent of collective bargaining, in which managerial authority has to be shared among executives and employees alike. In politics, that kind of thing might lead toward multiracial democracy. In business, it might lead toward what used to be called industrial democracy or, at the very least, the multilateral regulation of markets, particularly for goods deemed socially valuable.

In defending the culture wars' racial orthodoxy from Guinier's critiques, Clinton defended the market version of democracy as head-to-head competition shorn of historical or social context. In other words, Clinton defended the managerial, the unilateral, and the monopoly version of majority rule, a version where the winners can make the rules that allow them to keep winning indefinitely. This move was crucial: that particular 1990s style of economic success depended on downsizing, reengineering, merging, acquiring, and related forms of highly mobile investing that in turn depended on the concentrated power of large shareholders and executives over their employees, who would have voted against their disposability. Managerial sovereignty, invoking market forces as its ground of authority, would have been challenged by Guinier's antimonopolistic, civil rights–based notion of power sharing and consensus decision making in groups.

Clinton flatly rejected the key elements of Guinier's thought—racial consciousness, equality, historical memory, power sharing, and placing competitive outcomes in a social framework. Her ideas reflected crucial parts of the country's cultural capability for understanding how truly democratic voting procedures might work. Although it is risky to play what-if with history, we can speculate that without the culture wars' reduction of the cultural knowledge required to understand her ideas, Guinier would have been appointed to the Department of Justice and would have helped create a more coherent discussion of race and culture in national life. Had *that* happened, the country may well have had the intellectual resources it needed to avoid the simpleminded controversies over affirmative action that dominated the mid-1990s.

— 5 —

From Affirmative Action
to the New Economy

By 1994, culture warriors had largely discredited the concepts of cultural and civil equality, had cast race consciousness as dangerously divisive, and had reestablished market competition as the best solution to social ills. They had used the Guinier nomination to split open a liberal civil rights community already riddled with stress fractures. Thus, when conservative politicians and activists shifted the spotlight to affirmative action in 1993 and 1994, they could count on reduced cultural intelligence about the meaning and effects of those programs. This reduced intelligence also dimmed the electorate's ability to understand affirmative action's economic implications.

The Real New Economy

In California, Pete Wilson had already served as mayor of San Diego and U.S. senator before he became the state's thirty-sixth governor in 1991. He won reelection to a second term in 1995 and thus was California's governor throughout the legendary 1990s, which started with a terrible economic downturn and ended with the dot-com boom and the Internet-fueled, information-technology (IT)-driven New Economy. On the surface, the historical progression would seem to be that the old economy's leading industries—aerospace, automobiles, and so on—were allowed to die so that the new leaders—IT, biotechnology—could come to the fore. California seemed to be a successful laboratory experiment in Schumpeter's famous "creative destruction," in which a free market does not artificially protect declining industries but transfers its resources to domains of new and greater value.

Wilson was a socially moderate free-market Republican whose economic principles were deemed correct by enough voting Californians to earn him reelection as the economy was beginning to turn around in 1995. The creative destruction model—decline-reinvestment-renewal—concealed a major transformation in California's social structure. The state was participating in a national pattern, which was the stagnation or decline of the medium-to-good incomes that had defined that postwar trademark of American life, the mass middle class. In the nearly two decades that had followed the oil crisis and recession of 1973, average wages corrected for inflation had barely budged. During the Bush I administration (1989–1993), median household income actually fell 5 percent.[1] The spectacle of enormous wealth that marked the 1980s and 1990s alike took place at the top of the wealth and income pyramids, whose occupants did exceptionally well: by the end of the 1990s, wealth inequality in the United States was approaching the 1920s record, which it would surpass by around 2005.[2] These and similar trends amounted to a decline in the share of national resources going to the middle class. The process had begun long before Wilson arrived in the California statehouse: during the late 1970s and 1980s, white-collar cadres had done nothing while mass layoffs overtook what had once been a flourishing blue-collar middle class. Political and business leaders offered lots of explanations and excuses, but at the end of the day, the excuses did not really matter. The country's business leaders had calculated that they could make higher returns on investment outside of U.S.-based manufacturing, and they steadily eliminated a large percentage of the country's manufacturing jobs. By the 1990s the American layoff machine started to buzz through the white-collar cubicles.

This was the special feature of the California recession: it offered the country the spectacle of mass layoffs for the largely college-educated white-collar middle class. The state had fewer jobs in 1994 than in 1990, when the recession began. State unemployment rates were about 3 percent higher than in the rest of the country and by 1993 approached 10 percent.[3] The aerospace sector, a cornerstone of the state's Republican Party and symbol of its faith in continuous upward mobility, lost almost 150,000 jobs, around 45 percent of the total loss.[4] The sacrosanct California middle-class cushion—ever-inflating housing prices—deflated, in some cases by more than 25 percent.[5] The trademark institution of the California middle class—public higher education—suffered dramatic budget cuts that were never fully reversed, even during the late 1990s boom.[6] In 1992 and 1993, the Field Poll found that more than 90 percent of the California public perceived that they were living in bad economic times.[7] In short, the state whose reputation was based on offering the middle-class dream for all comers, and which had drawn large migrations of people of color as well as whites with this dream, showed that even its white middle class was vulnerable, disposable, and finally not economically important.

If you are a governor presiding over the worst economic period since the Great Depression, one that is cutting into your political base, what exactly do you do? One possibility would have been some kind of Keynesian—or Earl Warren–style—intervention, that is, government-led investment in public infrastructure from roads to schools to universities to bullet trains and high technology that could create or attract new industry and new well-paid jobs.

Wilson took a cheaper road. California's biggest problems, he claimed, were criminals, immigrants, and the poor, for they burdened social services, caused high taxes (which he raised substantially soon after he took office in 1991), and forced businesses to take their jobs out of state. Wilson sponsored two ballot propositions that prevailed in November of 1994: Proposition 184 mandated very long sentences for a "third strike"—a third felony, whether that felony was violent or not; Proposition 187 denied social services to undocumented residents, including schooling for their children. Since the voting population had a far higher proportion of the white middle class than did the state population as a whole, Wilson could appeal to the interests of voters while ignoring those of low-turnout communities. Both propositions passed with little trouble.

In January 1995, following these victories, Wilson delivered what may have been the most unpleasant inaugural address in California history. He described California as an erstwhile "valley of promise" that was beset by illegal immigrants, dangerous criminals, and unemployed unwed mothers, all assisted by that great enabler, failed government programs. "We must choose whether California will be the Golden State—or a welfare state. It can't be both," Wilson intoned. "The people" in Wilson's account wanted to know not, for example, what was happening to middle-class corporate jobs, but why the "welfare system taxes working people who can't afford children and pays people who don't work for having more children?"[8] "We must free our people, and release their creative energy," he exclaimed. But the seekers of creative freedom first had to eliminate illegal immigrants, deadbeat dads, and the racially coded "fatherless child of a teen mother [who] becomes a teen predator, and the trigger man for his gang." Though Wilson did not mention affirmative action as an equal scourge, it was in the same month, and in the same spirit, that Wilson's appointee to the University of California Board of Regents, Ward Connerly, announced his investigation of "racial preferences" in UC admissions.

The attack on affirmative action was in part another diversion: the public might have asked why state leaders had not built a new University of California campus in thirty years, during a period in which the state's population doubled and the gross state product tripled.[9] Instead, their leaders encouraged them to ask why some Chicanos were getting into UC Berkeley without 4.0 grade point averages. On a deeper level, the culture war on affirmative action did not only divert attention from economic policies; the culture war actively affirmed the Right's inegalitarian economic policies. To see this, we need to understand the structure of the affirmative action debate.

Targeting Affirmative Action

By 1995, several conservative legal foundations had been litigating campus issues for years and had scored victories against race-conscious programs at the University of Maryland and elsewhere.[10] The issue got national attention during the Wilson-Connerly campaign to end affirmative action at the University of California, which succeeded in July 1995, and which rallied support for the passage of Proposition 209 in November 1996, which prohibited affirmative action in all state government, and whose campaign Connerly chaired.

The issue was ready to explode after the racial controversies that emerged from Governor Pete Wilson's success with Proposition 187. Some credit for the new targeting of UC admissions went to a family called the Cooks, who were repeating the complaint of the 1978 Supreme Court *Bakke* case regarding a rejection from a family member's preferred medical school (in a twist on the *Bakke* case, he was rejected from UC San Diego but accepted where Bakke had sued for admission, at UC Davis).[11] The issue's life depended on Wilson and Connerly's orchestrated campaign. Affirmative action, they argued, put a person's race ahead of his or her individual merit in a hiring or admissions process. Though they sometimes acknowledged the country's history of racial discrimination, Connerly and his allies linked affirmative action to two negative phrases: "racial preferences" and "reverse discrimination." Once they put it in these terms, affirmative action critics made two related and effective points.

First, they argued, affirmative action was exactly the kind of racial thinking that landmark federal antidiscrimination legislation had outlawed. Proposition 209 was called the California Civil Rights Initiative, and its language deliberately echoed the Civil Rights Act of 1964: its first clause read, "The state shall not discriminate against, or grant preferential treatment to, any individual or group on the basis of race, sex, color, ethnicity, or national origin in the operation of public employment, public education, or public contracting."[12] Advocates for an affirmative action ban cast themselves as civil libertarians who were following in the footsteps of Martin Luther King Jr. Connerly put his opposition to affirmative action at UC in these terms, and regularly associated himself with King's legacy.

The second argument was that valued goods such as places in highly selective universities should be allocated through fair and open competition. If members of a racial group got extra points for race—and indeed routinized admissions processes at large public universities often did give points for this—then the principle of fair competition would be violated. Putting these two arguments together, affirmative action critics could present themselves as defending individual rights and achievements against both racial discrimination and the skewing of fair market competition.

The UC administration's response was coherent and under ordinary circumstances might have prevailed. At the fateful Regents meeting in July 1995, UC president Jack Peltason described the results of a review of UC admissions: the programs were "in the American egalitarian tradition," he said, sought only to remove barriers to access, and were essentially sound. He also described some immediate reforms. He announced the termination of automatic admissions for UC-qualified students from underrepresented groups (affecting the Davis and Irvine campuses) and the extension of "more comprehensive review" from underrepresented applicants to all applicants (affecting the Berkeley and Los Angeles campuses). Many campuses had been evaluating students who were underrepresented and those who were not in different ways, and were indeed out of compliance with *Bakke* and related decisions. Peltason also noted that "admission by exception" (for students who did not meet minimum academic standards, and which included athletes, musicians, other special talents, children of alumni or Regents, etc.) amounted to 4.5 percent of admissions systemwide, had been falling in recent years, and would be monitored for any overreliance on race and ethnicity. He further announced the opening of race- and gender-targeted faculty and staff recruitment programs to all comers.[13]

In American political life, it is hard to defeat a group that occupies the traditional high ground of individualism and market competition. Arguments about the true nature of merit, the historical legacies of racism, and the effect of racialized power relations were generally correct, but they lacked the simple fit with the conventional wisdom on the anti-affirmative action side, which said with great consistency (1) never discriminate on grounds of race and (2) ensure a level playing field. Citations of the real views of Martin Luther King Jr. on the need for ongoing affirmative intervention in unjust situations were countered with stories about the children of black surgeons being preferred over those of white coal miners' daughters. To the traditional pro–affirmative action claim that one needed awareness of race to defeat racism, opponents said that with skin-color racism largely a thing of the past, it was time to take a next step, "beyond race." The Regental bans on affirmative action in the University of California passed by votes of 14–10 and 15–10, and in the following year, Proposition 209 passed with 54 percent of the vote, and survived court challenges.

The De-integration of Elites

These critiques of affirmative action would have had less hold on the California imagination had they been applied to government jobs in the California Department of Transportation or Department of Finance. They became generally interesting only when applied to the highly selective world of the most prestigious University of California campuses. The state's higher education system was in principle open to all regardless of means: when Pete Wilson had attended Boalt Law School at UC Berkeley (class of 1962), it was nearly free. In that period, UC's flagship campuses had been relatively easy to get into, even with average SAT scores: in the 1950s, Berkeley accepted the vast majority of in-state students who applied for admission.[14] But as noted above, in the thirty years prior to the 1995 affirmative action debate, a period in which the state population had doubled, the state had not built a single new UC campus.[15] Similarly, the particularly savage state budget cuts of the Wilson years had further limited program expansion while forcing the university into double-digit annual increases in student fees. In spite of the increased fees, UC remained inexpensive compared to elite private universities like Stanford and Caltech, and its comparably high-status campuses were especially coveted. By 1995, UC had become a scare resource, increasingly difficult to attend both academically and financially.

Ward Connerly received enormous press coverage when he initiated his review of the university's admissions practices with a special focus on their race-conscious aspects, asserting as his premise that prized places at UC Berkeley and UCLA were going to mediocre students of color. Connerly complained to the *New York Times* that "we have a system where we're turning away white and Asian kids with 4.0s on a wholesale basis and admitting blacks and Chicanos with 3.3s."[16] In effect, Connerly invited rejected white applicants to trace their disappointment to admitted students of color, whose overall records of achievement were never described. The governor contributed to the line of thought in which black and Latino admitted students could seem to be the beneficiaries of an obsolete form of charity. In an op-ed piece a month before the Regents' vote, Wilson wrote that affirmative action had become "expressly based on preferential treatment in the form of quotas . . . that made race and gender determining factors."[17] He made any race consciousness in the admissions process sound like "a little bit pregnant" or "I just cheated a little": once you skewed fair competition with a little racial or gendered factoring, put your thumb on the scale just a little, added just a few points here and there, called just a couple of line shots the wrong way—and just one or two of these could be a determining factor in any tennis match—then you were, Wilson claimed, effectively making race and gender "determining factors."

Defenders of the UC admissions process did point out that every qualified student was in fact admitted to a UC campus, though not always to their first-choice campus. But since the crucial element in the *Bakke* case had been that race could be considered as only one among many factors, Connerly and Wilson were now arguing with at least prima facie plausibility that many UC campuses were out of compliance with a *Bakke*-type meritocratic shrinking of the importance of race, since any Chicano admitted to Berkeley with a 3.3, at a campus that could have filled its whole freshman class with 4.0s, had to be there because race had overridden everything else.[18] And since the issue for rerouted white students was not that they were rejected from UC, but that they would have to go to college at UC Irvine or UC Davis instead of UC Berkeley or UCLA. Connerly and his allies overturned affirmative action not to protect white access to higher education, but to protect white access to its most exclusive sites.[19]

The long-term impact of the debate was to further lower the public's understanding of higher education through repeated assertions that UC students of color were unqualified, less qualified, undeserving, less worthy, and generally of dubious merit. Students of color who felt stigmatized by affirmative action were largely stigmatized by the trashing of affirmative action in this period. As U.S. society increasingly solved deindustrialization with layoffs and imprisonment rather than employment, and three-strikes discourse spread images of inner-city youth as criminally defective, the war against affirmative action cast those neighborhoods' college-bound members as academically defective. A group stigma that affected black and Latino youth was being applied to high school dropouts and college graduates alike: all were said to have received some undeserved coddling from the liberal system, and though the college kids were not dangerous to life and limb, their inadequacies were cast as dangerous to white college applicants and to the economy. Not only had race-conscious practices been eliminated; the underrepresented students who had sometimes benefited from them were marked as undeserving and even dispensable elements of their own society.

The predicted results were quick to follow. The UC Board of Regents measures, reinforced by the ballot on Proposition 209, resulted in marked reductions in the presence of African American, Native American, and Latino students at several of UC's campuses, particularly Berkeley and Los Angeles. The measures also stimulated a widening gap between the proportion of these underrepresented minorities among California high school graduates and their proportion in UC as a whole; UC never caught up with the available proportions of black and Latino high school graduates and in many cases continues to fall farther behind.[20] In highly selective units at UC, underrepresented group enrollments collapsed: when the first post–affirmative action class arrived at Boalt Hall Law School at UC Berkeley in August 1997, it had exactly one black student. This student, Eric Brooks, gamely noted that he had "been given a unique opportunity to work to make needed changes and improvements for future students of color at Berkeley," but there was something uncomfortably similar to James Meredith's isolated arrival as the first black student at the University of Mississippi thirty-five years earlier, though Brooks did not need a national guard escort. After making some adjustments in their admissions practices and greatly increasing recruitment efforts, Boalt's 1998 figure improved from 1 to 9 (in a class of 275).[21] By 2004, the number had increased further—to 15.[22]

Anti–affirmative action leaders had a simple response to anticipated or plummeting enrollment of underrepresented groups in high-prestige schools: it was the way things ought to be. At UC, "the number of underrepresented minorities is going to go down," Connerly noted to the *Los Angeles Times,* but this made good sense: "If you give someone a preference, and then you take that preference away, the numbers are going to go down."[23] Critics of affirmative action generally assumed, as did Connerly, that the students from underrepresented groups had been academically inadequate and had been unfairly admitted ahead of their more qualified white and Asian American peers. Those rewards for the undeserving were now at an end.

The Culture War for the New Economy

Critics of affirmative action enjoyed almost unbroken success in the period between the defeat of the Guinier "quota queen" nomination in early June 1993 and the Republican loss of the California governor's office in November 1998. Because Proposition 209 withstood its major court challenges, the proposition's outlawing of race- and gender-conscious admissions and hiring became a part of the state constitution. The attitudes and policies that the attacks embodied became part of California's social landscape.

At the same time, that landscape was rapidly being equated with the Internet era. The day the Regents eliminated affirmative action at the University of California remained the best-known 1995 date in the state for just another three weeks, until August 9, when Netscape's initial public offering (IPO) of stock broke all previous records for first-day market capitalization. This IPO helped kick off the stock market and real estate booms of the second half of the 1990s, led by tech stocks and high-tech-related salaries. Silicon Valley reestablished itself as one of the centers of the economic universe, and though its leading industries were as likely to promote racial segmentation and stratification as the agricultural economy whose land they consumed, much of the public seemed to equate a high-performance economy with persistent racial inequality.[24] Immigration remained a smoldering issue, particularly in the middle- and lower-income central cities and inner-ring suburbs, which hosted most of it. The major immigration issue for California leaders was how to liberalize H1-B visas for high-tech foreign workers, especially from Asia; most white-collar employees and affluent homeowners accepted the steady decline of California's previously legendary public services, with the worst decline in terms of per capita income reserved for higher education.

The attacks on affirmative action did function in part as a *distraction* from the economic policies that were the primary source of the economic fear and insecurity most Californians had experienced. But we are now in a position to see that this branch of the culture wars did much more. It affirmed a concrete *economic* vision based on its antiegalitarian model of sociocultural life. This model, we will recall, claimed first that the majority's rules should govern minorities, and second, that race consciousness hurt individual rights. These elements led to a third, the real payoff, which was that racial equality was a form of serious injustice. The revalidation of disparate outcomes meant that justice was again being done. Though adherents of this view often recapitulated traditional stereotypes of black and brown mental inferiority, they could now claim, in the culture-wars environment, that this was not a sign of their own prejudice but of a market-driven, performance-based order. Connerly and others continued to trace efforts to reduce educational stratification by class and race to "the political correctness mind set," which was in turn an attempt to suspend market-style standards of objective performance.[25]

Through their attacks on affirmative action, the culture wars helped transform the impact of the New Economy on California and the United States. They defeated the idea that the student bodies of public universities should be roughly representative of the population's racial composition. They defeated the goal of interracial equality, which affirmative action critics painted as a great injustice, achievable only through unfair, inefficient interference with free competition. The culture wars cast expectations that the New Economy would benefit the whole society as the groundless complaining of the intellectually deficient.

Sure enough, the dot-com boom was also an inequality boom, in which the top 1 percent of the California population received 70 percent of the additional wealth, with most of that going to the top 0.5 percent.[26] Rather than this being an affront to the egalitarian spirit that had supported broad social development first for all whites and gradually for all citizens, it was seen as the effect of the socially neutral workings of meritocracy. The new inequality became the conventional wisdom of political and business leaders in the very period in which the "golden age" middle class was becoming increasingly diverse racially, propelled in large part by more equitable public university admissions. Once affirmative action was out of the picture, the California spotlight shone more narrowly than ever on the big, big money, which in popular Silicon Valley tributes like Michael Lewis's *The New New Thing* flowed naturally to the big, big talent.[27] Real value was not traced to labor anymore, whether that be the labor of the world's best engineers who immigrated from one of India's technical institutes or the labor of the unschooled rural workers who cleaned and patrolled the labs and factories. As a result, it became increasingly difficult for leaders to see the relevance of the overall population of California to the present or future. It seemed so much more efficient to shower resources, educational and financial, on the 1 or 2 or at most 10 percent who were said to have the best ideas that supposedly made all the money in the New Economy.

As the 1990s continued, more and more of the college-educated middle class came to feel that there was something economically illogical, and profoundly nostalgic, about the civil rights era notion of progress, in which states like California would celebrate the increased numbers of black and Latino students at Berkeley and UCLA and hope to continue the trend. Most media discussions were of wealth and crime, and higher education was left to its own devices. Public universities around the country thought about money too, and spent the later part of the decade trying to recover from the cuts of the Bush I recession period. Social equality fell off the radar, and media discussions suggested that most of the white middle class felt that if students of color could not keep up with the New Economy, their increased representation in the best institutions was a waste of time and money. If black and Latino enrollments dropped by a third, or half, or more, whites might feel badly. But the culture wars helped ensure that there would be no reason to change the outcome.

In this way, the narrow and petty issue of helping more white students get into UC Berkeley came to seem part of promoting economic progress. Future success depended on intense competition among individuals so that major resources would go only to those most likely to contribute to the breakthrough products and brand-new industries of tomorrow. If globalization meant competition and hierarchy, and demanded that all countries make their societies competitive and hierarchical to match, then the lesser members of those societies must be expelled to lower and less expensive institutions of the type that matched their contribution to the high-tech future. The culture warriors' ideal of color blindness matched this vision in which egalitarian outcomes were a feature of a less efficient industrial past.

Golden-age California had promised a decent middle-class life for all, including, in a far more limited way, for the African American migrants to defense plants and the Mexican American immigrants to the construction, agricultural, and hospitality trades. Silicon-age California promised something different: an end to the alleged inefficiencies of that broadly based and increasingly multiracial middle class. Its features included financial markets abstracted from their social and cultural worlds, leading industries run by an elite as male and nearly as white as any in American history, and, for the black and brown youth who were said to be unworthy of UC Berkeley, the largest, most expensive prison building boom in history. Between 1984 and 2004, while per capita funding for K–12 education grew 26 percent in constant dollars, and health and human services grew 34 percent, prison expenditures grew 126 percent. That bill was paid in effect from funds for universities, which declined by 12 percent in constant dollars during that period.[28]

Thus, the state's biggest "golden age" style investment in public services was now radically antidevelopmental, and it flowed directly from the world-view of the culture warriors.

— 6 —

The Battle for Meritocracy

Visions of general development never entirely disappear, and the era of the culture wars was no exception. Like other Americans, Californians in the 1990s had inherited decades of clichés, hopes, desires, and complicated experiences of what life in a golden state could be like. Actually, existing California had been racist, divided, monopolistic, and unequal: agricultural land ownership had been more concentrated in California than in the Midwest, its railroads were especially ruthless, its real estate empires were as deceptive as any in history—at least until Florida came along—and immigrants from China, Mexico, and the Philippines had received even worse treatment than that accorded to the Depression-era Okies, whose violent and degrading reception had been bitterly recorded in John Steinbeck's *The Grapes of Wrath* (1939).

But the flip side was just as dramatic, grounded as it had been in a sense of freedom and possibility without end, associated with cars, cheap housing, endless mobility, outdoor living, beaches, surfing, sunshine, backyards, and good jobs, as well as wealth, glamour, and Hollywood stars. This version of California sold endless copies of *Look* and *Life* that pictured white folks gathered around the barbeque with a dad who had been home from work for an hour by 6:30 p.m., as clean breezes wafted into the living room through wall-to-wall glass sliding doors that stayed open most of the year. The California historian Kevin Starr once described this California as an Oz-like protectorate, where ordinary people "were able to concentrate on the business of living, which for them was the life of emotion and imagination—and having adventures."[1]

Though these kinds of dreams were largely available to whites, the dreams were not limited to them. In 1994, not long after the Rodney King verdict revolt and in the midst of Governor Pete Wilson's anti-immigration campaigns, the novelist Walter Mosley, best known for his Easy Rawlins mysteries set in mid-twentieth-century black Los Angeles, described the desire that drew black migrants from places like Houston's poor third ward:

"You could tell by some people's houses that they came to L.A. to live out their dreams. Home is not a place to dream. At home you had to do like your father did and your mother. Home meant that everybody already knew what you could do and if you did the slightest little thing different they'd laugh you right down into a hole. You lived in that hole. Festered in it. After a while you either accepted your hole or you got out of it.[2]

Postwar America was supposed to allow the popular majority to climb out of whatever hole it was in. California had built a postwar public sphere—roads, schools, hospitals, universities—that gave a larger majority a shot at climbing out. California was not alone: the postwar United States, like postwar France, postwar Mexico, and many other postwar countries, had been rebuilding itself to support a broader base of its population than ever before. In the 1990s, hopes for this kind of general development persisted. Memories of dreams unrealized endured in expected shapes of things to come. And they appeared as anomalies and ambiguities and contradictions in the official record.

A Surprising Popularity

One set of anomalies appeared during the affirmative action culture war. In March 1995, the *Los Angeles Times* published a very interesting poll. It found that the vast majority of Americans believed that racial discrimination remained an important national issue. Seventy percent of the poll's respondents confirmed that they "don't think we are close to eliminating discrimination" as a society. Ninety percent of African Americans claimed that discrimination is not close to ending, and, interestingly, 68 percent of white men agreed.

If the poll's majorities did not base their skepticism about affirmative action on the rather foolish belief that discrimination was dead, did race consciousness really bother them? Actually, not that much. The *Times* poll also found that most groups *supported* standard types of affirmative action. In every group other than white men, a majority backed affirmative action by a ratio of 2 to 1. This majority support extended to set-aside programs, that is, programs that offered "a set percentage of federal contracts to qualified minority-owned businesses." Only 20 percent rejected all affirmative action.

The main case in which majorities did balk was when affirmative action appeared to set aside individual merit. This has been the origin of the perennial hostility to "quotas" and goes a long way toward explaining the greater hostility toward affirmative action of white men, who had received much public instruction on how their true merit was being ignored. But all groups, including African Americans, rejected the use of minority status as an automatic override of individual qualities.[3]

This poll suggested that majorities of all groups (with the partial exception of white men) *supported* affirmative action as long as it did not mean the nullification of prior judgments about individual merit. The term "quota" created a backlash because it suggested exactly this rejection of individual qualities, and not because majorities inherently opposed the use of race for purposes of outreach and inclusion. When affirmative action seemed tied to inclusion, to fairness—to what I have called general development—it polled well. Polls suggested that affirmative action could—and in most jurisdictions did—survive the culture-wars rhetoric of racial preferences.[4] This was a fact that culture warriors well knew.

The Established Model of Meritocracy

Given restricted but solid majority support for affirmative action, conservatives could best sideline it and its accompanying specter of equality by casting its programs as violations of individual merit. They had to show that affirmative action did not expand and improve meritocracy but damaged it instead.

The kind of meritocracy that *was* threatened by affirmative action was a narrow and hierarchical variety that had emerged from eugenics and standardized testing and that produced a bell curve of intelligence in which only a tiny minority of the population was truly gifted and capable of running society. Another, broader notion of meritocracy was being developed through practice more than principle by the sheer broadening of educational and economic access in the postwar years. A society with strong cultural capabilities would have been able to see a concept like meritocracy as susceptible to multiple interpretations—seeing variations of meaning is a hallmark of cultural capability. But affirmative action and meritocracy were both vulnerable concepts, for they were riddled with tensions that reflected American society's racial conflicts. Meritocracy was torn between two major meanings—an established, dominant meaning, and a second, emergent one. Culture-wars rhetoric discredited affirmative action by blocking the emergence of a broader meritocracy and insisting on the older, narrower meaning.

The strength of the concept of meritocracy lies in its core idea that social position and economic resources should be assigned by merit rather than by birth, wealth, race, color, gender, national origin, personal connections, or any other characteristic not tied to actual performance.[5] Since it opposes power based on such factors, meritocracy has frequently been a central component of political reform movements. Faced with a rapacious, mediocre aristocracy, a corrupt municipal government, or a captive insurance commission, reformers may invoke the concept of meritocracy to replace inherited wealth, political cronies, and incompetent puppets with people trained to perform a function according to professional standards.[6]

But though it was clear that merit had something to do with competence and skill, the question remained as to how merit should be defined. The main terms of debate were variants of "nature" versus "nurture": Was merit an innate ability that should be measured through aptitude tests? Or was merit the result of education and experience that should be measured through concrete achievements? The idea of measuring an innate ability— for example, general intelligence as "IQ"—exerted a continuous fascination. So did the related but different idea that rewards should follow actual results, particularly in an obsessively commercial nation where market returns were a common measure of both products and people. Both of these notions of merit have democratic and elitist variants. The idea of measuring innate aptitude gained strength from the racist goal of identifying innate superiorities among whites or Protestants or Northern Europeans in contrast to Europeans from the Mediterranean coast. But measuring innate aptitude also appealed to those who wanted to reduce the elitism of colleges like Harvard by finding able students from poor or rural backgrounds in the country's remote outposts.[7] Since their subjects were normally young people who had few or no accomplishments to display, "aptitude" seemed like a fair substitute for achievement. The standardized test that has served as a gatekeeper to the country's colleges and universities was for decades called the Scholastic Aptitude Test (SAT), bearing witness to its historical associations with military ability tests, the search for innate general intelligence, and eugenic refinements, but also to the pursuit of rare talent in obscure locales. The SAT has been renamed the Scholastic Assessment Test and has been redesigned and redeployed in the wake of sweeping critiques from researchers and major educational leaders. Both notions of merit retain their appeal—the unveiling of ability that the world has not allowed to be revealed, and detecting concrete achievement that reveals a mixture of ability, effort, and vision.[8]

American society would appear to want it both ways—to reward both aptitude and achievement. We appear also to want to hang on to the idea that innate ability really does exist, perhaps because that makes it easier to justify unequal outcomes—some people just *are* better than others, so it is natural for them to have more. Into this ambiguous and conflicted state we also need to inject racial and other forms of cultural diversity. When it comes right down to it, and you have nearly fifty thousand applications for a freshman class of about five thousand, as UCLA had in 2007, how do you actually compare each individual applicant to all the others? How, above all, do you compare *diverse* applicants, ones whose individual qualities are at least partly incommensurable?

I will call the familiar, hierarchical model of merit "meritocracy I," and note that its influence has come in large part from its claim to solve the problem of large numbers of diverse applicants. Meritocracy I has been embodied in the SAT, which addressed the problem of large and diverse numbers by seeming to offer an objective, quantified, transcultural measure of an innate characteristic. The "SAT score" was this number—1140 combined, or 1570, or 830, and it supposedly indicated vastly different abilities and different powers of taking advantage of educational opportunity. Such tests had the trappings of the quantitative sciences and were starkly different from a more qualitative, individualized process in which an applicant would submit a portfolio or would audition before a panel of judges, though these processes have survived in fields such as architecture, dance, graphic design, the fine arts, and advertising.

Ironically, the quantitative testing procedure we now associate with individual evaluation, polemically contrasted by culture warriors with the allegedly group-based treatment of race-conscious admissions, turned out to *replace* a review of concrete individual achievements like a sculpture, a science-fair project, mathematical problem sets, signal processing algorithms, or even essay exams in high school courses. Multiple-choice tests also eclipsed the grueling battery of substantive tests that dominate selection procedures in countries—Japan, France, Denmark, South Korea, Singapore, and so on—that do markedly better than the United States in measures of educational attainment. Meritocratic testing flattened individual features into one or more numbers that allowed for the convenient comparison of unlike candidates by translating their differences into a single but largely fictional aggregate. Meritocracy I created an abstract monoculture in which every citizen could be ranked on one uniform scale, ironically obscuring the individuality that it was supposed to represent and protect.

This traditional meritocracy inevitably expressed itself as a rank-ordered hierarchy. The whole point of meritocratic evaluation was to assess in order to rank, sort the great from the good, and create a pecking order. It would be a more functional pecking order than an aristocracy of birth, but it would be just as rigorously and persistently stratified. Meritocracy I always claimed to be fair, and often sought to be, and yet it has never sought equality. If a population is still in a condition of rough equality, then in this model a valid meritocratic sorting has not actually taken place. If a society is roughly equal, it is not meritocratic. The reverse is equally true: if a society is meritocratic, it cannot possibly be egalitarian.

This spirit of inequality continued to flourish after World War II, throughout the democratic booming of public higher education. Spots in elite universities were as coveted as ever before, and only a few public university campuses competed with Princeton and Stanford for stature and influence. The masses would go to college, but not to colleges like those two. Pecking orders were maintained by testing regimes, federal granting patterns, differential resource allocations, and popular legends. Even the University of California, which uniquely sought to be a system of equals, was surrounded by a folklore that stereotyped its newer campuses as the "cow college" or the "party school" and that enforced the preeminence of its flagship sites at Berkeley and Los Angeles. The cream was to stay at the top of a social system in which an increasingly large percentage of the population would become college educated. When this stratified model threatened to erode, as it often did in the 1960s via protests, in the 1970s with early affirmative action, and in the 1980s and 1990s around multiculturalism, theorists and politicians would carry more cement to the foundations. The cement consisted of works like Richard J. Herrnstein and Charles Murray's *The Bell Curve: Intelligence and Class Structure in American Life* (1994), which insisted at great length on the narrow distribution of high intelligence, on its lower incidence among African Americans, and on the causal roots of social inequality in unequal intelligence. Such arguments regularly renewed the marital vows between meritocracy I and alleged hierarchies of ability.

An Emerging Model of Meritocracy

Meritocracy I was not egalitarian, and it functioned as an *alternative* to a democratization of the university in which the whole society would eventually pursue top-quality higher learning. This model reserved a dominant role for elites in a representative democracy, staying true to its original nineteenth-century purpose of keeping the country in the hands of a "natural" aristocracy. These facts were not lost on the general public. One sign of their awareness was that even the enemies of affirmative action felt the need to make their version of meritocracy seem more inclusive than its color-blind rules allowed.

A striking example appeared in UC Regent Ward Connerly's proposals to end affirmative action at the university. Given his hostility to the use of racial identity as an admissions factor, it was surprising to see that he included personal and subjective elements in the process he recommended. The formal Regental action proposed that after January 1, 1997, the "University of California shall not use race, religion, sex, color, ethnicity, or national origin as criteria for admission to the University or to any program of study," but then went on to charge the Academic Senate with developing "supplemental criteria" for admissions under which "consideration shall be given to individuals who, despite having suffered disadvantage economically or in terms of their social environment (such as an abusive or otherwise dysfunctional home or a neighborhood of unwholesome or antisocial influences), have nonetheless demonstrated sufficient character and determination in overcoming obstacles to warrant confidence that the applicant can pursue a course of study to successful completion, provided that any student admitted under this section must be academically eligible for admission."[9]

Though this remarkable statement was couched in Charles Murray–style rhetoric about the "culture of poverty" that allegedly reigns in certain minority communities, the fact remained that Connerly's own proposal to end affirmative action simultaneously called for broadening merit beyond the limits of numerical scores. The proposal's language acknowledged the reality of social disadvantage and of its impact on the perception of merit and its distortion of meritocratic outcomes. The language allowed for hardship to be measured subjectively, through the perceptions of those who experience it, and not only externally, through an instrument like parental financial records. The language stated that assessment should focus on likely performance rather than alleged innate ability. Finally, the language assumed that UC would be better if its notion of merit were broader.

Thus Connerly's proposal to end affirmative action incorporated the classic assumptions of the liberal social development agenda. Rather than trying to decide whether his language was sincere or cynical, we could see it as a pragmatic recognition that a more egalitarian notion of meritocracy—I will call it meritocracy II—was popular enough with both the Regents and the public to require its inclusion. We can generalize that people liked the general idea of meritocracy because it rewarded individual effort and accomplishment, but only as long as it did not simply replicate existing inequalities. Cultural and social analysis of meritocratic testing—and many people's concrete experience—had shown that these tests on the whole attributed more merit to the socially advantaged. Most of the public wanted a better model than this and were moving from the established model of meritocracy, which sought quantified ability free of sociocultural context, to an emergent model that could account for social inequality and cultural difference. Connerly and Wilson had to go some distance to accommodate certain elements of the emerging model even as they tried to keep the conservative social results of the older one.[10]

The core idea of meritocracy II had been around forever: intelligence is spread widely rather than narrowly in human societies. The historian Christopher Lasch called this idea the "democratization of intelligence" and argued that the nineteenth-century United States believed this to be the "central promise of American life."[11] He contrasted this democratization with the concept of social mobility, which he claimed was a later and poorer substitute for the expansive vision of a United States based on universal education. This earlier ideal was applied by white men only to other white men. But its goal was to make "every man really free and independent," in Orestes Brownson's phrase, and to advance society as a whole rather than only its leading sectors. As intelligence was unlocked throughout the population, "social mobility" would in reality mean the mobility of an entire society as it evolved as a complex ensemble.

This general model has been a recessive strain in American thinking, but from time to time it enjoyed a resurgence. The 1960s and 1970s formed one such period. Some schools dropped numerical scholarly rankings and expanded resources. I attended one such school in the 1970s—Loyola High

School in Los Angeles—where the elimination of posted class rankings co-incided with the introduction of new courses and the general expansion of the curriculum, including a cosmopolitan course called World Religions, which marked the first time I thought of the United States as part of a clearly not-very-American world. The basic idea behind the reforms had been that *competition* for *scarce* resources damaged or blocked the experi-mentation and the collaboration that would lead to higher achievement. The Jesuit faculty had temporarily suspended the Darwinism of meritoc-racy I and assumed that an emphasis on cooperative advancement would make not only for a more peaceful high school, but also for a higher-achieving one. We still had our GPAs and SAT scores to reveal or hide. But we also had a place where a reduction of visible inequalities, combined with greater cross-racial experience, made the secret ingredient of higher perfor-mance and general development seem to be equality itself.

Meritocracy II circulated as a tradition, a promise, and a hope, tied very much to middle-class ambitions in both the nineteenth century and the twentieth. Its core features can be listed as follows: first, a vision of the "democratization of intelligence"; second, a determination to develop that broadly distributed intellectual capacity with an inclusive educational sys-tem; and third, a belief that general development was better served by equal-ity than by stratification.

In their periods of resurgence, these ideals had concrete effects. When meritocracy became more open, more cultural, more developmental, and indeed more accurately reflective of society's capacities, it excluded fewer people and advanced more. As the 1970s advanced, gradations of merit re-mained firmly in place, but more African Americans and Latino Americans were admitted to selective high schools and universities. There were many new admissions for *middling whites*. The California Master Plan for Higher Education implied that not just the best whites but *all* whites could go to college; for a time it seemed that the United States would have the most democratic higher education system in the world.[12] A racial compact ac-companied this vaunted education boom: middling white folks would not be hurt by any additional inclusion of people of color because egalitarian-ism would help both groups. Affirmative action could flourish in an age of expansion. There was a hardheaded way of putting this point: race con-sciousness was okay with whites as long as it did not cost them anything. But there was a more idealistic side as well. Programs did not have to be color-blind as long as they produced general advancement. Baby boom democratization meant that fewer white children had to suffer visible stigmatization as nonexcellent. Whites mostly assumed that this new and broader form of meritocracy could include and develop everyone while treating race and gender as add-ons, "plus factors."[13] But they had reason to be generous about this, because whites could go to a University of California campus without being clearly superb. They could get into medical school just by working harder in college than they did in high school. They could move up without being in the top 0.1 percent or 1 percent of their class but in the top 10 percent or 15 percent or even 50 percent of their class. The white majority was benefiting from the replacement of market-driven hierarchies in public higher education with an inclusive, developmental model. Society also benefited from this new model, since it was getting a much higher-quality middle class than it would have otherwise.

When meritocracy II resurged in the 1980s and 1990s, it took the more explicitly racialized form of multiculturalism and various kinds of race-conscious programs; it was propelled by scholars and advocates acutely aware that civil rights openings had not eliminated racial disparities. It occurred after deindustrialization and the Reagan-era downsizing of public services made American society again a market-style zero-sum game. In retrospect, it sometimes seems that conservatives had no trouble taking an economically fearful white middle class and convincing them that their real problem was poor people of color. But in fact such arguments had to be carefully engineered. And they had to discredit not only welfare programs and school busing, which had never been popular, but also quasi-universal state university admissions programs, which in fact were popular. In the wake of meritocracy II's partial successes from the 1950s through the early 1970s, culture warriors had to put the majority of whites at odds with a system that had helped them for years. Culture warriors stressed the tax costs of inclusive programs, and they played a whole deck of race cards. But there was also a hidden ingredient that allowed them to cement their mid-1990s gains against affirmative action.

The Culture War for Rank Meritocracy

This element appeared in two affirmative action decisions in the *Hopwood* cases in Texas, often described as *Hopwood 1* and *Hopwood 2*.[14] *Hopwood* began when four white residents of Texas named Cheryl Hopwood, Douglas Carvell, Kenneth Elliott, and David Rogers were rejected for admission to the 1992 entering law school class at the University of Texas at Austin. The four sued the law school on the grounds that "they were subjected to unconstitutional racial discrimination by the law school's evaluation of their admissions applications."[15] By discrimination, Hopwood et al. meant that Mexican Americans and African Americans were assigned a status different from that of whites for getting the same score on a numerical scale known as the Texas Index (TI). The index had three broad categories, much like the bell curve that still dominates thinking about merit: presumptive admit, presumptive denial, and a middle "discretionary zone." A Mexican American applicant with a 197 TI score was a "presumptive admit"; a white applicant with the same score would be in the discretionary range, and might well be rejected. Three of the *Hopwood* plaintiffs had a score of 197 and were denied admission.[16] Hopwood's own score was 199, at the bottom of the "presumptive admit" range, but the chairman of the admissions committee dropped her into the discretionary zone for reasons I discuss below.

Did these four applicants suffer so-called reverse discrimination? No, said the federal district court in *Hopwood 1*; yes, said the Fifth Circuit Court of Appeals in *Hopwood 2*, and that decision stood until the University of Michigan *Bollinger* cases were decided by the Supreme Court in 2003. It is fairly clear that the law school's procedure violated the *Bakke* precedent by placing different applicants on different numerical scales solely on the basis of race.[17] But the Fifth Circuit Court of Appeals, in *Hopwood 2*, went beyond a critique of the mechanism to a rejection of the *Bakke* principles behind it.[18] The *Hopwood 2* ruling meant that no school in the Fifth Circuit's area could take race into *any* account in admissions "for the purpose of (1) obtaining a diverse student body; (2) altering the school's reputation in the community; (3) combating the school's perceived hostile environment toward minorities; or (4) remedying the present effects of past discrimination by actors other than the law school."[19] The university could consider race only in order to "remedy the Law School's own discrimination."[20] In a view at the heart of the culture-war critique of affirmative action, *Hopwood 2* defined race consciousness as an illegal and destructive element, and did so through a plausible reading of conservative Supreme Court precedent. The decision affirmed two of the major elements of the culture-war tale of affirmative action: racial equality was an illegitimate goal, and race-conscious methods deprived worthy whites by wrongly elevating lesser members of favored minorities.

But these resounding themes obscured the major narrative of the lower court (*Hopwood 1*). The lower court detailed the credentials and qualifications of the rejected applicants, on whom it lavished uncomfortable attention. Hopwood was the strongest applicant, right on the borderline of the presumptive admits. But the head of admissions, after a review of her file, dropped her to "the discretionary zone because, in his evaluation, she had not attended schools that were academically competitive with those of the majority of the applicants." Her application omitted both letters of recommendation and a personal statement. Elliott was an accounting major with an undergraduate GPA of 2.98. Carvell ranked 98th in his class of 247 at Hendrix College in Arkansas; one of his recommenders described his performance as "uneven, disappointing, and mediocre."[21] Rogers had a GPA of 3.1 from the University of Houston–Downtown, where he had moved after flunking out of the University of Texas. All four files were reviewed by a committee of three people; admission would likely have followed had two of the three members found them distinctive or special in any way. But they did not. *Hopwood 1* found that the four plaintiffs were rejected not because of the law school's racial remedies but because of the workings of the "discretionary zone." All four candidates were clear examples of white educational mediocrity: they came from middling white backgrounds, and had been passed over largely in favor of other middling whites with sometimes worse scores than theirs.[22] *Hopwood 1* put this fact of white mediocrity out in the open. *Hopwood 2* ignored it.

Once again, meritocracy I was too punitive and narrow to be applied systematically, and the lead judge in the *Hopwood 2* decision had to bend it to detect Cheryl Hopwood's merit. "While the use of race *per se* is proscribed in state-supported schools," he wrote, "a university may reasonably consider a host of factors. . . . A university may properly favor one applicant over another because of his ability to play the cello, make a downfield tackle, or understand chaos theory. . . . [I]ndividuals, with their own conceptions of life, further diversity of viewpoint. Plaintiff Hopwood is a fair example of an applicant with a unique background. She is the now-thirty-two-year-old wife of a member of the Armed Forces stationed in San Antonio and, more significantly, is raising a severely handicapped child. Her circumstance would bring a different perspective to the law school."[23] This was true: Hopwood may well have brought a heightened motivation and understanding to disability or malpractice law or made another special contribution; the admissions committee could have admitted her with this "tie-breaker" had she actually turned in her personal statement. But were the *Hopwood 2* judge to have made this case systematically, it would have opened the door to meritocracy II, where *everybody's* individual circumstances create, define, and express their personal merit. And so he stuck, incoherently, with meritocracy I, and with its fiction of an objectivity not violated by mothering the disabled but violated by race. The "plus factors" that colleges can consider, according to *Hopwood 2*, are those like football ability that avoid questions about restricted resources, structural racism, underdevelopment of human capacity, growing inequality that traps whites as well as people of color, and every single nonelite person's dependence on social investment for his or her individual advancement.

In the end, the two courts offered conflicting descriptions of the woes of middling whites. *Hopwood 1* unearthed a story about how meritocracy damages a large and worthy but unexceptionable portion of the white applicant pool. The plaintiffs, it said, had been damaged not by racial classification but by being unable to distinguish themselves from the pack. That court held that such applicants were *supposed* to be damaged in this exact way— damaged by the ordinary operation of meritocracy 1, with its emphasis on ranking based on quantitative measurements. *Hopwood 1* held tacitly to the meritocracy II model in that it saw the effects of meritocracy I's equation of meritorious with narrow selectivity and had a sense that though the four plaintiffs would have benefited from law school, and perhaps benefited society in turn, they had no admissions claim under standard meritocracy I rules. Their claim was no better than that of 109 other nonexcellent whites, and some additional number of non-excellent applicants of color.

Hopwood 2 hastened to bury this story. Meritocracy, it said, is tough, but it does not reject whole chunks of currently average but potentially highly-competent whites. If these middling whites were rejected, it could only be the result of racial remedies and their minority clients. The fault lay not with meritocracy I and its indifference to expanding facilities and general development, nor with the post-1980 decline of inexpensive public higher education, but with the reverse racism of affirmative action.

The first story rears its head from time to time—rank-meritocracy, meritocracy I, hurts the great majority, including the masses of whites. But the *Hopwood 2* story remains pervasive—rank-meritocracy hurts the majority only when race remedies distort it. The first story implied the need for renewed social investment—new campuses, new fields, new levels of access— and stressed the lost human potential and general advancement as we agonize and delay. The second story made wider investment unnecessary, saying we need only to restrict access more rigorously to the campuses we already have.

In its ratification of unequal outcomes, its contentment with racial disparity, its indifference to general development, *Hopwood 2* was an unqualified triumph for the culture warrior. It encouraged the return of a white amnesia about harms done to people of color. It encouraged the same amnesia about harms that restricted development did even to whites. The culture-wars attacks on academic affirmative action reduced the presence of underrepresented groups in high-status public universities. These attacks also reduced white willingness to build major social institutions that provided for the development of their own communities. One longtime observer of the American racial scene has noted that the country does not need white racism to control blacks—it has more material means for that—but needs white racism to control whites.[24] The same can be said of the war on affirmative action, which helped dramatically to reduce white expectations for the expansion of the higher education that had made most of them middle class.

The effects of this culture-wars shift became more entrenched as the 1990s continued. American society resigned itself to meritocracy I while allowing admissions loophole language about hardship and non-racial exceptions, creating a kind of meritocracy I+. This version reinstalled a conservative bedrock beneath the diversity talk, restoring test scores, rank-hierarchy, the scarcity of high-quality resources, and the aura of a small, elite group of talent at the top. Race, class, gender—especially the ideal of racial equality—were shorn of their implication of a more broadly developed society and were returned to the status of Justice Powell's 1978 "plus factors" that could be extended or withdrawn at the pleasure of the small groups that do the picking for prestigious institutions. Basic racial integration returned to its dependence on a scarcity-based ranking system, although it was only the suspension of that system that had produced the integration gains of the post-1960s period.

Without the cultural capability to imagine social solutions to stratification and decline, whites too were increasingly dependent on private and individual stopgaps—family wealth, student loans, credit card debt, and part- or full-time employment during college—that held back educational gains. Everyone paid more individually, and expected more individually, but often did not get more individually; nor did society, judging from stagnant or falling educational statistics and from income stagnation for all but the top 10 to 15 percent.

The attacks on affirmative action restored an older form of meritocracy that in turn sharply limited the range of options available for moving forward. As specific social goals were placed outside the pale, market solutions saw their status rise. In this way, the academic culture wars directly contributed to the New Economy's overemphasis on finance and technology as the true sources of the betterment of humankind. It looked increasingly like the college-educated middle classes would entrust their own advancement to business and market forces, or not advance at all.

— 7 —

Diversity in the Age of
Pseudointegration

In the wake of the setbacks of the 1990s, advocates for racial progress in education made their last stand around the concept of *diversity*. In the later 1990s, they began to win significant victories. In California, they won state funding for outreach programs at UC when the governor's house returned to Democratic Party hands in 1999. In 2001, they persuaded the UC Regents to rescind their UC-specific affirmative action prohibitions. In that same year, the president of the University of California proposed dropping the requirement for the first half of the SAT test, suggesting that the university "require only standardized tests that assess mastery of specific subject areas rather than undefined notions of 'aptitude' or 'intelligence.' "[1] The alternative to an overemphasis on SAT-style tests and numerical formulas was to be "comprehensive review," which would restore the evaluation of individual achievements, including those that had a racial dimension.

Diversity won its most convincing victory in 2003, in the Supreme Court decisions about the use of affirmative action at the University of Michigan. Though this friendly word had fallen prey, like all race words sooner or later do, to systematic conservative attack, diversity had become by the end of the 1990s the center that *could* hold, the basis of a broad, temperate racial consensus that had endured all the controversy since the term had been codified into constitutional case law by Justice Lewis F. Powell in *Board of Regents of the University of California v. Bakke* (1978). Since major compromises had already been made, and the opposition just kept coming and coming, why not defend diversity with whatever it took? *Bakke*'s claim that diversity was a compelling state interest was rejected in *Hopwood v. Texas* by the Fifth Circuit Court of Appeals (*Hopwood 2*, 1996; see chapter 6) and was challenged again in the two University of Michigan affirmative action cases that the Supreme Court decided in June 2003. For advocates of both affirmative action and stronger forms of racial justice, diversity became the line in the sand. And *Bakke* was their *Roe v. Wade.*

The majority in *Hopwood 2* correctly noted that the courts had not explicitly affirmed Justice Powell's diversity defense of the use of race in admissions. In overturning *Hopwood 2*, Justice Sandra Day O'Connor's majority decision in the Michigan Law School case, *Grutter v. Bollinger*, finally did just that. Her decision was remarkable for its pervasive, even repetitious endorsement less of the law school's admission practices than of Powell's theory of diversity as the dominant, indisputable justification of the use of racial categories. O'Connor's decision intensified conservatives' anger at what they called the court's endorsement of racial preferences.[2] But others observed that, though race consciousness may have been unappealing, "everybody from President Bush on down likes the result of an integrated leadership."[3]

There was no actual evidence for this generalization and quite a bit of evidence to the contrary. The praise for diversity in the University of Michigan's amici briefs did not reflect a reality of American leadership: their only example of achieved racial integration was the enlisted ranks of the armed forces. In the years leading up to the *Bollinger* decisions, the concept of diversity had been taken in quite a different direction—toward the stratified society enforced by meritocracy I and away from the will of the multiracial majority.

Marketizing American Race

One influential pruning of diversity's possibilities emerged from the multicultural debates of the 1990s and appeared in David A. Hollinger's lucid, confident book, *Postethnic America: Beyond Multiculturalism*. Hollinger avoided the tone of cultural rivalry and insult by accepting cultural difference: he agreed at the start that a unified nation need not have a unified culture. But he wholeheartedly *rejected* ethnic identity. For those who thought multiculturalists were the proponents of open, flexible, negotiated systems of cultural and political relations, and that liberal nationalists like Arthur Schlesinger, Jr. were rigid and coercive, Hollinger had just turned the tables. For it turns out, he claimed, that multiculturalists have a rigid, fixed idea of identity while unhyphenated American nationalists uphold voluntary affiliation and cosmopolitan free exchange. The reason that multiculturalism falls short, he said, is that it is just too ethnic. In opposition to multiculturalism, to pluralism itself, Hollinger advocated a "postethnic" perspective. This perspective "favors voluntary over involuntary affiliations, balances an appreciation for communities of descent with a determination to make room for new communities, and promotes solidarities of wide scope that incorporate people with different ethnic and racial backgrounds." Postethnicity was neither multicultural nor pluralist, but cosmopolitan. While "pluralism respects inherited boundaries," "cosmopolitanism is more wary of traditional enclosures and favors voluntary affiliations. Cosmopolitanism promotes multiple identities, emphasizes the dynamic and changing character of many groups, and is responsive to the potential for creating new cultural combinations."[4]

Dynamic, changing, multiple identities that led to new combinations were certainly a reality of American and global racial life. The problem with Hollinger's formulation was its false contrast between postethnic and ethnic identity, one in which mere ethnic identity was fixated on settled boundaries and unchanging racial essences. In fact, the traits he claimed for cosmopolitanism actually belonged to a pluralist tradition that included W. E. B. DuBois and Horace Kallen, Angela Davis and Martin Luther King Jr., Stuart Hall and Patricia Williams, all of whom saw racial identity as a fluctuating sociocultural phenomenon that both acknowledged settled historical patterns of differentiation *and* what we now variously call hybridity and multiple identities.[5] This was not simply a matter of giving appropriate credit. Racial pluralism had generally claimed not that personal identity was fixed and given, or that individual liberty and choice were irrelevant, but that hybridity, mobility, and freedom *coexisted* with a group-based life that societies assigned to the members of groups, particularly those that were disfavored. This meant that democracy depended on recognition of the political and economic realities created by that group life—by systemic racial inequalities, by ongoing racial disparities, by racism past and present. This historic cosmopolitan pluralism insisted that democracy required consulting the members of racialized groups about the effects of their racialization. It also required that cultural knowledge be brought to bear on legal, social, and economic questions. It further required that the experience of ordinary people of their sociocultural system guide the writing of policy.

Hollinger's cosmopolitanism in effect offered a market model of racial, ethnic, and social identity, which by contrast insisted that the individual be perpetually adaptable and flexible rather than reformist or oppositional. Pluralism, in this view, reflected a kind of nationalist protectionism, one opposed to the free flow of goods and services and ideas and identities. Cosmopolitanism envisioned a marketplace in identities where individuals consumed rather than sued, and where the long labor to redesign legal, political and economic institutions could be as overlooked as it was in the American version of globalization. Once the curtain was lowered on society, pluralism could be seen as stuck in the past along with blue-collar manufacturing, well-paid union jobs, and bureaucratized social services.

Unfortunately for the postethnic model, the history of racial progress in the United States derived at every point from race-conscious critiques of existing arrangements. Race consciousness was the prerequisite to detecting empirical racial disparity in the first place. Hollinger-style replacements of pluralism with cosmopolitanism, consigning racial protest, Black Power, and so forth to the historical graveyard, encouraged the reader to set aside the dependence of American social progress on the political equivalents of managed markets. Civil rights scholars and activists had in fact argued for decades, even centuries, for open, flexible, democratic racial relations, yet in the name of pluralism and race-conscious equality.[6] Mixed economies, combinations of price signals, multiple desires, and intelligent collaborative economic design had their sociocultural equivalent in the civil rights reconstruction of equitable social processes, in full recognition of the way that individual identity was simultaneously voluntary *and* involuntary, chosen *and* imposed, mixed *and* differentiating.

In the postethnic model, progress had never come from the collaborative social labor of thousands and millions of people, acting in the name of the issues that emerged from their own experience, including the experience of race-based inequality. By turning this history inside out, and tracing change and advancement to postethnic cosmopolitanism, Hollinger in effect argued that progress was now to come from market-like systemic deregulation. This in turn shifted legitimacy away from the racialized plaintiffs in cases like *Ward's Cove Packing* (1989) and toward the deciders, selectors, and managers occupying the major choice points—the Harvard admissions committee, the boardroom of a Fortune 500 company.

The Powell Precedent

The postethnic model rejected the agency that members of groups assert on the basis of their sociocultural positioning. And yet it was hardly an original position in American thought. We saw a major resurgence of this thinking in the attacks on political correctness and in corresponding Supreme Court decisions, especially *Bakke*, which announced the primordial yoking of the culture wars to diversity. Postethnicity was a bridge between the Supreme Court's two foundational diversity decisions.

The crucial opinion in the first of these, the *Bakke* case (1978), had been written by Justice Lewis F. Powell, a genteel southern aristocrat who had been something of a racial moderate while chairing the Richmond, Virginia, school board during the years of "massive resistance" to school desegregation in the wake of the *Brown v. Board of Education* decision (1954). Throughout a long period of engagement with the racial politics of his native Virginia, Powell had tried to split the difference between white segregationists and the black civil rights movement. The latter's vision of racial equality was honored largely in the breach, but was still a galvanizing public ideal at the time that the Supreme Court took up Allan Bakke's suit against the UC Davis medical school's affirmative action program.[7]

This program resembled others in resting on the Civil Rights Act of 1964 and on subsequent executive orders to act affirmatively to ensure equal treatment without regard to race.[8] These measures did not mandate cross-racial equality of result, but they did erode the facially neutral yet disparity-producing mechanisms that had historically blocked such equality. The UC Davis medical school, which opened in 1968, set up a task force that was given eight of fifty (and then sixteen of one hundred) places in each entering class to consider offering to disadvantaged students.[9] These early remedies were somewhat mechanical, for their focus remained on "the *number* of 'affected-class' members represented in the workplace, not on systems and organizational change."[10] What was as important as their flaws, however, was that these remedies went beyond nondiscrimination toward changing the racial proportions of the larger medical profession.

In his *Bakke* decision, Justice Powell rejected the medical school's admissions program on the grounds that its "two-track" system, one for whites and one for "minorities," when held to the standard of strict scrutiny appropriate for all racial classifications, did not serve a "compelling state interest" that would justify its violation of the Fourteenth Amendment's equal protection clause.[11] The most influential aspect of the decision was its distinctive mixture of allowed and disallowed objectives. Powell famously allowed university admissions programs to pursue "the educational benefits that flow from an ethnically diverse student body."[12] At the same time, he struck down three other goals of UC Davis's pursuit of equality—countering the ongoing context of social discrimination as practiced by whites, correcting the racial imbalance in the medical profession, and increasing the supply of physicians to underserved communities. Powell's line between permitted and prohibited goals became highly influential. First, social goals that acknowledged race as an important factor in shaping society were prohibited.[13] Elite groups such as medical school admissions committees were not to act on behalf of members of racialized groups who had engaged in popular struggles for racial equality. Second, these elite groups *could* act in their own self-interest, which lay in pursuing a racial diversity that enhanced their own quality and influence. Most attention has been focused on Powell's finding that race could be used only as a "plus factor," which meant that the candidate had been consistently compared to all others, and no numerical goal or quota had been established.[14] But it is important to notice that Powell's notion of diversity had changed the subject away from racial discrimination as outlawed by the Fourteenth Amendment and other legislation.[15] As Powell had it, "The atmosphere of 'speculation, experiment and creation'—so essential to the quality of higher education—is widely believed to be promoted by a diverse student body. As the Court noted in *Keyishian* [1967], it is not too much to say that the 'nation's future depends upon leaders trained through wide exposure' to the ideas and mores of students as diverse as this Nation of many peoples."[16] Powell in effect limited race to an expression of the First Amendment rights of elite universities to pursue academic freedom and quality as they saw fit.[17]

Powell's claim about the benefits of diversity was true as such, and has been verified by subsequent research.[18] But in advancing this claim, he contrasted the nonremedial pursuit of diversity with remedial racial classification. He rejected all attempts of members of racial groups to change their collective social status except for those relatively few, narrow cases in which a specific, present inequality was clearly caused by the defendant's explicit and intentional actions. Powell thus insulated the concept of diversity from the legal pursuit of racial equality. "Ethnic diversity," he wrote, "is only one element in a range of factors a university properly may consider in attaining the goal of a heterogeneous student body. Although a university must have wide discretion in making the sensitive judgments as to who should be admitted, constitutional limitations protecting individual rights may not be disregarded." Powell in effect de-raced diversity.[19] Powell protected not the rights of the groups discriminated against, but the right of the university to run itself as it saw fit.

This meant that in Powell's diversity framework, diversity was the expression of an institution's freedom to choose particularly attractive individuals, and was about ensuring this freedom for powerful institutions like the source of Powell's preferred admissions model, Harvard College. Diversity did not reflect regulatory mandates but their effective absence. Diversity acquired social influence not as a moderate mode in which to pursue racial equality but as an *alternative* to that pursuit. Lawful racial remedies, Powell held, consisted not of restricting middle class or executive choice for egalitarian ends, but of liberating choice from those ends. The white professional middle classes certainly had different taste in their associates in 1978 than they had had in 1958 or 1878, and the would be different again by 2003, but in all three centuries members of the professional middle class used thinking like Powell's to identify racial justice with their own racial preferences in the making of their own institutions.[20] Diversity reflected the managerial authority of elite decision makers, not a social group's right to restrict that elite's power of discrimination.

Diversity as a Market Standard

Justice Powell's *Bakke* decision became the cornerstone both of affirmative action programs and of a highly functional white racial consensus. The consensus settled into a managerial phase, where race could operate as a plus factor in otherwise standard procedures for acceptance into middle-class gateway institutions like colleges and corporations. The consensus formally opposed racial discrimination. At the same time, it decertified the claim for racial equality.

After Powell's decision, the Supreme Court steadily retreated from the *disparate impact* measure of discrimination, which had construed Title VII of the Civil Rights Act of 1964 to forbid "not only overt discrimination but also practices that are fair in form but discriminatory in practice."[21] Racial inequality lost its earlier status as an overriding and singular concern that deserved society's undivided attention. In 1978, the year of the *Bakke* decision, William Julius Wilson summed up the trend in the title of his book *The Declining Significance of Race*, which lent the imprimatur of a prominent black scholar to the retreat from race-conscious programs.[22] Debates about affirmative action and racial justice of course continued, but the policy mainstream was dominated by arguments among members of the racial consensus, and they agreed—as its members usually had from E. L. Godkin in the 1860s to Saul Bellow and Glenn Lowry in the 1980s—that diversity was good and discrimination was bad.[23] Now that the doors of colleges and businesses had been pried open by the law, racial balances would change gradually, they said, one meritocratically selected, due-processed, minority individual at a time. The consensus hardened through the 1990s, when, as we have seen, Bill Clinton dropped Lani Guinier as his nominee to head the civil rights division of the Department of Justice, and did so in part because members of his own policy group, the Democratic Leadership Council, claimed that Guinier's views "fall way outside the American tradition of equal opportunity, individual versus group rights, and majority rule."[24] Diversity was the pivotal concept through which the college-educated middle classes could officially reject racism and yet tolerate, even perpetuate, racism's traditional symptom, racial inequality.

When the Supreme Court again considered affirmative action in higher education, Justice O'Connor's decision in *Grutter v. Bollinger et al.* (2003) was remarkable for its deference to the Powell opinion. O'Connor construed Powell as mandating a bowing to educational authorities: "The Law School's educational judgment that such diversity is essential to its educational mission is one to which we defer. . . . Our scrutiny of the interest asserted by the Law School is no less strict for taking into account complex educational judgments in an area that lies primarily within the expertise of the university."[25] O'Connor also adhered to the *Bakke* decision in insisting that the Court could approve only a "narrowly-tailored" plan that adhered to the strict-scrutiny standard for all racial classifications, beefed up in the interim by various employment cases in which the Court had struck down all affirmative action programs that attempted social remedies.[26]

The O'Connor decision included language about the evils of racial exclusion; it argued that group diversity reduced racial stereotyping and made for more competent civic engagement. But since O'Connor adhered to the strict-scrutiny criterion for racial classification, this classification not only had to be flexible and individualized, but also had to fulfill a "compelling state interest." What, exactly, was the compelling state interest in achieving the educational benefits of diversity? Was it Powell's "robust exchange of ideas"? O'Connor tried this out, but here she was not convincing.[27]

The turning point came when O'Connor cited the needs of business and the military: "These benefits are not theoretical but real, as major American businesses have made clear that the skills needed in today's increasingly global marketplace can only be developed through exposure to widely diverse people, cultures, ideas, and viewpoints. . . . What is more, high-ranking retired officers and civilian leaders of the United States military assert that, '[b]ased on [their] decades of experience,' a 'highly qualified, racially diverse officer corps . . . is essential to the military's ability to fulfill its principle mission to provide national security.' "[28] Educational diversity rose to the level of compelling state interest when it could be shown to serve the marketplace and the military enterprise now globally intertwined with it.[29] Diversity was particularly important at elite universities and their law schools because these institutions provided the nation with its future leaders.[30] Diversity may in some sense have improved the quality of that leadership, but O'Connor stressed that diversity made the institutions that formed economic and political elites appear legitimate to the rest of the public.[31]

The two justices closest to the culture warriors—Antonin Scalia and Clarence Thomas—dissented from this decision with undisguised hostility. In his dissent, Thomas was particularly annoyed by the claim that the educational benefits of diversity, which he derided as "racial aesthetics," represented a compelling state interest. But this melodrama veiled the underlying agreement between the two sides. O'Connor and Thomas shared a belief that racial classification and race-oriented action were justified only in cases of actual ongoing racial discrimination, which they could never find, and in cases of national security.[32] O'Connor took a step beyond Thomas in tacking onto military security the domain of economic competitiveness. Her understanding of the utility of diversity was broader than his, but the principle was the same. Diversity had nothing to do either with racial equality or with the cultural agency of ordinary people or groups. Both the right-wing and centrist positions in this discussion took place on culture-wars terrain. For both sides, diversity was either an input into military and economic security or it was irrelevant. O'Connor's decision, read as a victory for affirmative action, was in fact a victory for the market's management of society, and for the decision makers who performed that management in the place of everybody else.

Diversity as Market Stratification

The diversity consensus had major conceptual and political limitations, but these were sidestepped by defending diversity on the grounds of its popularity. Diversity *was* popular—among the professional middle classes and institutional leaders who had come to rely on affirmative action for even rudimentary integration. National leaders had certainly become convinced that some measure of racial diversity was a vital performance enhancer for the national economy. If you are going to race in the Alps in the Tour de France, you need to train in the mountains in your own country, and the same was true for firms that hired Indian software designers or sold television programming in Latin America.[33] Diversity entered and exited the Michigan case with an enormous elite-level prestige, a prestige that rested on the claim that for businesses competing in overwhelmingly nonwhite global markets and for armed forces fighting with 40 percent minority personnel, diversity *worked*.

But the question remain: Works to do what? What kind of racial and economic structure would diversity produce? Culture warriors saw stratification as natural and civil rights as the opposite—as a restraint on market efficiency. Would diversity overcome this culture-wars trajectory to real social effect?

The answer at first looked somewhat ambiguous. Take the military's racial composition. The armed forces' Michigan brief noted that "nearly 40% of the U.S. military's rank and file are minorities, as are almost 20% of officers on active duty, according to Defense Department statistics. Those numbers have jumped dramatically from the early 1960s, when fewer than 2% of officers were minorities."[34] On the one hand, the officer corps had half the proportion of people of color as the rank and file. On the other hand, it had ten times the proportion of minority members that it had had forty years before. The military credited its "limited" race-conscious personnel policies for what appeared to be deliberate and reasonable racial progress—a little slow and incomplete, and yet steady and continuing.

Similar ambiguities marked higher education. In 1940, the national college and university population was 97 percent white. By 1995, it had become 85 percent white. As for faculty, by the year 2000, "85 percent of all full-time faculty members and instructors were white, compared with 86.5 percent in 1992 and 89 percent in 1987" (the national population was 75 percent white).[35] In terms of gender, "the proportion of women among full-time faculty members increased to 36 percent in 1998, up from 27 percent in 1987."[36] White student representation fell only 13 percent in sixty years. And yet the shift was steady and real, and white overrepresentation in education, as compared to the general population pool, had dropped to 10 percent.

Though we may wish to read these numbers as a slow but uniformly positive advance toward ever-increasing integration, a closer look suggests something less clear. In the years between 1976 and 1999, African American undergraduate enrollment as a proportion of total enrollment went from

9.6 percent to 11 percent, a change of about 1 percent in nearly twenty-five years.[37] Most of the improvement in black enrollment took place during the first and most aggressive phase of affirmative-action programs from the mid-1960s to the mid-1970s, and these were driven in large part by social protest.[38] In a study I coauthored at UC Santa Barbara, we found that the percentage of Latino faculty doubled from 1975 to 1995 (2.5 to 5.5 percent of tenure-track faculty) and then stagnated after 1995; we found that the African American percentages doubled from 1.5 to 3 percent in the same years and then stagnated as well. In both cases, most of the gains were in place by the late 1980s.[39] The situation improved in later years, but only slightly, resembling the pattern for California overall. Plateaus defined PhD statistics as well: in the field of literature, the number of African American PhDs held steady through the mid-1990s—at about 18 *individuals* per year nationwide.[40] A study of changes in black enrollment at the flagship campuses of the fifty states found that between the years 2001 and 2004, twenty-five flagships either increased black enrollment or maintained the previous level (all but three of these increases were under 1 percent over four years, and the largest was 1.9 percent); twenty-five saw a decrease (including UC Berkeley, Penn State, Virginia, Georgia, Michigan, Illinois, Iowa, Maryland, and Rutgers).[41] Thirty-five flagships had proportions of blacks that were below that of the share of blacks in the college-age population, the exceptions being states with small black populations. Integration—again, defined as parity that could lead to equitable development—was neither steady nor consistent, and in many cases was moving in reverse.

In spite of the language of diversity that calls for diverse leadership, integration remains much more likely in lower-status institutions. The most selective UC campuses, Berkeley and UCLA, continued to have declining enrollment from underrepresented groups into the 2000s; the less-selective Riverside campus has increased enrollment from those groups, while at Santa Cruz and Irvine enrollment from those groups has stayed about the same.[42] A similar stratification marks the relation between high school and college, in which a long boom in underrepresented minority students in the California graduating high school class did not produce a matching boom in UC enrollment.[43] Looking at the situation nationwide, a recent Century Foundation report found that "74 percent of the students at the top 146 highly selective colleges came from families in the top quarter of the SES [socioeconomic status] scale (as measured by combining family income and the education and occupations of the parents), just 3 percent came from the bottom SES quartile, and roughly 10 percent came from the bottom half of the SES scale."[44] Not only are the higher levels of an institution or industry consistently less integrated, but there is evidence, again, that integration is moving sideways and sometimes in reverse.

Though the situation is complicated, we can isolate some of the factors at work. One is sheer demographic change. Just as the gross national project can grow simply because the size of the population grows, much statistical integration is the result of population shifts. Where the presence of people of color does show clear increases, as is the case in some educational categories for Latinos and Asian Pacific Islanders, these gains are no more than proportional to the very rapid growth of these two groups in the general population.[45] Thus the integration of K–12 schools in such states is not so much the result of enlightened diversity policies as of demographic mini-revolutions. And since some of the minority growth reflects continuing white flight, "integration" can be another word for segregation.

There is a second factor at work that overlaps with the first, and that is economic stratification. The lower levels of an institution or sector as measured by income or status integrate fairly readily as whites "retreat upmarket" to more lucrative opportunities. Much agricultural work, construction, elder and disabled care, and other difficult physical labor in states like California and Texas is now performed by Latinos; much mom-and-pop retail in Southern California is handled by Asian Americans. The integration of more poorly paid employment categories reflects labor market stratification and segmentation rather than diversity and integration. More accurately, such diversity bypasses integration for de facto segregation between levels or sectors of the labor force.

Something similar happened in education. The proportion of women who were "full-time professors and instructors working at private research universities . . . *declined* between 1992 and 1998—from 31 percent to 26 percent."[46] The entire period of significant increases in integration after 1970 coincided with a near doubling of the proportion of faculty who worked part-time—from 22 to 42.5 percent.[47] Thus some progress toward racial and gender integration can be traced to the declining status and working conditions of large sectors of college teaching. Service work integrated early and quickly compared to higher-paying professions and executive positions. The sectors of higher education most like service work have seen increased integration over time, while the integration of higher-paid research faculties lags well behind.

Minority growth and inequality are readily symbiotic, and they suggest one overriding interpretation of the present state of American society: we are managing our diversity through stratification. We can conclude that, as the "minority" population of the United States got larger and more influential every day, the white majority regarded it with a mixture of interest and fear, a mixture made more volatile by its dependence on the minority's presence as a cheap and flexible labor force. This dependence has coincided with increased economic instability. Much of the American middle class has seen long-term wage stagnation, and its former birthrights, like low-cost public college degrees and affordable coastal suburbs, have become the preserve of the upper 10 or 20 or 2 percent of American incomes. Instability, coupled with growing inequality and declining access, has decreased the middle class's inclination to share. There is evidence in the form of housing, schooling, and other forms of everyday voluntary segregation that the white middle class tends to regard the bulk of the laboring minority populations as low-cost toilers rather than colleagues, neighbors, and fellow citizens. In states like California, the result has been a decreasing willingness to fund services that are perceived to serve large minority populations, from public health care to K–12 education. Observers of political life have correctly noted that as primary and secondary education became preponderantly black and brown, per capita taxpayer funding declined.[48] Most higher education leaders sincerely lament this situation, and yet they must work to avoid a similar fate by maintaining their funding levels, which they do by affirming their rigorous standards, their recondite technological research, their special packages for top students, and the brute selectivity that intensifies stratification between research and teaching colleges. Stratification has become a primary mode of professional-middle-class self-defense, made all the more attractive because, while in reality it holds the line against the racialized masses, it is apparently color-blind and supportive of diversity.

The Middle Class Helps Its Own Decline

The bad joke is that the middle classes are increasingly holding the line against themselves. Stratification has meant the stratification of the middle class as well, with its corporate-oriented professionals mixing in college with its teachers and nurses and then never meeting again. The middle classes tolerated and even demanded racial stratification. They supported a model of diversity that undermined remedies for racial stratification that were triggered from below. They were then left with no remedy for economic stratification occurring within their midst. Having largely cooperated with the culture warriors, they lacked the cultural capability to criticize a university system that increased inequality where it had once reduced it. Many members of this middle class missed the stratification of their class because it appeared to them in the guise of *racial* stratification—a false guise, but to many, a familiar and tolerable one.

An example of this mistake came from the town where I live, Santa Barbara, California. Because of high housing costs in this coastal California city, middle-income whites without inherited equity were buying houses in less expensive Latino neighborhoods. At the same time, they sent their children to school in majority-white neighborhoods elsewhere.[49] One majority-Latino school district had 105 white school-age children, while its elementary school had 18 white children enrolled. Another Latino-majority neighborhood that had become a favorite of white buyers had 308 white elementary-school-age children and 37 white children in its elementary school.

Interviews suggested that the whites had looked at the lower test scores of those schools and assumed that they were the unchangeable result of low-income, working-class kids whose parents did not know or did not care about educational quality. The whites missed the fact that their new neighborhoods were mixed working- and middle-class Latino neighborhoods, that some of their Latino neighbor kids were going to private schools themselves, that "Mexican gentrification" was upgrading the facades of houses all over their neighborhoods, and that these were houses for which their Latino buyers had also paid between $550,000 and $900,000 or were paying $3,000 a month to rent. If many of the parents spoke Spanish to each other on the porch, their kids were playing in English on the front lawn.

The white arrivals could have said to themselves, well, I'll assume my new Latino neighbors are as interested in good schools as I am. I'm putting my kids in this school, and together we're going to force the school district to give us what we need to make this school good. School "diversity" will be a strength—for example, all the kids, regardless of their home language, will be bilingual by the sixth grade. A few white parents felt this way, and a more widespread version of this attitude would have reduced inequality among the district's white- and Latino-majority schools. But it would have required that whites see such racialized inequality as abnormal. It would have helped, too, if they saw such inequality as an attack on their own status and security as middle or working class. After all, the school district was accepting second-class performance for all schools not in neighborhoods that were solidly upper or upper middle class and overwhelmingly white.

But by and large, after two decades of culture wars, which plastered over any holes that the more egalitarian, Keynesian postwar period had opened in two centuries of racial loyalty, middle-class whites now lacked the cultural knowledge to link their own prosperity to cross-racial equality. Nor could they link this equality to the social intervention that historically had created it.[50] Instead, Santa Barbara, like towns and suburbs all over the country, got neither the segregation nor the integration of their elementary schools, but schools that have a small minority contingent (white in some cases and Latino in others), often as low as 10 percent. The Santa Barbara middle class—real middle-income people, teachers and sales managers and personal assistants and firefighters and police—got increasing stratification in its own ranks, and schools too weak to reverse this stratification.

What should we call this pattern? A major report on the subject was called *Resegregation in America's Schools*, and "resegregation" was not too strong a word to describe recent changes. Very few whites expressed segregationist intent, and yet liberal as well as conservative whites did and do seem to prefer environments that are very white—70 percent, 80 percent, 90 percent white—even if those environments make no contribution to social development. An alternate term for this quasi-segregated and stratified condition is "pseudointegration." By "pseudointegration" I mean a state that formally rejects racial segregation without leading to producing racial integration. The term refers to a condition in which the legal possibility of integration (the end of segregation law and so on) leads neither to proportional representation of population groups in an institution, nor to political equality between the designated peripheral group and the historic core—what used to be called power sharing—nor to what used to be called "social equality," meaning the integration of informal social life. By "pseudointegration" I mean something other than "not yet integrated," other than the idea in which progress this decade or the next or the next will see African Americans and Latinos in boardrooms and university labs in about the same proportion as they are found in the population. By "pseudointegration" I mean a condition that replaces *both* segregation *and* integration, has its own identity, and is possibly permanent. By "pseudointegration" I also mean the condition rationalized by "diversity," that substitute for egalitarian measures. Diversity and pseudointegration were mutually entrenched by the culture wars' shift of the country's racial understanding.

The age of pseudointegration had the following features: First, most national leaders accepted that diverse neighborhoods, schools, and businesses offer their members clear advantages in performance. Second, this diversity would not lead to programs that sought racial equality. Third, this diversity did not lead to integrated institutions, since the white majority had abandoned anything but lip-service to participating in them—including white-minority institutions like public elementary schools. Fourth, any reduction of disparate impacts would come from the market, when reduced disparities might in some way serve the interests of companies, customers, and their pliable governments. Fifth, the market would operate with elite but not mass or popular guidance, and would be expected to create social spaces—neighborhoods, malls, universities, and private medical clinics—where whites form the large majority and where they retain monopolies on selection and governing.

Though much of the white middle class did not join the Right's culture-war mudslinging, they rode on its coattails, accepting the economic benefits of tax revolts, defunded public services, gated communities, abundant low-cost labor, wage stratification, and exclusive schools, as well as the accompanying elite decision-making structures.[51] All this has been achieved at a high cost: while basic integration has languished, inequality has increased, the economic majority has stagnated, stratification has intensified, and yet the discretionary powers of gatekeeping institutions have been repeatedly affirmed.

The ideal of diversity is in a perverse sense the culture warriors' greatest achievement, for it is perfectly compatible with the market value of facially neutral procedures and the market naturalization of unequal outcomes. Diversity expresses the apparently color-blind version of an antiegalitarian racial consensus that protects the insulated social spaces of the professional middle class while supporting the economic disparity that makes its fortune. In the wake of the diversity settlement, we will have pseudointegration indefinitely. We will have it until the white college-educated middle classes recommit themselves to linking quality to racial equality and prosperity to racially proportional outcomes. By the early 2000s, the culture wars had at least temporarily destroyed this group's capacity for making these links and had insured that it would continue to lose economic ground.

— III —

Market Substitutes for
General Development

— 8 —

Facing the Knowledge Managers

Higher education went from the frying pan into the fire through most of the 1990s. The decade started with attacks on political correctness and multiculturalism. It continued with cuts in public funding and successful challenges to affirmative action programs. It carried on with debates about meritocracy and diversity, and established the framework which would support the post-9/11 attacks on faculty politics. Culture warriors used each issue to weaken the credibility of higher education as a source of reliable, independent knowledge. This did not mean attacks on science and engineering research, but on fields associated with the expansionist, majoritarian "golden age" boom of the 1945–1975 period. Culture warriors discredited the postwar case for cultural equality where that would mean racial equality, thereby reinforcing inequality, resegregation, and pseudointegration. Culture warriors discredited what I have called meritocracy II, which rejected the necessity of hierarchical outcomes and reinforced professional, peer-reviewing communities. We now turn to the third, directly economic dimension of the culture wars, where the culture wars fulfilled their aim as an economic war on the power and resources of the mass middle class.

The 1990s elevated knowledge to a central place in the economy and intensified the claims that the university would be central to future prosperity. The one thing all Americans seemed to agree on was that the United States was a "knowledge society," its economy was a "knowledge economy," and the present age was the "age of information." This vision had already had the major social effect of supporting widespread indifference among political and business leaders to the fate of blue-collar workers: mass layoffs in steel, autos, and manufacturing in general came to be regarded as the natural effect of economic evolution. When mass layoffs became more common for

125

white-collar workers in the 1990s, a similar logic was applied to them: technology was enabling the elimination of routine white-collar jobs as it had for routine production in the 1970s and 1980s.[1] Workers would thrive, wrote Robert B. Reich in *The Work of Nations* (1991) and Daniel Pink in *Free Agent Nation* (2000), if they became entrepreneurial knowledge workers who created their own destiny by giving the high-tech network economy what it needed most—new knowledge.

But how would the relationship between knowledge and finance be determined? The power of knowledge to influence the bottom line required respect for nonfinancial factors. This meant that financial outcomes would be shaped by the authority of expertise, which was becoming more flexible and democratic. They would also be shaped, in evolving post-1960s principle, by processes of cross-cultural negotiation with the expectation of rough equality. As we have seen, the culture wars had undermined the credibility of both cross-cultural negotiation and egalitarian meritocracy. These were serious losses to society's cultural capability, which it would need to handle balanced, sustainable, long-term social development. The culture wars also targeted a third dimension, which was the subordination of market forces to this general development. If democratic cultural processes and goals could be made to seem threatening, disruptive, and inefficient to sound economics, more restrictive models of financial government could step into the vacuum.

Resurgent finance needed to do something about academic labor. Academia had supported much of the most sophisticated white-collar brain work, and in the knowledge economy the work of this group was more essential than ever. The college-educated work force was increasingly multiracial, international, and accustomed to intellectual and even political independence, and all of this had achieved visible form on college campuses. Did this conjunction of knowledge production and cultural independence mean that knowledge workers would make rules that managed the market forces to which they were ultimately exposed? Could they influence and redirect business leaders? Would academic workers be Peter Drucker's "intellectual capitalists," owning the means of knowledge production and thus ultimately controlling production's financial rules?[2]

A Financial Revolt

Investors did seem to have been persuaded as a group that knowledge was the central indispensable element of the New Economy. But this did not mean they had any interest in being replaced by intellectuals and scientists as the nation's capitalists. The United States may have embraced knowledge capitalism, but it had not embraced *post*capitalism. People who invested capital in the 1990s were as interested as they had been in the 1980s or 1920s or 1820s in controlling how their capital was used. It seemed paradoxical to some, but the same years that intensified the influence of knowledge work intensified the power of financial control. This business trend also swept governmental thinking, which focused increasingly on the bottom-line aspects of their not-for-profit sectors, like higher education for government and research and development for industry. The U.S. vice president wrote *Common Sense Government: Works Better and Costs Less* (1995), claiming that his National Performance Review had shown that governments needed to pay more businesslike attention to their "customers." In Australia, Britain, and New Zealand, national university systems became subject to ever-increasing pressure to show direct returns to the economy.[3] In the United States, business leaders called for corporate-style management measures to be applied to universities.[4] More than thirty states had imposed financial cutbacks on higher education by 1995; most had launched accountability programs that increased monitoring of universities' financial results. Universities responded: most were translating patent regulations into more persistent attempts to extract royalties from their faculties' discoveries. Financial auditing had a firmer hold on education than ever before, and this was no less true when the financial object was intellectual property.[5]

University leaders were trying harder than ever to march in step with leaders in business. The general trend was clear. After 1980, finance had taken hold of corporations with a vengeance. Finance theorists increasingly demanded that firms dump 1970s-style social goals, union-style employee protections, and anything else that distracted them from the maximization of profit and of shareholder wealth. For most of the twentieth century, publicly held companies had dispersed corporate ownership among thousands of shareholders while effective control resided in the hands of upper managers.[6] In the 1980s, financiers and their academic allies began confronting the independent manager head-on. Some influential finance professors— Michael Jensen in particular—claimed that declining corporate profits in the 1970s could be traced to the refusal of upper managers to heed the call of owners for maximum returns. He and others accused managers of hoarding "free cash flow" instead of handing it over to its rightful owners through dividends. In a widely noted essay entitled "Eclipse of the Public Corporation," Jensen advised shareholders to replace top executives with merger and acquisitions specialists who would more perfectly reflect the profit focus of large investors.[7] The boom in mergers and acquisitions in the 1980s was undertaken by investor groups who claimed to be disciplining both "redundant" employees and entrenched—read autonomous—executives. The infamous Michael Milken was especially good at stigmatizing executives whom he regarded as unresponsive to his definition of shareholder interests.[8]

Measured by the transfer of wealth, the shareholder's revolt was a big success. The financial historian Doug Henwood determined that "from the early 1950s through the mid-1970s, firms paid out about 45% of their after-tax profits in dividends." But "from 1990 to 1995, nonfinancial corporations paid 78% of their after-tax profits out as dividends."[9] On the basis of calculations like these, Henwood concluded that nonfinancial firms were giving more of their revenues to shareholders than at any time since World War II. Though many shares were owned by pension funds, the overall effect was to transfer wealth up the ladder to the very top; leading financiers had initiated nearly all mergers and acquisitions activity and benefited disproportionately.[10] Investors thus increased their share of after-tax profits by about 75 percent, which implied substantial decreases for business development, employee salaries, and R & D.

The shareholder's revolt was in essence the triumph of financial control within business culture. In the financial view of business, "financial tools . . . measure performance according to profit rates. Product lines are evaluated on their short-run profitability and important management decisions are based on the potential profitability of each line. Firms are viewed as collections of assets earning differing rates of return, not as producers of given goods."[11] Though financial management may seem to have lacked subtlety, since it drove major decisions on the basis of daily, monthly, and quarterly numbers, it had more subtlety than traditional scientific management, for it worked at a distance. It did not require constant surveillance. It established the ends but not the means: it granted all sorts of latitude to workers and managers on the job even as it tightly controlled the measurement of the results. Finance was perfectly capable of a hands-off approach to the actual labor of knowledge workers, and was perfectly suited to controlling the high-tech companies of the New Economy and their potentially freethinking employees.

All of these practices elevated investors over other corporate constituencies—employees, customers, the local community, the national economy, and of course the knowledge producers, whose interests, even if sometimes served by financial goals, were subordinated to them with an increasingly self-righteous militance. As the 1980s became the 1990s, profits and stock prices became virtually the only remaining standards of managerial success. This meant that cultural factors and goals—human resource management, company climate, employee relations and group communication, managerial structures and their psychological effects, and the "higher ends" of John Kenneth Galbraith's "technostructure"—came to have an increasingly public-relations function that helped keep employees quiet or helped ease them out the door.

The shareholder's revolt profited from its own form of culture-wars rhetoric, for it tirelessly attacked excessively humanistic managers who had been running companies for themselves and their employees and their customers and their communities and not exclusively for investors. Employee knowledge was cast as self-serving; embedded organizational knowledge was described as superfluous; relatively egalitarian collaboration was considered a source of weakness. The shareholder revolt took the same hostile stance toward multilateral negotiation, political equality, and economic parity that culture warriors took toward similar qualities in the political and academic realms.

Managing Empowerment

Sometime in the 1990s the effort to apply tough new business principles to knowledge workers produced a field that for a time was called "knowledge management" (KM), and which later evolved into "innovation management." Proponents of KM agreed with Drucker and other management theorists that workers with bachelor's and postbachelor's degrees were bearers of intellectual capital. Knowledge management also stressed that knowledge work entailed qualified independence.[12] It rejected the simplistic entrepreneurial rhetoric that defined Reagan-era finance culture to stress the "idea of community" that supported the innovation that high-tech success required. KM was a fan of "teams" and endorsed a "community of practice" like that established at Xerox's legendary Palo Alto Research Center in the 1970s.[13] It held that the most fundamental "learning happens in groups." In these groups, individuals would have enormous intellectual latitude as well as the inspiration, intellectual guidance, and continuous feedback of passionate colleagues. The resulting synergies, in most KM views, produced breakthroughs that for individuals would have required rare individual genius. Everyday working genius could instead by supplied by a community of practice.

"Knowledge management" acknowledged the importance of culture and, at the same time, subordinated it to financial goals. KM wanted to improve the freedom of the human interaction that enhances knowledge work while translating individual labor into value for the firm. KM had two main ways of seeking this synthesis. It aimed to stratify knowledge workers into clearly identifiable subgroups, which would then receive disparate treatment. Second, it aimed to transform "human capital," owned and controlled by employees, into what the field called "structural capital," controlled by the company. We will look at these features one at a time.

Though KM advocates agreed that most employees were in some sense knowledge workers, it sought not to cherish all knowledge workers equally but to discriminate against whole categories of them. Its goal was "identifying which human capital generates wealth" and which should be drastically cheapened.[14] This sorting was of the utmost importance. A distinctive feature of the New Economy was the ease with which even those technologies that had barely been invented were commodified—that is, copied and mass-produced at rates that could destroy the original creator's profits. KM was part of a system that hoped against hope (and against the economic evidence) that "the greater the human-capital intensity of a business—that is, the greater its percentage of high-value-added work performed by hard-to-replace people—the more it can charge for its services and the less vulnerable it is to competitors." The reasoning here was that a company could thrive when it was "even more difficult for rivals to match those skills than it was . . . for the first company to replace them."[15] KM was thus not window dressing, but the life-or-death creation of the human capital that would allow a firm to survive in the cutthroat New Economy.

A particularly good exposition of the KM strategy appeared in a book by Thomas A. Stewart called *Intellectual Capital* (1997). At the time, Stewart was a member of *Fortune* magazine's board of editors; he later became editor in chief of *Harvard Business Review*. Stewart distinguished between three different types of knowledge or skill. There are "commodity skills," he wrote, which are "readily obtained" and whose possessors are interchangeable. This category includes the "pink-collar" work that involves skills like "typing and a cheerful phone manner." The second type is "leveraged skills," which appear in many firms but which are especially important to a particular firm's business model. The third type is "proprietary skills," which Stewart defined as "the company-specific talents around which an organization builds a business."[16] The knowledge manager must nurture and cultivate the third, proprietary type of skill and stamp out (or radically cheapen) the first, commodity-kind of knowledge worker.

Stewart sorted skills and workers into four categories in order to simplify the manager's task (see Table 4). Each of these categories is made up of knowledge workers. But only one of them, Stewart said, adds real value to the firm: "A company's human capital is embodied in the people whose talent and experience create the products and services that are the reason customers come to it and not to a competitor. That's an asset. The rest—the other three quadrants—is merely labor cost."[17] The formula was simple and plain: squeeze costs, nurture assets, and remember that most people are merely cost.

The knowledge manager's responses are expressed in the second line in each quadrant. For the lower-left quadrant, which includes lower-skill knowledge workers, the solution is to buy machines and eliminate the workers. One example is customer service operators who route calls according to type. These can be replaced by phone menu systems. The low-value-added workers who are hard to replace (upper-left quadrant) are necessary to the firm but not valued by its customers. They "have learned a complicated set of ropes but don't pull the strings."[18] Such workers include "skilled factory workers, experienced secretaries," and back-office bookkeepers. The latter, for example, have accounting skills as well as plenty of informal knowledge about how the particular company works. They have experience-based cultural knowledge that cannot be easily codified and transferred, and that helps them figure out what anomalous figures mean, since they have seen them before, or which routes of project approval are slow and which are fast. Such knowledge directly improves efficiency and profits in various ways. Tough luck: they may be trained, intelligent, valuable, and even necessary,

Table 4 Types of knowledge workers (and appropriate actions)

Difficult to replace, low value added	Difficult to replace, high value added
INFORMATE	CAPITALIZE
Easy to replace, low value added	Easy to replace, high value added
AUTOMATE	DIFFERENTIATE or OUTSOURCE

but they are not perceived to contribute directly to the firm's main sources of profit. Thus a good knowledge manager should try to codify some of their informal knowledge, disregard the rest as irrelevant, and outsource as many of these workers as possible.

The same goes for the workers in the lower-right quadrant. The firm should try to get rid of them (through outsourcing) or differentiate them from other firms' similar workers. This group could include people with expensively acquired, difficult knowledge, like code writing in a customized programming application, but who nonetheless are similar to their counterparts in other companies. These folks must be transformed into distinctive specialists, or they must be fired and their functions given to a company that specializes in them. This is a quadrant stocked with good university graduates: they finished school, did well, are highly educated, hardworking, and intelligent, but are too similar to their counterparts from other colleges who work in similar firms to add unique value. KM saw good college graduates as well-credentialed variants of other production workers: there was nothing wrong with them, exactly, but they did not contribute the only thing that counted in the New Economy—unique comparative advantage. Stewart was codifying the major development in attitudes about white-collar labor workers in the 1990s, which was that, for the most part, they were as disposable as their blue-collar brethren before them.

The Star Quadrant

In this model of KM, only one type of knowledge worker deserves full capital support. That is the one who is both hard to replace and who adds lots of value to the firm's product (upper-right quadrant). These knowledge workers add major value because their knowledge is *proprietary*. Knowledge managers thus have to be cheap with three of four categories of knowledge worker so they can make the maximum investment in the high-value remainder, from whom most earnings and security flow. Note again that future knowledge workers do not get into the capitalized, protected, pampered quadrant by being competent or even brilliant. They get there by being competent, brilliant, and unique.

The importance of uniqueness to KM cannot be overstated. Uniqueness did not mean unique genius or originality. Uniqueness was not an intellectual quality at all. It was a property category: uniqueness meant sole ownership. Knowledge by itself did not produce profits in the New Economy.

Proprietary knowledge produced big profits. Proprietary knowledge was the only really valuable (though not the only necessary) knowledge for a simple reason. Because of the ease with which high-tech products could be commodified, firms throve not through niche maintenance but through control. Be first or second in every market or get out, said General Electric's lionized CEO Jack Welch, and he sold even profitable GE divisions that could not make that cut. The process of commodification was good for consumer budgets but it was hell on profits. The really big money came from managing not for market innovation but for market domination. Only proprietary knowledge offered real capital and security in an age of turbulent markets.

During the 1990s firms were being told to use knowledge managers to select in favor of the knowledge that would bolster "increasing returns." Large existing sales of a product like Microsoft's unloved but unavoidable Windows operating system meant that more people were willing to pay more money for it. This pattern broke with the traditional demand curve, which predicts that larger production runs lead to lower prices.[19] An earlier term for increasing returns was "monopoly rent," the use of which would have denied that there was anything special about new technology, since capital formation has always depended in large part on rent as a mechanism for increasing the rate of profit over the rate that would obtain in a truly competitive market."[20] Monopoly returns are greater and more secure than competitive ones—compare Microsoft's 1990s position to the much weaker one of hard-drive manufacturer Seagate, also a well-managed early entrant in its field, a leader of the steady exponential increase in the density of disk-media storage, and yet financially far less stable than Microsoft because of uncontrolled direct competition. The conflict between Microsoft and the federal government that ran through most of the 1990s concerned Microsoft's right to require purchasers of its operating system to buy other Microsoft products, particularly its Web browser. These tie-ins had given Microsoft near-monopoly market shares that had allowed it to collect rent-like profits.[21] The New Economy was most new in favoring some industrial sectors, like electronics, pharmaceuticals, and software, over previous leaders, like energy and autos. But it was not new in the sense that its leading companies stayed ahead by limiting the choices of customers to whom they could then charge rents. Business was looking to knowledge management to turn a worker's ideas into a proprietary product that would return a rent-sized profit. The "rentier" were the firms that would receive the lion's share of investor capital, thereby lofting their stock prices, executive compensation, the prestige of their sector, and the global stature of American business.

For employees, the crucial fact was that only one type of knowledge worker would have access to capital. In stark contrast to Drucker's prediction of a new age of widespread intellectual capitalists, elite knowledge workers had access to capital only because they served equity markets and consumer markets as interpreted by financial managers, and not because their intellectual capital now drove the financial kind. After a nod to the finance-serving skills of one category of knowledge worker, status deteriorated rapidly. In the KM scheme, the remaining three classes of knowledge workers would be treated as ordinary labor, whose cost would be cut as much as possible. These knowledge workers would be micromanaged, surveilled, downsized, temped, or outsourced—automated and informated—treated in other words like "semiskilled" industrial workers or service workers, like the "second-class citizen" Drucker thought lacked the ability and education to be a knowledge worker. The brilliance of knowledge management, from the company's point of view, was to have created a new hybrid—a *service-knowledge worker*, an information worker who was smart and cheap *and* fully manageable and ultimately interchangeable with someone much less costly and troublesome, whether that be a call-center worker in Sioux Falls and then Bangalore, India, or a radiologist in Mumbai.

The Cubicle Humanist

I have pointed out that in the KM system the vast armies of college graduates would not be funneled to the winning quadrant but would be dispersed through all four quadrants, and therefore be fungible, disposable, outsourceable and vulnerable as a group. It was not hard to guess the default quadrant for the humanities major. Humanities research was already seen as economically trivial.[22] Humanities *graduates* were, to the contrary, a centerpiece of the system of corporate workforce preparation that rested on the college degree. Humanities majors were the generic college graduates.[23] They were employable not because they could use and extend the great traditions of art and letters but because they had two other qualities:[24]

1. They were professional processors of information. They had "communication skills," the possession of which was often the employee trait most desired by personnel directors in standard surveys. As col-

lege graduates with professional experience, they would in an earlier era have been candidates for the peer-based forms of professional self-governance Galbraith had identified with the advanced technostructure, and which formed the basis of "meritocracy II."

2. They were ideal cultural managers. In theory, their education had prepared them to interact with rather than confront and challenge people across cultural, racial, and national lines. Since they could communicate equitably across borders, and work outside of traditional international and colonial hierarchies, they would be the exemplary intermediaries in the famous new "network economy."[25]

Though they lacked the technological expertise to design, operate, and manage value-adding technical systems, humanities majors had skills the contemporary economy needed, and they would be readily hired into it. They showed the same intelligence, initiative, and entrepreneurial energy that companies looked for in engineers, financial executives, and other star employees. They also had the skills associated with majoritarian capitalism and could contribute to its increasing diversity.

In tandem with other culture-war attacks on these qualities, knowledge management dismissed their economic value. Nontechnical college graduates, KM declared, simply did not offer the company proprietary knowledge. They were associated in nearly all businesses with the vital but ordinary interconnective tissue of the networked organization but were not seen as a direct source of profits so much as a part of institutional support. They could aspire to middle management but would not secure a position squarely in the profit chain. Business at one time needed huge numbers of these college graduates to operate its enormously large and expensive infrastructures. Business was still enormously large and expensive, but it was now focused on liquidating or cheapening the personnel not tied to its proprietary products.

Knowledge management linked big returns to protected technoknowledge and linked culture to background support systems. It admitted the necessity of culture but cheerfully defined it as a handmaiden to economics. The star quadrant would take nearly all of its members from the technical fields. The exceptions would be found in highly specialized, stratified niches in fields like media and law, and the most valued former humanities majors would have to become professionals like intellectual property lawyers with a direct connection to creating and defining proprietary knowledge.

Structural Capital

Once KM had slotted knowledge workers according to their relevance to the firm's proprietary goods, its other major goal followed rather easily. That goal was to convert human to structural capital. Most experts offered the knowledge manager the kind of advice that Stewart did: Recognize brainworkers and their importance. Give them the resources they need.[26] But do not get permissive and go too far. One consultant noted that knowledge communities can get cocky and independent. "Fund them too much, and you'll start to want deliverables. You won't get what you want. You'll get what the community wants to deliver."[27] Too much independence for the professional-managerial class (PMC) would become a threat to the process by which knowledge was put to profitable use. Toward the end of the 1990s, as elite knowledge workers became scarce or mobile enough to strike good deals for themselves, they caused all sorts of corporate complaining about the pampering of coders who acted like teenagers and the rise of a bratty class of "gold-collar workers."[28] The bargaining power of the members of the PMC—to say nothing of self-management—allegedly interfered with the task of maximizing their knowledge's value to the firm.

The only real question for the firm, as Stewart put it, was "how to own human capital."[29] Though he celebrated "employee capitalism" in which high-value-adding knowledge workers got to share ownership through fancy compensation systems, he argued that the company must "contain and retain knowledge, so that it becomes company property."[30] The company needed to convert its human capital to its own proprietary "knowledge stocks" and "knowledge flows." Company-owned knowledge was what Stewart called "structural capital." Only structural capital directly served the firm.

The KM model thus steered companies away from letting knowledge workers manage their own work directly. These workers posed permanent loyalty problems, since they could easily care more about their project or intellectual challenge or profession than about the firm they worked for. Managers, on the other hand, were paid to serve the firm, and could be trusted—given the appropriate financial controls—to make decisions that favored the firm.

The knowledge company would thus have a management structure that was more flexible and more informal and more casually dressed than management of old, but otherwise just the same. "The leading social groups" of the New Economy, Drucker admitted, will be "knowledge *executives* who know how to *allocate* knowledge to productive use" (emphasis added). Knowledge executives would not produce but would allocate knowledge. To do this job, they would set themselves apart from ordinary knowledge workers. Perhaps the knowledge economy had as big a gap between labor and management as the older industrial one. Once Drucker started down this road, he went all the way on it. "The post-capitalist society," he continued, "will be divided by a new dichotomy of values and of aesthetic perceptions. It will not be the 'Two Cultures'—literary and scientific—of which the English novelist, scientist, and government administrator C. P. Snow wrote in his *The Two Cultures and the Scientific Revolution* (1959), though that split is real enough. The dichotomy would be between 'intellectuals' and 'managers,' the former concerned with words and ideas, the latter with people and work."

Thus, even as he pictured knowledge workers helping to move the economy toward postcapitalism, Drucker sustained capitalism's traditional, defining split between worker and manager. Drucker and most other sages of flexible, networked firms tossed out much of the old baggage of scientific management—the knowledge worker innovates as well as implements; the manager allocates and guides but does not monopolize thinking and planning—yet the blending of functions between worker and manager did not prevent the continuation of the traditional management–labor hierarchies, with financial control vested squarely in the firms. Possessing intellectual capital would *not* make a knowledge worker a knowledge manager.

As much as they beat around the bush, Drucker and others were repackaging an old Marxist truth about capitalism: capitalism operates by converting the labor of the worker into the capital of the firm. The reason for this was old as well: high rates of capital accumulation—high enough to please investors—were thought to depend on managers deciding unilaterally on the uses to which capital would be put, including how much would be given back to labor. The sole exception to this managerial control was the investor, since managers were indeed bound to stock prices and other financial indicators of investor opinion. In contrast, consultation with labor was minimized, since labor could not be trusted to pay itself little enough or to fire itself (in spite of a growing history of union "givebacks"). Labor relations were often conflicted at high-tech companies: high levels of trust, collaboration, and even influence for leading scientists and other brain workers coexisted with the compartmentalization of financial matters and intensified levels of secrecy about business strategy.[31] The firm's dependence on the high-end worker's intellectual capital would not be allowed to turn into dependence on the high-end worker. Knowledge workers did not have an obviously larger place in major financial decisions than did other kinds of line workers or cubicle dwellers. They may have had more control over the immediate process of creating knowledge. But they did not, through this knowledge, have more input into the executive suite. The purpose of KM was to prevent humane management from eroding the boundary between highly competent employees and financial decisions.[32]

From the scientists' point of view—and from that of the cubicle dwellers of the other three quadrants—KM missed the real challenge of the knowledge economy. The real challenge was *not* how to turn new knowledge into sustainable profits, since this was a permanent issue in the history of capitalism about which a great deal was known. The real challenge was how to overcome the dualism between finance and "culture" in the life of the firm. The incentive was not simply ethical, though that was part of it—the professional middle classes expected to be treated like accomplished, productive, deserving human beings and not like cogs in the machine. The incentive was also improved financial efficiency. Simple profit maximization that took no heed of the lifeworld of the firm's knowledge workers was not optimal: "human relations" management theory, many empirical studies, and the strong growth rates of "low-conflict" economies had shown this again and again.[33] As the environment for knowledge companies became more competitive, the products more complex, and the processes of production more intricate and difficult, more organic approaches to management—even self-management or self-organization—would have become more lucrative. The scratching tumult, uncertainty, and anxiety introduced by the 1980s and 1990s traditions of perpetual financial maneuvering might have been replaced by structures that better reflected the innovation process, the firm's capacities, and perhaps collaborative employee assessments of business and wider public needs. The firm was, ultimately, a social institution. But financial control blocked the complex signals by which its public life could be registered and developed.

Finance worked in parallel with the culture wars, undermining the corporate cultural movements that had emerged from the crises of the 1970s. KM did not reconnect finance to the labor process, but maintained its separate superiority in a superficially humanistic way.

Postcapitalist Glimmers

KM put universities in an awkward position. On the one hand, their product—knowledge and knowledge workers—was celebrated as never before. On the other hand, their product was a secondary input, a raw material like any other. With KM, knowledge's application would be decided by a financial system that had little contact with its production or with its social context and potential use. Educators often claimed that the producer-manager relation was flexible, that advanced scientific research had much weight in negotiations with industry, that knowledge really was the heart and soul of the economy. Could the university translate this thinking into a continuing cultural transformation of the 1990s corporate system?

The university did seem poised to extract a theory of postcapitalist management from its own practices. Its schools and departments enjoyed an unusual amount of autonomy from the central administration. Since this was long tradition, they did not have to spend too much time fighting about it. Within departments, principal investigators (PIs) ran their laboratories as semi-independent operations. They shared some common overhead expenses—staffing costs, communications, energy, building maintenance—via the university, but their labs' success depended on their ability to function as permanent fund-raisers. They often supplemented their federal grants, which were already enormously time-consuming to acquire, with research sponsored by private foundations and businesses. They built and supported their own research staffs, planned and performed their research entirely on their own, interacted with their professional peers as they chose, and developed and transmitted their results according to their own judgment. All of the diverse but interlocking activities that went into a successful lab were directed not by distant administrators but by the PIs and postdocs and teams of colleagues who were directly involved in the research. PIs also had many other responsibilities, including traveling to report to federal agencies, share research results, and raise further funds, and this meant that day-to-day research was often relatively self-organized. PIs were increasingly likely to work with their counterparts in industry, to consult with industry directly, to have contact with "angel" financiers and venture capitalists, and to start their own companies. They were doing some of the development in R & D along with their expected research.

At the core of this model was the independent knowledge worker—not free of obligations and ties, but able to pursue these in continuous contact with the work itself. The best part of Drucker's theory of the "intellectual capitalist" was its vision of a New Economy of craft workers—the return of the artisan to the complex economy.[34] The university was a setting in which this craft worker operated in dialogue with the modern economy. The 1990s university might have decided to show the way toward the team-based, administratively "de-layered," socially oriented, creative knowledge environments on the grounds that it had learned to reunite economic with cultural knowledge, and could show business how to operate in a complex, post-hierarchical, decentered, borderless, more egalitarian world.[35]

Academic humanists played a part in the university version of Drucker's postcapitalism. They retained significant control of their research product. This was in large part because they were also their product's major consumer. They generally signed copyright over to academic presses, but because of the absence of a commercial market for scholarly articles, faculty retained low-cost access to these articles for research purposes. The national disciplines constructed a miniature market that, like the market for private placements of venture capital, operated largely through peer review. Virtually no money changed hands, but this was less important than the fact that the members of the research community had almost complete control over its structure and the research uses to which its knowledge would be put. Researchers controlled production through their standards of consumption, embodied as professional evaluation. Presses and their editors had financial responsibilities that researchers did not, and yet they depended on the opinion of those researchers to move the product. Though this kind of "market" could not be scaled up for technology-rich commodities, it did harbor enormous experience with a nondualistic production process in which financial issues remained answerable to intellectual and social standards.

The story of the 1990s New Economy had two potential endings. In one, the university would be harnessed by KM and its kin so that it provided intellectual ingredients with a minimum of interference in the financial system. Here, the university "businesses" itself in order to attract industry funding and to develop its inventions through industry partners. In the other ending, university-industry partnership would also take place, but would adapt the networked craft-labor model that had been doing quite well in the university. This would likely have produced sustainable economic growth, since financial goals would have been keyed to realistic appraisals of a technology's potential as well as of its social effects, which in the dot-com era they largely were not.

This latter ending lost out to the first. The reason I have given here is that KM, the managerial technique that was supposed to reflect the cultural specificities of knowledge workers, was little more than an extension of the culture war, which continuously eroded challenges from political, social, and cultural systems to neoclassical economics. One example of the culture wars' economic impact was the academic humanities, which entered a period that mixed intellectual advancement with steady financial decline.

— 9 —

English's Market Retreat

I will use literary and cultural study (LCS) as my emblem of the humanities' reaction to the changing environment outside the university as the twentieth century wound down. Along with history, the study of language and literature remained the largest field in the humanities, and literature was arguably the most persistently introspective about its place in the academy and the world.

This introspection was intensified by the collapse of the academic job market for literature PhDs around 1970. The market took about fifteen years to improve, and never fully recovered. To the contrary, it intersected with the rise of the use of non-tenure-track faculty in colleges and universities across the country. A major study of professional employment conducted by the Modern Language Association (MLA) in 1998 implied that the recession of the early 1990s may have been the end of any chance for a return to normalcy: "During 1991–93, when the number of full-time positions advertised in the MLA's *Job Information List* declined by 29% in English and 14% in foreign languages, part-time and temporary positions across higher education grew by 17% in four-year institutions and 40% in two-year colleges. In 1970, 22% of the faculty nationwide consisted of part-timers, but by 1993 the face of higher education had changed so drastically that *part-timers constituted 40% of the faculty.*"[1] After five years of the New Economy boom, an analysis of the 2001–2002 MLA job list suggested that the situation was, if anything, a little worse: the placement rate in full-time tenure-track jobs was 46 percent in English, about the same in foreign languages excluding Spanish, and 62 percent in foreign languages including Spanish.[2] Literary and cultural studies thus appeared to have developed a semipermanent 50 percent under- or unemployment rate. Those humani-

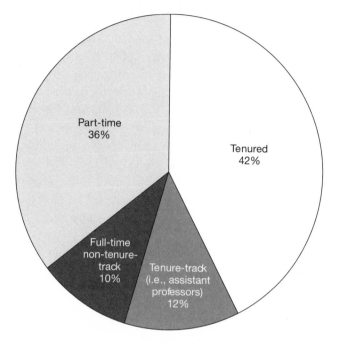

Figure 1. Estimated percentages of faculty members in different categories, four-year English departments, 1996–97. Source: Philip Smith, Marcia Dalbey, David Laurence, Adalaide Morris, Stephen Olsen, James Papp, Barry V. Qualls, and Eric Sundquist, "Report of the ADE Ad Hoc Committee on Staffing," *ADE Bulletin* 122 (1999): 11, http://www.ade.org/reports/staffing_rpt.pdf (accessed August 26, 2006).

ties faculty who looked at staffing reports would see charts like the one shown in Figure 1.[3]

Not all the numbers were even this good: a 1999 survey conducted by the Coalition on the Academic Workforce found that the percentage of instructional staff counted as "full-time tenure track" had fallen to about 36 percent. Advancement was a particular problem, especially for women, where after thirty years of attention to gender equity, women were still best represented as instructors, lecturers, or adjuncts and worst represented among the tenured ranks of major research universities.[4] Such low rates of full-time, secure employment are obviously very significant for white-collar workers, and resemble those of young high school dropouts from disadvantaged neighborhoods.

Year after year of this kind of job shortfall—some years much worse than 2001–2002—produced outcries in official places. Writing in *The MLA*

Guide to the Job Search (1996), one observer exclaimed, "Since the mid-1970s, incalculable damage has been inflicted on thousands of aspiring academics as the academic pipeline continues to disgorge people into a marketplace saturated in most fields. Preventing such dysfunctional imbalances in the future should have a high priority in the making of national, state, and institutional policies."[5] This sentiment was endorsed by the MLA's *Final Report* in the following year.[6] Every committee established by a professional organization in the humanities denounced the trend toward the cutting of tenure-track positions and their replacement with nontenure-track faculty, whether part-time or full-time.[7] The labor crisis in the humanities was common knowledge, and a leading response to it, unionization by graduate students and adjunct faculty, became persistent national news in the 1990s.

With all this depth and intensity of concern, what would fields like English do to right themselves in the new business environment?

Roads Not Taken

One possible response was open rejection of the university's increasing economic determinism. I earlier associated this rejection with the philosopher of postmodernism Jean-François Lyotard. Literature and philosophy are gold mines of antideterminist thinking. Using this tradition would have required the cultivation of a nonmarket understanding of value and mode of life. It may have emerged from some combination of literary aestheticism, with its rich romantic, bohemian, and spiritualist traditions: the critique of financialization, the defense of craft labor of all types as a primary source of value, and the theory of sustainable development. Research in the study of literature and culture could have made common cause with literature itself as it advanced largely outside the academy, and with the social sciences.

The academy had supported and might have continued to support this anti-determinist thinking. It was a fountainhead of what had been called a liberal society—of what I have described as an *economic majoritarian* society, whose college-educated middle class worked within market relations but did not exactly follow them, and which off-and-on supported universal higher education and racial equality. The university had justified its increasing influence on two basic grounds—its majority status and its expertise. The public university had grown by offering major expansions of the majority's expertise. The public university, many held, was to transform knowledge elites into a knowledge majority, which might finally fulfill the country's democratic promise. This sense of the destiny of majoritarian expertise expressed itself in slow but growing support for civil rights, and in indignation at the irrational brutality of the Vietnam War and at Nixonian abuses of power. As I have noted before, we cannot identify this middle class with enlightenment, for it was also attached to racial hierarchy and world economic supremacy. But overall it was an improvement over its precursor leadership groups, and its key activity was to *manage* markets with its expertise. Its long-term effect—and evolving goal—was society's general development.

The humanities might also have been renewed by the advancement of literary and cultural study to the point that it could be widely seen to lead to valid cultural knowledge. LCS research could build on its existing analysis and interpretation of important texts in order to define and address the major problems of this and other ages. LCS disciplines could remain pluralistic, in that a large proportion of research would carry on as it has. But graduate programs and much research could be reoriented toward practices that would make concrete contributions to understanding the complex relations between culture and society in an era of continuing socio-cultural disaster in most regions of U.S. influence. In departments of literature, two fields that could clearly expand at the expense of others would be (1) composition studies, including various kinds of creative writing, journalism, and new media composition, and (2) the study of contemporary literature and culture, where thousands of poets, novelists, and dramaturges, fully engaged in the analysis of their times, died on vines that lacked the basic cultivation LCS continued to lavish on Shakespeare and Joyce. University administrations could support these moves, for they would see them as efforts to recover from the culture wars and actively build external communities for LCS research and jobs for LCS students. The investment might not pay off for years, but universities could be persuaded that this was exactly the kind of long-term development of cultural fields that served both knowledge and society. LCS's overall philosophical motive would be its direct and central contribution to cultural problem-solving and to human development.

But that would be a project of long-term reconstruction, and it was perhaps too much to hope for in the midst of the culture wars on humanistic knowledge in particular and the university in general.

English's Market Default

The culture-wars script appeared in LCS in this form: rather than putting the development of cultural understanding ahead of market logic, LCS leaders criticized the impact of markets on academic labor while continuing to adapt to them.

The authors of the MLA's *Final Report* (1998) recognized that there was nothing new either about the job crisis or about the shift in higher education employment to contingent faculty: a similar report in 1970 had sounded the same alarms.[8] The 1998 findings also noted that literature departments were caught up in national if not global economic trends. At the same time, they rejected the relentless pressure to downsize higher education. In particular, the *Final Report* insisted that it was unacceptable to replace full-time with part-time faculty as an ongoing strategy. It was clear by then that what had seemed a stopgap solution to temporary budget crises had become instead a standard practice, much as mass layoffs had become a solution to financial problems in large corporations. The *Final Report* proclaimed that "excellence in education for present and future students *depends on an increase in full-time tenure-track faculty positions*."[9] It also argued that the value of education could not be properly captured by market calculations: "Of course the object of business corporations is to make a profit, while the object of institutions of higher education is to acquire and disseminate knowledge as well as, most important, to develop in students sophisticated intellectual strategies they will use for the rest of their lives, in and out of the workplace."[10]

Reading through statements of senior LCS faculty of the period, it was not difficult to find rejections of market measures of educational value. For example, the critic Robert Scholes, who would become MLA president in the early 2000s, recommended fundamental changes in the literature curriculum in order to restore a "modern trivium" that would be based on "a canon of concepts, precepts, and practices rather than a canon of texts." This trivium would "encourage textual production by students in appropriate modes." The outcome would be students who could "situate themselves in their own culture" and presumably participate in its creation. Scholes's calls for a new basis for criticism's social engagement rested in part on his belief that LCS could engage the outside world across a gap "between the values of the humanities and those of the powerful worlds of business and public life."[11]

But though the official statements contained good ideas—departmental self-study that would lead to reimagining "the size and shape of the graduate programs they offer," or the formation of alliances between tenure-track and contingent faculty, or better public explanations of the purposes of higher education—they did not call for interventions in the university's institutional conditions. The pervasive assumption was that self-study would lead to reductions in graduate programs, "where numbers of students are not being placed in the positions for which they are trained." Since this was true in even the best-known departments in the profession, it was a recipe for national cutbacks in the number of graduate students being trained. Similarly, graduate programs were to become more oriented toward teaching and less toward research. Departments should also provide "specialized counseling for graduate students interested in learning about employment opportunities outside the academy" and should prepare many of their graduates to move away from the academy altogether. Any expansion of the graduate curricula should move graduate students into the teaching markets that national trends suggested were likely to expand—community colleges and even high schools.

These recommendations flowed from the MLA's remarkably consistent acceptance of the "market" as the arbitrator of the shape of the profession. (This view was not unique in the humanities disciplines: for example, many historians thought about their profession in the same way.[12]) The 1970 MLA report held that the problem with English was market "oversupply." The 1998 *Final Report* cited the 1970 report's analysis of the *Sputnik* boom in university hiring and then applied a market analysis to the alleged post–cold war bust. The MLA authors repeatedly defined the job crisis as a market imbalance. It arose, they say, from "the misperception of 'an endless need'" for humanities faculty that "spawn[ed] a professional supply soon to be so out of phase with marketplace demand." And again: "At some point . . . a limit on the capacity to fund new positions for faculty members was inevitably reached and the market for new PhDs saturated." This definition of the problem predetermined the solution: market imbalance is always corrected by the restoration of market equilibrium. Accordingly, the *Final Report* noted that one of its three main objectives was "to adjust the job system so as to balance the number of jobs available with the number of qualified PhDs." "It is imperative," the authors insisted, "that graduate programs make adjustments appropriate to the realities of the job market." The market expressed a certain demand to which responsible programs must adapt.

This view persisted into the 2000s. The MLA's "Professionalization in Perspective" report that analyzed 2001–2002 job market data not only took as its starting point the oft-lamented "oversupply" but made the extraordinary statement that "the history of this oversupply is the history of our profession."[13] This claim was factually untrue: there were also periods of undersupply, but they all occurred more than three decades before the professionalization report was published. It would have been interesting to see whether there were causes of those earlier faculty shortages that were more profound—and more supportive of LCS—than the inevitably mentioned baby boom and cold war defense spending.[14] It would have been interesting to inquire how other fields, particularly economics and the health sciences, had managed to make their funding grow even in bad economies and boom in good ones. It would have been interesting to factor in the basic fact that LCS's potential market had *grown* every year between 1970 and 2005, in the steady increase in the number of students who started college nation wide. But the MLA's limited market thinking made such inquiries unnecessary.

This market orientation began to infiltrate assumptions about the production of humanistic research. Not only were LCS scholars generating too many graduate students, but they were writing too many articles and books. In the 1990s, two MLA presidents expressed concern about publishing— one (Patricia Meyer Spacks) about graduate student publishing and the other (Elaine Showalter) about the publishing of criticism in general.[15] An MLA committee was formed, and it produced a report called *The Future of Scholarly Publishing* that made a number of practical recommendations.[16] These focused on how departments and their university administrations could achieve greater awareness of the market conditions that were making it less and less likely that tenure candidates could publish their research in order to keep their jobs. The English professor and magazine essayist Louis Menand suggested replacing the dissertation with a series of papers, and though he had some good intellectual reasons, his underlying assumption was that literary scholarship suffered from massive oversupply. This trend culminated at the end of 2006 with a lengthy report from the MLA Task Force on Evaluating Scholarship for Tenure and Promotion, which offered sound, intelligent recommendations for adapting tenure requirements to a dead market and, in effect, accepting permanent austerity.

Though clarity about external conditions is always good, the general tone in LCS was one of market determinism: Stephen Greenblatt, the MLA president who in the early 2000s got the ball rolling again on the publication issue, wrote that

> many factors are involved here, but the core of the problem—which extends beyond our fields to such disciplines as philosophy, musicology, and anthropology—is systemic, structural, and at base economic. Under financial constraint, universities have been unable to provide adequate support both for library budgets and for university presses. Responding to the pressure of shrinking budgets and of skyrocketing costs for medical, scientific, and technical journals, libraries have cut back on the number of books that they purchase. And university presses, suffering severe financial losses as a result of this shift in library purchases and a general decline in book sales, have cut back on the number of books they publish annually in certain fields.[17]

The iron logic of these cascading cutbacks was correct but incomplete. It was inevitable only when the "many factors" mentioned at the start are excluded—the culture wars' tarnishing of the humanities fields, the failure of these fields to redefine and articulate their public utility, and their market fatalism in itself. The MLA analyses simply argued that under existing market conditions there was an oversupply of humanistic publication. The market would be insisting that scholars cut back. Departments and reviewing agencies would need to recognize these cutbacks as inevitable. To further and falsely naturalize this lowered market demand, the publication report suggested that stressing quality over quantity would "reduce the flow of both books and articles that do not greatly add to current scholarship in their field."[18] The incorrect implication here was that the humanities disciplines had long been ignoring market forces and had been stressing quantity over quality. The new introduction of market awareness would put an end to that and would restore the quality control to scholarly publishing that peer review (coupled with requirements creep) had not supplied. The result would be a reduction of quantity and an increase in quality thanks to the market's logic of austerity.

In its attempt to be realistic about economic forces, LCS learned one-half of the lesson of business. It was the half the culture wars taught again and again: the market was to be adapted to, not to be criticized or changed. The market model blocked rather than answered a simple question: who or what decides the level of demand? The other half of the lesson of business, the half LCS ignored, was the requirement to respond to "market" environments by increasing one's own influence over the market's demand decisions. This meant learning how to *manage* markets—how to discover hidden demands, how to create demand for products one thinks are important, how to adapt the market to one's output, how to subordinate markets to the needs of one's "customers," not to mention the wider society. These were all lessons that craft-labor professionals had to master if they were to thrive or even survive in complex economies.

LCS was indeed thinking about its markets, but only halfway. It launched itself into a twilight zone between commercialism, which it shunned, and market management, which it did not practice. Having spent a century in quasi-managerial organizations, it had learned again and again that they are vulnerable to economic forces but had discovered little about how to manage those forces. As a result, LCS was cooperating in a downsizing that it resented, was discouraging the creators of its main product (cultural knowledge), and was turning more of its students into lower-division teachers in the very moment when these positions were being pushed to the edges of the knowledge economy.

Austerity in Practice

An illustration of LCS market thinking may help clarify these points, and it comes in the form of an accomplished humanist-administrator. Carol T. Christ was an English professor at the Berkeley campus of the University of California, and in the 1990s became dean of humanities, then provost, and then executive vice chancellor at that campus; in 2000 she became the president of Smith College. In the midst of an impressive ascent through the administrative ranks at a complicated institution, Christ wrote an article in an MLA publication, *Profession*, on the subject of "retaining faculty lines." Christ's piece offered a helpful guide to administrative assumptions for uninitiated faculty. Although the topic suggested that she might be interested in helping LCS departments increase demand, her article was divided into a half that expressed a traditional humanistic vision of shrunken graduate programs, and a half that offered a similarly reductive account of resource allocation.

Christ wrote that she evaluated departmental requests according to the three factors of workload, service to the institutional mission, and "excellence." The first of these clearly responded to existing demand, as measured by factors like undergraduate enrollment. The second sounded like it might harness accounting to substantive educational goals and might offer scope for thinking about building future demand. But Christ did not describe the positive value of any humanistic discipline in itself or for its students or its institution. Nor did she offer a general description of the university's mission as a whole or that of the liberal arts.[19] The closest she came was to say that "English language and literature has long stood at the center of American conceptions of a liberal arts education; it does not face the challenges that confront small foreign language departments, for example, departments of Italian."[20] The university mission thus sounded like another index of existing demand, with the proviso that for some larger fields demand was either built-in, or, for reasons of tradition or ideology, would be treated as though it were. This might explain why Italian would struggle to claim a bigger piece of the institutional mission while English would not: though foreign language skills were not obviously less important to an educated public than was a knowledge of Shakespeare, departments of Italian did have lower enrollments than departments of English.

Christ defined her third criterion, "excellence," as a combination of "research productivity," "quality of departmental governance," "quality of teaching," and "vigor of intellectual life." Such content generally boiled down to a combination of the department's rank and status in the field combined with its apparent ability to turn new resources into still higher status. Excellence was in essence a measure of whether or not the department was a good investment: excellence meant that it was likely to offer a good return.[21] Though Christ, like nearly all other administrators, would never have put it so crudely, excellence was an index of a department's present position on the market, measuring the demand for its research, its consulting networks, the job offers received by its faculty, and its overall prestige. Thus Christ's third criterion echoed the other two. The first assessed existing student demand, the second expressed the university's demand for the department's services, the third assessed demand in the profession, government, and industry. Christ's three mechanisms of evaluation were three ways of responding to current market conditions, rather than remaking them. They fit well with English's tendency toward self-imposed austerity.

Market Victims

Austerity economics had a large social cost. It encouraged employees, including faculty and other professionals, to be market adapters rather than market makers. It located guiding agency in abstract demand rather than in organizations and people. This view has gradually become a pillar of conventional wisdom in the college-educated middle classes, including in their weaker sectors like college English. By contrast, 1990s top executives did not buy austerity for a second. Their job in the New Economy, as in the old, was to try to control markets in order to stay on top and ahead of them. Some of the biggest companies in the world, like Citibank and General Electric, tied their survival to dominating instead of merely competing in markets. Imagining themselves living "inside the tornado" of hypercompetitive global capitalism, executives felt a permanent obligation to lead, manage, control, engineer, dominate, and subordinate markets to their needs. Wherever English departments might have looked, organizations had problems with markets and were trying to refashion them. English might have noted this refashioning and learned some new moves.

But LCS scholars who researched the history and theory of the New University were unable to break with the market determinism that was common in their field. A good example of this predicament appeared in Bill Readings's widely read *The University in Ruins* (1996). Readings was utterly opposed to the trend toward "the exclusive rule of business management" in the university. He blamed market ideology for this and blasted its alleged henchman, the concept of "excellence." Excellence, he argued, lacked the qualitative, substantive content of academic disciplines, and stood for nothing more than a field or concept's market value. Excellence "allowed for the increasing integration of all activities into a generalized market, which permitted a large degree of flexibility and innovation at the local level."[22] It was the proxy for knowledge-based capitalism and its networked and flexible corporation. Unfortunately, the terms of Readings's analysis opposed market logic without subordinating it, and so robbed the humanities of an opportunity for redirection or resistance.

Readings's main example of corporate educational thinking was a report for UNESCO called *The University as an Institution Today*, by Alfonso Borrero Cabal. Readings started from a familiar dichotomy in which "economic criteria and cultural development are at odds." By this he meant a system in which culture—supported by genuine higher education—was regulated "in terms of cost and benefit."[23] It was true that strict cost accounting was irrelevant or worse for advancing conceptual development in all intellectual fields: some in business were aware of this problem, which stimulated corporate interest in the kind of academic research that a bottom-line orientation forbade. Readings was certainly right that the university should (and does) go much farther than industry in creating knowledge whether or not it offered a commercial payoff. That in turn meant that the university would have to continue to treat most knowledge and all "cultural development" in nonmarket terms.

Readings was particularly concerned by a passage in which Borrero Cabal called for better administration of planned global development. "Planning, execution, evaluation," Borrero Cabal wrote. "The natural actions of responsible persons and institutions. They make up the three important stages that complete the cycle of the administrative process. In logical order, planning precedes execution and evaluation, but all planning has to start with evaluation."[24] Readings interpreted this to mean that "the language in which global discussions are to be conducted is not that of cultural conflict but of economic management. And the language of economic management structures Borrero Cabal's analysis of the university around the globe."[25] Readings claimed, overall, that "the idea that the sequential processes of business management are the 'natural actions' of 'responsible persons' may come as a surprise to some of us. What kind of 'responsibility' is this? Clearly not that of a parent to a child, for example."[26]

It was true that Borrero Cabal used an inflated accountability rhetoric popular with high-level administrators who constantly strain to stay on business's good side. But Readings's response was disastrous for the non-market thought he claimed to prefer: he tainted any kind of planning as selling out to for-profit market forces. He sounded unaware of the long history of "planned economies," "government planning," "industrial policy," "market-state coordination," and even the corporate world's own "strategic planning," all of which had consistently come to blows with the profit motive.[27] He favored the metaphor of parenting, which was unfortunate as a metaphor for teaching, inapplicable as an image of faculty-administration interactions, and inappropriate as a description of government administrators' relations to their society.[28] Readings simply ignored several of the crucial elements of the kind of administrative process Borrero Cabal was talking about: it was collaborative and iterative, meaning that draft proposals had to be revised in view of local or public response; it was future oriented, meaning that it did not simply respond to current priorities and market hierarchies; and it proposed specific goals that were associated with the prospect of social and international development.

For all its faults, Borrero Cabal's administrative planning was not the same as following markets, but was an attempt to manage or control them in a world where corporations largely dominated governments. In the process of critiquing Borrero Cabal, Readings reproduced LCS's inability to translate its accurate sense of the market's limitations into a means of managing them, or even to understand those who attempted this management.

Literary Theory's Market Foundations

The dead end of the aversion to market management appeared in Readings's solutions. He disapproved of the old humanistic mission of forming organic national communities by forming common cultural identities. At the end of his book he called on the university to create "the community of dissensus" instead. In this "inoperative" or "unavowable" community (Readings was invoking the philosophers Jean-Luc Nancy and Maurice Blanchot), "members do not share an immanent identity to be revealed," nor do they seek consensus or any other kind of unity. They instead exist in a network of obligation, of reciprocal debts which cannot be discharged, of thickened and finally unknowable social bonds.[29]

In calling for inoperative communities, Readings explicitly rejected the legitimacy of either individual or collective agency. He was right to say that individuals do not achieve full autonomy, groups do not achieve true consensus, and community obligations in all their complexity cannot be truly known. But Readings took this to imply the necessary and desirable absence of efforts to steer the apparatus. The inoperative community had no "power to name and determine itself; it insists that the *position of authority cannot be authoritatively occupied.*" Thus individuals had no right to try to "regulate the reciprocal debt." Such communities must be "understood on the model of *dependency* rather than emancipation."[30] Loss of agency was not an unfortunate by-product of Readings's vision of the "posthistorical university." It was its explicit goal.

The default result of avoiding administrative agency was, unfortunately, the rule of the market itself. The practical effect was the misguided abandonment of the attempt to govern the organizations of higher education or, more to the point, to revise LCS teaching and research so that they increased their public without selling out to it. Readings's moralistic antimanagerialism was *not* required by his correct claims about the epistemological gaps and tangles in our knowledge of the webs of power and obligation. Contra Readings, the basic purpose of management was to make timely decisions in the pursuit of goals without ever waiting for complete information about the environment. Management in the LCS context could well have been functioning in accordance with an antifoundationalist theory of "governmentality," one with a better Heisenberg uncertainty principle for organizations than that found in the average business school. But it was not: LCS scholars were finally more comfortable with losing to market forces than with everyday efforts to manage them.

Roots of Managerial Incapacity

Bill Readings was not a bad student of LCS traditions, but to the contrary an extremely good one. His thinking had sources in literary theory and philosophy, which tended to move from a habitual dichotomy between culture and markets, and from a generalized opposition to market forces, to an opposition to managing markets even through cultural knowledge. Part of the opposition to managing markets stemmed from the difficulty that criticism had in sustaining individual agency. It had grown comfortable with a tradition that developed with rejections of romantic subjectivity in Irving Babbitt and T. S. Eliot, reappeared in New Criticism's vision of the poem as a system-equilibrium, and continued through raging individualists like Harold Bloom who nonetheless subordinated individuality to higher or invisible systems of nature, spirit, language, or consciousness. This tradition of criticism, in spite of its variability, tended to undermine the agency that was a prerequisite to managing market forces.[31]

A second part of the answer lay in what came to be called the "American Foucault." The reference is to Michel Foucault, the renowned analyst of society and systems of power. Foucault may well have been the most influential thinker in the human sciences of the last quarter of the twentieth century, having inaugurated new directions in the study of clinical medicine, the penal system, sexuality, social policy, and many other fields. In literary and cultural study, one of his most influential themes was subjectification, referring to the way that structures of power do not simply control individuals, but constitute them. Foucault himself was deeply interested in how such structures were resisted by individuals and groups in a wide range of ways, ways that included social movements, sabotage, institutional obstruction, sexual practices, and the "care of the self." But in the United States, scholars seized more on power than on resistance. Foucault's sophisticated model of systemic social forces came to reinforce the existing tendency in LCS toward weak models of subjectivity.[32]

The sophistication of the model, at least in LCS, tended to overwhelm analysis. In one particularly famous tour de force, Foucault insisted that power was *neither* "a group of institutions and mechanisms that ensure the subservience of the citizens of a given state," *nor* "a mode of subjugation which, in contrast to violence, has the form of the rule," *nor* "a general system of domination exerted by one group over another." On one page he had thus disposed of all the modes in which power had most often been critiqued. Power was instead "the multiplicity of force relations immanent in the sphere in which they operate and which constitute their own organization." He was right to insist that power was a multidirectional process of transformation that worked on its objects from within, that was inseparable from those objects, and that incorporated reversals, contradictions, and disjunctions. In contrast both to earlier Marxist claims that the working out of contradictions would eventually generate a break and a new system, and to the neoclassical economics that posited market-led returns to equilibrium, Foucault insisted that contradiction was exactly how the system laboriously sustained itself. And yet, in a further twist, even as power succeeded, it did not present a stable, visible, familiar target: power was not "a unique source of sovereignty," but "the moving substrate of force relations which, by virtue of their inequality, constantly engender states of power, but the latter are always local and unstable."[33] Power was immanent rather than institutional and most effective when it seemed ineffective, even invisible.

Foucault's model was a genuine advance, and yet scholars tended to conclude that all this meant subjectivity was only subjugation, even a trick, and perhaps what a psychoanalytic thinker like Jacques Lacan had said it was: a mask over a permanently changing and incoherent entity we merely call the self, a mask that was never of our own making. Thus the theme of emancipation that had been so important in the 1960s and some of the 1970s became suspect and even self-deluded. Influential works were written with titles such as *The Novel and the Police*. Sayings were coined such as "there is always resistance, but never for us."

It is easy to understand why countless scholars placed enormous emphasis on the power of power. Given the way it saturated all of reality, including our own minds, what kind of individual or organization could actually manage it? Theorists set to work on this problem, and sometimes produced important new syntheses. One thinks of Stuart Hall's arguments about producing antiracist scholarship while discounting essential racial identities, or Ernesto Laclau and Chantal Mouffe's 1985 book *Hegemony and Socialist Strategy*, which offered an antifoundationalist account of the formation of powerful political blocs that could ultimately alter larger systems. Apparent opposites were combined—flexibility and justice, openness and power. New social movements, including the much-discussed anti-AIDS group ACT UP, showed that decentralized organization and guerrilla tactics could work better than organizational consistency and bureaucratic command. But it was almost impossible to imagine, from within LCS, a way of developing this kind of institutional agency. To put it reductively, LCS's Americanized Foucault delivered strong systems and weak subjects. This view ironically recapitulated the model of strong markets advanced by the culture wars.[34]

One critic who, like Hall, Laclau, and Mouffe, sought some pushback against the system, was Judith Butler, whose *Gender Trouble* became a classic of the 1990s. In her accounts, systems of power inadvertently led to their own partial and provisional undoing. As one example, she wrote that "if the suppression of the body is itself an instrumental movement of and by the body, then the body is inadvertently preserved in and by the instrument of its suppression. The self-defeating effort of such suppression, however, not only leads to its opposite—a self-congratulatory or self-aggrandizing assertion of desire, will, the body—in more contemporary formulations it leads to the elaboration of an institution of the subject which exceeds the dialectical frame by which it is spawned."[35]

Many readers worked through these subtle and conflicted formulations for their capacity to point toward moments in which individuals, bodies, and elements of the system itself were not simply determined by the system. These efforts were repaid, but in very small and incremental ways. Resistance largely consisted of the system's own failure to reproduce itself, and not of any individual or collective agency that achieved some kind of even limited and partial control. LCS theory of the Foucauldian period offered only weak, indirect, highly mediated agency and thus little in the way of institutional or market management.

In addition to traditions of romantic individualism and American Foucauldianism, a third source of LCS's weak managerial capacity was its attitude toward the relation between cultural and social forces, the latter often going under the name of politics. Around the time he was serving as MLA president, Stephen Greenblatt said, "I cut my teeth in Berkeley in the 1970s in heroic times, times that fancied themselves as heroic, and was very dubious even then that getting these literary readings right was going to have a direct political effect on the world. The other extreme position, the one, say, that Auden reached, namely that literature makes nothing happen, is also not true. The goal is to find the middle space, in which you understand that you're participating in a small way in an indirect and glacially slow shift in collective understanding."[36]

Certainly Greenblatt was right that literary criticism will never lead to revolution, but who thought that it would? Who said social change was a one-stop linear process? This false fusion is invoked so that Greenblatt can reject it, leading to a rejection of strong agency (for example, as expressed as "heroism"), and an assertion of a split between politics and knowledge. A bridge then has to be built between them, which requires a whole career of scholarly labor, and the existence and the labor of the bridge affirms the separation of the two realms. Culture cannot then be known through agency or action, all cast as the realm of politics, but through LCS operating as a lower science.[37]

This paradigm shaped the important methodology of New Historicism, which throughout the 1990s set the limit of LCS mainstream engagement with the "social text," beyond which fields like postcolonial studies or queer theory could not go without risking their mainstream professional audience. There was a culture-wars element at work in Greenblatt's and similar statements, and it implied that literary and cultural study would not produce the kind of knowledge that could manage social systems, including markets. The implication was that cultural research, even when conducted by a New Historicist like Greenblatt, would separate cultural researchers from the social systems in which their materials have their existence, and where their findings could have major impact.

Critics like the ones I have cited produced some of the strongest work of the thirty-five-year period of LCS's market decline. Their professional influence was justified, and yet it was in part malignant. The market decline and advanced LCS thinking were related. LCS scholars regularly attributed change to systems rather than to selves or groups. At the same time, they were uncomfortable with methods of actively managing those systems and their institutions, viewing such intervention, depending on who they were, as too social, or too unliterary, or too naive, or too conservative. Locating the winning force in systems, yet not believing in direct control over them, LCS scholars at best had little idea of how markets might be shaped, and at worst gave markets intellectual encouragement. Having accidentally internalized a culture-wars market vision, LCS scholars waged a culture war on themselves.

— 10 —

The Costs of Accounting

Culture warriors paralyzed their most easily labeled antagonists in the academy—the humanities faculty whose traditions had for centuries subordinated market forces to human welfare in the broad sense. The culture wars were so effective at normalizing market precepts that as public universities struggled in the early 1990s and early 2000s and lost ground to their private counterparts, a new financial language appeared on campus without debate or even an interpretive framework that would help to understand its effects.

The Looming of Finance

Following the California state budget squeeze of 1993 and 1994, University of California senior vice president for business and finance V. Wayne Kennedy linked the success of the university's public mission to better financial management:

> Recognizing that faithful stewardship of the public's investment in the University of California is a top priority for our administration, the university is strengthening its business focus and is now in the second year of an ambitious program to overhaul and update its business practices with the expressed goal of enhancing institutional accountability. We are strengthening our system of controls as we continue to evaluate and redesign the university's fundamental business processes. We are replacing outdated business systems and practices with methods comparable to those utilized by the nation's leading corporations.[1]

Using terms that had become common during Governor Pete Wilson's administration, Kennedy redefined the university's constitutional status of "public trust" as a "public investment." The production of value depended in some large part on a "business focus." Business focus boiled down to more economical forms of financial supervision. Although the "business" of the university was knowledge, the university's financial systems came to loom alongside research results as an index of quality.[2] Financial accounting became a language of public explanation, and it was certainly more accessible than that of expert peer review.

Most universities gradually improved their accounting systems over the 1990s. They used better computer systems to automate information collection that was still done by hand, enhanced inventory tracking, and generally upgraded computer hardware and software to allow for something closer to real-time monitoring of cash flows. The quantity and quality of financial information seem generally to have improved. How much money these improvements actually saved is less clear. The University of California administration was in the unusual situation of having attracted the critical attention of a tireless, quantitatively oriented, retired physics professor from its Berkeley campus, Charles Schwartz. In a long series of 1990s papers that scrutinized the university's public budgets for administrative costs, Schwartz was unable to detect savings.[3] To the contrary, he found that administrative costs grew even during the period of budget cuts.

National trends showed the same pattern. Administrative costs and personnel grew steadily in good times and bad, and certainly at a higher rate than the growth of faculty. A 1990 study found that "the category of 'other professionals'—academic support personnel filling such roles as financial aid counselors, auditors, research specialists, and systems analysts—had increased by more than 60 percent between 1975 and 1985, a period during which the size of the average faculty increased by less than 6 percent."[4] Another study found that in the twenty-five-year period between 1976 and 2001, "administrative staff employment in colleges and universities increased substantially, by about 50.1%. During the same period, the employment of non-faculty professionals mushroomed by a whopping 239.3%—that is, at a *much* faster rate than that of the faculty (75.8%) and of teaching and research assistants (about 63.1%)."[5] Whatever else new management theory was doing on campus, it was not saving money by simplifying administration and reducing staff.

If the categorical statements about the value of business methods were not designed primarily to cut costs, what were they doing? They had a rhetorical dimension, of course, since nods to business were by the 1990s generally taken as mandatory proof of a cooperative attitude toward society's leading members. It is useful to think of finance as a symbolic system among other things, a prestigious language for explaining university operations to the outside world. The primary audience in this outside world was the business and political leadership that also spoke the language of finance, and that looked for financial returns on investments of public and private money alike. This leadership also recognized in the language of finance this symbolism of outreach to its own perspectives and interests.

Financial accounting was not a restraint on growth but a definer of growth, one that defined meaningful growth in financial terms. Much of the growth at universities in this period derived from two factors. The first was mission creep. Universities took on many new tasks, most of them not directly educational. Many involved financing, notably the expansion of private fund-raising, especially at public universities, into a permanent, large-scale campaign that came to take up much of the time of the academic administration. A second factor consisted of responses to new external rules. These two functions developed symbiotically, since much of the compliance to outside agencies involved the monitoring of the new money operations. Summarizing the explosion of reporting requirements coming from public commissions of higher education, legislators, boards of trustees, state and federal agencies, and the like, one set of veteran experts concluded that "the result again was more paper, more reporting, and, not surprisingly, more personnel, some of whom were charged with explaining to governing boards just why administrative costs were increasing at such an alarming rate."[6]

There is thus much reason to believe that corporate methods were not only ends in themselves but also a means of tightening the university's dependence on outside agencies. Educational leaders had lamented this dependence in the 1950s and 1960s in relation to the federal government. The same issue was becoming more acute in relation to industrial sponsors. The culture wars, with their relentless attacks on nonmarket values, helped many participants to feel that these changes were not only inevitable but progressive.

The Evolution of Financial Influence

An interest in rationalizing academic management was hardly new in the 1990s. In the early 1900s, some academic leaders had thought that Frederick Taylor's scientific management could be applied to the unruly university.

After World War II, business was remodeling itself along the lines that the sociologist Neil Fligstein described as the "financial conception of control."[7] Financial measures tended to supercede other estimates of a company's status—strong product development, institutional stability, marketing innovation, community relations, and so on. In the 1980s, the rise of the "leveraged buyout"—in which a small company uses money borrowed at high interest rates to take over a much larger one—hinged on the commodification of the firm itself, which was treated as a product that could be bought, sold, divided up, and resold like suburban farmland or a truckload of firewood. Financial measures became more elaborate, accurate, comprehensive, and instantaneous, and came to play an ever larger role in the strategic planning and operations management of American companies. They tended to become the final judge of the quality of both the company and its management decisions: the value of a CEO was and still is readily and popularly measured by his or her impact on the company share price. Many such measures were obviously not relevant to the university as such, but as financial performance gained in status and influence, it came to loom larger in university administration.

There was one area in particular where it was easy to tell the story of the university as the story of money, and that was the school endowment. During the 1990s, most endowments enjoyed many years of double-digit growth: in fiscal year (FY) 1999, growth averaged 11 percent, and in FY 2000, the decade ended on a strong note with 13 percent average growth. It was impossible for administrators not to be a little preoccupied with growth like this, which seemed to make many new things possible.

University endowments also reflected the decade's growth in economic inequality. The wealthiest endowments tended to do the best: endowments worth more than $1 billion in FY 2000 grew not at 13 percent but at 29.2 percent. In contrast, endowments valued at $100 million or less grew that year at less than one-third the rate of the majors.[8] Harvard had the biggest endowment at the end of FY 2000 ($18.8 billion) and also a very large growth rate of 32.2 percent. Duke University and Notre Dame's endowments grew 59 percent that year.[9] On the whole, the richest got richer faster than everyone else. *Business Week* noted that in 2003, "just 20 institutions received $6.2 billion, or more than a quarter of all higher ed donations." They correctly concluded that private fund-raising "exacerbates the inequality gap between the mostly affluent students who attend the elite schools and the middle-class and poor ones who mostly enroll in less prestigious ones."[10]

The secret of the biggest growth was private placements with venture capital firms.[11] "These arrangements required that university fund managers be as sophisticated as their Wall Street peers. They also required secrecy about investment strategies, which were closely held proprietary information generally developed at arm's length from the administration and certainly from students and faculty. The only workable form of oversight over investments was financial accounting. The returns were easy to see, and the managers of endowments at Harvard, Yale, and elsewhere became stars in the investment world.[12] Their endowments had little to do with campus culture, and had become more than ever a part of Wall Street culture.[13] This influence was not linear: the university's interest in endowment returns that thrashed market averages did not directly determine labor and other administrative policies. But the pronouncedly antiunion positions of major universities during the 1990s certainly resonated with conventional Wall Street wisdom about the tie between the strict minimization of present and future labor costs and the value of an enterprise in the eyes of investors. Administrative cultures deselected people who could not work well with the world outside the university, meaning with the business and financial leaders who were taking an active role in academic affairs. Such matters as union negotiations were seen as a net drain that could only interfere with the positive gains of investment management. With endowments, size did matter, and it mattered more and more as public funds were inexorably scaled back all over the country. Critics did note that endowment size did not necessarily correlate with educational quality, but size did not obviously *hurt* educational quality and in any case became more urgent as education leaders came to conclude that 1960s or even 1980s levels of public support for higher education were gone for good.[14]

In addition to intensifying investment management, university administrators, who had lost confidence in the stability of both state and federal funding, became increasingly interested in raising private funds. They committed more university resources to expanding development offices. Development officers went donor hunting all across their alumni base, their local business community, and even their own campuses. English professors began to have the strange experience of being asked to meet with development people who would describe them as hidden assets in the university's fund-raising agenda. The UC flagship campuses at Berkeley and Los Angeles announced capital campaigns of more than $1 billion apiece, and competed for the private contributions that at one time had gone largely to private universities, many of them small and poorly endowed.[15] Public universities announced a lengthening sequence of billion-dollar endowment campaigns, which by the 2000s included the University of Pittsburgh ($1 billion by 2007), the University of Missouri at Columbia ($1 billion by 2008), the University of Iowa ($1 billion by 2005), the University of California at San Diego ($1 billion by 2007), along with larger campaigns at more senior public flagships (half of the twenty-one in the billion-dollar sweepstakes were public).[16]

Fund-raising brought new waves of wealthy potential donors onto campus and made their interests, viewpoints, and concerns central to the academic enterprise. A donor might have a special interest in an autism clinic, or terrorism studies, or global environmental management, or soft functional materials, and his or her donation could create a new program where none had previously been desired or planned. Usually these investments were in important areas, and university officials conducted careful and skillful dialogues with potential donors to help match their interests with existing academic needs. There were also boondoggles, like the financier T. Boone Pickens's $165 million gift to Oklahoma State University for athletic facilities.[17] In such cases, academic direction depended on the preferences, and sometimes the narrow-minded whims, of powerful outside figures. General statistical patterns could be observed: wealthy donors tended to be older, and the most generous donors were on average older still; it was not entirely surprising that major gifts appeared to go disproportionately to the health sciences. In most cases, wealthy donors had succeeded in their own fields by carefully evaluating investments and their returns.[18] Many thus expected reports on how their gifts were paying off, and sometimes keyed future gifts to benchmarks established with earlier gifts. Donors often saw themselves as representatives of the public interest, but they naturally represented their own interests in a giving process that did not override but certainly influenced normal academic planning and review.

In each of these areas, external institutions and individuals increased their capacity to affect and monitor the university's management of its own affairs. Again, this was not new. While serving as the president of the University of California in the 1950s and 1960s, Clark Kerr had sharply criticized the growing influence of federal research agencies over hiring and firing decisions, the structure, size, and budget of various departments, the allocation of physical space, the construction of new buildings, the creation of "new classes of administrators," and the expanding relative size of administration overall.[19] For Kerr, the university was already serving as " 'bait' to be dangled in front of industry."[20] But in the 1990s, the fish had became fishermen and were increasingly private, increasingly focused, increasingly individual, and increasingly sophisticated in their use of financial measures to evaluate the university's output as it was relevant to them.

Financial Incentives in Academic Planning

In addition to its focus on endowments, the 1990s university developed new financial strategies toward its educational mission. The most important and enduring of these was the cluster of techniques that has gone under the name of responsibility-center management (or RCM, along with related names such as revenue-center or activity-based management). RCM was developed during the 1970s and twenty years later was continuing to spread across the country.[21] It sought to inject financial incentives into the budgeting decisions that schools, departments, and other units were making. Because the facilities, administrative, and other general costs were not charged to schools and departments but were paid by the central administration, RCM advocates alleged, these costs were not factored into academic decisions at those levels—how many new faculty to hire, which courses to shrink or expand, and so on. RCM sought to bring a complete budget to each unit so that each unit would know its total costs and its total revenues.

Universities and corporations alike had long used versions of centrally allocated, incremental budgeting, meaning that most or all units used the previous year's budget as a base; their budgets were then cut or, more commonly, augmented from that base. This made it hard for organizations to respond to new opportunities, whether they were product lines, research topics, or student enrollment shifts, since in the main the only funds available for new allocations were funds beyond those of the previous year's budget. When the organization was growing quickly, as companies and universities were doing in the 1950s and 1960s, new programs could be built with new money. When there was little or no new money, as in the 1970s, early 1990s, and early 2000s, new programs died before they were born. In a rapidly changing environment, companies and, to a lesser extent, colleges and universities could miss out on new growth areas (new product lines, new federal grant opportunities) because they did not have the resources to build the facilities, hire the faculty, and do all the other things required to set up activities that would be valuable in the years to come. This problem was worse for public universities, whose relatively small endowments and, in most states, constant enrollment pressures meant that even small downturns in state revenues could bring development to a halt. Public universities in states with chronic budget problems, like the University of Massachusetts, the University of Michigan, or the State University of New York, were in danger of falling farther and farther behind in a death spiral in which losses (of students, faculty, grant funding) were met with ever-weaker countermeasures, which allowed the losses to continue to grow.

RCM was part of a larger business movement that reflected managers' growing interest in retaining control while reducing the costly bureaucratic layers that had traditionally been responsible for it. It was associated with total quality management (TQM), which grew from the generally good idea to move decision making away from central administrators and toward line workers and shop-floor supervisors, who were closer to actual problems and could therefore come up with quicker and better solutions. These hands-on decisions would not occur unless employees had enough autonomy to make them more or less on their own. TQM would monitor the quality of the decisions by their financial effect, yet measures had to be calibrated to fit the smaller units that were making the decisions. Managers would know the results, but so would the line workers, who would be given financial information so that they could adjust their own activities according to their results. The method was sometimes called "open-book management." The bad news for employees was that they would be held responsible for the financial effects of their work, and this would be especially bad news if even high-quality work did not improve the numbers: quality and financial results were treated as the same thing. The good news was that employees could in theory see the basic company numbers and had somewhat more autonomy from central administrators to determine their own work practices. The other good news was that this limited self-management seemed to be more effective financially than was executive authority.[22]

We can simplify the detail-oriented practice of RCM into four main features.[23]

1. *Decentralizing costs and benefits.* Operating units like schools, divisions, and departments would know their true costs, not just for telephones and office staff but for building maintenance and mortgages, water and electricity, and other expenses traditionally picked up by the central administration as overhead. The university would no longer take care of this overhead invisibly while also holding all revenues generated from

enrollments and then returning some portion as the unit's annual budget. Courses, majors, and programs that lost money would need explicit compensation from other programs in the unit that made money. Transfers from profitable to unprofitable units were still permissible, but only after the real amount of such transfers was clearly understood by all parties.

2. *Financial incentives.* As a result of knowing the costs of their teaching and research, faculty would have financial incentives to evaluate their programs with their costs and revenues in mind. While finances were not meant to outweigh educational considerations, they were meant, in the RCM scheme, to become intrinsic to academic planning.[24] The firewall between educational and financial metrics was to be torn down, even though everyone involved could tell the difference between the two categories.

3. *Transparency and iterative collaboration.* Although RCM might be used by administrators to assert control over academic programs, advocates repeatedly insisted that the implementation had to be a collaborative process between faculty and administrators. The budget was to be transparent, and everyone's costs and revenues were to be known by everyone involved. This knowledge would at first be shocking and painful. An account of RCM discussions at UCLA described faculty members' indignation at one another's long-distance bills and express-mail charges, and transparency was shortly abandoned as too divisive.[25] But these sorts of failures were to be taken in stride at the early stages of a multiyear procedure of community and institution building. When in late 1997 I asked the provost of the University of Illinois at Urbana-Champaign about the school's campus-wide RCM-like budgetary overhaul, he replied that "we try hard to refer to our effort simply as 'budget reform.' There are some RCM-like elements in the design, but the overall system is some distance from having a classic RCM form. By avoiding labels that imply a set model, we have managed to keep the focus on improving practice through an iterative process, rather than driving the campus toward an up-or-out decision on a package."[26] The idea was that with the proper leadership and an organized process that could develop trust over time, most faculty would come to contribute to decisions that would be better because they were based on wider consultation and fuller financial information than had ever before been the case.

4. *Educational strategizing.* As a result of budgetary decentralization and new levels of financial clarity, educational choices would be more

rigorous. RCM advocates made an apparently paradoxical claim. "A major thrust of RCM, in fact its original raison d'être, was sensitivity to the marketplace. RCM quantifies the revenues and costs of all programs and demonstrates that the underlying academic or institutional value of a program is independent of whether it is subvened or not."[27] By seeing just how expensive a high-quality, low-revenue program was, one supposedly could defend it with the strength and purpose that its quality deserved and its costs demanded. One set of RCM theorists put it this way: educational programs generate revenue (or lack thereof) *and* "mission attainment." "One might say these represent 'love' and 'money.' [A provost will] expand a program if the extra love plus the extra money exceeds the variable cost of expansion. . . . By doing this [the provost will] produce more value overall than if [she] considered either love or money alone."[28] In other words, the value of intellectual output ("love"), in the form of grammars of languages spoken by six hundred people or of commentary on the later Milton, certainly had nonfinancial value, and this was on par with quantified revenues. Both educational and financial outputs were valuable. The latter would not be allowed to replace the former: finance would be used simply to assess the economic costs of educational "mission attainment," which would then be paid for in ways people could agree on.

The road to RCM was paved with good intentions, and it had potential to create more clarity, more collaboration, even something like more democracy in setting institutional directions. It has enjoyed a fair amount of success in various institutions.

But its success has been largely proportional to two factors, one well-known, the other less so. The first is the process of implementation: where this was gradual and inclusive, RCM improved at least the budgeting process, if not academic planning overall. The second factor, however, has been the context of implementation, where the culture wars were constantly putting nonfinancial "mission attainment" on the defensive.

The Limits of Finance

RCM had in principle solved one perennial problem of budgeting, which was that budgets traditionally had been established by a small set of administrators in consultation with financial professionals. RCM imagined wide-ranging discussions among all interested members of the university community, ones structured and long lasting enough to allow the views of culturally quite different units to appear in the mix. Advocates were aware that cooperation among units required "leadership," which generally mixes persuasion with coercion: USC's experiment with RCM may have gone very wrong had that university's president not unilaterally rejected some units' plan to improve their revenue statements by getting a quick bump in enrollments through lowered admissions standards.[29] To arrange for English and engineering professors to agree on planning principles would require skillful orchestration and negotiation. In this sense, since it acknowledged different stakes for different units and did not try to eliminate variation, we could hope that RCM might have evolved into the multiculturalism of budgeting.

But the cultural context elicited different impulses. Though RCM did not insist as culture warriors did on a core budgetary culture, it adhered to two of their prime directives. The first was a sharp dichotomy between financial and educational matters, which reflected the culture warriors' distinction between economic and sociocultural development. The explicit aim of RCM was to support varied academic units by using finance as a universal language, one to which all separate strategies were finally accountable. Planning would proceed by establishing profit and loss figures for each unit and then covering losses in one unit with profits in another—as long as those losses could be justified as part of "mission attainment"—which was in turn embedded in accounting measurements. Finance was the privileged language of reality. How the institution was doing was first and foremost a question of its economic situation. Though skillful practitioners would not be too rude about it, the bottom line was comprised of dollars and cents.

The hierarchy of measures in which finance came first was signaled by language like that cited above, in which money is money and education is "love." This language is deeply misleading: Education cannot be divided into functional and emotive halves like this, nor can its functional side be equated with money. Education is not a form of goodwill, nor is humanistic knowledge a heartwarming sideshow, the academic equivalent of an evening with family by the fireside. The university is in general not-for-profit, meaning that it exists to *spend* money on making citizens, engineers, writers, and the other forms of what is sometimes called "human capital" and that can also be called the creative capability of always-evolving society. Culturally speaking, RCM reinforced the culture-war belief that education is a commodity as measurable as any other, and that administrators must sort the disciplines according to those that supposedly pay and those that supposedly do not. RCM is thus as hard on educational development—as dismissive of education's internal logics and conceptual independence—as any form of financial accounting.

At all campuses where I have had direct experience, administrators showed official esteem toward the educational mission and the liberal arts. They were not a mercenary lot, having after all chosen education over bond trading, and they appreciated the broader value of education. But it was hard for anyone to fight numbers with philosophy and love, especially under nonstop post-1970s financial pressures. The defenses of nonquantitative educational goods were abstract, long-range, and, in cultural fields, labeled "political," and the culture wars drove this last stake deep into the ground. Thus an urban planning school's investigation of contemporary school or housing discrimination would ask for funding in a context in which UC regent Ward Connerly was trying to outlaw the collection of racial information of any kind. Nonquantifiable benefits were harder to justify than were quantifiable ones. When the overall university was divided into cost units, accounting gave programs that attracted outside funds—materials science, mathematical finance—a natural advantage over those that provided services, required public sector involvement, criticized policy, developed human capabilities, or rested on self-sponsored research that lacked external markets (anthropology, classics). Returns on investment were potentially damaged by controversy, and yet controversy was built into most cultural study. The lack of paying customers now quantified by RCM, then combined with the presence of debate, threatened to keep cultural disciplines in a permanent state of underdevelopment. This was certainly their fate during the years of austerity. As the 1990s advanced, downturns coupled with accounting standards took a toll on dreams of the new: new programs, new disciplines, new combinations, new ideas that could not yet—or would never—acquire markets and revenues.

RCM rode the culture-war current in a second way. This was reflected in its hostility to budgetary equality among different disciplines and units. It started with the valuable idea that universities could not just keep adding everywhere, but translated this into the culture-warrior notion that relative equality was a violation of financial principles.

It is important to remember that universities had brought some fields of knowledge to great heights by defying market judgments about them.

American history is a good example, where the enormous range and depth of past decades of academic literature greatly surpasses popular media representations of the subject, dominated as they are by presidential and military history. Universities boomed intellectually through the postwar period's genteel socialism: by paying the overhead and related costs for all departments regardless of income, they ensured all disciplines the basics of a decent living. This internal sponsorship led to gradual reduction of teaching loads even in fields that lacked extramural support. As humanities course loads at research universities went from six or eight a year to four or five (still twice as high as loads in science and engineering), historians were able to increase and improve their output, and there is some reason to believe that the post–World War II renaissance in historical study—and the new, formalized cultural and social knowledge about the contributions of women domestics, African American professionals, Chinese railroad workers, Native American belief systems, immigrant farm and factory laborers—owes much to better research conditions for the relevant nonmarket fields. As a result of this revenue sharing, university fields developed a kind of general parity during the boom years, and certainly an equality of expectations for research and teaching performance that benefited every field of endeavor as well as the country as a whole.

In the RCM system, this kind of general provision was redefined as a subsidy that the institution provided to low-income areas. Since RCM advocates were not right-wing political activists, they did not criticize "administrative handouts" and complain about "university welfare" for the humanities. Nonetheless, they challenged the concept of general provision—on sound technical grounds—*without* insisting on a good basic income for all fields regardless of their financial capacity. This would not have been an endorsement of ongoing growth for mediocre and declining areas, but would instead have meant relative equality for fields that the *academic* planning process had endorsed, in the shape in which it had endorsed them. In this non-RCM system, educational value would have been the baseline, where good work on Milton and good work on carbon nanotubes produced similar amounts of intellectual value. Enormous variations in *financial* resources would then have to be judged by their necessity or by their effect on intellectual outcomes. The shoe would sometimes be on the other foot: were financial measures found to oversupport some fields some of the time, judged by their intellectual merit or social value, lucrative fields might now and then be trimmed. Informal evidence suggests that this rebalancing regularly occurred, leading to the revenue "subsidies" that RCM systematically opposed.[30]

To each according to her intellectual need? It may have been academic quasi-socialism, but some version of that process of *educational* benchmarking (and evaluating financial distribution on those grounds) enabled the postwar university to reach unprecedented research heights.

In the world of the culture wars, inequality is natural and equality the result of unnatural intervention. Something like a bell curve was the normal distribution, while anything flatter meant monkey business, usually for populist political ends. Whatever its expressed intentions, RCM challenged the academic reality that culture warriors disliked, namely, the intellectual greatness that arose from collaboration enabled by shared resources and driven by curiosity or social goals. RCM was right to say that universities must have accurate, detailed budgetary information about all the moving parts of the complex institution, including one's overhead expenses. But RCM intensified the existing divide between financial and academic factors, where the academic was increasingly at the mercy of the financial. The university already knew how to worry about money. What was needed was a system for explaining nonquantitative educational benefits to a deeply money-minded culture, and this is what RCM made even more difficult. It instead perpetuated the duality of love and money, and campuses logically gravitated toward investing in fields close to the market. RCM was of little use in helping universities support the inventive teaching and novel research that were their main reason for existing, precisely because they would not be supported by its already existing customer base.

The rise of accounting intensified the first two dimensions of the culture wars: it offered color-blind budgeting that demoted other forms of value, and it defined merit in what we can call market-plus terms—merit was market value plus a little intrinsic intellectual value. Accounting further consolidated the culture wars' third dimension: it confirmed the market not as academic servant but as academic master, the de facto final authority on the health of the enterprise.

—11—

The Problem with Privatization

Accounting improved some aspects of university management. But as its, authority increased in university systems, particularly in the public systems, it was much easier to continue with the larger culture-wars project, which was the liberation of private interests from public goals that were apparently too egalitarian and expensive.

Universities were not an inherently easy sell for the market vision of human nature. Their expansion after World War II had underwritten the large postwar middle class, and public universities were largely responsible for the widespread improvement in the American population's general educational attainment, which in turn is widely regarded as a major source of the economy's health during that period. To put it another way, the success of higher education showed the dependence of American business on high-value public expenditure. Affluence could be traced directly to public funding and not just to private profits. The enrollment boom was paid for by populations that had become at least temporarily persuaded that they would get something good by spending public tax money.

They spent it more freely than they have ever since. The conventional wisdom in higher education today is that while public education is more crucial than ever, there is no will to support it with public funding. Studies of actual funding levels bear out this view. One by the Urban Institute showed that higher education's share of state appropriations nationwide fell from 6.7 percent to 4.5 percent in the last quarter of the twentieth century. More recently, steady or slightly declining appropriations, in real dollar terms, have not kept up with increasing enrollments. An analysis by the State Higher Education Executive Officers Association (SHEEO) found that per-student allocations in fiscal year 2005 reached their lowest level in twenty-five years. Even after starting to recover in FY 2006, they were still about 15 percent below their FY 2001 level ($7,371 per student FTE).[1] Since no one wants to beat her head against a brick wall, most educational leaders have come to say that colleges and universities should adapt to the new political reality of a permanently downsized public sector. This has generally meant only one thing—replacing declining public money with increasing private funds. This shift from public to private funding sometimes goes by the name "privatization."

Most commentators saw a silver lining in all this. One important example was the book by Robert Zemsky, Gregory Wegner, and William Massy on "responsibility-centered management" that I discuss in chapter 10, "The Costs of Accounting." Its authors were three influential educational administrators and analysts, and they called on universities to realize that they must become "market-smart and mission-centered."[2] Like many other observers, they lamented that universities now "pursue their own, as opposed to the public's agenda." On pressing issues like the "continuing deterioration of public schools," universities "have been seen as neither the problem nor the solution."[3] But Zemsky et al. argued that universities could keep their unique mission while being "market-smart," and, in fact, that they could keep their mission only by facing, using, engaging, and mastering markets.

Zemsky and his colleagues' initial example of this successful strategy was the University of Michigan (UM). Faced with a deindustrializing state economy and falling tax revenues in the early 1980s, UM decided to diversify its income sources. It increased private fund-raising, continuously raised tuition, and supported entrepreneurial faculty members in their quest for larger shares of both federal money and industry sponsorship. Zemsky et al. portrayed this as a great success on two separate fronts. First, Michigan succeeded in the market, especially when compared to peers who stuck with the public sphere. "In the 1970s Michigan and UC-Berkeley received roughly the same levels of core revenue. Three decades later, however, Michigan's core revenues exceeded those of Berkeley by more than $400 million per year," the result of "revenues earned mainly in the marketplace."[4] Second, Michigan's privatization (my term, not theirs) correlated with a *stronger* public purpose. "Not so coincidentally, we believe, the University of Michigan also played the leading role in the decade's most important litigation concerning higher education. In defending its use of race-conscious admissions policies, the University of Michigan and its tough-minded, market-smart administration demonstrated what a mission-centered institution can accomplish in the defense of public principle."[5]

When universities help themselves they help society, the authors claimed, invoking an American tradition of seeing civic-spirited liberal capitalism as the source of a revitalization of public universities. They advocated a combination of "market-smart" and "mission-centered." By "market-smart," they appeared to mean two main things: (1) an acceptance of the shift from general public funding to a "user fee" model in which students and their families pay privately for their education; and (2) the use of financial measures to improve productivity. I have already criticized the second of these (chapter 10, "The Costs of Accounting"). An equally tricky issue is the first aspect of market thinking, in which higher education replaces lost public funding with higher student fees. We need to ask—If various commentators are right that entrepreneurship and partial privatization mean both more money and stronger *public* purpose, why would anyone oppose privatization?

Grounds for Skepticism: The Michigan Downside

Zemsky et al. made a familiar kind of claim, which implied a causal relationship between "going to market" and newfound wealth. The claim is unfortunately familiar in a less positive sense: they do not provide evidence of this causal relationship between "going to market" and *new* revenues. For starters, I have been unable to verify Zemsky et al.'s claim of a $400-million-dollar gap between Michigan and UC-Berkeley.[6] Even were the figure correct, Michigan's overall revenues come largely from *non*market sources. Much of the university's new money was public research funding: 60 percent of federal research money goes to the health sciences; Michigan has a large health sciences operation; and overall federal contracts and grants volume more than doubled in the twenty-five-year period in question and grew even faster in health-related fields. With its enormous medical centers and other high-volume science operations, UM was a principal beneficiary of this federal boom. Since UC Berkeley lacks a medical school, a more accurate comparison would be between UM and the UC Berkeley and UC San Francisco campuses combined. If the comparison is done this way, the gap disappears.[7]

On the private side, Michigan did very well with philanthropy. But it is not clear what relation this success had to market-mindedness. UM already possessed a venerable and powerful fund-raising operation, particularly with its alumni base, which is the largest in the United States, and UM receipts did not outpace philanthropic growth for American universities as a whole. UM did reap major new revenues through steep and continuous tuition increases, augmented by expanding each class's proportion of out-of-state students (who comprised 40 percent of entering first-year students by 2005). But much of these revenues replaced lost state funding rather than offered new money. Increasing "user fees" is a traditional strategy that is fully compatible with public funding and does not in itself signal a new adaptation to market forces.

As is also typical of the standard equation of market forces with greater wealth, Zemsky et al. did not factor in the costs of the strategies they describe. Although the University of Michigan remains one of the world's great universities, its rank has declined, at least judging by *U.S. News & World Report*'s infamous reputational survey, where UM fell from eighth to twenty-fifth place between 1987 and 2003. UM's dependence on tuition revenue has not helped its selectivity: more than 50 percent of all undergraduate applicants were admitted in 2005, which makes UM about half as selective as UC Berkeley, somewhere between UC San Diego and UC Santa Barbara.[8] UM's high proportion of out-of-state students has not helped its original mission of educating the population of Michigan itself. Michigan remains well below the national average in the percentage of the state's population that receives bachelor's or advanced degrees: one study calculated that merely catching up to the national average would require Michigan to increase the rate of growth at which bachelor's degrees are obtained from 1 percent to 37 percent by 2015.[9] The focus of the University of Michigan's flagship campus on out-of-state tuition dollars could not support this public mission. While UM has done an effective job of protecting its Ann Arbor flagship, it has not protected the quality of the UM system, of Michigan higher education overall, or of higher education access for the residents of the state.

Something similar can be said about the composition of UM's student body. UM lost African American enrollments during the first wave of fiscal crises in the 1980s and has only slowly gotten most of them back (African American enrollments in the freshman class of 2005 comprise 7.2 percent of the total, about half the African American proportion of the state population).[10] After strenuous efforts in the 1990s, the University of Michigan still has a Pell Grant rate half that of UC Santa Barbara's; at the other end of the income spectrum, more than half of Michigan's 2003 freshman class came from families with six-figure incomes in a state where only 13 percent of families earn that much.[11] The university's involvement with the Bollinger affirmative action cases was less an example of public leadership than a mandated self-defense, one that might have been avoided had UM been able to "afford" college preparedness and other recruitment programs for in-state students of color.

All these considerations suggest that "privatization" is not a recipe for improved fiscal, intellectual, or sociocultural health. It serves as such a recipe only within the ideological framework of the culture wars, in which market forces are always invigorating and never interfere with legitimate missions. In the real world, "market failure" is commonplace, particularly in the creation of services. Zemsky and his coauthors knew this perfectly well, and yet the cultural environment licensed them to write as though they did not. Privatization would need to work harder and better than this to make a valid case for itself—outside the world the culture wars made.

College Admissions: The Skew Toward Financial Returns

We might be particularly suspicious of privatization's effort to apply market standards to education when we recall that the university already had another, complexly evolved system of measurement in place, commonly known as meritocracy. Students have always been subject to open competition for test scores and grades—lots of them, every academic term. Faculty members had always had publication records, patents, prizes, awards, and a teaching rating from each student, every academic term. But these intellectual assessments could not be equated with market measures. They referred to standards of intellectual quality that had emerged over decades from within intellectual disciplines and that were continuously updated and refined by evaluating their outcomes. An optical processor chip, for example, was not rated on its financial returns—though it had great future expectations—but by its functionality as a solution to problems with existing bodies of established knowledge. Classroom standards were the same, where innovation and transmission were brought together.[12] Intellectual returns were noneconomic, had much longer horizons, and did not exist in the world as a "rivalrous" form of property (where one person's use diminished that of someone else). They also actively sought spillover effects, where their value would travel beyond the ownership boundaries of the inventor or patent holder to affect society as a whole.

Throughout the 1980s and 1990s, intellectual factors tried to hold their own in admissions policy. Students still applied for places on the basis of their academic achievement. They were not thought to be admitted because of their future economic value to the university. Universities certainly hoped for future philanthropic returns that would follow from preparing the best students for lifelong success. Alumni cultivation had become a systematic practice by the 1920s, and top schools succeeded beyond all expectations— by the decade 1994–2003, Princeton received a remarkable 54.6 percent of its nongovernmental revenue from alumni; the comparable figures for Yale and Harvard were 52.7 percent and 41.8 percent, respectively.[13] But even as admissions officers sought a "well-rounded" class that included future moguls as well as future artists, students were in principle admitted on the basis of their ability to contribute to the academic and extracurricular life of the university, and not on the basis of their ability to contribute to its bank balance. "Needs-blind" admission—admission that looked at qualifications and not a student's ability to pay—remained the gold standard of admissions ethics.

But as cost pressures increased in the 1970s and 1980s, throughout this period admissions practice evolved toward the money. A series of books about the admissions rat race drew the attention of students and parents to the compromising of the meritocratic rules they had sought to master.[14] Many of these analyses focused on affirmative action, but other forms of preference attracted increasing attention. The best known was preference for athletes, and a second type that received increasing attention was the "legacy preference"—the admissions advantages offered the children of alumni, particularly of wealthy alumni with a history of philanthropy. The legacy preference had produced a spin-off sometime during the 1970s at some private universities, like Duke, that wanted to compete toe to toe with Stanford and Princeton and thought they needed more money to do it. This spin-off was the "development admit"—a wealthy student whose family might become first-time contributors to the university if a relationship could be established by admitting their child.

This mercenary side of admissions became a national story during the Supreme Court consideration of affirmative action at the University of Michigan (see chapter 7, "Diversity in the Age of Pseudointegration"). A *Wall Street Journal* reporter had been assigned to cover that story and to find a new angle on it. Though feeling little hope of success, the reporter, Daniel Golden, began to examine the case materials. He noticed that one of the undergraduate plaintiffs had been a legacy applicant, and had received 5 extra points (out of 150) for being the child of a UM alum. Golden wrote a series of articles on legacy and development admissions that criticized what was in effect an affirmative action program for the already advantaged and, in some cases, the wealthy and well connected. The articles became a book, and Golden elaborated the damage done to the careers of brilliant but "un-hooked" applicants who were knocked out of contention by a "legacy establishment" that used elite universities to perpetuate its lion's share of the country's wealth and power.[15]

In examining this kind of admissions, let us first look at the bright side, where legacy and development admits offer a classic example of market engagement in the university arena. Everyone can claim good intentions and moderation as they synthesize market demands with the world of knowledge and describe a win-win outcome. In a case like Duke's, where in one period 3–5 percent of each class consisted of development admits, university leaders could argue that these wealthy students brought resources that made things better for everybody. Their full tuitions and family contributions to scholarship funds subsidize low-income students: development admits could be cast as a low-key "Robin Hood" project in which the university took from the rich to give to the poor. Later on, major gifts from wealthy alumni would allow the university to keep fighting cancer and addressing global hunger. On university campuses the rich are parted from their money not by the owners of racetracks and the builders of luxury yachts but by the stewards of teaching and research for the general good. The children of the rich are tutored in the world's problems in the liberal classroom, increasing the likelihood that they will lead useful rather than idle lives. In the context of such arguments, even a 5 percent set-aside for the wealthy seems a small proportionate sacrifice for a large return. It seems an excellent example of balancing the mission with the market.

But there are many problems with this approach.[16] The first is that it grants wealthy donors greater and often undue influence on institutional priorities. I broached this issue in chapter 10, "The Costs of Accounting," and it is a serious matter that has not received enough significant analysis from administrators. To recap, the cultivation of wealthy prospects takes a great deal of time and significant money, and administrators are under pressure to make the university seem as congenial to the donor as possible. Controversial issues or faculty members may be kept out of sight, and may receive fewer resources than they otherwise might. A brisk, efficient atmosphere is presented as the campus norm, though the struggle for new knowledge is anything but efficient in the standard sense. The interests and priorities of donors go to the head of the line, bypassing the normal campus planning process. Disciplines that faculty members may have rejected as too expensive or too far from existing campus strengths may become major sites of campus investment once seeded by outside funds. Some portion of intellectual leadership shifts off campus to the movers and shakers who also make the wider society attend to their concerns. The influence of the donor may be increased by the presence of his or her child on campus, who may in effect function as a native informant or spy on classroom proceedings and enable the parent to offer real-time criticism of academic activities. In short, the campus may become less an alternative to the society's and the economy's conventional concerns than an echo and extension of them—indeed, an important endorser of those concerns through the imprimatur of its academic independence.

A second problem is that the argument for development admits lacks the intellectual dimension that is essential to the arguments for diversity. Diversity theorists argued that people of color, by virtue of their personal experience, cultural differences, distinctive perspectives, and, in many cases, their unusual socioeconomic challenges, make a unique intellectual contribution to the community. No one makes a similar *intellectual* argument for the unconventional insight that the wealthy bring to the classroom or lab.

Third, in contrast to the admission of members of underrepresented racial groups, development admits serve the institution's private interest without serving direct public goals. Fourth, development admits create a double standard when they are coupled with the rejection of race- or gender-conscious affirmative action. Why should anyone balk at giving one applicant 20 points for being black when another receives a special, customized review process for being rich? Though most university officials favor some version of "comprehensive review," in which race, gender, and other background factors—including family wealth—can be taken into account, this stance does not solve the deeper problem at issue here.

The Tuition Trap

The deeper problem is that private philanthropy can erode support for the public, "general fund" base for public higher education. Lessons from private higher education have been transferred indiscriminately to public universities, in spite of stock differences in endowment base and student constituency between otherwise similar private and public universities. The boom in giving to education over the past twenty years has convinced many observers that philanthropy *can* replace public funding: the comments of highly knowledgeable figures like Zemsky and his colleagues are typical in this regard. I address the financial claim below. Here my point concerns the damage privatization does to general support for public funding of public institutions.

It is worth recalling that the general-fund model of educational funding regards all levels of schooling as sources of general social and economic development for all members of society. In chapter 6, "The Battle for Meritocracy," I called this meritocracy II, a model that imagined education reducing inequalities of expertise among strata, enhancing everyone's individual potential, and making the country more prosperous and equitable. When postwar universities aimed at this thing that throughout this book I have called general development, they established relatively broad and equitable forms of access. Sometimes this meant open admission for all applicants. Other times it meant selective admission with near-zero tuition—anyone with a good academic record could attend. At other times it meant affirmative action, outreach to underrepresented groups, and aggressive financial aid. In all cases, the goal has been the proverbial level playing field, in which general development rested on general rules and general access.[17]

We have seen that the culture war on affirmative action did much to destroy this vision among whites by convincing them that universities— particularly public universities—no longer offered a level playing field to *their* children. After several years of renewed assault in the early 1990s, "racial preferences" had become the explanation for why their white children were rejected by the taxpayer-funded flagship schools that offered the diploma that could give them a boost. The discourse of undeserving minorities ignored the fact that the multicampus University of California had sought to become a system of equals so that all admits, whether to Berkeley or Irvine or Santa Cruz, would attend an excellent school; it also ignored the decline of public investment that would have built more new campuses while making "flagships" of all the existing ones. Legacy and development admits also obscured the egalitarian vision. They said that wealthy kids, who should have aced their SATs and gotten excellent grades because of all the tutors and small classes they had already had, were entitled to buy their way to the head of the line. On top of this, as I have said, these admits were just about the money—there were no social goals to soften the blow.

The same problems affected public universities that increased their tuition on a regular basis. Such increases reduced the public's sense of the affordability and accessibility of the schools that it thought it funded through its taxes. One study conducted for the University of California noted that "voters who say that UC is unaffordable and out of reach are far less likely to say UC provides a high-quality education, contributes to California's health care system, is a valued presence in the community, or even treats its employees well."[18] Though this 2005 survey showed substantial public support for the state's public research university, and for its combination of public status and high quality, it also revealed a "tuition trap" stalking public higher education.

The tuition trap goes like this: The public is worried about college affordability, but its public university raises its fees. The university thus implies it does *not* actually depend on public funding, since it has the private resource of higher tuition at its fingertips. The university may also deepen this impression—that it can do without more public funding—by saying how good it is in spite of public funding cuts. Even worse, it may declare strong public funding a thing of the past in order to justify tuition increases or expanded fund-raising. Taxpayers then reasonably ask, if the university does not need more money, why does it keep raising fees? And since it keeps raising fees, why should we give it more public money?

The overall effect of all these moves—attacks on affirmative action admissions, then coupled with legacy and development admits and tuition hikes—has been to deepen the public's cynicism about the university's mission. If the university is just another cog in an economic system that is about getting ahead, charging as much as you can, maximizing your returns, and buying your way to the top, why *should* the general public pay for it? Why should the general public, whose income has stagnated for thirty years, give more taxes to a system that lets the top 1 percent purchase a VIP seat, or that favors applicants from six-figure families?

Being "market smart" in admissions has not only introduced injustices and hidden financial transfers; it has also damaged and eclipsed the vision of general development on which mass higher education depends. Admissions and tuition policy have become yet another arena of culture-wars effects, in which market forces and hierarchical development have seemed acceptable substitutes for equal access and general advancement.

Inevitable Stratification

Supporters of privatization have often invoked the truisms that markets enforce fiscal discipline, tell institutions what the customer wants, and fully support successful ventures. They have moved from there to the implication that universities could replace *all* their lost public funding with private funding, and even increase their funding overall. Zemsky et al. implied this in the passage I noted at the start of this chapter. The claim has been the major safety valve for public fund cutters. Well, advocates say, it is not *good* that the states are cutting funding for the economically and socially essential service we know as higher education. But we can always replace cut public funds with private money in the form of higher tuition. And we can smooth out the peaks and valleys with financial aid and private philanthropy.

The latter claim has made superficial sense, since by the early 2000s there was much new wealth at the top to be soaked up by higher education. But there was a lot of smoothing to do. The State Higher Education Executive Officers (SHEEO) plotted state expenditures per "full-time equivalent" (FTE) student against FTE enrollment growth and generated the visual roller coaster displayed in Figure 2.[19]

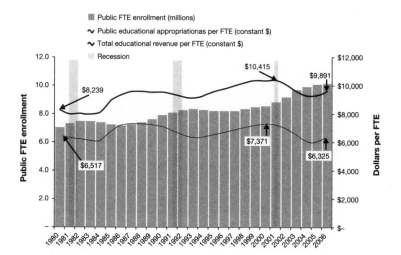

Figure 2. Nonmedical FTE, educational appropriations per FTE, and total educational revenue per FTE, in public higher education, U.S., fiscal 1980–2006. Source: SHEEO SHEP, http://mlis.state.md.us/other/Funding_Higher_Ed/2007July 9_SHEEO. pdf (accessed Nov. 15, 2007).

This graph told a sad story of public expenditures in what looks like a country that has suffered a series of coups d'état. But what goes down has seemed always to go back up again. So could private funding not act like fiscal lithium and at least smooth out the wild budgetary mood swings, or even provide some steady growth?

University budget officers, anxious to keep their institutions from appearing needy, seemed inclined to match the bad news of public funding with the good news of private money. The University of California offers a good example of back-to-back budget slides, shown to its Board of Regents in November 2006 (see Figures 3 and 4). If you take these budget slides together, and do not notice the enormous difference of scale, you might think that they cancel each other out: declining public funds can be replaced by private fund-raising.

To see whether this was really true, and whether the University of California could made up for recent cuts with other sources of income, I conducted a study with several UC colleagues—Henning Bohn (economics, UC Santa Barbara), Calvin Moore (mathematics, UC Berkeley), and Stanton A. Glantz (medicine, UC San Francisco). We were asked by the University of California's Academic Senate Committee on Planning and Budget

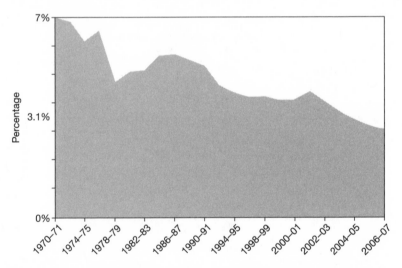

Figure 3. University of California's share of state general fund. Source: Office of the President, *2007–2008 Budget for Current Operations* (November 2006), Display 6, p. 40 (http://budget.ucop.edu/rbudget/200708/200708-budgetforcurrentoperations.pdf (accessed Oct. 21, 2007).

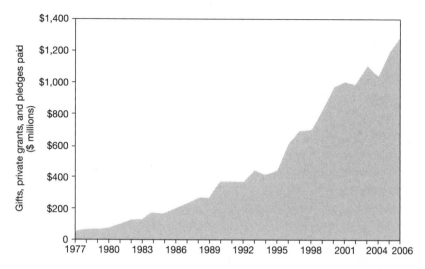

Figure 4. Private support (University of California). Source: Ibid., Figure 3, Display 12, p. 93.

(UCPB) to provide a comprehensive analysis of past and likely future state funding trends for the University of California. Our report analyzed the impact of two waves of major cuts in state funding to California higher education and examined four scenarios for recovery from those cuts.[20]

The results were not encouraging. We looked at "UC Core Funds"— excluding the medical centers, contracts and grants, and other business operations—in order to focus on funds that administrators could allocate for essential campus operations.[21] We confirmed the story told in Figure 3—a dismal tale of an overall trend of declining education funding in a state with one of the largest concentrations of wealthy individuals and industries in the world. We quantified the declining state share of "UC Core Funds" (down to 45 percent around 2005 from 60 percent in 2001), and the state's declining contribution measured as a share of personal income. We found that the university's recipe for recovery, the May 2004 "Higher Education Compact" among UC, California State University, and the governor of California, which had promised five years of increases in state funding starting in 2006 (initially 3 percent and then 4 percent a year in the last two years), was in fact a recipe for further funding declines locking in budget cuts. By 2010, we calculated, UC would be about $1.2 billion a year behind its extrapolated 2001 funding level, and twice as much behind its extrapolated 1990 funding level (on a base of about $3.3 billion in state general fund

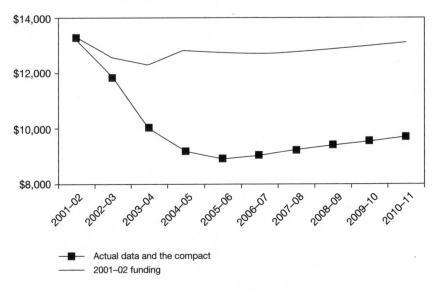

Figure 5. State funding per student (in real dollars). Source: Christopher Newfield, Henning Bohn, and Calvin Moore, *Current Budget Trends and the Future of the University of California*, May 2006, http://www.universityofcalifornia.edu/senate/reports/AC.Futures.Report.0107.pdf (accessed October 30, 2007).

money in 2001). The funding gap could also be expressed as a quantity per student (see Figure 5).

Since the Compact did not in fact protect public funding, we suggested that such protection required a return to the 2001–2002 trajectory. We also noted that a recovery of the funding levels associated with UC's traditional quality, measured as student-faculty ratios and other data, required a return to 1990 levels of contribution, measured as a share of state personal income (an increase from the 2001 level of 0.29 percent to 0.36 percent over a period of five years).

These conclusions were greeted within the UC Senate and administration with a combination of agreement (with the calculations) and pessimism (about the "political realities"). No one in a position of responsibility felt that UC could ask the state to move to a higher level of funding. No one thought asking for a higher fraction of personal income would work with the public. Some observed that any request for a state funding increase from UC would be accompanied by a parallel request from Cal State, meaning that UC's $1.4 billion request would come to well over $3 billion a year once our companion system got involved. Arnold Schwarzenegger had promised both wealthy and working-class constituencies that he would hold the line on new taxes, and he was set to remain governor for the rest of the decade. Every discussion seemed to show that the way to greater public funding was entirely blocked.

Our report, however, included another scenario, which we called the "Public Funding Freeze." We imagined the following, not unlikely, situation:

> Another downturn in state finances and continued political opposition to tax increases prompts state and University leaders to reluctantly conclude that it would be better to conduct an organized shift away from public funding than to suffer further uncertainty amidst a new cycle of budget crises. They decide to become a "state-assisted university" and to "privatize" centrally and systematically. State leaders agree to cap the General Fund at 2005–06 levels (in nominal dollars), to allow the General Fund share to decline to 15% of the university's overall budget (or about 1/3 of the "core") by the end of 2010–2011.
>
> Under this scenario, undergraduate fees rise as quickly as seems politically prudent; graduate and professional school fees rise to "market" levels as rapidly as possible; annual increases are routine and significant. Nonresident tuition (NRT) is raised even higher. UC also allows the share of in-state students to fall so that they can be replaced by high NRT-paying non-state residents. Most state leaders expect that over a further 10-year period (ending in 2020–2021), General Fund contributions decline to levels already achieved by the flagship public campuses of several states, including Colorado, Michigan, Vermont, and Virginia (8–10% of the overall budget, or 18% of "core" funds in Vermont's case and 22% in Michigan's case). . . . The University loses an additional $1.7 billion each year beyond the Compact's funding level, including the costs of increased financial aid to offset increased tuition.[22]

We then calculated the reduced public contribution: for example, the public spends half the share of its income on UC that it had a decade earlier (down to 0.15 percent of per capita personal income by 2011).

Our main interest was whether private funds could replace public money after all these cuts. The philanthropic picture was bleak:

> By 2010–2011, the General Fund is $1.11 billion below the level anticipated by the Compact, and has an additional half-billion dollars in financial aid

obligations to cover. The administration looks to endowment sources to make up the shortfall. Taken all together, UC's various endowments approach $10 billion, and pay out close to $400 million a year. But 97% of giving to the university carries restrictions, so very little of this money is available for support of core functions. For the endowment to pay out $1.1 billion, it would need to be nearly $25 billion, putting it at the level of the oldest and largest endowments in the country. But to obtain one billion dollars in unrestricted payouts, the University would need to raise $25 billion in unrestricted gifts, which, given the normal rate of restrictions on fundraising, would require a far larger amount. In addition, to reach the 2001–02 funding level, more than $54 billion in unrestricted endowment would be needed. These efforts would come on top of normal fundraising. To put this number in perspective, every man, woman and child in the state would have to contribute about $1500 to an unrestricted endowment fund, one devoted exclusively to the University of California.[23]

UC officials would clearly need to turn to tuition increases to fill in the multibillion-dollar gap ($2.5 billion below the 2001 pathway). Tuition in this scenario would increase annually until it was more than $15,000 a year in constant dollars, matching the highest public university levels in the country. We projected a significant loss of student enrollment at all but the two flagship campuses, those that could compete successfully for a national student body with Michigan, Columbia, and similar schools.

The outcome of all this would be the end of the UC "system" as we know it. The "One University" would have become impossible financially, and administrators would reduce their ambitions and services to fit their finances. Many campuses would no longer function as full research campuses, and would offer more of the cutbacks they had already been offering their students: larger classes, less advising and counseling, older equipment, less personal attention of the kind that can turn middling into excellent students. These cutbacks would be particularly noticeable in graduate programs, where funding would fall further behind that of peer institutions and all campuses would lose most of their best applicants to more affluent institutions. Political and educational leaders would promise that high tuition would be accompanied by high aid, but this is easier said than done as financial aid comes head to head with the needs of core operations. Student bodies would lose their disadvantaged members in higher proportions, undoing recent strides toward equitable racial representation. In addition to reducing educational capacity, campuses would be forced to degrade working conditions, meaning fewer and smaller raises, more departures of the most productive faculty for greener pastures, and lower retention of key staff and skilled technicians. The outcome would be something like what Michigan, New York, and Texas have now: systems where relatively poor and academically struggling institutions coexist with one or two research flagships in a phrase stratification.

Ending Quality for All

Although the culture wars have seriously damaged the prestige of public funding, it is important to see behind the ideological curtain. It was public funding that built the University of California as a system that could take *all* academically qualified students and give them a roughly equal education. Berkeley was more famous and had more Nobel-prize winners than Irvine, San Diego, or Santa Barbara, but massive public funding took the new campuses of the 1950s and 1960s from zero to sixty in the university equivalent of about five seconds. Within a few years of their founding, even the new UC campuses had superb programs and high-quality faculty that brought advanced research into the classroom. As time went on, the different rankings of the campuses would even out: by the late 1990s, six of UC's eight general campuses were members of the prestigious American Association of Universities. By 2000, UC San Diego, created in 1959 from the Scripps Institute, led the UC system in federal research expenditures, appeared above UCLA in some rankings, and had one of the most successful technology-transfer programs in the world.

Having a whole system of high-quality research campuses made an enormous difference for the college-aged population. It meant that UC-qualified high school graduates—technically the top 12.5 percent of all graduates—would not have to compete with one another solely for places at one of two flagships (though Berkeley and Los Angeles remained the most coveted campuses). If fifty thousand California high school graduates were eligible to attend UC, then all fifty thousand could attend a top-ranked UC research campus, rather than, say, eight thousand going to a flagship (like Austin in Texas, Madison in Wisconsin, Ann Arbor in Michigan, Chapel Hill in North Carolina, Gainesville in Florida, Urbana-Champaign in Illinois, or Buffalo and Stony Brook in New York) while the other forty-two thousand highly qualified students made do with the more limited opportunities of a regional state college.

There is a school of thought that says that this kind of college stratification does not matter—the main thing is to get students through a two-year college at least, or any kind of four-year college, since the salary and public payoffs of attaining these levels are measurable and sufficient.[24] There is no doubt that excellent faculty are to be found at community and regional state colleges, along with wonderful teaching and academic experiences that change people's lives. State colleges also train the majority of practitioners in fields like nursing, teaching, and social work, fields that have a high social value without an equally high wage.

But there are major economic and sociocultural losses when a state sends only a fraction of its highly qualified high school graduates to a major research university and assigns the rest to state colleges. Studies of these differences are incomplete, but we can extrapolate from clear differences in conditions and mission. State colleges have fewer resources, offer less or little research, and generally place fewer of their students in positions of social or professional leadership. Students coming out of them have lower incomes than students from major research universities (public or private) and pay less in taxes back to the states that educated them. On average, state college graduates have more limited prospects. States that send a higher percentage of their public university students to regional rather than research universities have lower average incomes, and, we can infer, more socioeconomic stratification within their college-educated middle classes.[25]

These differences in social impact between public research universities and state colleges rest in large part on the different educational missions of these institutions. Put simply, research university undergraduates are more likely to be exposed to both the *results* of advanced research and the *process* through which research creates new knowledge.

As one example, the structure of an undergraduate education that includes research was articulated by a University of California task force. The group divided the components of such instruction into a three-part system called TIE:

- Transmitting the Knowledge Base
- Initiating Intellectual Independence
- Emphasizing Independent Inquiry[26]

In a research university, knowledge transmission is largely the domain of "lower-division" instruction, which takes place in the first two years of the four-year program. In principle, during next two years, and especially the senior year, students develop the practices of intellectual independence. This independence is crucial to both creativity and leadership. It is also the essential ingredient of the "lifetime learning" that the contemporary economy is said to require. Finally, the third component offers actual experience with independent inquiry. This experience takes place largely outside of the "push" medium of the classroom, is fully interactive, and requires the student to originate, initiate, problem define, problem solve, and think outside the proverbial box. The "independent study" is one familiar venue for this activity, as is directed research, in which an undergraduate prepares for a career as a knowledge creator in his or her own right.

It is worth emphasizing that research faculty do not see independent inquiry as an add-on or special challenge for only the most gifted students, but as the destination of undergraduate education overall. The UC task force described these individualized forms of instruction as "the crowning accomplishment of instruction in a research/scholarship/performance-based university."[27] This vision has also long been the core strength of the liberal arts college, where small numbers of undergraduates work in small groups with faculty to produce their own independent research in the form of a final project or senior thesis.

We can say, then, that the genius of public education has been high quality on a mass scale—the equivalent of a senior thesis for everybody. The genius is *mass quality*. The means is achieving *independent inquiry for all*. In mass public systems, that role has fallen largely to the major research university.

There is thus an obvious comparative advantage in a system with ten research campuses rather than with one or two flagships in conjunction with many lesser ships. The advantage is clear from the perspective of human development, since a much higher proportion of qualified students is attaining the state of creative independence that is this development's central feature.

The advantage of a system of roughly equivalent research campuses is also clear in the salary markets. Studies of wage shifts in the 2000s noted that the gap between workers with only bachelor's degrees and those with advanced degrees was widening more quickly than that between college-degreed workers and those workers with only high school diplomas. Between 2000 and 2005, the real wages of college graduates actually *declined* by 3.1 percent. On the other hand, the wages of workers with PhDs increased by almost 3 percent, and those with professional degrees by more than 10 percent.[28]

This gap is not a cause for celebration: The advantages of professional degrees owed much to high barriers to entry, that is, to licensing protectionism that prevented most of the competition with lower-wage foreign workers that helped drive down wages in most other sectors: "It is in the middle—where many four-year college graduates work—that imports, overseas outsourcing and technology seems to be reducing U.S. employer demand most significantly, and thus restraining wages."[29] But some of the wage difference stemmed from what the advanced degrees represent: higher levels of training and more developed capacities to innovate and restructure systems on an ongoing basis. At research universities, undergraduate instruction comes closer to offering the features of postgraduate education. It gives graduates a better chance of acting to improve complex situations rather than simply adapting to them.

We are now in a better position to see the crisis that privatization has posed for undergraduate instruction at public universities. The components of intellectual independence and independent inquiry described by the UC task force on undergraduate education are labor-intensive: the best versions involve senior faculty working with groups of two or three students, or with students one-on-one in the tutorial structure that was devised at Oxford and Cambridge for England's upper classes. At public universities, instruction is precisely that component that depends almost entirely on state appropriations: private giving, as we have seen, is almost always restricted, and goes to targeted research, sports, trademark-building projects, and the other special interests of donors. When state funds are cut, instruction is cut: faculty are not hired or replaced, more teaching is done with less expensive lecturers and teaching assistants, class size is increased, and classes are dropped. The first classes that are dropped are the small and advanced classes that are not "efficient" from a budgetary point of view. In the most recent round of cuts, the economics department on one UC campus redefined a "seminar" class size from 15 to 50 students, which made an obvious mockery of a concept designed to encourage full student participation and active learning. A biology department on another campus reduced its "capstone" seminar requirement from two courses to one, and a history department eliminated its seminar requirement altogether. In short, private funds do not pay for teaching, and the most vulnerable teaching is the labor-intensive kind with the greatest returns for both individual and society.

The president emeritus of one of the tiered state operations, the University of Wisconsin system, has studied the effects of "de facto privatization." She concluded that it is mostly likely to divide public systems into two major groups. One group, "specialist" or regional universities, focuses on satisfying current workforce and public needs by continuing and upgrading established disciplines. The second group is the "creative university," which "looks not to respond, but to create the future by making large investments in new interdisciplinary research fields (nanotechnology, biotechnology, and so on) that use the intellectual resources of the university in new, team-oriented ways." These creative universities will consist almost entirely of public flagships like Wisconsin-Madison, Michigan–Ann Arbor, Minnesota–Twin Cities, and the like, and of course, of wealthy private universities. "Ironically," she wrote, "private research universities may be better equipped to fulfill this public purpose of creating the future than traditional public universities."[30] The result would be a clear stratification between private research universities, whose limited scope means that their graduates form a small elite, and the public systems that teach the overwhelming majority. In this privatizing world, "public universities [meet] their public purpose primarily through applied research and educating graduates for life and the professions, as private universities increasingly take over cutting-edge research that enables the nation to grow intellectually and economically in the future."[31]

Such a situation spells the end of the majoritarian vision of quality for all. It erroneously reseparates creativity and the masses in order to save money in the short term. It revitalizes a class system that belonged to the assembly-line approach to labor management that the knowledge economy had supposedly made obsolete, while damaging both social justice and economic effectiveness. When forced to participate in this return of social and economic leadership to a small elite through the downgrading of mass higher education, the public university sides with the backward current of contemporary history I have linked to the culture wars, undermining general development and its broad public constituency in one misguided move. It is no wonder that senior education leaders have started to think the worst: the president emeritus of the University of Michigan wonders whether "one might . . . conclude that America's great experiment of building world-class public universities supported primarily by tax dollars has come to an end."[32]

The logical conclusion here is stark: high-quality, large-scale public education requires strong *public* funding. Private funding does not come in sufficient supply to support core operations: teaching lower-division courses, writing tutorials, calculus and bench laboratory experience, language instruction, seminar interaction, independent study, and well-staffed large lectures in which students continue to get adequate personal attention. Personal attention is the core element of high-quality mass higher education: the brilliant top will do fine on its own, but the other 95 percent—with plenty of potential but with less experience, training, entitlement, and confidence—need the kind of highly developed teaching infrastructure that costs serious money. The point is worth repeating: high-quality education for *elites* is cheap, since there are not that many students involved.[33] High-quality education for the great majority is expensive, and private sources are unable to support it.[34] Private funding works at some exciting, creative, but narrow margins of higher education, while doing next to nothing for the instructional core on which its public mission depends.

— 12 —

The Failure of Market Measures

I will start this chapter by reversing the emphasis with which I ended the last one. I note, therefore, that private funding *does* help some highly focused activities that are too new or advanced to have acquired a constituency. Advanced research is a good example of an area where privatization can work wonders. Specialized legal clinics that provide free advice on health insurance law for poor or unwell clients who cannot afford to hire a private attorney are another example. If these are interests of a faculty or administration, and of real social benefit, why not try to find a small group of special financial supporters rather than lay yet another claim on an overstretched state general fund? Or to take another example, why not accept a wealthy family's offer of seed money for an autism clinic, even though it means diverting public money from other areas in order to build and operate this good unit toward which state money never would otherwise have flowed?

Moving inventions into society is one of the great things that the university does. "Technology transfer" is a general term for the process that leads from inventions in university science and engineering fields to things that people can use in their everyday lives. The term refers to many different aspects of the process whereby discoveries move from "bench to bedside"— from a concept that gets proven out in the lab to a product that improves or saves the lives of many people. In general, technology transfer has great social value and is a central part of the university's public mission. It is often boosted by infusions of private money that come at the right time, or are focused on the right research objective, or leverage insufficient public funding so that a project can leap a difficult hurdle. The question here is not whether or not technology transfer as such is a social good—it is. The question is not whether private-public partnerships should exist—they should.

The question is whether the discourse of privatization skews technology transfer such that its public value is distorted or reduced. Like every other university activity, technological research and development have been operating in a culture-wars atmosphere that assimilates social purposes to market forces. Could culture warriors show that market forces and their financial incentives improved the quality and quantity of research in ways that neither social nor intellectual goals could? Was the market now doing for science what blue-sky curiosity and public funding had never done?[1]

The Social Roots of Research

Culture warriors had their work cut out for them, for even neoclassical economists agreed that innovative research required public investment. Their key insight was that "market failure" characterizes innovative research. This does not mean that research fails markets, but that markets fail research: market calculations cannot correctly estimate basic research's future value. The future value of such research is possibly large but actually unknown. Since the future value is incalculable, anyone rigidly calculating the future value of basic research will perceive investment risk to be infinite, and will logically put their money into an activity whose returns are more predictable. To make matters worse for market measures of R & D, firms also know that they are unlikely to capture more than a small fraction of the overall value of the patent for their own organization. Individual firms are thus less likely than they should be to invest in R & D that might have had a large monetary and social value some time in the future.[2] Kenneth Arrow made the point with particular directness in 1962: "We expect a free enterprise economy to underinvest in invention and research (as compared with an ideal) because it is risky, because the product can be appropriated only to a limited extent, and because of increasing returns in use. This underinvestment will be greater for more basic research."[3] The more innovative the research is, the less likely the market is to fund it correctly.

Such considerations led many mainstream economists to advocate substantial public support for basic research in the mid-1950s. The costs of long-range research that was too great for any one firm would be shared by society. Economists offered good neoclassical reasons to support the National Science Foundation and similar institutions that offered public subsidies for activities whose public value far exceed the profits that any single firm could expect to recoup. These economists showed that financial incentives would in general fail to support an optimal or even adequate level of basic research. The only solution was public subsidy. Research would serve the market eventually, but only if it was not measured by market returns.

Contemporary economists have made similar arguments. In a series of articles and a comprehensive book on the economics of intellectual property (IP), the economist Suzanne Scotchmer has confirmed in various ways that "for investments in R&D, unlike ordinary capital, the social value of a marginal investment is not equal to the private value": the social value is often greater, and investing in it cannot depend on market incentives like IP ownership for an individual person or firm.[4] This key conclusion was repeatedly confirmed by the work of other economists as well as by business historians and entrepreneurs. The 1990s start-up founder Charles Ferguson noted that the failure of the efforts of major technology companies to start an Internet on their terms was directly attributable to the companies' attempts to design it around their proprietary technology.[5] The success that we know as the Internet today was publicly funded, nonproprietary, multicentered—and was established long before anyone could imagine making any money from it.

Such analyses could lead to recommendations for a publicly debated industrial policy. In the United States, where industrial policy is unthinkable, ad hoc public investments have taken place anyway. At the end of the 1990s, the Clinton administration launched the National Nanotechnology Initiative, and not long afterward, in 2001, California governor Grey Davis persuaded the state legislature to give $300 million in state funds to start the California Institutes of Science and Innovation at the University of California. Scotchmer has recommended the creation of an international research funding consortium along the lines of similar international bodies for intellectual property regulation, trade agreements, and the like, based on the findings of orthodox economic modeling.

The public origins and benefits of basic research have been apparent in the industrial regions and networks for which the United States has become renowned. Silicon Valley and Route 128 depended on private capital but functioned well because of distinctive sociocultural features: a concentration of human capabilities, unintended network effects, informal knowledge circulation, fortunate, unplanned collaborations, massive public investment (decades of defense money in Silicon Valley), and major universities.[6] The cultures of such regions have also been unusually good at articulating the social dimensions of innovation systems: these descriptions included Richard Stallman's Free Software Foundation, which has sought to keep software development nonproprietary; Tim Berners-Lee's understanding of open access, which influenced his development of the universal resource locater (URL), the *Wired* crowd's fascination with self-organized systems; Lawrence Lessig's free culture; and Manuel Castells's elaborations of the network society; not to mention a widespread interest in applying chaos theory, complexity theory, and fractal mathematics to sociocultural systems.

To be taken seriously in American political culture, the thinkers behind these concepts have at some point claimed to be following the market. But in reality the market was only a piece of the overall operation of these nonlinear organizations and networks of organizations. When we view the source of a systemic intensity like "regional advantage" in all its sociocultural complexity, we see that the transfers of information and interests and motivations and attachments look superficially like markets but are almost wholly social and nonfinancial. *Most* of this transmission is *free*. Quite a bit of it is paid for publicly, and collectively. To collect a toll would block much of it from taking place. The cost of monitoring and charging would be greater than the *financial* value of the transmissions, which at an early stage in a long-term creative process have in fact no financial value. The innovation capability of the overall system depends on its collective activity—on a vast collaborative labor that no one directs.[7]

The university fits right into the country's actual innovation system. It is the paradigmatic instance of "free" in the sense of open, of collaboration with low overhead, of ideas developed with knowledge and not money in mind, of cross-subsidies that enable complex work to continue longer than markets would let it. Technology transfer in its broadest sense—as the process of moving inventions into society—is one piece of a system of agents interacting with mixed resources, mixed motives, and complicated aims (for-profit, not-for-profit, short-term, long-term, educational, instrumental). Sometimes patenting an invention can help continue the development process: there are cases where patents are required to attract private investment at a pivotal stage, or to enable inventor control so the invention develops in an optimal direction. This does not mean that patenting is a universal solution or has no downside: broad studies of patents show that their *average* value is very low; furthermore, the large majority of patents do not normally recoup their costs of prosecution.[8] Given the realities of the innovation system, tech transfer would ideally stay flexible around the issue of IP, use proprietary structures only where they added clear scientific and social value, and focus on preserving the research communities on which progress depended.[9] Like all innovation processes, tech transfer would be regarded as a market failure but an intellectual and institutional success.

The Tech-Transfer Tale

But technology transfer came of age in an era in which acknowledging social and collaborative forces was increasingly difficult. The tech-transfer process was defined by the Bayh-Dole patent legislation of 1980, which, along with related legislation and court decisions, gave universities ownership of the intellectual property created by their employees through government funds.[10] In subsequent years, continuous advocacy tightened the perceived causal link between increased disclosures and patenting activity on the one hand, and the university's ownership stake on the other. Though the Bayh-Dole Act may have been most important in the boring details that helped standardize licensing processes among the federal government's many funding agencies and helped support new research partnerships, the act came to be identified with the power of market incentives to inspire science and technology through intellectual property ownership.

The standard survey of tech-transfer results has been conducted each year since 1996 by the Association of University Technology Managers (AUTM). This organization has also dominated the story about how technological innovation actually works. For example, the 2004 survey framed its statistical results with the following highlights:

- The U.S. Patent and Trademark Office issued more than 3,800 U.S. patents in fiscal year 2004 to universities responding to the AUTM Licensing Survey; less than 250 were issued to universities in 1980, the year the Bayh-Dole Act became law.

- In the U.S. alone, 567 products based on university or nonprofit research results were introduced in fiscal year 2004, and more than 3,100 new products have entered the marketplace since fiscal year 1998.

- Today's product development activity contrasts sharply with the situation before Bayh-Dole, when the government held title to patents discovered with federal funding. A 1968 study found that no drug to which the government held title had ever been commercially developed and become available to the public. By 1980, 28,000 government-funded patents had been issued by the U.S. PTO and were gathering dust.[11]

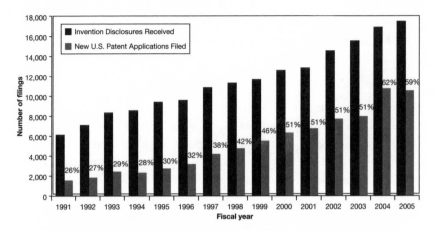

Figure 6. New patent filings and invention disclosures received, 1991–2005.
Source: Association of University Technology Managers, "AUTM U.S. Licensing Survey: FY 2005" (2007), 5, http://www.autm.net/events/file/US_LS_05Final(1).pdf (accessed October 22, 2007).

These points offered a typical mixture of statistical reporting, as in the ambiguous second bullet point, and repeated references to a pre–Bayh-Dole dark age, as in the first and third bullet points. In reality, scholarly studies of Bayh-Dole's effects do not confirm the simple linear connection between university title and commercial development.[12] But AUTM regularly asserted a causal connection between the Bayh-Dole regime and these major increases in patenting and product development.[13]

To continue the storyline, AUTM's presentation featured a continued rise in the volume, the value, and the economic importance of university-based tech transfer (see Figure 6). The clear implication here was that Bayh-Dole enabled steady annual increases in invention disclosures, patent filings, and the public benefit of new products.

The same trend appeared in the graph of licensing income, the majority of which came in the form of licensing royalties (see Figure 7). By 2004, universities had a combined total of nearly $1.5 billion in gross licensing income (before various costs and inventor share payouts). The continuous rise appeared to correlate with a constantly increasing contribution to economic growth. AUTM also reported a less steady but overall increase in the annual number of start-up companies that came from university sources, totaling 4,543 between 1980 and 2003. There thus seemed to be a link con-

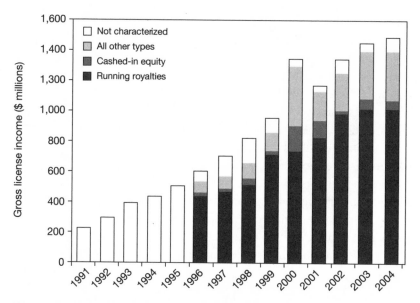

Figure 7. Gross income received, United States, 2004. Source: Association of University Technology Managers, "AUTM U.S. Licensing Survey: FY 2004" (public summary version), Figure US-27: Gross Income Received by Income Type, All U.S. Respondents, 2004; http://www.autm.net/events/File/04AUTMSurveySum_USpublic.pdf.

necting patenting, revenues, start-up activity, new products, and hence new sources of economic prosperity.[14]

But in reality the financial picture was much more mixed. The vast majority of universities involved in tech transfer received fairly small revenues from them. Of the 196 institutions reporting, around two-thirds made $1,000,000 or less in licensing income. About 30 institutions made more than $7.5 million each, and eight more made more than $5 million. The kind of numbers that affected research budgets were limited to a small number of very large players: MIT, Stanford, Harvard, Columbia, the University of California, and the University of Pennsylvania, and a few others. Although some newer entrants had risen in the ranks, mostly through a small number of blockbuster patents, the universities that made lots of money on patent licensing were generally those that already had lots of money.[15] The same skew was apparent in the figures for large patents. Patents that yielded more than $1 million a year in income comprised 1.5 percent of the total (or 167 licenses).[16] AUTM reported that 66 institutions had one of these. AUTM also reported that three institutions had more than ten "mega-licenses," meaning that a minimum of about 20 percent of the licenses held by this top 1.5 percent were held by approximately

5 percent of this group of institutions. Such figures suggest that the tech-transfer system offered plausible financial incentives—in the form of a good shot at major income—to only the top fifteen or so universities. Michael Crow, while the head tech-transfer official at one of these dominant powers, Columbia University, advised the journalist Jennifer Washburn to assess a university's tech-transfer chances as follows: " 'Look at the list of top university royalty earners that AUTM publishes.' . . . Any school whose tech-transfer activities 'rank below fifteenth' on that list . . . doesn't have the research capacity, talent, or resources it takes to do commercialization successfully."[17]

The implication here is that tech transfer has skewed and partial market outcomes, but strong and important psychological effects. The chance for a large payout may stimulate certain scientists to go to new lengths to produce viable results. Actual market results are far smaller than the hopes they stimulate. Perhaps because of the limited revenues, AUTM began to place greater emphasis on scientific and social arguments for tech transfer.

Returns at the Top

What if we focused on the lucky few? A good example is the University of California, which has ten campuses and the largest tech-transfer operation in the country. The numbers look good in the initial aggregate. In the 2000s, the number of inventions reported each year increased from under 1,000 to closer to about 1,300 in five years. The overall number of active inventions went from 4,481 to 6,618, while the number of inventions earning royalties increased from 767 to 1,088.[18]

But a further look revealed another story. In the first five years of the 2000s, patents actually issued were up and down (easing from FY 2000 to FY 2004 from 324 to 270; for the UC system as a whole, there were 270 patents issued in FY 2006).[19] Overall licensing revenues were up and down. The same was true for licenses or options issued—down from 249 to 204 in FY 2004 and back to 226 in FY 2006.[20] Total licensing revenue was $88 million in FY 2002, $80 million in FY 2004, $93.5 million in FY 2006—again defying a strong trend or a large yield.[21]

Such data suggested that even the most powerful tech-transfer operation in the United States was not a growth machine. It fluctuated with the business cycle and other factors. The data also suggested that UC tech transfer was not on its way to providing a meaningful revenue source for research or anything else. In FY 2003, federal research funding to UC amounted to nearly $2 billion; overall extramural research funding was around $3 billion;

UC's overall budget, excluding the national laboratories, was $13.8 billion in that year.[22] Thus UC's patent royalties for FY 2004 were about 2.67 percent of its overall research funding. If strategically applied, such an amount could make a difference to a handful of programs, but it was destined to remain a fraction of overall research.

Unfortunately, we are not done whittling away at the funds made available to the university through technology transfer. Further losses can be noted in Figure 8. Various inventor shares took almost 40 percent of revenues, and net legal fees another large slice. This left about one-quarter of gross revenues, or just under $20 million, in that year to the campuses. It is reasonable to assume that the bulk of this went into covering either the indirect costs of research or direct costs that the granting agency was unwilling to pay, and in the case of some foundation and industry gifts for research, these can be considerable. The amount of royalty income that

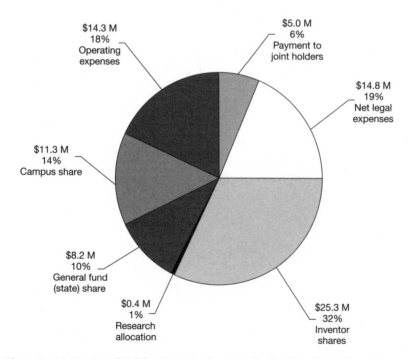

Figure 8. University of California patent income distribution, FY 2004. Source: Suzanne Quick, "Technology Transfer Statistical Highlights, FY 2003–2004," Technology Transfer Advisory Committee, UC Office of the President, March 10, 2005, slide 19 (in author's files).

went back into research was, in this year, $400,000 for the UC system as a whole. This small number is somewhat greater than 0.01 percent of UC's research budget for that year (net income overall was about 0.67 percent of research revenues).[23] No one would be pleased with this figure (or that of any other major research university) as a "return on investment."[24]

UC's size and increasing decentralization did not overcome another feature we noted in AUTM's national numbers, which was the skew in licensing revenue toward a small number of blockbuster patents (see Table 5). The top individual patents paid out extremely well. But in FY 2004 UC had 6,618 "active inventions," of which 1,088 had at some time earned royalties. The top five produced one-half of all revenues, and in FY 2006 that percentage had fallen, only slightly.[25] (Here UC did better than average, for AUTM's 2000 survey found that the top five inventions at an institution generate on average 76 percent of total revenues.)[26] About 15 percent of all UC patent revenues came from the top single invention, the hepatitis B vaccine, whose patents were by the early 2000s about twenty-five years old. Such figures suggest that the vast majority of all active licenses return next to nothing. A comparison of figures for inventions and licenses shows that 84 percent of UC's "active inventions" did not have an active license. Even a strong and fairly decentralized tech-transfer performer like UC did not break the national pattern of a remarkable disproportion between its top patents and the rest. Nor could an increased focus on patenting ensure increased innovation of the kind that led to revenue: only two of UC's top 25 patents had been disclosed after 1996.

The point here is not that the University of California and American research were doing badly. To the contrary, they were producing the normal market results of doing research very well, which (with rare exceptions) is to spend lots of money rather than to earn it. The market results of innovative research are, *as* research results, close to nil. This is as it should be: the purpose of innovative research is innovation—discovery, invention, and scientific progress. This research has great long-term and social value that could not be captured as licensing revenue or estimates of the market value of patents.

The contribution of the research university can best be appreciated in broader, postmarket terms. The research university was designed to investigate every topic of conceivable public interest, from astronomical physics to agricultural genetics and everything in between. Major commercial returns accrued to research in a fairly narrow band of fields largely found in information technology and biomedicine, though there are exceptions (among UC's top producers is the Camarosa strawberry, a standout in a list of mostly health-related royalties). Nearly all research produced value for society by feeding into further research in the continuing process of expanding our knowledge of everything under the sun. Some of this knowledge would eventually produce profitable products and perhaps new industries, but it belonged to a tiny

Table 5 UC Top-earning Inventions
Year Ended June 30, 2006

Invention (campus, year disclosed)	$ (Thousands)
Hepatitis-B vaccine (SF, 1979 and 1981)	15,299
Treatment of intracranial aneurysms (LA, 1989)	8,763
Dynamic skin cooling device (IR, 1993)	7,037
Interstitial cystitis therapy (SD, 1980)	6,439
Egf receptor antibodies (SD, 1983)	5,750
Subtotal (top five inventions)	**43,288**
Biodegradable implant Coils (LA, 1998)	4,429
Camarosa strawberry (DA, 1992)	2,666
Cochlear implants (SF, 1979)	1,735
Firefly luciferase (SD, 1984)	1,645
Chromosome painting (LLNL, 1985)	1,598
Energy transfer primers (BK, 1994)	1,578
Nicotine patch (LA, 1984)	1,116
Feline AIDS virus diagnostic (DA, 1986)	1,041
Ventana strawberry (DA, 2001)	908
Liposome storage method (DA, 1984)	867
Fluorescent dyes—calcium (BK, 1984)	854
Laser/water atomic microscope (SB, 1989)	735
Magnetic resonance imaging (SF, 1976)	715
Universal oligonucleotide spacer (BK, 1996)	577
Aids for learning disabled (SF, 1994)	573
Diamonte strawberry (DA, 1996)	514
Fluorescent conjugate probes (BK, 1981)	492
Human cytomegalovirus diagnostic (SD, 1982)	484
Novel phosphorus fertilizers (RV, 1990)	363
Radionuclide imaging method (SF, 1989)	324
Total income (top 25 inventions)	**66,502**
Total income (all inventions)	**93,500**
Percentage of total from top 5 inventions	**46.3**
Percentage of total from top 25 inventions	**71.1**

This list is limited to revenue-generating inventions that have been commercialized.

Source: http://www.ucop.edu/ott/genresources/documents/OTTRptFY06.pdf (accessed Nov. 15, 2007).

minority of research activities. The rest of the published knowledge would result in *public* benefits that could not be harvested and captured by any one firm or group of firms: this included most public health knowledge, as well as research in scientific fields like geology and mathematics. New algorithms in conjunction with empirical geological science might improve earthquake prediction, saving countless lives and perhaps much property damage, but the amount of money a particular firm might make (training personnel in interpretative techniques, packaging and distributing software) would be minute by comparison.

Because overall profits for even the most important discoveries are negative to small, and because blockbuster patents can never be predicted or planned, universities cannot base research or other programs on tech-transfer income. Universities cannot steer research programs on the basis of explicit financial incentives. No office of research that seeks to support a *range* and *diversity* of research—a broad, complex intellectual enterprise—can make funding decisions with licensing goals uppermost in mind. This is just as well, since, to repeat, the *market* value of nearly all socially useful research is a fraction of that research's social value. The larger value of the research enterprise cannot be discerned by focusing on market outcomes.

Most practitioners understood these facts. By the 2000s, many technology managers were moving away from simple monetary defenses of tech transfer toward more developed discussions of benefits for research consortia and partnerships and for society as a whole. But much damage remained to be undone. Without intending it, tech-transfer advocates had generated their own culture-wars discourse, one in which tech transfer could best be measured in market terms and was, at the same time, evidence of the value of market incentives. Tech transfer thus dovetailed with the efforts of culture warriors to show that educational aims should be subject to the vision and rules of the marketplace. Most policy makers, encouraged by narratives emerging from the tech-transfer community, defended technology transfer as a direct service to market expansion structured by financial incentives.

In so doing, most tech-transfer advocates misstated the actual market outcomes of technological research. They undermined arguments for public support and open communication of research results. They made it harder to work out equitable compensation for participants who were at a distance from the licensing, start-up, or other transfer arrangements. They distracted attention from the long-term public value of this research. They weakened interest in transfers that avoided exclusive licenses to individual companies. They did not properly conceptualize or fund research consortia based on intellectual property pooling and nondiscriminatory licensing. They tied academic research to market measures of success in spite of the evidence that this would not improve research and might actually damage it. In the dot-com period and its aftermath, when it might have become clear that market measures were failing technology transfer, tech transfer, within the gravity field of the culture wars, became a discourse devoted to markets.

— 13 —

Hiding Culture's Contribution

Market thinking saw cultural disciplines as second-class: they made no money now and obviously never would. This assumption was as pervasive in academia as it was in business itself, and was blandly assumed by administrators, scientists, and humanities scholars alike.

But in the real world, science made no money either. That is, basic research cost money, enormous amounts of it. Science made money once it had been developed into commercial products, but that was a separate process that occurred almost entirely outside the university. Product development was also a net money loser in most of its early and pivotal stages. The culture of start-up companies reflected this fact with its folklore of "burn rates," as companies raced their technology-development process against a money clock that was always threatening to run out. The gap between an exciting technological breakthrough and a successful product became famously large and famously difficult to cross: during the technological boom years of the 1990s, a popular technological determinism that asserted the inevitable profitability of new technology was flattened by serious pro-tech critiques like *The Innovator's Dilemma* and *Inside the Tornado*.[1] Science cost money and technology cost money and money would be earned only well down a development road that would not be traveled by the university itself.

This statement flies in the face of two entrenched dogmas on university campuses. The first of these is that scientific research brings in money from the outside, and therefore earns money for the university. The second is that fields that cannot obtain much extramural funding—qualitative disciplines like art history and cultural anthropology—cost money and are a liability. We have already encountered these dogmas embedded in misleading dichotomies like "love versus money." Now I need to suggest why both

208

dogmas are wrong, and how correcting them challenges core culture-warrior doctrine.

Social Value Minus Cultural Knowledge

First, let us recall this doctrine. The culture wars described the market as the sole repository of collective economic wisdom, and as a result academia's ties to industry were readily cast as intrinsically valuable, as a sign of academia's new willingness to reform and change, and as the main source of value creation. In contrast, disciplines that focused on basic skills, on the past, on difficult and controversial social and cultural domains, meaning fields like sociology, anthropology, history, literature, philosophy, music, drama, classics, and linguistics, in short, studies of the whole spectrum of human life and culture summed up in French academia as the "human sciences," lost money, caused trouble, and were not seen as part of society's economic engine. When that engine faltered cultural study could be cast as an expensive luxury; resources should, in culture-war doctrine, be diverted to the rock face of technological innovation.

This doctrine appeared unintentionally in various domains: in accounts of technology transfer, as we have seen, and even in official descriptions of the university's social importance. For example, sometime after the year 2000 the University of California's main Web site came to feature a link to an elaborate list of UC contributions to the California economy. This made good political sense: universities were trying to talk to state legislators in their basic language of economic gain. Thus UC president Robert C. Dynes noted that "our research leads to an average of three new inventions every day, and the UC system leads the American higher education community in the generation of new patents. Those innovations lead to new products; the products lead to the creation of new companies and even new industries; and those companies generate good, new jobs for Californians."[2]

But it turned out that only some fields were part of this economic contribution. UC commissioned a report about UC research called "California's Future: It Starts Here."[3] Though the report ran 374 pages, the humanities and social sciences were all but nonexistent in it: sociology and anthropology, the "Democrat" disciplines in culture-war surveys of faculty politics, did not appear once. The fairly quantitative field of political science was equally invisible, though one would think it might have made contributions to understanding the famously dysfunctional California political system that helped necessitate the report in the first place. Though the state's racial diversity was arguably the single most important determinant of its present and future direction, cultural, ethnic, racial, sexuality, and gender studies did not make an appearance. "Arts and Culture" showed up in the report as public service programming.[4] They also appeared in a section on "Quality of Life Impacts," along with "community outreach and volunteerism," "athletics and recreation," and "conference services and housing facilities."[5] The word "literary" appeared in the entire report exactly once, in the following sentence about a public art installation at UCSD: "Projects include Terry Allen's 'Trees'—three preserved eucalyptus trees encased in metal, individually known as the Music Tree, Literary Tree and Third Tree—installed between the Campus Library and Faculty Club."[6]

Though the official report was right to note that UC contributed to the aesthetic and recreational lives of the public, it assumed that the human sciences did not *produce knowledge* in the conventional sense and did not contribute to the state's economic development. In this sense, culture—and cultural study—did not contribute to the state's future.

Mysteries of Indirect Cost Recovery

The absence of cultural knowledge from notions of social value reflected and reinforced the two dogmas that say that technology makes money and culture loses it. The factual error at the heart of the story begins to appear when we pause to look at indirect cost recovery (ICR). This is one of the least appealing of university topics, but it is simpler and about ten times more important than it sounds. "Indirect costs" are little more than the overhead on an activity, and in particular, on research. The standard situation is that a university faculty member applies for and obtains a research grant from a federal agency. If that person's university has a 50 percent ICR rate, or overhead rate, this means that 50 percent of the amount of the direct costs of the grant will be charged to the agency in addition to direct costs. If a faculty researcher obtains a grant of $100,000, an additional $50,000 will be given to the researcher's institution by the granting agency. The cost of the grant to the agency will be $150,000, the researcher will have $100,000 to spend on conducting the specific research, and the university will have $50,000 to cover its overhead. Direct costs involve the costs of the specific grant—the portion of the salaries of the principal investigator and research assistants that are consumed by grant activity; buying equipment and materials to be used in the research; and travel costs and similar expenses. Indirect costs go to the university primarily to pay "facilities and administrative costs . . . that are incurred for common or joint objectives and, therefore, cannot be identified readily and specifically with a particular sponsored project."[7] Clear examples are power bills, building maintenance, capital upgrades required by a number of research programs that share a building, environmental mitigation, and staff costs in the grant's primary departments.

The actual formulas are often Byzantine, but the basic idea is that many of the costs of research are shared over a large number of grants and over a long period of time, and that each grant should pay for a piece of these common facilities and administrative structures. Everyone agrees that basic facilities are indispensable to the ongoing success of a university's research operation: the university has to have the buildings and experienced staff in place before it can be a strong contender to get any grant money at all. Facilities and administrative structures must also be continually refreshed and upgraded if the university is to stay competitive. With modern science, these costs can be extraordinary: a building housing one unit of a school of engineering's research operation can cost $100 million to construct, to say nothing of costs of operation.

The assumption that most observers make is that researchers apply for money that will cover all the direct costs of the research they propose. In addition, they assume that the negotiated rate of indirect cost recovery similarly covers the research's indirect costs in terms of building maintenance, staff time, and so on. Once these assumptions are in place, the market view of university research takes hold: if both direct and indirect costs are covered by extramural grants, then administrators can transfer some ICR from the science departments that earn it to social science or humanities departments that do not. Administrators can do this either because ICR exceeds actual overhead costs so they can use the surplus to pay for other university expenses far from the origin of the grant, or, as most believe, because they skimp on expenses in the science departments (confiscating money that should pay for adequate staffing and proper facilities) so they can pay bills for the soft disciplines, which loses money. Making matters worse, scientists do face shortages and real deprivations. A significant campus research program may gross $100 million in federal contracts and grants, and generate around $50 million in overhead, and yet the science faculty that generate most of this money still cannot replace office furniture, hire clerical assistance, or repair leaky faucets—unless they pay for it directly from their grants.

But in practice the founding assumptions are incorrect. In many cases, the research's *direct* costs are more than the agency is willing to pay to support them. An even worse story must be told about overhead, or *indirect*, costs. Accounting studies show that "research at [universities] is *not* fully funded by external funding sources." The basic reason is quite straightforward: in order to help its faculty conduct research, the university allows and even encourages faculty members to accept grants from agencies that do not pay the full overhead costs of their grants. Such agencies include those of the federal government, where the negotiated ICR rate is almost always below actual overhead costs. Such agencies also include the many nonprofit foundations that have explicit policies of not paying full overhead. A third group of agencies is corporate partners, who can negotiate lowered overhead on a case-by-case basis. In UC, if sponsored research is classified as a gift—meaning it requires no reporting and no deliverables—its overhead rate can be as low as 2 percent. In other words, virtually no external sponsor of research pays its share of actual indirect costs. A UC Senate investigation concluded that "external studies of under funding have consistently put total recovered overhead at about 33% of modified direct costs—a dramatic shortfall as true costs appear to be in the 61–67% range."[8] This means that, on average, universities are recovering about half of their actual overhead costs.

Table 6 shows a sampling of ICR shortfalls. A few universities have minimized the gap between their actual costs and their negotiated rate of ICR, but most have not. The gap between actual and recovered costs would then be multiplied by the dollar amount of the research operation to yield the amount that scientific research actually costs each campus. Oddly enough, some of the largest gaps occur at some of the largest research operations in the country (Washington is always near the top in overall federal contracts, Harvard is a perennial front-runner, and the UC campuses as a whole have more than $2 billion just in federal contracts). If an "average" campus has $200 million in research, and the gap between actual and recovered costs is "only" 5 percent on a 50 percent negotiated ICR rate, the university needs to find nearly $7 million a year of its own money to cover the costs of conducting extramural research.[9]

The actual situation, however, is generally much worse. The federal agencies listed in Table 6 are among those who come closest of all research sponsors to a full recovery rate; some percentage of research occurs with much less or even very little ICR. When all these sources are pooled together, the negotiated rate turns out to be far higher than the *actual overall* rate of recovery, which at UC is only 33 percent. If the gap between actual and recovered indirect costs is not 5 percent as posited above but 50 percent, then the university needs to find ten times the subsidy money assumed above, or closer to $70 million of its "own" money. The actual gap is somewhere in between these figures, but even if it hovers nearer the low end, such rough calculations suggest that the costs of research are a very serious chronic budgetary issue.

The clear conclusion is that extramural research is *not* a moneymaker for universities. Research is, to the contrary, a major cost, and is one of the important sources of the continuous above-average price inflation in higher education that torments parents by producing continuous tuition hikes.

Table 6 Organized research facilities and administration rates, selected research universities

	Most recent submitted estimates of actual costs (%)	Negotiated recovery rate (%)	Cognizant agency
Harvard University	72.9	67	HHS
MIT	69.2	65	ONR
Johns Hopkins	67.7	63.1	HHS
University of Washington	64.4	56	HHS
Stanford	58.8	56.5	HHS
Penn	58.5	57	HHS
University of Minnesota	53.6	49.5	HHS
Georgia Tech	50.5	50.3	ONR
Penn State	46	45	ONR
Utah State	40.2	42.4	ONR
UCSD	64.5	56	HHS
UCLA	60.7	54.5	HHS
UCSF	58	54	HHS
UCD	71.2	52	HHS
UCR	60.3	50	HHS

HHS, U.S. Department of Health and Human Services; ONR, Office of Naval Research.

Courtesy of Charles Louie, vice chancellor for research at the University of California at Riverside, 2007. F&A data is available through a variety of resources, including the Council on Government Relations, web sites of universities, and a number of federal agencies who maintain this data. The data obtained here is publicly available, and no single organization is responsible for providing it.

Research does many other good things—it creates knowledge, enlightens humankind, improves long-term economic health, raises the quality of life, enhances the reputation, status, and social influence of the faculty, and allows the university to continue to get more grants to do more research. But scientists do *not* earn net income for the university through their grants. They do *not* send money over to the alleged money losers that populate the cultural fields. Although it is certainly true that administrators deprive grant getters by diverting a portion of ICR funds to cover expenditures at a distance from the faculty members who generated them, grants never earn enough to cover their own costs. And they never will. Many technical reports confirm this analysis, and some universities are honest about this, but most are not clear about the basic fact that "all research is subsidized research."[10]

We now turn to our next question: subsidized by whom?

The Financial Contribution of Teaching Culture

The most immediate answer is that research is subsidized by graduate students. They are paid relatively low wages and are easily hired and fired. Universities offer themselves and their industrial partners a large number of very bright, highly motivated young people who are trained in the latest techniques, and who are paid salaries that range between $15,000 and $25,000 a year. The research university thus offers corporate sponsors high-quality scientific labor at a fraction of its market cost. This helps explain science managers' defense of the university's distinctiveness even as many political and business leaders call for the university to be more like a business. Were the university really to be a business, it would in theory really have to pay market wages, meaning that it would have to pay young scientists and technologists like employees rather than like graduate students, and this would significantly increase overall research costs. (University technology managers tell me that their rule of thumb is that industry can cut its cost for high-risk, long-term research to about ten cents on each dollar it would spend in its own laboratories.)

The more general subsidy for research comes from the public, through the tax and tuition money that pays for teaching. General fund and tuition money flow to course enrollment in varying degrees, since both taxpayers and students are paying first and foremost for instruction. States normally appropriate money to public universities according to enrollment: some of the money pays direct costs of instruction like faculty and staff salaries, and some pays indirect costs, like the building, equipment, administration, course materials, and utility costs that are part of the teaching enterprise. Private universities do something similar with tuition money: most have formulas to ensure the fair funding of teaching "workload." As a result, departments that have lots of majors or enrollments generally get proportionally more money for faculty and staff salaries, more money for new hires, more teaching-assistant funds, and so on. States often set an amount that they will pay to instruct each student. The formulas can be arcane, but the basic idea is that allocations should generally reflect instructional load, especially since instruction has long been seen as the university's core service to society.

What this means is that we can in principle calculate what individual departments or divisions "earn" based on their student enrollment. We can also find out what their actual budgets are. We can then see whether the university is actually paying every department what it earns through teaching, or whether it is getting more or less than what it expects to get for its teaching effort.

Table 7 offers one example of such a calculation. These are actual, though simplified, figures from a flagship state university with a complement of additional professional schools that I exclude here. The "earned" figures are a product of the division's instructional load multiplied by the amount of public money that is sent by the state per student. The private university equivalent would be the tuition revenues generated by student enrollment. "Actual revenues" reflect what the university administration then really gives each division. "Research awards" refer to extramural contracts and grants from all sources, including industry. These figures include money for both direct and indirect costs, at various rates.

The normal way to read such a table is to look at the last column. When we add teaching revenue to research revenue, and then divide by the number of faculty FTE (not shown), we could apparently conclude that both sides of campus contribute funding in their own ways. The humanities and social sciences contribute with more teaching, and the sciences and engineering with more research. When you add the numbers in the last column, this story goes, "Funds generated" by engineering faculty are double those of the professional school faculty and more than double those in the human sciences. Natural and physical science faculty are in between, but closer to engineering. Hence, we seem to have learned yet again that science and engineering faculty earn the bulk of the money and then have to share a piece of it with their poor relations in the human sciences. Any administrator trying to maximize return

Table 7 Earned versus actual instructional revenues (averaged by division, 2001–2002)

Division	Earned instructional revenues	Actual revenues	Ratio of actual to earned revenues (%)	Research awards	Funds generated (total, including gifts)	Funds per faculty FTE
Professional school	869,000	2,433,369	279.8	2,668,012	4,075,309	251,562
Arts and humanities	56,684,987	25,665,591	45.3	1,542,992	60,942,496	230,922
Social sciences	40,820,389	15,732,870	38.5	1,673,422	43,194,634	294,743
Natural sciences	40,336,121	30,309,471	75.1	55,437,901	97,870,016	400,811
Engineering	11,398,652	24,348,696	213.6	43,382,033	64,420,069	530,250

on investment would think, according to this logic, that she should stop hiring literature professors and only hire engineers.

But if we look at the fourth column, "Ratio of actual to earned revenues," we see a more startling picture. Were the sciences subsidizing the social sciences and humanities, one would predict departmental budgets in the latter divisions that are larger than what these departments earn through their teaching. A department like English or art history would, according to this standard assumption, keep its teaching money, hang on to the tiny scrap of ICR it may generate with its minute grants, and then extract some ICR money from a science or engineering grant on top of that. In reality, the opposite is the case. At this particular public university, humanities and social science departments keep only a portion of their enrollment money, less than one-half and one-third, respectively. The sciences do somewhat better but are not at 100 percent. By comparison, engineering receives double its teaching workload money. The professional school receives closer to three times its workload money. Were this a medical school, the gap would be far larger—each student could receive six to ten times the allocation for the general campus student. It is worth reflecting on the lessons of column 4, and not just on the more familiar lesson of the final column.

The lessons of column 4 can be generalized as follows:[11] First, if these figures are at all typical, humanities and social sciences disciplines are not getting a piece of the science and engineering action, but are sending a piece of their action to the sciences and engineering. The human sciences cannot generate much external support, and thus depend largely on teaching revenue. They teach more courses than science faculty and conduct their research on the margins of their workweek and in many cases out of their own pockets. To make this situation worse, the university represented in Table 7 takes a portion of the human sciences teaching money and gives it to the sciences. In this case, this is not a small slice: it is half of the humanities instructional money and close to two-thirds of the social sciences money. Topping it all off, the university lets everyone think that the science and engineering fields that are getting such a large share of human science teaching revenues are in fact the generous if sometimes unhappy subsidizers of the "soft" fields. It appears that the humanities and social sciences are major donors to science and engineering budgets, while being told that they are actually living off those budgets. In other words, both dogmas about university research are wrong. In fact, science and engineering cost money, and humanities and social science teaching subsidize it.

Second, humanities and social science students receive a cheap education, one in which they get back less in terms of fees than they put in. Some of the differences *are* justified by the higher costs of instruction in fields like chemistry, which require laboratory equipment that fields like economics do not. (This is the number one retort to the analysis I have just offered, and it is true to a point: the costs of instruction are higher in bench sciences. But much of that difference is in *research* costs, and in any case this does not change the fact that the money arrow flows *to*, and not away from, science and engineering.) The "higher costs" rationale can and does slide over into justifications for sometimes gross inequalities in equipment, ones in which fields like music and art history cannot afford new practice instruments or digital projectors. The assumption developed over many years that the arts, humanities, and social sciences do not need great equipment comes to guarantee that they never have it. Their students learn to do without, and in the absence of some vital forms of technology, may learn less than they otherwise would. The myth of the science subsidy underwrites the second-class education that many if not most public university students receive in cultural and social disciplines.

Third, the arts, humanities, and social sciences are being underdeveloped relative to their social and even their financial capacity. The greater infrastructural costs in science and engineering should not be allowed to conceal the fact that the arts, humanities, and social sciences would be much stronger locally and nationally were they to keep more of "their" enrollment money. Drama and music departments, for example, tolerate dilapidated conditions that would be unthinkable in any self-respecting engineering department: first-rate soundstages, rehearsal areas, digital playback equipment, lighting, and a tripling of staff could turn a mediocre drama department into a national center of innovation in its field, and would in addition attract the kind of private philanthropy that more often flows into science and engineering. But a hierarchy of needs is ingrained in university culture. The humanities and social sciences generally ask for trickle-down funding from other divisions, even though much of that money was "theirs" to begin with.

I say all this *not* to foment class war between the arts and sciences. The disciplines are complementary, their faculty members largely agree on educational matters, and science and engineering research requires more, not less, funding to do what it needs to do. But, to sum up these points, we do need to realize the following: First, the common view that market-oriented fields earn while sociocultural fields take is false. Second, the humanities and the social sciences have a legitimate claim to a larger share of such a university's resources, even in market terms based on their earnings from their "customers," the students. Third, the sociocultural fields are direct financial contributors to the financial base for technological R & D and to technological progress as such. This contribution should be acknowledged and honored—and also correctly compensated.

Finally and most broadly, even the market power of the innovation system is being threatened by misplaced market values. By equating commercially oriented research in technology with profitability, and culture with cost, culture warriors helped obscure the budgetary reality that successful tech research depends on public subsidies—subsidies funneled in some significant part through teaching in cultural fields. Quite to the contrary, culture warriors helped persuade policy makers that public subsidy for basic research was not so necessary, since science, once given the incentive to produce for business, would more than pay for itself. Policy makers were happy to believe this tall tale, since it justified their continued cuts in public outlays for higher education. As a result, the country has been less prepared than it otherwise would have been to pay openly and publicly for the breakthrough science or the new industries that might have given it a step-function advantage over its global competitors. Marginalizing cultural study on ideological grounds and then obscuring its economic value, while simultaneously denying the central role of public life and public funding to economic progress, culture warriors shot their own economic goals in the foot. The culture wars fed the odd decadence of the current situation, in which hidden teaching subsidies in cultural fields veil the rot left behind by falling public support—even if only temporarily.

— 14 —

Half-Suffocated Reforms

Concerns about the university's business deals are as old as the university itself, but by the late 1990s they had become widespread. By that point, campuses seemed to have completed their fusion with the wider marketplace. Athletes had become human billboards for sporting goods companies while their coaches collected large endorsement fees. Campus centers had assumed most of the functions of suburban shopping malls. Student credit card debt came to grow as quickly as the size of ever-increasing student loans. A large portion of campus Internet traffic was devoted to consumer uses like downloading music files. Universities tried to attract the most affluent demographic by marketing themselves as prestige brands. In short, everyday student life seemed to be as much about buying stuff as it was about learning things. After two decades of public funding cuts, Bayh-Dole, and definitions of education as a private interest, commerce had moved from the edges to the core of the academic mission. Decades of the culture war had made alternative paradigms very difficult to imagine.

Lowered Resistance to Business

When they began to appear, the critiques of the late 1980s assumed a traditional polarity between academic and commercial goals. For example, the president of Yale University claimed that commercialization placed the faculty member at odds with his or her academic responsibilities. He described a systematic tension between "the private, proprietary corporation, whose norms are competition, efficiency, and 'profit maximization,' and whose goals are short-term, and the traditional university, which is non-profit and whose goals are intellectual, civic, and long-term." He claimed that "the burden of maintaining a teaching program and two separate research programs, where the results of one research program are to be widely disseminated and the results of the other may be required to be kept secret in the pursuit of economic success, is more than even the most responsible faculty member can be expected to bear."[1] As the 1990s advanced, more systematic research on university-industry ties began to appear: the landmark study *Academic Capitalism* nicely summarized an international cycle in which cutbacks in public funding increased the university's dependence on corporate funding, which encouraged universities to build up areas that corporations would support.[2]

But by that time, political and cultural alternatives to business governance had lost most of their prestige. The New Economy was in full swing, and the university's main constituency was a professional-managerial class (PMC) apparently committed to technological and market cures for all economic, social, cultural, physical, and even emotional problems. The 1980s authors had assumed that their audience would immediately accept and recognize a basic distinction between profit-driven commercialization and knowledge in the public interest. But this was exactly the distinction that the Reagan-Clinton era had all but erased. By the late 1990s, leaders and citizens alike appeared to assume that society's core function was to stimulate economic growth and that financial incentives were the most efficient stimulant. It was a short step from there to the belief that the "businessing" of the university would lead to the mutual enrichment of the university and society alike, again proving the world-historical greatness of American capitalism, the envy of the world. The commercialization of everything, especially technical knowledge, was what social theorist Louis Althusser might have called the spontaneous philosophy of the PMC.

This was a far cry from the traditional concern of educators, which had been to preserve the university's independence from society's rulers. This had meant freedom from the direct control of the church or the crown or an elected state authority or big labor or big business. It had meant freedom from any ruling ideology, for society's conventional wisdom blocked the pursuit of both truth and justice. In the period after World War II, university leaders were most concerned about the impact of the federal government on academic freedom. As I have noted in chapter 1, "The Three Crises and the Mass Middle Class, and chapter 10, "The Costs of Accounting," leaders of federally sponsored golden age-universities, like Clark Kerr, lamented that the university's "directions have not been set as much by [its] visions of its destiny as by the external environment, including the federal government, the foundations, the surrounding and sometimes engulfing industry."[3] As we saw in chapter 3, "The Discrediting of Social Equality," some of the conservative criticisms of the liberal university spoke not only for traditional canons and values but for the free play of intellect. As early as the 1970s, however, a more powerful threat appeared on the horizon, one that represented private rather than public interests. In chapter 2, "Declarations of Independence," I described how the paradigmatic "postmodernist" philosopher Jean-François Lyotard regretted that the intertwined pursuits of truth and emancipation had become increasingly subordinated to economic optimization.[4] The stated concern of all such analyses has been that the university could be subject to a social determinism that would destroy its core function, the creation of knowledge, since creation by its very nature can be subject to no pre-existing law. The only solution was for society to guarantee the university's intellectual independence even in the midst of its financial dependence. If society could not protect the university's academic freedom because society pushed too hard for an economic or ideological contribution, the university, properly speaking, would cease to exist.

We have traced the arguments whereby the culture wars knocked this historic defense of the university out of position, and it was natural enough for academic business to fill the breach. The new century brought a new wave of attempts to cope with the university's contradictory position as an independent partner for society, a society increasingly defined as commerce. These scholarly reactions to the university's twenty-first century predicament marked the beginning of a new consensus about realistic university reforms. These books and articles made for an interesting kind of mystery reading. There was plenty of evidence of unsavory institutional environments suggesting major crimes to come. But there were no dead bodies, and only a hint of smoke from a gun.

The reform consensus started from a now-familiar doctrine: American capitalism is here to stay, and in any case it has always been the university's environment. There is therefore no point in expecting a clean break between higher education and the marketplace. At the same time, the university's core mission is noncommercial and not-for-profit. To pursue its educational mission, the university cannot be a business; 1990s demands to make the university resemble corporations failed to grasp how universities work. Even as the university must work with business, and acknowledge that it can learn much from the best business practices, educational goals should remain distinct from commercial ones. The university and business are partners that should not fuse, neighbors that need good fences, friends that must remember that opposites attract. The reform consensus gave up on a categorical contrast between academic and economic goals while insisting that the university and society could agree on strategic differences based on mutual respect.

But what policies would arise from this general model? What practices would ensue? Would business and academics govern the university together? One limited occurrence—when the Swiss pharmaceutical company Novartis placed its representatives on a research board in the College of Natural Resources at UC Berkeley in exchange for multiyear funding—had turned into the textbook picture of what *not* to do. How would the partnerships evolve when the New Economy crashed?[5]

Three quite good books encapsulated the elements of this consensus as it wrested with new particulars.[6] I examine the strengths but also the conceptual weaknesses common to these books, which are really the weaknesses of a college-educated middle-class culture faced with a culture-war's market ideology that has served and, at the same time, undermined that class. The culture-wars framework pressured these authors to perpetuate the market conditions that they critiqued and, it is worth seeing how these very good authors held up.

The Market and Its Failures

Of these three representative works, David L. Kirp's *Shakespeare, Einstein, and the Bottom Line* wins the award for best title.[7] This book also offered the moment's best survey of market-led changes across the full range of educational settings. The modern university has been compared to a medium-sized city, and Kirp's book was a primer in the staggering variety of functions in which the contemporary university is involved. It had chapters on undergraduate admissions, business schools, distance learning, Web-based humanities consortia, university-industry research collaborations, law schools, and much more. In each case, Kirp described a "business vocabulary [that] reinforces businesslike ways of thinking." In most cases, he suggested that business improves some functions while damaging others. In the book's parting shot, he said that universities have made deals that only Faust could love.

One of Kirp's best examples of the Faustian bargain was the response of the Darden School of Business at the University of Virginia to continual cutbacks in state support. Originally, one educator notes, the state university had a deal with the public: "In return for financial support from the taxpayers, these universities would keep tuition low and provide broad access, train graduate and professional students, promote arts and culture, help solve local problems, and perform ground-breaking research."[8] As we have seen, states had on average reduced their share of public universities' operating expenses by around 30 percent since the early 1980s. Those units that could follow the money did exactly that, and no unit was in a better position to do this than the university's business school.

At Virginia, the Darden business school had responded in a variety of ways. It increased its tuition base by expanding the size of its classes. It expanded the resources it devoted to fund-raising. It fought to reduce its contribution to the overall university's infrastructure, helping to increase the gap between rich and poor units in the university. It expanded its lucrative executive education program, and at least informally required most faculty to participate in it. The business school allowed some portion of this instruction to be proprietary, in violation of traditional academic standards of open publication. Darden faculty also appeared to do less research than their peers at similar schools, as they shifted some of their professional activity into preparing executive seminars that not incidentally paid them at much higher rates than did their regular courses.

We could add three other concerns about this arrangement to Kirp's long list: Customized, pricey corporate seminars were likely to tell their paying customers what they wanted to hear, casting doubt on the academic freedom of the enterprise and the quality of the knowledge produced. Such seminars siphoned much of their proprietary material from the public domain, making them vehicles of a dubious privatization of intellectual property. Finally, executive education allowed wealthy businesses and businesspeople to bypass public education altogether, making them even less likely than they already were to support public education with their tax contributions. Of course, few businesspeople pay for continuing education in the conscious hope of hearing flattering propaganda, but suspicions about the product and its apparatus reached a pitch of tragic irony when Kirp cited a letter from the University of Virginia's founder, Thomas Jefferson, complaining as though it were yesterday that legislators "do not generally possess information enough to perceive the important truths, that knowledge is power, that knowledge is safety, and that knowledge is happiness."[9] Kirp concluded this chapter with the crucial question: "Can a university maintain the intellectual world that

Thomas Jefferson sought to represent in his design of the Lawn—professors and students with diverse academic interests coming together in a single open space to pursue and create knowledge—if learning becomes just another consumer good?"[10]

Eric Gould raised similar questions in his book *The University in a Corporate Culture*. While Kirp was a policy professor at a large public university, Gould was an English professor with an understandable interest in giving the liberal arts something important to do. He saw corporate culture as a challenge to the university and especially to what he called democratic liberal education in John Dewey's sense. Early on, Gould presented the calling card of the reform consensus, namely, treating the current form of capitalism as a determinant fact of life. "The search for important knowledge in technoscience is not going to slow down. University bureaucracies are not going to look less like corporate bureaucracies in the future. Students are not going to cease to search for credentials for the workplace. Neither are they going to have fewer problems financing their education. Discipline-based knowledge in the arts and sciences is not going to become less professionalized. The old ideal of a liberal education as something that is pursued for its own sake is most unlikely to have a revival." Gould showed how the capitalist university was devoted to economic functionality, and at one point he provided a particularly good summary of this operation's major components: "quality management criteria and strategies drawn from the world of business; an emphasis on marketing, visibility, and public image promotion; accounting concerns for contribution margins and the perennial cost effectiveness of learning; decentralized power structures with incentives for growth and gain-share revenues; the redistribution of labor—in this case away from tenured to part-time and adjunct faculty; the development of sophisticated ancillary products, patents, and services; a vague rhetoric of excellence that replaces specific details of what an education is about, and, of course, research and other financial collaborations with the corporate world."[11]

One of Gould's best examples was the tuition spiral.[12] For most of the twentieth century, universities—especially public universities—tried to minimize tuition costs in order to maximize public access. It was hoped that every qualified person could go to college without regard to his or her ability to pay. Academic qualifications trumped financial ones, and the role of financial aid was to bridge the gap between educational cost and student income. As we saw in chapter 11, "The Problem with Privatization," the college admissions office has become an important component in the institution's overall financial strategy, where tuition rates, financial aid, and even admissions themselves have become weapons in the college's competition with its peers for the most desirable students.

Gould's crucial point was that even on its own terms this market system does not work properly. Tuition costs—growing at about ten times the rate of family income between the mid-1970s and the mid-1990s—have never stopped rising at well above the rate of overall inflation and have done as much damage to the university's image as culture-wars attacks on "tenured radicals" and their ilk. The damage is clear when we consider the impact of rising tuition on student finances: Nellie Mae, the student-loan provider, "found that the average student-loan debt had more than doubled" between 1991 and 1997; in addition, "the average credit card debt for the class of 2002 was over $3,000."[13] In that year, "39 percent of students [were] graduating with 'unmanageable levels of student loan debt' "; for African American and Hispanic students, the levels were 55 percent and 58 percent, respectively.[14] To keep things at even this low level of control, four-fifths of all undergraduates work in college, one-third of them full-time, the other two-thirds an average of twenty-five hours a week. Other reports have suggested that educational debt levels have reached the point that they are forcing graduates out of public service and into income-maximizing posts in the private sector, regardless of the actual goals or values of the graduates.[15] As funding levels drop, many states are seeing declines in college participation rates; overall, the United States was thirteenth in college participation rates among industrialized nations in 2000, and its position has worsened somewhat since.[16]

Ironically, the victims of the university's tuition and admissions strategies include not only students and the public but the university itself. Department of Education statistics covering the same time frame—the mid-1970s to the mid-1990s—show that an incredible 400 percent increase in charges for tuition, room, and board translated into "a modest 32 percent increase in current-fund expenditures per student."[17] What is the source of this enormous gap between the university's gross and net increases in income? Apparently, less than we assume went into administrative growth, and a bit more into research. "The major area of expenditure growth was in financial aid (scholarships and fellowships) to students, which increased fivefold in public universities and sevenfold in private universities."[18] Universities have been boosting tuition and also boosting financial aid, resulting in an increasing number of students attending college at a discount off the actual cost of their education. "For every dollar colleges have tacked on to tuition since 1990, they have kept just 46 cents."[19] The combination of high tuition and high financial aid may allow universities to use well-off students to subsidize poorer ones. But it is also used to chase the small pool of highly qualified and affluent students who are given aid on the basis of "merit" rather than "need." "Thus," Gould concluded, "we have the curious situation in which most families—probably three-quarters of those with children attending or seeking to attend college—have to borrow money to send their children to institutions that are in turn struggling to keep their discount levels at 30 percent."[20]

Gould correctly concluded that the ultimate culprit was the market model of unregulated competition for the "best" students. "So long as we insist on promoting higher education as a relatively unregulated market system, modeled on the corporate marketplace, the rich will get richer and the poor poorer, a number of schools will die off or reduce their quality, and there will be fewer places for the growing number of students."[21]

Taking Kirp and Gould together, readers could come to a remarkable conclusion. Market forces endangered the academic mission of the university, *and* they endangered the financial health that markets were supposed to help. The culture-wars veneration of markets was not improving the university's control of its finances, but undermining it.

The Dangers of Financial Interest

This brings us to Derek Bok, president emeritus of a school unlikely to succumb in any Darwinian market struggle, Harvard University. He was nonetheless as vexed as the other two authors. He began *Universities in the Marketplace* by noting that commerce was once "largely confined to the periphery of campus life: to athletic programs and, in a few institutions, to correspondence schools and extension programs. Today, opportunities to make money from intellectual work are pursued throughout the university by professors of computer science, biochemistry, corporate finance, and numerous other departments."[22] Bok gave great credit to market forces—at times bending over backward to show his respect—and also claimed that there was little hard evidence that financial interests have changed academic standards or the direction of research.[23] And yet he shared the consensus view that a clear distinction must be made between commercial and educational goals. Education has always been concerned with "helping to develop virtue and build character" and develop a practical ethics. The reason Princeton should not put a banner that says "Things Go Better with Coke" over Nassau Hall is that selling goods conflicts with pursuing education: "Such a message would be damaging to students and demoralizing for many members of the faculty who believe that their academic careers and the institution where they work stand for aims and ideals that transcend money."[24] I have discussed the impact of market theory on the costs of research in the previous two chapters.

Bok offered an especially good account of the market's shaping of research directions. While corporate support remained less than 10 percent of the total support for academic research, it had a glamour, an intensity, and a financial potential that swelled its influence in the unending quest for funds. Faculty who have corporate support are more than twice as likely "to be influenced by commercial considerations in choosing their research topics."[25] Business makes the most money off proprietary knowledge, meaning knowledge that allows a firm to avoid competing with many similar versions of the same product; as a result, corporate partners routinely request publication delays and confidentiality with university personnel that can suppress the open circulation of research knowledge.[26] In addition, research tools and materials in the biological sciences are the corporate property of individual firms, and these firms have sometimes required researchers to sign secrecy and patent agreements that give the owners of materials "reach-through" rights to intellectual property created with those materials. Since the Bayh-Dole legislation requires university employees to assign title of any inventions over to their (nonprofit) university employers, such transfer agreements can create serious and expensive legal conflicts.

Even as they are expected to set an example for their faculty employees and enforce federal law, universities may also steer research toward money rather than knowledge. In one particularly pointed passage, Bok wrote,

> Columbia, Duke, and several other medical schools have formed consortia to bid for contracts from pharmaceutical firms to test new drugs. In many cases, the principal purpose is not to secure opportunities for cutting-edge research, but rather to earn money that can be used for other purposes. Schools that benefit in this way clearly have a financial stake in retaining the business of the companies whose products they test. To that extent,

they have an incentive to avoid results that will disappoint their corporate sponsors. Nevertheless, like individual investigators, medical schools seem unwilling to admit that their financial interests could possibly affect the results of research performed within their walls.[27]

Here Bok summarized the logic of the financial incentives that shape the business of science. Each actor behaves rationally, and usually with good intentions, but the system's alleged invisible hand leads, not necessarily but quite possibly in at least some cases, to misdirected, unnecessary, or tainted research. As Bok noted rather witheringly, "Scientists with corporate ties naturally deny that financial interests will have any effect on their scientific work. Nevertheless, a number of investigators have shown that researchers reporting on the efficacy of drugs produced by companies in which they have an interest are more likely to report favorable results than scientists without such ties. Other studies have shown that clinical trials funded by drug companies are far less likely than independently funded trials to arrive at unfavorable conclusions."[28] These studies were not widely known even among academic scientists, nor were they warmly received. But such studies are now routinely detecting major statistical anomalies in privately funded research.[29]

Bok returned several times to the practices of medical schools, where the potential for abuse was arguably the most advanced. The American health industry is troubled, to put it mildly, by lagging health outcomes at enormous cost compared to other industrialized countries.[30] Medicine was the origin of the "social trusteeship" model of professionalism, a tradition stretching back to the Hippocratic oath, but it may be the profession that has become the most completely suffused with commercial factors. The ethical stakes are very high, for in contrast to other commercialized fields like engineering and law, medical faculty work directly with human subjects. Bok mentioned the best-known case at that time, that of Jesse Gelsinger, a patient at the University of Pennsylvania who died in the course of a gene therapy trial conducted by an institute whose director had a large and undisclosed financial stake in the company that funded the research.[31] Bok showed that this kind of practice reflects the wall-to-wall presence of drug and other health corporations in medical education. "Fortunately," he observed, "universities have not yet allowed companies to tout their products in campus classrooms."[32] "Not *yet*" is the operative phrase, and once again Bok's overview is worth quoting at length.

At the periphery of the educational process, however, advertisers wait like predators circling a herd of cattle and occasionally manage to pick off some careless member that strays too far from the group.

The clearest example has occurred in medical schools where large pharmaceutical firms and medical supply companies have become very wealthy at a time when traditional sources of funding for medical education have tended to dry up. These trends have created a vacuum major corporations are all too willing to fill. By now, corporate representatives commonly recommend speakers paid for at company expense and help shape the content and format of continuing education courses by giving ample subsidies that help medical schools operate their programs at a profit. These practices are clearly worrisome. Although the lecturers subsidized by industrial sponsors may be accomplished faculty members and the quality of the programs is often high, speakers paid for by a pharmaceutical firm and selected from an approved company list cannot be assumed to be as objective and disinterested as university instructors ought to be.[33]

Commercial considerations could in this way modify the professional judgment of practicing physicians. Bok noted too that commerce has also influenced the shape of medical research and scientific knowledge. "Pharmaceutical companies naturally tend to support programs on diseases commonly treated with expensive drugs. Although the presentations may not tout any particular product, they do promote the use of an entire class of drugs. Moreover, subsidized programs seldom emphasize preventative measures and other alternatives to drug treatments. In these ways, the subsidized programs can be slanted not by what they put in but by what they leave out."[34]

In spite of these serious problems, the economic environment discouraged reforms. Though medical schools could always create their own more balanced programs, "subsidized programs tend to win out. This is particularly likely when schools treat continuing medical education as a profit center to finance other faculty activities."[35] Reforms were made even less likely by the obstinacy of many science faculty and administrators. Even measured criticisms like Bok's, backed by statistical evidence derived from large samples, were usually met with blanket assertions that financial incentives could not and do not affect the scientific method.

This impenetrable, outmoded objectivism was the real beneficiary of the "science wars" branch of the culture wars. Alan Sokal and his allies may have believed that they were defending the scientific basis of progressive enlightenment. But the more important effect of their success was to damage the kind of historical and contextual arguments, whether coming from epistemological radicals or from worried university presidents, that could demonstrate the impact of financial interests on scientific knowledge. These important books on university reform have been forced to proceed without the benefit of public respect for qualitative and contextual analysis. They have nonetheless successfully described a wounded if not a dead body, and, in the form of financial interests, smoke if not a gun.

The Limits of the New Consensus

We now arrive at the larger question of how best to respond to the chronic, escalating crisis in university affairs. The reform consensus that emerged from books like these implied that the best opening move was to pay more critical attention to the main problem areas. Medical schools, business schools, and undergraduate admissions were at the top of the candidate list for an ongoing and thorough assessment of the impact of business practices on higher education. A fourth trouble spot was for-profit distance learning, though this was more thoroughly treated by other authors, most critically by David Noble, and has not taken off as once expected. Another utterly central problem has been the explosive growth of the adjunct and part-time teaching force, though this was also more thoroughly treated by other authors and publications, such as the journal *Social Text*.

Another move was regulatory, and it is interesting to note that the author with the warmest words for market mechanisms, Derek Bok, also called for the most direct crackdown on market abuses. He recommended that researchers disclose the financial interests that support their work even when federal and other regulations do not require them to do so. Financial disclosure policies are becoming more common in professional journals, and though this trend will probably continue, these policies are resisted by many faculty members.

Bok also noted a limitation to the disclosure rule: "Repeated disclosure of financial conflicts may deepen the public's suspicions about the objectivity of academic research and thereby place universities and their scientists and scholars under a cloud."[36] He thus took the opportunity to suggest something stronger: "Universities should flatly prohibit their scientists from performing research on human subjects if the work is supported by companies in which the researchers have significant financial interests, whether from consulting arrangements, gifts, retainers, or stockholdings."[37] Although such reforms can disadvantage academic scientists, they would help generate higher industry-wide ethical standards and protect the integrity of academic research.

The reform consensus thus brings us to this point: it accepts the primacy of the market in American life and education but calls for regulation of market interests in the creation of knowledge. It makes valid suggestions for how to do this. But at this point the three representatives I discuss here arrived at the end of the line. The authors were aware of this, for they were quite pessimistic about the possibility of getting reforms of market forces to go even this far. Much of the problem was the absence of powerful interests pushing such reforms. Students could not be relied on to preserve academic goals, either because they were too inexperienced or too careerist to care. Faculty— at least those with influence in science, technology, and medicine—turned out to be not so much champions of scholarly values as willing and sometimes arrogant commercializers, pressuring administrators and staff to bend the rules that protect the university's interests.

It is striking how often faculty who in general favor conflict-of-interest laws in public life have been unwilling to apply similar standards to themselves. As Bok noted, the National Institutes of Health diluted its news disclosure rules in 1989 when faculty strenuously objected, and that pattern has repeated itself regularly since. The case of tobacco companies' sponsorship of research on their products is a case in point. No industry has a longer, more reprehensible, more proven, or more penalized reputation for the deliberate distortion of research results on the health effects of its tobacco products. Individuals, groups, and governments have won a large number of judgments against these companies, which was made easier by the discovery of documents showing conspiracy to mislead the public going back at least to 1953.[38] In 2006, U.S. District Court Judge Gladys Kessler handed down a racketeering conviction of tobacco-company research organizations such as the Council for Tobacco Research and the Center for Indoor Air Research in *United States of America v. Philip Morris, Inc. et al.*[39] The University of California Academic Senate got involved in this issue when a unit at UC San Diego, in a majority vote, banned its members from accepting funding from tobacco-related sponsors and the ban was overturned by university officials, which meant that faculty could not vote to restrict their own members from accepting tobacco-related sponsors. A wide faculty Senate majority endorsed the idea that academic freedom meant that faculty could not impose a ban on taking research money from proven research defrauders.

After the racketeering conviction, the Regents considered passing a university-wide ban, and the Senate again voted to oppose a ban on tobacco money. The Regents replaced the ban with a disclosure rule, to which most Senate faculty continued to object. While such situations have been complicated by the fact that regulations do impose partial restrictions on a researcher's academic activity, this kind of prohibitionist stance raised the obvious question of whether faculty would accept restrictions on money from other industries where the evidence of research fraud is strong but not quite so overwhelming, and where the stakes are even larger—the impact of petroleum use on global climate change is a clear example. Given faculty hostility to regulation, even when coming from other faculty and in situations where research distortion has been shown, our three authors were right to assume that reforms would not emerge readily from faculty groups.[40]

In the absence of an established reform constituency, Bok, Gould, and Kirp retreated to a conceptual solution in which they themselves did not wholly believe, and that was a foundational contrast between commercial and academic values. Kirp, for example, offered a fascinating chapter on Dickinson College, whose new president began remaking this liberal arts college by hiring an "enrollment manager" with the power to trespass on faculty turf (like the curriculum) if it would improve financial outcomes, and by hiring a marketing consultant, who redefined the college's image with whatever he found out from focus groups. But in fact the commercial barbarians decided that the college's values are "Freedom + Guidance = Growth," which could best be expressed in the slogan "Reflecting America, Engaging the World." The new regime decided to renew "the link between liberal learning and the world outside Carlisle [Pennsylvania]," to start programs to send their students all over the country and the world, and to develop "citizen-leaders" by "crossing borders" and becoming more representative of the U.S. population. The least one can say is that the marketing professionals ended up sounding more like the democratic humanist philosopher John Dewey than did the academic philosophers Kirp quoted, for the marketers appeared to reject the classical bourgeois contrast between liberal and practical knowledge, and they set the college on a more progressive liberal arts trajectory than it had pursued before.

Kirp also had a pair of chapters on New York University and its apparently successful efforts, as one observer put it, to "spend [its] way into high society." Kirp claimed that these advocates of the "star search" strategy had plenty of stars to be crass about. He also observed that bulk purchases of stars means the great exploitation of adjuncts: "Twenty-seven hundred adjuncts, almost the same in number as the tenure-ladder faculty, teach 70 percent of the undergraduate classes, a figure considerably higher than at comparable universities" (34). Undergraduates recruited to study with stars are subjected to a "bait and switch" in which their actual instructors turn out to be usually dedicated but always overworked "permatemps," as these instructors came to be known under eerily similar circumstances at Microsoft.

Certainly NYU's administrators and trustees were primarily responsible for this situation, but so were its humanist faculty. The stars of the philosophy department, for example, implemented a system that term after term minimized their contact with undergraduate students; the use of adjuncts and graduate students for this instructional work was central to their recruitment of additional stars. This group came off as an oblivious academic gentry, far more concerned with the politics of their colleagues than with the exploitation of younger philosophers in their own departments. They appeared consumed by a self-interest so narrow that it threatened their ability to perpetuate their own profession. The humanists in Kirp's chapter on the University of Chicago were similarly dogmatic and disappointing.

While NYU's "academia" faltered, its "commerce" glittered. The dean of NYU law school was the author of something called "A Commercialist Manifesto," whose slogan was, "We are a business, deal with it. . . . Go to the market and create greatness."[41] These were words that he lived by, and at previous jobs, Kirp reported, this dean ended a free law clinic's pro bono policies and tried to name Florida's leading public law school after a successful trial lawyer in exchange for a $10 million donation. And yet, for Kirp, this dean's effect on NYU was largely positive. "An entrepreneurship that defies the conventions of legal education," he noted, "isn't necessarily antithetical to academic excellence."[42] The dean himself came off as a cutting-edge humanist. We do not only care about our ranking, he said, for we tried to "create a niche outside the hierarchy, as the place where you do cool things."[43] His goal, he said, was "making the world a better place through law. This capacity to look for ideas, to find contingently right answers—that's what the money goes to support." We might note the additional irony that Kirp had no stories of abusive labor practices at NYU's law school. The field that was closer to the market was on the surface farther from academic labor exploitation. For the humanities, the case was the reverse, with an apparently corrosive effect on the social intelligence of its faculty.

We do not need to take the commercialist dean's manifesto at face value in order to identify the core problem with the reform consensus. It wanted to limit the impact of market forces on the academic mission, and yet it accepted the market as inevitable and irresistible. It knew that commercial and educational goals were not simple opposites, and yet it defended education by contrasting it with commerce, and at the same time it, would say that commerce was good or at least inevitable. The consensus pointed toward a case-by-case evaluation of this or that academic activity with this or that set of academic and industrial partners, and the rejection of categorical a priori judgments was a genuine advance. And yet the consensus could offer no replacement principles by which hybrid activities might be judged. After thirty years of financial pressure, and fifteen years of culture wars, nonmarket fields had no vision for higher learning that was better or at least different from that of their market competition. What problems could be solved by research that rested on public funding? What kinds of discoveries needed not to be patented? What issues required well-funded and highly sophisticated qualitative methods that led to new cultural knowledge? What kinds of cultural capabilities did the university need to develop, and what unique good would they do? Even the classic issues of the postwar period—international conflict resolution, race relations, democratic accountability, economic equality—were little more than names lacking vital academic content. And they were as likely to appear in presidential education commission reports and on the Web sites of Republican senators as in the official positions of academic senates.

The reform consensus overstated the internal coherence of capitalism and thus its inevitability. It understated the university's nonmarket value. This consensus was itself an intellectual effect of the culture wars, of a reduced cultural capability that has meant we are less able think beyond the boundaries of market thinking.

This was not an abstract failing, for the university in the 2000s was more than ever in need of elements that markets did not support. Public universities needed past cuts in per capita general funding reversed, and markets did not support that. Universities needed new types of public engagement with the academic research that its practitioners controlled, and markets would not help that. Universities needed to restore respect for their collaborative processes and their traditional commons of shared resources, and markets were opposed to that. Universities needed to reverse their increasing dependence on temporary, adjunct, and student instruction, and markets would block that. Universities need to reverse decades of affirmative action fiascos and move steadily toward racial equality, and markets were certainly not helping with that.

The logic of the situation suggested that universities would decide to jump the market fences and try something else. And yet even their best thinkers held back.

— IV —

The New War—and After

— 15 —

The Blame-Academia Crowd:
Culture War After 9/11

What happened to the culture wars in the 2000s? They spread and intensified in the political sphere, as various Republican masterminds kept voters'
attention focused on one values-related liberal outrage after another. Gay
marriage and the Terri Schiavo euthanasia case joined perennial standards
like abortion and affirmative action in maintaining the political polarization that remained the Right's best chance to control the large social majority from its minority position. The academic front also saw more than its
share of action. Veteran culture warriors like Lynne Cheney used the attacks
of September 11, 2001, as a springboard for a renewed round of accusations
against universities as such.

Triumph and Danger

In the political sphere, the contested 2000 presidential election led to a con-
clusive triumph for the hardworking network of right-wing activists that
had been aiming toward that kind of victory for several decades. A conservative majority at the top of the judicial branch gave the executive branch to
a Republican candidate whose political machine was fully interconnected
with a conservative infrastructure—including the Federalist Society—that
included several of the justices who formed that majority. By Inauguration
Day 2001, culture warriors had control of all three branches of the federal
government and the majority of the nation's governorships and state legislature, extensive power on the local level, and the ability to frame major
media discussions of economic and social issues. "Free market" principles
were by then well-established national and journalistic common sense.
Forms of social development that did not rely solely on market mechanisms

had to prove themselves in the face of categorical skepticism that felt free to dismiss specific evidence.

What followed George W. Bush's inauguration is well known. The new president revived the Reagan-era tax-cut politics that the Clinton administration had interrupted or softened, revived Reagan-era attacks on public services, revived Reagan-era business and environmental deregulation, and revived enduring right-wing cultural themes, which were implemented in such forms as escalated attacks on lesbian and gay "lifestyles," renewed efforts to block family planning at home and abroad, and the steering of unprecedented amounts of public funds toward "faith-based" organizations.[1] Before the end of the Bush administration's first year, the September 11 attacks on the World Trade Center and the Pentagon prompted the declaration of a war on terror, the invasions of Afghanistan and then Iraq, exploding war expenditures, a booming federal deficit, and an economic recession, all of which coincided with further tax cuts that disproportionately favored top income brackets and additional cuts to the public infrastructural basis of general development—higher education, local health care, and the like. State budgets suffered all over the country, and public universities saw their funds take their second serious hit in a decade, in some cases experiencing reductions of 25 percent.[2] Economic inequality increased at an intensified rate.

The Bush II era represented the integration of all three dimensions of the culture wars on the new majoritarian America of the postwar era. We can recall these dimensions in the form of a summary table (see Table 8). All the challenges persisted in a way that alarmed much of the Right. The U.S. population was more multiracial than ever before, reflecting the fact that the U.S. economy was more dependent than ever on immigrant labor from Asia and Latin America. The electorate continued to harbor strong majoritarian assumptions, and the dot-com era had convinced the college-educated middle classes yet again that they would inherit the economy. Brain workers were the new "productive class," and the Right had to remain vigilant lest this class go beyond its support for the Bill Clintons of the world, start to sympathize with displaced blue-collar workers, and begin to vote again for more expensive public services that might retrain, reactivate, and develop the entire society. Though market ideology was firmly in control, its advocates were always concerned that obvious market failures abroad (Russia, Argentina) and economically successful "social states" elsewhere (Germany, Japan, Sweden, and in a different way, China) would lead to revisions in official market thinking

Table 8 The culture wars in three dimensions

Domain	Epoch-making challenge	Middle-class bulwark	Emerging nonconservative middle class
Politics	Multiracial mass democracy	Expert rule; no power sharing	Majoritarian democracy via antielitist meritocracy (meritocracy II)
Economy	Decline of profits, rise of knowledge-workers	Market-led growth, interpreted by financial interests	Planned mixed-economy; mass affluence via valuing of labor and public systems
Culture	Civil rights "science"-movements rooted in qualitative, context-specific, cross-cultural knowledge	White or "West" supremacism in the form of cultural hierarchy	Cultural and social equality leading to "human development"

at home. The same was true of rising insecurity and of the continuing decline of labor conditions for manufacturing and even many service workers: would these chickens ever come home to roost? More subtly, the collaborative networks of college-educated people had worked wonders in the business world: would these expand into some rethinking of politics? Although the civil rights movement seemed dormant, partner benefits for gay couples were quietly spreading through corporate America, and the prospect of gay marriage was a constant reminder to conservatives that they did not control the culture in the same way that they could control the government.

Economic Interests on the Academic Front

For culture warriors, academic knowledge continued to be a problem. During the Bush II administration, cultural scholars, those time-honored culture-war targets, were joined in the crosshairs by scientists. Although the "science wars" offshoot of the mid-1990s had been important, it had attacked not scientific knowledge but socially minded interpretations of science coming from cultural scholars. The new targets were the scientists themselves; those who came under fire in the 2000s worked on climate change, missile defense systems, stem-cell research, sexually transmitted diseases, and many other topics. As the Bush administration got fully under way, scientists found the membership of professional review committees altered, report contents changed or suppressed, and in some cases their data requested, challenged, and denounced in congressional hearings.[3] The targeted scientists appeared to share only research findings that challenged the conventional wisdom that underwrote major Republican constituencies such as the petroleum and defense industries, which did not welcome academic results regarding climate change, human rights, or international law, or right-wing Christian organizations, which did not like academic research on human reproduction, abortion, sexuality, or discrimination law.

The military was a pillar of Republican strength, but even here the university intruded. The university conducted much defense research, including a great number of the military's most advanced projects. Some work that seemed quite remote from weapons development nonetheless had military applications and received military funding.[4] The funding encouraged faculty and universities to maintain their relationships with military agencies, although these relations were never too popular with the faculty as a whole. Given the obvious conflict between open research and military secrecy, and between the university's liberal culture and most U.S. military interventions, why would the government not conduct classified research in its own laboratories, where it could maintain high degrees of secrecy and security, and then subcontract major functions to private companies with extensive security capacities and no history of political or intellectual independence? As it turned out, the Bush administration came up with a business solution to this problem.

One of the universities most involved in defense research was the University of California, and it had honed explanations for this involvement during the decades that it had exclusive control over three national weapons laboratories, including the one at Los Alamos, New Mexico, that had developed the atomic bomb and had remained centrally involved in enhancing and multiplying U.S. nuclear stockpiles in subsequent years. UC generally defended its management of the labs by saying that its world-class expertise in the underlying science guaranteed the quality and integrity of the defense work. But it also argued that academic freedom made a difference too, and the government sometimes chimed in on this topic. For example, a commission convened by the secretary of energy claimed:

[T]here is an independence of thought at the [university-run] laboratories that allows the staff to speak freely, to propose new ideas and to oppose what they perceive as an unwise course of action advocated by others.

It is manifested by such things as testimony to Congress and advice to the Executive Branch of the government that are independently formulated; technical breakthroughs in weapons safety before such need was officially identified; and the refusal by the laboratories to follow instructions blindly. We believe such qualities to be of long-term benefit to the nation. Their preservation is clearly associated, in large part, with the University environment, in the judgment of people both inside and outside the laboratories. We concur.[5]

The university and its governmental partners repeatedly maintained that the university presence assured not only the best expertise but also intellectual freedom and professional independence from economic and political interests.[6]

The Bush administration effectively ended this tradition for two of the three national laboratories when it rebid the contracts for the Los Alamos and Livermore labs with the new requirement that any university applicant take on industrial partners who would be primarily responsible for lab security. The University of California took on three such partners: Bechtel, BWX Technologies,* and Washington Group International,† all of whom had experience as military contractors and expertise with nuclear materials. The partners formed a limited liability corporation called the Los Alamos Nuclear Security (LANS) LLC, and did indeed win the contract to take over the management of the Los Alamos laboratories from the University of California. Although university officials continued to insist that their management of laboratory science would carry on the labs' traditional intellectual mission, the Los Alamos scientists were now in fact corporate employees who answered to an LLC lab director who in turn answered to a governing board that did not report to anyone in the university administration.[7] The lab's intellectual property (IP) was signed over to the new corporation, ongoing pension obligations were assumed by the Department of Energy, and the majority of the laboratory management fees were to go to Bechtel and the other corporations. The university remained the most visible partner,

---

* now part of Babcock & Wilcox.
† now part of URS Corporation.

and continued to be named in press coverage of environmental problems and of plans to manufacture a new generation of nuclear weapons at Los Alamos. But a federal laboratory and the long-term public investment it represented had in effect been privatized: its operations were now controlled by a for-profit limited liability corporation to which the university belonged, its IP had been absorbed into business operations, and its independent scientists were now answerable to LLC managers.

The LLC contract was itself a symptomatic violation of academic standards of open publication, being declared a trade secret by the company and withheld from most of the university's administration and from its Academic Senate until well after the negotiations were complete and the LANS LLC had been in operation for nearly a year. In the Spring of 2007, the Academic Senate's Committee on the National Laboratories was dismayed to learn that the DOE contract had a no-exit clause, and that it would likely require the accelerated manufacture of nuclear pits for next generation warheads. News of this no-exit clause had apparently been withheld from top university officials, including the president. Whatever its long-term outcome, the change in the status of Los Alamos symptomatized the ascent of market over academic powers, the injection of the profit motive into the heart of national security science. The change was a minor but functionally important triumph for the long-standing efforts of culture warriors to subordinate the university to political and economic forces. It was another example of the culture wars at work far from their supposedly native ground of affirmative action controversies, Western Civ courses, and the like. And the LLC contract showed how subtle culture-wars moves could be, for almost no one in the university even realized that Los Alamos was no longer their lab, or that independent faculty oversight had been gutted.

Bush conservatives were quite consistent in their efforts to reaffirm executive authority over the three areas we have discussed—cultural relations, business affairs, and politics. Reinforcing top-down authority had long been a central goal and genuine accomplishment of the culture wars. The main energy was spent on the broader political front,[8] but the culture warriors never forgot for long about academia. Even as the government needed the research university for the military and civilian technology that would keep it on top in the world, the university embodied three central counterpropositions that we have examined: cross-cultural negotiation and equality, the compatibility of broad meritocracy and majoritarian economics, and the priority of knowledge work to political authority, usually called academic freedom. Throughout the early 2000s, the Right was in need of a broad strategy for weakening these tendencies in relation to executive authority. It found that strategy right after 9/11, and maintained it throughout the Bush II administration.

The Un-American University

On November 11, 2001, a previously obscure but extremely well-connected conservative organization, the American Council of Trustees and Alumni (ACTA), published a report entitled "Defending Civilization: How Our Universities Are Failing America and What Can Be Done About It." The body of the report was eight pages long, and about half of that consisted of quotations. The rest of the report comprised an appendix with two main sections, one called "Public Responses" (to 9/11) and the other "Campus Responses." Each section consisted of statements from various individuals. The entirety of the "Public Responses" section, less than a page in length, came from President Bush, senate Republican leader Trent Lott (joined by Democrat leader Thomas Daschle), and New York's Republican mayor Rudolph Giuliani. By associating these statements with a New York Times/CBS poll (September 25, 2001) that found that 92 percent of respondents thought that "Americans Should Take Military Action Even If Casualties Occur," the report suggested that these leaders represented the general public position. While the "Public Responses" were the carefully prepared statements of a select handful of top officials, the "Campus Voices" consisted of 115 extracts taken from Web sites, student newspapers, daily newspaper editorials, and the like. These all appeared to quote statements made to crowds at public rallies, letters to the editor, and other similar sources. None seem to have been uttered by a professor or a student during class.

The "Public Responses" claimed that it was not only America that was under attack, but humanity, democracy, and freedom itself. They also claimed that we already knew everything we needed to know about the situation, and could act accordingly. The key statement came from then-mayor of New York Rudolph Giuliani: "We're right and they're wrong. It's as simple as that. . . . The era of moral relativism between those who practice or condone terrorism, and those nations who stand up against it, must end. Moral relativism does not have a place in this discussion and debate."[9] Thanks to the work of the culture wars and their ideological apparatuses, Giuliani could simply refer to and lament the "fact" of pervasive moral relativism, so self-evident had the culture wars rendered it by 2001.

"Campus Reponses," on the other hand, ranged from questions, skepticism, and historical contextualizations of the 9/11 attacks and the U.S. military response to angry rejections of this response and categorical rejections of U.S. leaders and their claims to goodness. The range of campus responses includes the following statements, as numbered in the report:

1. "I was cheering when the Pentagon got hit because I know about the brutality of the military. The American flag is nothing but a symbol of hate and should be used for toilet paper for all I care." Freelance writer at Brown University protest.
2. "What happened on September 11 was terrorism, but what happened during the Gulf War was also terrorism." Professor of English, Brown University.
3. "The ultimate responsibility lies with the rulers of this country, the capitalist ruling class of this country." Mathematics instructor at City University of New York teach-in.
10. "Anyone who can blow up the Pentagon gets my vote." Professor of history, University of New Mexico. The professor later apologized for making the comment.

The report's authors appear to have combed the national press for the strongest examples they could find; these headliners taper off fairly quickly to comments like the following:

14. ". . . the actions taken by the terrorists on Tuesday are not completely unwarranted. We try to forget about the way this country behaves internationally—that we too often behave as terrorists." Student at University of Michigan and columnist for the Michigan Daily.
15. "[We should] build bridges and relationships, not simply bombs and walls." Speaker at Harvard Law School.
18. "What the U.S. calls counter-terrorism is terrorism by another name. Operation Infinite Justice—the Bush administration's code name for proposed military action against terrorists—is 'cowboy law.'" Professor of linguistics, MIT.
19. "It disturbs me to see all the flags out supporting the slaughter." Student at University of Wisconsin–Milwaukee protest.

Another cluster later on reads as follows:

63. "Our grief is not a cry for war." Poster at New York University.
64. "Recycle plastic, not violence." Poster at Hunter College.

65. "A lot of people are saying we created this monster. What goes around comes around. People are forgetting about the past." Student, Hunter College.

66. "There is a lot of skepticism about the administration's policy of going to war." Professor of communications, New York University.

67. "[It is] ridiculous for us to go and kill more people because of what Bin Laden did." Student, Columbia University.

68. "No racist scapegoat, no racist war, we won't take it anymore." Chanting students, University of Michigan.

69. "For this to turn into an excuse to have a war and kill more people, it seemed like it would just be too horrible." Student, Wesleyan University.

70. "War Is Also Terrorism." Harvard sign.

71. "One, two, three, four—we don't want another war! Five, six, seven, eight—stop the violence, stop the hate!" Student protestors in Harvard Square.

72. "To declare war, in this case, is a dangerous use of metaphoric language: it dignifies terrorist acts and implies a war with terrorists could end with a peace treaty. We must resist calls for revenge or retaliation." Professor of anthropology, MIT.

73. "Students at several colleges walked out of classes and held protests Monday in response to U.S. military actions in Afghanistan. The rallies—at Bryn Mawr and Haverford Colleges, the University of California at Berkeley, and Wesleyan University—attracted hundreds of students although many students did not attend or held counter-protests backing the government's response to last month's terrorist attacks."

74. "Revenge Is Not Justifiable" and "No Racist War." Signs at the University of Michigan.

75. "We need to think about what could have produced the frustrations that caused these crimes. To have that kind of hatred is a phenomenon we will have to try to understand." Director of the project on international intelligence at the Woodrow Wilson School's Center of International Studies, Princeton University.

As the report listed them, the "Campus Voices" ranged from angry denunciations to calls for understanding and further research, and yet the report lumped them all together as criticisms of America. Finding this hodgepodge badly organized, I decided to clarify the structure of "Campus Voices" with a basic content analysis.

A Range of "Campus Voices"

I divided the comments into several general categories, which I refined as I reflected on the content of the actual statements. The categories are listed below,
along with my classification of each statement by its number (I include my
notes on some borderline cases). I should point out that all categories are
meant to be descriptive rather than evaluative, and that in my view there are
justified as well as unjustified forms of anti-Americanism (as there are of anti-
French sentiment or anti-Canadianism, for that matter: the issue is the quality,
specificity, and clarity of the arguments and evidence for a particular position).

> A. Anti-Americanism: The United States and/or its leaders have been essen-
>   tially or inherently wrong, generally by being racist, exploitative, genoci-
>   dal, or terroristic themselves. Examples (of those cited above): 1, 10
> B. Blowback: The United States has been militaristic and/or terroristic
>   and/or exploitative of its allies, and is getting back what it dishes out.
>   Examples: 2, 3, 18, 65
> C. The "cycle of violence" is bad: War is not the answer to these attacks.
>   Examples: 19, 63, 64, 67, 68, 69, 70, 71, 72, 74
> D. Reflect and analyze: The attacks must be understood in their histori-
>   cal context (learn about root causes like racism, poverty, injustice, or
>   foreign policy bias, and change the nation's course as necessary).
>   Examples: 14, 15, 75
> E. The rest, including reports of others' activities, possibly misguided
>   steps taken by administrators against pro-war personnel, calls for ad-
>   ministrative action, and others.[10] Examples: 66, 73

My categories are arranged in approximate descending order of intensity.
While category B comments noted an action-reaction effect, category A
comments "blamed America" and described it as essentially (and not merely
sometimes) bad. Category B comments critiqued specific American policies
(or policy patterns) and not the country as such; they described a cause-
effect relation in which the United States has been an actor rather than an
innocent bystander, but not a systematically bad or dishonest actor. Category C includes comments that were antiwar without commenting on the
nature of American society, international relations, other causes, or deeper
remedies. Many of them were opposed to violence on principle, but many
others were opposed on the pragmatic grounds that it would produce more
violence in the future. Category D comments were the closest to being stan-

dard educational remarks, and often praised the traditional educational values of contextualization, analysis, and knowledge of the past. They were often but not always critical of specific actions and patterns in American policy, and sometimes suggested remedies. Category E is for "extra"—what was left over, including administrative actions from which the report's authors seem to have inferred antiwar bias.

Based on this typology, I have set aside category E responses and come to the following conclusions about the "Campus Voices."

Category A: Of the 115 citations, 6, or 5 percent, can be construed as anti-American in a classic sense. Only a couple of these are violent. Anti-Americanism was a marginal aspect of the "campus" response to 9/11. It was especially insignificant given the charged settings in which these comments were made, the heightened emotions during the attacks' aftermath, and the refusal of nearly all national leaders to acknowledge any American role in creating the socioeconomic conditions that facilitate terrorism.

Category B: 18, or 16 percent, of the comments noted that prior American actions could be interpreted as having provoked or given rational pretexts for the 9/11 attacks. Though they often noted that the United States had been violent, even terroristic, in its foreign policy, and that one ill turn is often followed by another, they did not state that this was an essential feature of U.S. society or that the United States deserved the attacks. Once again, the absence of any serious historical analysis in the American media or political system was no doubt a contributing factor: one sometimes shouts at people who are hard of hearing.

Category C: 42, or 37 percent, of the comments opposed war, further violence, interactive cycles of attacks, vengeance, or versions of "an eye for an eye." But they did not comment on the U.S. overall or blame anyone in particular.

Category D: 34, or 30 percent, of the comments were critical but primarily educational and contextual. They argued that future decisions should be grounded in broader and deeper understandings of the role the United States plays in world affairs and in the Middle East.

In short, only about one-fifth of the "Campus Voices" could by any stretch be construed as the "blame America first" folks repeatedly denounced in right-wing discourse. To be more rigorous, only one in twenty overall saw American policies and values as primarily responsible for the 9/11 attacks (category A). The rest of the one-in-five group sought to establish relation-ships between cause and effect in the world system (category B); while they did not blame the American system for the attacks, they did not believe that the United States was innocent—either of all wrongdoing or of contributing to enabling conditions. This denial of innocence ran afoul of the culture-war theme articulated by Giuliani, which went beyond calls for rebuilding and for trying and punishing the guilty to insist on an American innocence that would survive any and all possible inquiries and research.

As for the rest of the comments, about a third of the total were opposed to war, particularly war as an unreflective activity that does not wait to en-sure that it has the right culprit or that it might get at root causes. It is worth noting that the newspaper article accompanying the poll to which the report refers cited several citizens saying that they supported military action but hoped that the government would pause to find the guilty parties first.[11] Another third of the total 115 comments called for further research, reflection, and understanding. Most of these implied that reflection would lead to something longer lasting, more ethical, and probably more intelli-gent than war, and that the United States may have to talk or take less and listen or give more. But they were, generally speaking, educational com-ments, of exactly the type one would expect to find on a college campus where some of the invited speakers are senior faculty, deans, and other offi-cials responsible for ensuring an appropriate academic atmosphere even in a time of war. If one adds the category B comments to the category D com-ments (rather than to the category A comments, as I did earlier), and sees them as somewhat harsher attempts to show some historical causality be-tween American action and Al-Qaeda reaction, then calls for further teach-ing and research on the war on terror formed about half of the total. If we interpret category C criticisms of cycles of violence as attempts to establish the nonviolent preconditions of national learning, we can see 88 percent of the ACTA report's citations as compatible with or actively supporting the educational mission. If category A commentators showed the reasoning that led to their conclusions, their comments would have been educational too.

We thus have a range of comments, a large proportion of pedagogical ob-servations, a small number of denunciations of the United States as such, and a context of emotional turmoil after 9/11. We also have an institution, the university, that conceives of itself as a bastion of skeptical and always in-dependent reflection. Finally, since we are talking about a large, powerful country in a moment of conflict, we might assume that the American public would have been interested in the most accurate facts and the most complete, precise, and reality-based analyses it could find. We might assume that it would have wanted to hear as much as it could about causes and effects of wars on terror, about the place of the United States in the world, about attitudes toward its actions in farway places that turn out to be not so far way after all. We might further assume that it would have been willing to accept some extravagant and off-target claims as the price of creative thinking. Given all these, we are entitled to ask the ACTA authors, so what? What was so bad about what you showed?

Faculty Un-Americans

The report was not shy about telling us what was bad.

Page 1 of the report announced that while 92 percent of "Americans across the country" favored military action against those responsible for 9/11, academics refused to follow along.

> Even as many institutions enhanced security and many students exhibited American flags, professors across the country sponsored teach-ins that typically ranged from moral equivocation to explicit condemnations of America.
>
> While America's elected officials from both parties and media commentators from across the spectrum condemned the attacks and followed the President in calling evil by its rightful name, many faculty demurred. Some refused to make judgments. Many invoked tolerance and diversity as antidotes to evil. Some even pointed accusatory fingers, not at the terrorists, but at America itself.[12]

The report continued by contrasting faculty behavior with the patriotism aroused in Americans by 9/11 and Pearl Harbor, and claimed that faculty were unable to object to what was obviously a mass murder: "Although the public responded with clear condemnation of the terrorist attacks, many professors failed to do so, and even used the occasion to find fault with America."[13]

To my knowledge, ACTA and its allies never found a single faculty member in the United States who was unwilling to condemn the loss of life.[14] But the ACTA argument worked through a binary polarization in which such details were of no importance. The whole spectrum of Americans immediately grasped the whole true meaning of the attacks, which was that evil had attacked good. Real Americans responded in the right way, which was by "calling evil by its rightful name" (as the Bible tells us to) and rallying to the side of their country: they improved security, flew the flag, denounced the evildoers, and invaded Afghanistan. These Americans recognized that there was no hidden meaning or further subtlety in the attacks. They judged, condemned, and started to fight.

While this was happening, what did the professors do? They refused right judgment and clear action. Or to put it another way, they *taught*. They talked, thought, discussed, and analyzed. All these activities implied that things were not as simple as they appeared to be, that there was more than one meaning, that there was more here than good versus bad. The teach-ins, the rallies, the dialogues all said that there was something incomplete or wrong with the president and the mayor's analysis that good had been attacked by evil. The teach-ins and the dialogues implied that there was something to do besides denounce evil and make war upon it. Thinking, reflecting, researching, teaching: all these things define the university and were for ACTA the essence of weakness and equivocation, a genuine danger to the nation. In the report, thought is weakness and judgment is strength. Knowledge is confusion and conviction is truth. "Tolerance and diversity" will sap us while hate will prepare us. Self-criticism, Americans criticizing America, is a threat to the nation. More fundamentally, what threatened the nation was thought itself, thought not controlled by prior certainty.

ACTA could treat the comments from my categories A through D as though they were exactly the same only by assuming that analysis is a betrayal once the executive goes to war. To say "I was cheering when the Pentagon got hit" (1, category A) is the same for ACTA as saying "[We should] build bridges and relationships, not simply bombs and walls" (15, category D), which is the same for ACTA as saying "Recycle plastic, not violence" (64, category C), which is the same for ACTA as saying "There is a lot of skepticism about the administration's policy of going to war" (66, category C), which is the same for ACTA as saying "We need to think about what could have produced the frustrations that caused these crimes. To have that kind of hatred is a phenomenon we will have to try to understand" (75, category D). All these things—the rejection of the U.S. historical roles, values, and policies, observations about blowback, rejection of war as effective and/or ethical policy, and calls for context and knowledge—share an opposition to acting without cultural knowledge, to acting without political knowledge of interdependent systems, to acting without thinking on the basis of prior conviction of American rightness and superiority. ACTA in effect defined as disloyal comments that declined to respond to executive authority without thinking first.

ACTA's abused poll results conformed to a set of connections that Lynne Cheney and her circle had been promoting for years, and which the report spelled out like this:

> Moral relativism has become a staple of academic life in this country. At the same time, it has become commonplace to suggest that Western civilization is the primary source of the world's ills—even though it gave us the ideals of democracy, human rights, individual liberty, and mutual tolerance.
>
> Until the 1960s, colleges typically required students to take survey courses in Western civilization. Since then, those courses have been supplanted by a smorgasbord of often narrow and trendy classes and incoherent requirements that do not convey the great heritage of human civilization. Accompanying this basic failure is a campus atmosphere increasingly unfriendly to the free exchange of ideas. Students have reported more and more that they are intimidated by professors and fellow students if they question "politically correct" ideas or fail to conform to a particular ideology.[15]

Political dissent, in this view, stemmed from moral relativism on campus, which was itself the contradictory result of a dogmatic opposition to Western civilization. Faculty members could teach students to be moral relativists fixated on Western imperialism because colleges did not require Western Civ anymore, which is what you would expect given that the free exchange of ideas had been replaced by PC indoctrination. In short, university-based attempts to debate anything about "the West," which would obviously include critical perspectives on it, had become nothing more than attacks on American values and a threat to national security. In case anyone missed this point, or thought it exaggerated, "Defending Civilization" ended its main text with a historical parallel:

> In 1933, the Oxford Student Union held a famous debate over whether it was moral for Britons to fight for king and country. After a wide-ranging discussion in which the leading intellectuals could find no distinction between British colonialism and world fascism, the Union resolved that England would "in no circumstances fight for king and country." As the *Wall Street Journal* reported: "Von Ribbentrop sent back the good news to

Germany's new chancellor, Hitler: The West will not fight for its own survival."

Thus for ACTA, Hitler was launched on world conquest and genocide by the moral relativism of an academic debate. The description and the conclusions were ludicrous, and yet consistent with the culture warriors' claim that liberal debate weakens the nation and liberal debaters oppose its interests. They were also consistent with the parallel effort within the same right-wing circles to define Saddam Hussein as a new Hitler, the better to make him deserve military invasion.

This denunciation of universities was not a random eruption. The attack on the liberal culture of academia was coordinated and intellectually consistent with the attacks on political liberals by the media Right. The commentator Ann Coulter, trained, groomed, connected, and subsidized from her college days by the same concentrated right-wing network that founded and sponsored ACTA and the prominent activist David Horowitz's groups, was there to connect the dots in the title of her book, *Treason: Liberal Treachery from the Cold War to the War on Terrorism* (2003).[16] "The only way to talk to liberals is with a baseball bat," she said at one meeting. Liberals must be intimidated and terrified: "When contemplating college liberals, you really regret once again that [U.S.-born Taliban fighter captured in Afghanistan] John Walker is not getting the death penalty," Coulter reportedly said in an address to the Conservative Political Action Conference (CPAC). "We need to execute people like John Walker in order to physically intimidate liberals, by making them realize that they can be killed too. Otherwise they will turn out to be outright traitors."[17]

"Defending Civilization" was more scholarly than this, but it was a straight-up attack on academic cultural knowledge as not simply excessively liberal but also anti-American. Clearly conservatives saw the cultural front as more important than ever in an age where America had to wear the white hat in a global "clash of civilizations." The revived culture war was fused with the Right's political and economic agenda. In politics, a united, Christian, and sufficiently militaristic national culture would enable America to fulfill its historic, even biblical, destiny of world leadership or domination, "democratizing" and spreading free markets everywhere in its own image. The cultural front, as commentators have pointed out, would also help Republicans have the same minority control over domestic politics and resources. In economics, the Right's West supremacism was a convenient—

if transparent—cover for the occupation and forced Westernization of the world's second-largest oil reserves in Iraq. More systematically, conservatives continued to discredit and dismantle the public systems that were the only real competition in economic decision making to businesses. The university had been a widely popular success story for the public sector, and cutting it down to size had major practical impact: as prolific as the university had been in producing ideas that accelerated financialization, globalization, and other trends dear to the heart of the corporate world, the university also remained a source of a competing vision of a culturally dense, complex, rich, and multilateral civic world that could not and should not be ruled by dominant political or economic interests. In the early 2000s, the culture wars continued, as schematized in Table 9, and were more important than ever to the Right's twin projects of minority American rule in the world and conservative minority rule at home.

"Defending Civilization" used culture as an essential component of the campaign across all three dimensions. Once ACTA invoked its stark opposition

Table 9 Post–9/11 culture-war victory

Domain	Epoch-making challenge	Emerging nonconservative postwar middle-class orientation	The conservative restoration
Politics	Multiracial mass democracy	Majoritarian democracy via anti-elitist meritocracy (meritocracy II)	Elite core dominant at home; enlightened empire abroad
Economy	Decline of profits, rise of knowledge-workers	Planned mixed-economy; mass affluence via valuing of labor and public systems	Low taxes, high inequality, reduced social investment
Culture	Civil-rights "science"-movements rooted in qualitative, context-specific, cross-cultural knowledge	Cultural and social equality, leading to "human development"	West supremacism, loyalty to executive authority

between America and the university, the people and the professors, knowledge and authority, it could conclude that the survival of America depended on established authority convincing the people that academic knowledge is wrong.

Two Mainstream Impacts

The American Council of Trustees and Alumni was not a Goldwater-era fringe element. It continued its work through subsequent years, and in tandem with the conservative activist David Horowitz helped to create a controversy over academia's alleged liberal thought control with its report "Intellectual Diversity: Time for Action" (2005). The claim that academia lacked enough conservative opinion to be intellectually diverse was widely influential. It helped propel the introduction of Horowitz's "Academic Bill of Rights" into the legislatures of twenty-three states, and prompted hearings in the state of Pennsylvania. The story of anticonservative bias was told by U.S. senator Lamar Alexander (the former secretary of education under Bush I). At the opening of the Bush II administration's Secretary of Education's Commission on the Future of Higher Education, Alexander used the occasion to announce that the "greatest threat to broader public support and funding for higher education [is] the growing political one-sidedness which has infected most campuses, and an absence of true diversity of opinion."[18] Academia's alleged liberal bias was thus to be one of the starting points in this top-level national review.

The attacks on particular faculty and programs had to be renewed consistently in order to stay in the news. Hence Horowitz's book *The Professors* appeared at an opportune moment, as the Academic Bill of Rights was fizzling in most state legislatures, the Pennsylvania hearings were yielding little, and the Colorado investigation of Ward Churchill's alleged academic misconduct produced a report that had no immediate public impact. ACTA soon released another report, "How Many Ward Churchills?" in which it cast its usual blanket of suspicion over the university nationwide ("Is there really only one Ward Churchill? Or are there many? . . . WARD CHURCHILL IS EVERY-WHERE"). Their evidence that Ward Churchill was the presiding influence over the American liberal arts consisted of downloaded course descriptions for classes in "subjects such as women's studies, Africana studies, or global studies."[19] Although the University of Colorado denied being influenced by outside forces, ACTA's report kept Churchill visible in culture-warrior circles throughout the procedure that led to his dismissal. Another group, Campus Watch, maintained its attacks on Middle Eastern studies programs that seemed too critical of Israel's foreign and domestic policies, and continued the "Columbia Watch" campaign that, in conjunction with the David Project, had attacked programs and individuals in Middle Eastern studies so vociferously as to produce unusually strong defenses from administrators.[20] When this campaign stopped drawing so much press attention, it was renewed in the form of Horowitz's tour against "Islamofacism" in the fall of 2007.

The culture wars consolidated the Right and also transformed the academic center, where the wars had succeeded at backing liberals away from the liberal foundations of the "golden age" United States. My analysis of the larger "intellectual diversity" campaign and its empirical base appears in the appendix to this book. I conclude here by turning my attention to the nonconservative university vision and its stunted state in the 2000s.

Backpedaling and Downgrading

The university vision that I described at the start of this book led to a cultural capability that was both an intellectual and a political turning point. It allowed new understandings of the relation shared by sociocultural systems, material forces, and individuals. It justified the political and economic claims of the majority population that had started to attend college and move into knowledge work of both the blue-collar and white-collar kinds. The hallmark of the postwar university was "academic freedom" as the fundamental condition of creating and disseminating valid and useful knowledge. One result was the sort of intellectual liberty that challenged the status quo, not just now and then but all the time. Another result of the university's expanded intellectual scope was the cultural capability that enables individuals to see themselves as agents in complicated systems where they must work with (and against) people and groups quite different from them.

One cornerstone of modern cultural capability is in fact that thing culture warriors like to call "relativism," which is better labeled as "interpretive" knowledge. This framework was renewed and elaborated in various ways throughout the twentieth century, though it is at least as old as the pre-Socratic philosophers of ancient Greece. Interpretive knowledge sees truth as the result of a process, as being in large part created by human perception and action. The process is also social and cultural. It involves the pivotal skill of *interpretation*, since the truth is not given in advance of systematic encounters with the beliefs of others. The process of discovery also involves *negotiation*, precisely because others are involved—others with their own beliefs, evidence, and methods for talking about beliefs and evidence. This model is sometimes called the "pragmatic" theory of truth, and in the United States it is often associated with John Dewey from the early twentieth century and with Richard Rorty from the late twentieth century, who came to call it "antifoundationalism." Critics who label it "relativism" assert that it has no evidentiary foundations at all, but antifoundationalists argue that evidence is if anything more important in their model that in its "foundationalist" alternative, since no unmediated "correspondence" to reality can be taken for granted.[21] Though the view is often associated with the humanities, it has roots in the philosophy of science and now appears in places like management theory, particularly that which is concerned with creativity and innovation. Management writers can be found saying things like "interpretation plays in the space of ambiguity" that is required "for creativity to flourish."[22]

This interpretive understanding of truth is embodied in the modern version of academic freedom. For example, when the University of California adopted revised language on academic freedom in September 2003, it offered the following footnote.

> The revision of [the University's definition of academic freedom] does not distinguish between "interested" and "disinterested" scholarship; it differentiates instead between competent and incompetent scholarship. Although competent scholarship requires an open mind, this does not mean that faculty are unprofessional if they reach definite conclusions. It means rather that faculty must always stand ready to revise their conclusions in the light of new evidence or further discussion. Although competent scholarship requires the exercise of reason, this does not mean that faculty are unprofessional if they are committed to a definite point of view. It means rather that faculty must form their point of view by applying professional standards of inquiry rather than by succumbing to external and illegitimate incentives such as monetary gain or political coercion.[23]

Academic freedom was so important to the discovery of truth because it allowed for freedom of interpretation, revision, and reinterpretation.

Culture warriors have disliked this understanding of truth; it is fair to say that in most cases they dislike it so much that they cannot understand it. Conflicts over "PC" and "multiculturalism" and "intellectual diversity" have been embedded in a stark conflict between epistemological ancients and moderns. The ancients tended to look for truth as correspondence to a reality that is independent of research communities. If knowledge depends on contexts like professional research communities, they say, it is relative to those communities and *therefore* not truth at all.

The leading ancients in this battle have in recent years been outside academia, and one could understand why they would at first be skeptical of the objectivity or truth-making power of a peer process to which they do not belong.[24] University-based knowledge *can* become encrusted around a shared and unquestioned bundle of assumptions: in Thomas Kuhn's classic account of academic knowledge production, for example, the scientific community is often reluctant to take up epistemological challenges—be it Copernican astronomy or Einsteinian physics—that undermine well-established and productive paradigms. But the cure for this ossification is more of the kind of debate and exchange that the modern paradigm of academic freedom is designed to protect. All "moderns" adopted some kind of context-based epistemological position and put their trust in institutional and professional safeguards. The overall result has been the power to absorb heterogeneous data, interpret it with reference to explicit framing conditions, and then reinterpret it as new or conflicting evidence comes in. There is nothing very radical about this: it is the basis of academic knowledge in organic chemistry and art history alike, and it is particularly important—and endangered—in cultural controversies like those involving "radical Islam."

When professional academics appeared in major media venues, most did not do a good job sticking up for complex cultural knowledge and its professional base in interpretive epistemology. One example was the professor that the *New York Times* columnist John Tierney used to claim that "once liberals dominate a department, they can increase their majority by voting to award tenure to like-minded scholars. As liberals dominate a field, conservatives' work comes to be seen as fringe scholarship." Tierney's actual evidence for this familiar belief came in the form of a literary academic's denunciation of the entire peer-review process.

"The filtering out of conservatives in the job pipeline rarely works by outright blackballing," said Mark Bauerlein, a conservative who is an English professor at Emory. "It doesn't have to. The intellectual focus of the disciplines does that by itself."

"Suppose," he said, "you were a conservative who wanted to do a sociology dissertation on the debilitating effects of the European welfare state, or an English dissertation arguing that anticommunist literature from the mid-20th century was as valuable as the procommunist literature.

"You'd have a hard time finding a dissertation adviser, an interested publisher, and a receptive hiring committee," Bauerlein said. "Your work just wouldn't look like relevant scholarship, and would be quietly set aside."[25]

Bauerlein's claims were factually incorrect: critiques of the European welfare state are common, and many of them have been written by sociologists.[26] Similarly, admiring exegeses of anticommunist literature from the mid-twentieth century formed the backbone of twentieth-century literary criticism as it revolved around close readings of Ezra Pound, T. S. Eliot, William Faulkner, and others. The right-wing icon Ayn Rand has received serious critical attention.[27] But Bauerlein's claims were driven by an apparent belief that liberal monopoly was coming through the essential feature of professional life, through interpretive evaluation as grounded in the epistemologically modern process of expertise-based peer review. Conservative views were purged, he felt, not by liberal political attitudes but by the "intellectual focus of the disciplines" themselves. The problem with academia was not just the political views of its liberal faculty but the nature of professionalism itself, and professionalism was a problem because it was antifoundationalist and interpretive—very much like the study of culture as such. The whole process of creating knowledge, involving the review of vast literatures of existing materials, consultation and collaboration with other experts; all the conceptualization, applying for grants, archival work, lab studies, teaching, advising of grad students, presentations, critiquing, revising, publishing, rethinking, continuing, extending, further granting, further peer reviewing, further revising and publishing; the large complex system that makes up the scholarly enterprise, the enormous craft labor of it that involves hundreds of thousands of people at any one time: Bauerlein had apparently lost confidence that professionalism itself could produce truth or justice, and seemed happy to have some outside element intervene.

Another example of impaired liberalism was a piece by literary criticism's leading theorist of professionalism, Stanley Fish. In the summer of 2006, Fish responded in the *New York Times* to yet another skirmish over "advocacy" in the classroom. A lecturer at the University of Wisconsin-Madison "acknowledged on a radio talk show that he has shared with students his strong conviction that the destruction of the World Trade Center was an inside job perpetrated by the American government. The predictable uproar ensued, and the equally predictable battle lines were drawn between those who disagree about what the doctrine of academic freedom does and does not allow." Fish went on to claim that neither the defenders nor the detractors of the lecturer understood the real meaning of academic freedom.

> Academic freedom has nothing to do with content. It is not a subset of the general freedom of Americans to say anything they like (so long as it is not an incitement to violence or is treasonous or libelous). Rather, academic freedom is the freedom of academics to study anything they like; the freedom, that is, to subject any body of material, however unpromising it might seem, to academic interrogation and analysis.
>
> Academic freedom means that if I think that there may be an intellectual payoff to be had by turning an academic lens on material others consider trivial—golf tees, gourmet coffee, lingerie ads, convenience stores, street names, whatever—I should get a chance to try. If I manage to demonstrate to my peers and students that studying this material yields insights into matters of general intellectual interest, there is a new topic under the academic sun and a new subject for classroom discussion.[28]

Fish's definition of academic freedom followed directly from his decades-old defense of professional procedures, and reiterated the notion of valid knowledge—or "insights"—as that which is defined as such by the professional community—here, "peers and students." His position has always been close to Rorty's and that of other respectable antifoundationalists.

But the more the piece insisted on its notion of professional behavior, the closer it came to echoing culture-warrior attacks.

> There is a world of difference, for example, between surveying the pro and con arguments about the Iraq war, a perfectly appropriate academic assignment, and pressing students to come down on your side. Of course the instructor who presides over such a survey is likely to be a partisan of one position or the other—after all, who doesn't have an opinion on the Iraq war?—but it is part of a teacher's job to set personal conviction aside for the hour or two when a class is in session and allow the techniques and protocols of academic research full sway.

It is certainly true that professional teaching requires giving the "techniques and protocols of academic research full sway." It is also true that all norms of professional conduct forbid indoctrination and "pressing students to come down on your side": intellectual coercion is obviously out of bounds.[29] Professional protocols do *not*, however, require the setting aside of "personal conviction": the latter is a political-sounding phrase for what is actually accumulated professional expertise. When a teacher weighs various positions and then chooses one over the others on the basis of evidence and arguments, the teacher is "advocating" what he or she has judged to be the correct position, correct as determined by his or her best use of "the techniques and protocols of academic research."

Caught, perhaps unawares, within the culture-wars framework, Fish first fed the unfounded culture-war prejudice that the nation's professors are always about to fall off the wagon of dispassionate teaching and start pressuring students to agree with their politics. He then asserted that professional standards rule out the taking of a position, putting his thumb on the scale by calling this "advocacy" and "partisan advocacy." This had the disastrous effect of rendering invisible the professional standards within which faculty must take positions in the classroom, which leads not to neutrality and equal time for all possibilities but to expertly researched and argued advocacy of the truth (defined as everything that one's profession agrees that we know). In denying the existence of professional acts of concluding, Fish deflated the professional labor that creates the "position" (knowledge) that the "partisan" (scholar) "advocates" (argues) on the basis of his or her "identity" (expertise).[30] In other words, Fish claimed that the student's academic freedom and the quality of instruction are protected by the professor's *neutrality* and not by his or her *professionalism*. Once this idea was in place, then the processes of peer review that appeared earlier in Fish's piece no longer had a meaningful existence. "The moment a professor does embrace and urge [a viewpoint], academic study has ceased and been replaced by partisan advocacy. And that is a moment no college administration should allow to occur." Once a professor draws a conclusion, in other words, the judge of the validity of that conclusion is not peer review but a supervising administration.

The culture wars on the university did not cause this backsliding all by themselves, but they were the catalytic ingredient. They condemned both the content of academic cultural study and the process by which it creates knowledge of complex systems. In the process the culture wars created a void where the relevant cultural capabilities might be. Into the void rushed bloggers and columnists and writers, many of whom did everything they could to use arguments and evidence to explain difficult things. Into the void also came culture warriors like Horowitz and Coulter, who used intimidation and terror. This was terror as defined by the philosopher Jean-François Lyotard, who saw it as "the efficiency gained by eliminating, or threatening to eliminate, a player from the language game one shares with him."[31] From this culture-war terror came the air time that professional knowledge would not sanction—creationism to counter evolution, religion to replace public services, and the various alternatives to established climate science. From this terror came the decline of the interpretive capability to tell the difference, and the decline of the professional structures that could validate this capability. In the 2000s, the United States needed knowledge about cultural variation, knowledge about economic effects, knowledge about actual political forces. The United States needed this knowledge more than ever in order to live at peace in the world, to support the world's general development, to help solve the world's environmental and social problems—or at least to stop making them worse. But it was exactly in this period of the 2000s, in the moment of danger, when the culture wars made this cultural capability almost impossible to use in public and tarnished the university that had sustained it.

Conclusion:
Powers of the 100 Percent

In this book, I have analyzed the connections between two major, averse changes in American society. The first is the decline in public funding for the public university, which has affected far more students than has the more visible wealth of higher education's leading private universities. The second, starting in the late 1970s, is the decline of the economic fortunes of most of the country's population, and one that has continued through ups and downs into the present.

Public funding for public higher education as a share of state outlays is now about two-thirds of what it was in 1980. In the early 2000s, per-student expenditures in public universities fell by 15 percent. The situation has been particularly dramatic in California, a state whose early self-definition as a knowledge economy heralded cuts in public support for its academic knowledge "factories." The story can be quickly illustrated by Figures 9A and B.

The tables show that higher education is the only major sector of the California state budget that has grown more slowly than the population and the only sector to have less per capita funding in the early 2000s than it had in 1984. The winner has been the California prison system, whose real per-capita expenditures more than doubled during the same period. National figures show a similar pattern.[1] Across the country, the public university has had a harder budgetary time than any other major sector of public spending.

The decline of the U.S. mass middle class has been equally unmistakable. Though large majorities of Americans continue to believe that the United States is the meritocratic and upwardly mobile society par excellence, relative mobility is in fact 2.5 times higher in Canada and about 3 times higher in Denmark: the democratic-socialist bastions of Western and Northern Europe all have higher rates of upward mobility than do the finance-led

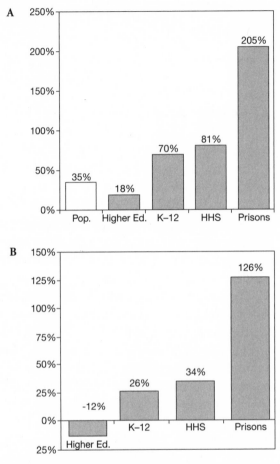

Figure 9. Population and expenditure growth, state of California. **A:** California population versus growth in general fund spending on the four largest state programs, 1984–2004 (constant dollars). **B:** Growth (decline) in general funding spending per capita on California's four largest programs, 1984–2004 (constant dollars). Source: State of California, Department of Finance tables, http://www.lao.ca.gov/laoapp/ LAOMenus/lao_menu-economics.aspx (accessed October 31, 2007), prepared by Jonathan Polansky.

market societies of Britain and the United States. The same is true for absolute mobility: men in 2004 made about 12 percent less at the same age than did their predecessors thirty years earlier. Median family incomes have done better because more women now have salaried jobs to contribute to the family total. Even so, family incomes have not kept up with productivity growth. These and related forms of majority economic stagnation have persisted in spite of several economic booms.[2]

In this book, I have sought not simply to describe the declining fortunes of the public university and of the U.S. middle class, but also to explain them. I have diverged from analyses that trace problems with public funding and with middle-class incomes to global economic changes and their related shifts in public opinion.[3] Though these changes matter, their effects have been greatly magnified by the work of the culture wars. Though the proximate causes of such complex changes are always long series of policy decisions occurring within myriad institutions, the changes have depended on the transformation in cultural climate to which the culture wars made pivotal contributions. I have described a decentralized and complex campaign to discredit the cultural foundations of a group that had come to threaten the position of traditional American business and political elites. That group was the increasingly multiracial, blue- and white-collar, college-educated middle class. I have been telling the story of what made this broad middle class and its signature institution, the public university, a danger to conservative rule, and of how the culture wars put this middle class back in its place, culturally, politically, and economically.

Culture wars have been a staple of U.S. history from the beginning of the colonial era. The wars I have discussed here, which crystallized in the late 1980s, were a belated but successful attempt to restore a conservative governing order whose credibility had been eroded by the Great Depression, World War II, and the obvious successes of the New Deal (chapter 1). A surprising range of activists and writers—including Malcolm X, John Kenneth Galbraith, and Robert Pirsig—worked both with and against the era's progressive model of social development to define a society run by and for a popular majority, a majority guided by knowledge of its own traditions and aspirations (chapter 2). These figures' rejection of elite economic and political interests was clear, as was the mixed working- and middle-class "front" they formed from very different positions. The growing harmony of the diverse elements of this progressive front was represented in simple ways by the participation of white college students in "Freedom Rides" and other aspects of the black-led civil rights movement, and in more subtle ways by cultural and social research on college campuses. Culture warriors were clear early on about how a progressive middle class could cement a majority coalition that would end conservative rule. The culture wars of the 1980s and 1990s focused on discrediting this new majority's intellectual and institutional foundations.

I have described the long counterrevolution in detail, focusing on controversial writings and policy statements in a range of venues. The new round started with conservative opinion writing, which became widely influential only when it was echoed in national media stories that denounced the study of race, gender, and sexuality, the humanities fields that did the bulk of the research and teaching in these fields, the students of color who seemed to benefit from them, and the universities that harbored all of these. I analyzed a central example at length: the late 1980s and 1990s campaign to undermine arguments for cross-racial cultural equality, which meant undermining arguments that justified the presence of the students of color who were then finally achieving visible numbers in high-status public universities. The crusade against "political correctness" (chapter 3) and against Lani Guinier's nomination to the Department of Justice (chapter 4) successfully hamstrung the case for racial equality. The path was clear for renewed attacks on affirmative action (chapter 5), which eviscerated a broader democratic understanding of meritocracy (chapter 6). This in turn obscured the need to expand high-quality facilities in public universities, leading to the rise of a weak notion of diversity that supported the widespread racial standoff I call "pseudointegration" (chapter 7). The intensified competition for existing university seats did not increase overall quality of educational outcomes, but it did make stratification and the cultivation of elites seem normal again.

The culture warriors had an obvious interest in making universities less liberal. But winning the battle over ideology was not the ultimate prize. The ultimate prize was the reduced cost and status of the middle class that the public university created. The American middle class is always politically sacrosanct, so downgrading it could not be announced as the goal; nonetheless this goal has been gradually achieved, as in part indexed by stagnating economic fortunes. A roundabout way was found to downsize the new middle class, and that was to discredit its cultural foundations. The middle class could rise on the basis of cultural egalitarianism, since it was not all white, and on the basis of an antielitist model of meritocracy, since it was not a small group of ultimate achievers, and on the basis of a willingness to control market economies, since it did not control the capitalist institutions that the market served. The culture wars on higher education cut the middle class down to size by undermining the popular belief in these interrelated ideas, a belief that had its most powerful mainstream embodiment in the public university.

The public university was a special venue for this economic majority. The university obviously had no monopoly on social wisdom—the university depended for its vitality and insight on a vast range of social movements and groups and often spoiled their grassroots knowledge. But the public university in full expansion brought disparate factions of the large majority together. This integration was functional, causing the military and corporate worlds to defend a soft diversity all the way to the Supreme Court. This integration could also produce new social rules and new leaders to apply them. The public university provided forums for students of all races to learn about each other, to diminish suspicion and fear, and to act together. When the culture wars weakened the public university vision, they weakened the broad, racially hybridized middle class that had been emerging from it. They weakened a mass middle class that had been overcoming the historical divergence between white- and blue-collar labor—the children of both were meeting in Atlanta, Ann Arbor, and Austin, in Madison, Berkeley, and Buffalo, in Gainesville and Grand Rapids, in Iowa City, Santa Barbara, Spokane, Chapel Hill, Missoula, Knoxville, and Bloomington—in college towns all over the country. This class was now more diverse than the professional-managerial class (PMC) that college had historically served. This new middle class had benefited from earlier movements that had pushed elites to develop society beyond the minimal requirements of business leaders. This class generally supported spending for the high-quality public infrastructure that, thanks to the civil rights movement, was becoming available to 100 percent of the public. When the culture wars weakened this multiracial college class, it weakened a progressive majority that had been getting expensive and demanding as it lay ever greater claim to the country's future.

Commentators often contrast cultural and economic issues. Some argue that "cultural values" serve as screens for real economic interests. The story I have told shows that this is a false dichotomy. Though issues like racial equality and "bell curve" meritocracy cannot be reduced to economics, leaders and voters alike were in fact pursuing their economic interests in culture-wars terms. For example, conservative attacks on affirmative action may have seemed like a diversion from the skewed tax cuts that did not actually help the white, middle-class people who voted for them. In fact, the attacks did help whites economically. Attacks on affirmative action renaturalized racial inequality, which allowed "voluntary" racial segregation to continue and spread, which in turn enabled white neighborhoods to protect housing price increases that they felt racial integration would jeopardize.

This same alignment of cultural and economic interests undermined public higher education. As we have seen, California's high school population was growing and diversifying in the 1990s, but the University of California had not built a new campus in thirty years. The attacks on affirmative action reignited at a time when taxes had just been raised to narrow a budget deficit, and when the value of investing in a growing population's education implied the need for further public outlays. The attacks managed to define UC as too open rather than too limited: since the alleged problem was too many spaces for Latinos at UC Berkeley, why bother to build another Berkeley? By making educational stratification natural, and limits seem efficient, the attacks on affirmative action saved California residents billions of dollars in multiyear educational investments.

Because their cultural and economic goals were so intertwined, the same conservative organizations—often the same authors or political figures—who railed against political correctness also denounced the public sector and steadily pushed for the privatization of government functions. This was entirely logical and consistent. Racial inequality and privatization were the Tweedledum and Tweedledee of the counterrevolution. And they each supported a crucial third theme: elite democracy, one largely liberated from the working class *and* the college masses.

Privatization has systematically diminished the public university's distinctive features. One of these was top quality at a low cost to the individual student and his or her family. The result of this synthesis was freedom to choose a field of study without overriding awareness of its future income potential. A further result was graduation with little or no debt, allowing the graduate from a low-income background to have the same shot as others at the freedom to take poorly paying but satisfying work, or a shot at international travel, or a shot at being a professional painter or dancer. The boom in student debt has reduced these freedoms, and likely reduced the socially valuable innovation that comes with them. In the professional schools, the tuition difference between top private and top public institutions is quickly disappearing. Though public law schools, for example, still expect taxpayer support, they decreasingly offer the low tuition that enables graduates to enter public-interest law.

All this is in keeping with the systemic changes in university business that I have discussed at length: knowledge skills without proprietary business potential were demoted (chapter 8); faculty learned to adapt to academic markets rather than lead or change them (chapter 9); financial measures were more likely to drive academic planning than the other way around (chapter 10); state appropriations were cut on the false assumption that private money could fill the gap (chapter 11); scientific research was said to make money for public universities when it in fact cost public money (chapter 12); the reverse claim, which was also wrong, was made for cultural and social studies, since these fields generally paid both for themselves and other fields through teaching enrollments (chapter 13); and even sharp critics of the effects of market forces on higher education could no longer picture the coherent alternatives (chapter 14). With the partial but continuing privatization of public universities, the market had become the medium and the message. Administrators looked to private funding to solve the problems that the ascent of private over public funding helped create. The fact remains that private funding can build great universities for elites, but private funding cannot and will not do the same for society's majority.

This is not to say that good things have not been happening for higher education: there are new fields, new research, new challenges, new students. There is also new money, though largely for universities that already have plenty of it. The new money, and many of the new fields, reflect the high-end concentration of resources in recent decades rather than its wider and highly productive distribution.

It has become hard to miss the disproportion of this expenditure and of its results. It sometimes reminds me of when I was a young and obsessive sports fan growing up in Los Angeles. My favorite local pro teams offered nonstop instruction in being good at only one thing. In baseball, the Dodgers of the period had one of the best pitching rotations in the history of the game, and an erratic, frustrating offense. When the offense failed in 1964, the Dodgers made it even worse by using off-season trades to improve their pitching again. This lopsided strategy worked for two years, and then fell apart. In football, the Rams had a similar problem: Great passing and defensive rushing, and pretty average everything else. They won their weak division year after year, only to lose their first postseason game just as often.

The United States in the twenty-first century is looking like the mid-1960s Dodgers writ large. It has put the best that it has into its business system, into buying and selling, into its executive compensation and stock prices, and into the world's most complex and expensive financial architecture. But it has neglected its public systems and done a below-average job with its human capital. The results are mixed, as can be seen in international comparisons of primary and secondary school students, or in health

care, where the highest costs in the world yield lower-tier public health results in the usual comparison groups. A similar fate has befallen public
higher education, where the top keeps climbing higher, and the rest run to
stay in place. The middle class that has been cutting public expenditures for
college may have thought that it was cutting other people's college, but this
has not been the case. There has never been a middle class in history that
was not created by public infrastructure—by facilities offering rough
equality regardless of personal means. As the middle class cuts public education, it cuts the conditions of its own existence.

The history I have told suggests clear cultural remedies. They do not fit
with the momentum of our recent mistakes, but they are achievable
nonetheless. First, racial equality needs to be reaffirmed as a value and as a
goal. By this I do not simply mean equal opportunity—thought that too is
rarer than we think—but general equality of outcome among racial
groups. Racial difference is not the only form of unjust stratification in the
United States, but it is the primary source of the current illusion that inequality is a natural fact and an index of liberty. The culture-wars notion
that inequality is inevitable and liberating has justified the withdrawal of
resources from poor communities. It has done the same thing to higher
education.

Second, the public university must be defined all over again as the place
where maximum access is synthesized with the highest quality. This was the
core insight of the system I have called "meritocracy II," which correctly understood talent to be widely distributed in the population. In this version of
meritocracy, talent exists everywhere in multiple forms and mysterious dis-
guises: thus most of it in our increasingly top-down society is going to
waste. Public higher education has been a place where that waste is continuously and drastically reduced, reduced by refusing to lower quality for the
students from economically limited backgrounds who are more interested
than ever in transforming their lives through college.

Third, the university needs to be understood as engaged in forms of individual and collective development that cannot be captured in economic
terms. Education cannot pay in this way. It must not be expected to. If we
are forced to use an economic term, the term for education would be "investment." But the realm of profits and returns simply does not fit with the
forms of growth, evolution, advancement, expansion, elaboration, discovery, and invention that education delivers to individuals and societies alike.
American capitalism is saddled with many intellectual limitations, and one

of these is that in the very period in which it became obsessed with innovation, it wrongly decided it could capture innovation in financial terms. This has restricted the forms of cultural creativity and labor that I have discussed, along with the options of the culture workers that come out of the humanities disciplines. But it has given science the same treatment, since there too most discoveries lead to other discoveries and not to products, and to far more public than to private benefit. Universities obviously need to keep good financial books and have systems that are efficient and effective. But they cannot function properly as capitalist institutions. Their work of labor-intensive, craft-based creation and teaching is noncapitalist. Since capitalism will continue to insist on bottom-line measures of their output, universities will at those times need to be frankly anticapitalist.

Fourth, access can coexist with quality only by restoring and increasing public funding for the public university. Private sponsorship can support novel and important programs on a limited scale; in public education, it is not enough to fund high-quality core operations. High-quality mass higher education requires mass public funding: there is no way around how the numbers work. Rising tuition costs have gotten college access and affordability onto the national agenda. The next step is for public universities to agree to stop raising fees in exchange for restored and augmented public funding. States should set a goal of getting public funding levels back to where they were in 2001, and then move forward from there. This clearly requires that universities continue to improve operations, make their budgets more transparent, and streamline administration. But it also means that states must fund public higher education at the levels required by their full educational missions—missions that must again come from concrete educational aims rather than from reactions to permanent austerity. It is only through public funding that the whole society can contribute to forming the next generations, rather than relying on the generally stagnant incomes of their students' parents.

Proper public funding should also be tied to reversing the growth of adjunct and low-wage teaching staffs. The shift toward academic permatemps has persisted through good times and bad, and has resulted in the de facto elimination of tenure for a large proportion of the faculty. More fundamentally, it has created an unjust two-tiered labor system. Public universities cannot model either a sustainable, desirable society or the creation of high-performance workers when they offer underpaid, dead-end jobs to much or most of their teaching staff. Rather than trimming their labor standards to fit their budgets, public universities need to seek the budgets that will uphold their labor standards.

Fifth, public universities need to insist on the value of understanding societies beyond their status as commercial markets. Although the culture wars sought to restrict the humanities and social sciences disciplines that seek this understanding, these disciplines will need to play an even stronger role than they have to date. The human sciences must explain in better ways what human development is, why it must be available to everyone, and what social investments and cultural practices will allow it to occur. They will need to explain again the power of the imagination. The imagination is always a kind of revolt, and the humanities fields have a long history of revolts on behalf of human development. These fields are particularly close to the ancient forms of human creativity, to intuitive modes of change, to the unquantifiable forces that comprise experience and history. This cultural knowledge and historical experience cannot be reduced to the market-driven model of economic development that U.S. leaders prefer. When public universities represent the public, this is something that they must say, and explain, and extend into the practical modes of life.

The human sciences have spent much of the last hundred years offering concrete answers to enduring social problems. They have expressed the prospects for majoritarian democracy in all of its concrete particularity. They have looked at the effects of every range of economic system both local and global, and they have celebrated work, art, writing, and science as versions of creativity that transcend economic rules as such. The humanities fields helped articulate early versions of cultural pluralism as a model of equitable cross-racial negotiation. They imagined equality as not only feasible, but as necessary to advancement.

To the charge that culture reflects subjectivity and human interests, the liberal arts fields have replied that these are strengths, for they manifest the kinds of freedom that progress and innovation require. To the disregard of experience by abstract economic and political discourse, the liberal arts have offered detailed descriptions of people's everyday lives. To the constant endangerment of good work in neoliberal economies, the humanities have displayed the innovation that comes from the self-managed craft labor we call art, and the spillover social effects that always exceed their market value. To the ongoing conflicts within U.S. democracy, and to the resegregation of much of our public life, the humanities have proposed equality across difference, turn taking, negotiating, and power sharing as just and sustainable modes of innovation.

Everyone in the university has a role to play. The human sciences have a role in describing how public systems actually work—how they enable informal knowledge and constant sociability and unquantifiable experience and everything we know as art and craft and passion and obsessive attention to getting things right. The professions have a role to play in maintaining their traditions of intellectual rigor, codification, public presence, and peer review. The university, across all its disciplines, has a role to play in maintaining its commitment to truth in a world of knowledge for hire, and by honoring the dissenters, heretics, radicals, troublemakers, and creators who have always practiced human development for all.

Culture-wars values have poisoned the American appreciation of public systems. They have helped the federal government focus increasingly on security and war and see health and education as entitlements to be cut. The corporation has rejected the social contract that enabled its own prosperity for decades. Neither the political nor the business system is currently able to confront the core problem of our time: in a world with six billion people, and four or five billion poor, how do we develop the whole of society and not just a protected minority? How do we have societies in which everyone prospers and not just a defensive and self-righteous elite—1 percent in Mozambique, 5 percent in Russia, and 10 percent, at most, in the United States?

For better or worse, the university has became increasingly responsible for imagining progress for the whole of society. Intellectually, at least, it is up to the task. But if it is to succeed, it will need a renewed financial base and a new confidence in its public mission.

Appendix:
Flaws of the "Liberal Bias" Campaign

The intellectual diversity campaign had two main institutional sponsors, ACTA and the Center for the Study of Popular Culture, the former co-founded by Lynne Cheney, the latter operated by conservative activist David Horowitz and renamed in mid-2006 as the David Horowitz Freedom Center.[1] The overlap between the two organizations is evident not only in their funding sources, but in their goals and materials: the ACTA report's recommendations on intellectual diversity, for example, are largely a paraphrase of Horowitz's brainchild, the Academic Bill of Rights, though the recommendations do not cite it. The joint campaign for intellectual diversity developed hand in hand with the steady intensification of the monitoring of the university by both the government and conservative groups. Many universities objected to new restrictions on visas for the foreign graduate students on whom their programs depended, to new export controls, to new lists of sensitive materials that could not be handled by people of certain nationalities or with other background features.[2] There was also resistance, though it was less official, to charges leveled at the university by conservative activists.

Although the monitoring of campus activities was sometimes compared to similar activities during the McCarthy period in the United States,[3] the historian of the McCarthy-era university, Ellen Schrecker, has pointed out one difference. "McCarthyism dealt mainly with off-campus political activities. Now they focus on what is going on in the classroom. . . . It's reaching into the core academic functions of the university."[4] The campaigns of the early 2000s cast a narrower net. As the historian John Munro observed, "The left had to be purged from the NAACP, the CIO, Hollywood, plus the Council on African Affairs, the Civil Rights Congress, the Jefferson School of Social Science, etc.,

etc.; then there was the left's leadership that was to be imprisoned, deported, and denied passports, plus the Congressional hearings that made many in a range of professions unable to get a job. Today, the job is easier: the intellectual left is concentrated in universities and colleges, and thus the Right's firepower is mainly concentrated on the campuses and their classrooms."[5] Regardless of the strength or weakness of the 1950s parallels, ACTA's report "Intellectual Diversity: Time for Action" offered a leading example of the 2000s strategy of moving into the core of the faculty's professional life.[6]

David Horowitz was equally active during this period. He pursued a traditional culture-war infrastructural strategy of building a cluster of organizations with the same agenda, activities, output, and even personnel, whose collective, mutually referential activities created the impression of a trend by gathering material from volunteers—in this case, undergraduates in various colleges and universities—and generating a blizzard of reciprocal citation. In addition to the center named above, Horowitz had established the Students for Academic Freedom (SAF) and was "involved with Campus Watch, Jihad Watch, Professors Watch and Media Watch; he was also connected to discoverthenetworks.org," another watchdog group.[7] In addition, he supported local campus activities, the most infamous being a UCLA blacklist of apparently radical professors ("the Dirty Thirty"), run by a twenty-four-year-old UCLA graduate and former SAF intern who set up a professor-rating Web site designed to resemble the site of the official UCLA alumni association.[8] Such sites mirrored each other's material and offered Internet news releases based, as we will see, on a very small amount of research, little or none of which was subject to quality control, and whose results were ambiguous and systematically distorted.

Horowitz's best-known initiative in this decade was the drafting and advocating of the Academic Bill of Rights (ABOR). ABOR declared that students should not be graded "on the basis of their political or religious beliefs," that "curricula and reading lists in the humanities and social sciences should reflect the uncertainty and unsettled character of all human knowledge in these areas by providing students with dissenting sources and viewpoints where appropriate," that faculty should not indoctrinate, and that "allocation of funds for speakers programs and other student activities [should] observe the principles of academic freedom and promote intellectual pluralism."[9] These positions were almost universally shared by faculty, with qualifications I mention later: the point of the campaign was to suggest that these principles had to be legislated because they were being violated on campuses across the country.

ABOR and its ostensibly liberal requirements were discussed in more than twenty state legislatures, and went the farthest in the state of Pennsylvania, where a very effective ABOR campaign was launched when a Republican activist approached a legislator at a fund-raiser with a story about a state college physics professor who used class time to denounce President Bush.[10] In July 2005, the Pennsylvania legislature established "a select committee to examine the academic atmosphere and the degree to which faculty have the opportunity to instruct and students have the opportunity to learn in an environment conducive to the pursuit of knowledge and truth."[11] Horowitz, ABOR's main advocate, said he felt this was "a tremendous victory for academic freedom." By "victory for academic freedom," he was referring in this case to the setting up of a political committee to monitor academia.[12]

Horowitz and ACTA claimed to call for the classic liberal virtues of freedom of inquiry and an impartial hearing of all opinions. They claimed that their target was political uniformity, and based this claim on surveys showing that academia was running 8 to 1 or 10 to 1 Democratic to Republican majorities on their faculties. Because of their safety in numbers, these liberals could allegedly misbehave and, more important, freely reproduce themselves. Conservative reports and the generally credulous journalistic accounts that spread them offered a range of anecdotes: sometimes a truth-seeking conservative student was humiliated by a dogmatic, Bush-bashing liberal professor. At other times invited lecturers were heckled by liberal students. At still other times exam questions were biased and grading disfavored conservative opinions.[13] These charges appeared on many conservative Web sites and in other media outlets, and were featured in major dailies like the *New York Times* via columnists such as David Brooks and John Tierney.[14] Conservative academics, such as the English professor Mark Bauerlein, were cited explaining how the numerical dominance of liberals informally but inexorably marginalized conservatives.[15] Conservative researchers sometimes confessed in their academic papers their sense of their own marginality: one author's statement, posted by the Students for Academic Freedom, declared, "The lead author, Christopher F. Cardiff, felt politically homeless through his first four opportunities to vote for president. Eventually, he found that his beliefs are best described as libertarian-tending-to-vote-Republican. As an economist, his chief research interest is education policy. His motivation to conduct this investigation arose from the monolithic political culture that his daughter seemed to confront (in his eyes) as she shopped for an undergraduate education."[16]

The kind of arguments about unfair majority power monopolies that conservatives had laughed at when described by, say, Lani Guinier, now founded the gospel of conservative victimization and motivated at least some of their research.

The most systematic public presentation of academia as a fount of liberal thought control again came from ACTA in the form of the report I mentioned at the start of this appendix, "Intellectual Diversity: Time for Action."[17] Building on a commissioned survey,[18] the report claimed that "today's college faculties . . . are overwhelmingly one-sided in their political and ideological views, especially in the value-laden fields of the humanities and social sciences."[19] The foreword declared, "The academy has become one-sided and coercive—indeed, even hostile, to a multiplicity of viewpoints. Study after study has documented the politically one-sided nature of the faculty. . . . Nearly half of students at the top 50 colleges ranked by *U.S. News & World Report* reported significant political pressure in the classroom, nothing short of a direct attack on their right and ability to learn."[20]

These were serious charges: not only were faculty expressing antiwar views and criticisms of authority outside of class; they seemed to be doing more or less the same thing during class time. But did ACTA really have the evidence of "study after study" for its main claims that (1) universities lack intellectual diversity, (2) faculty are exerting "significant political pressure" on students in class, and (3) faculty are therefore mounting a direct attack on students' "right and ability to learn"?

The last charge follows entirely from the first two, so I will look at those in turn.

The report sought to prove the first charge, the absence of intellectual diversity, by showing that faculty overwhelmingly self-identify as liberal rather than conservative, or as Democrat rather than Republican. Some surveys going back to the 1970s (mostly associated with Seymour Martin Lipset) showed that university faculty were generally more Democrat than Republican.[21] Some kind of Democratic majority would be neither news nor scandal: ACTA was looking for higher multiples of Democratic representation that would imply domination and hegemony.

The report's reference to "study after study" boiled down to two studies in the midst of the busy network of mutual cross-referencing. The first, by Stanley Rothman, S. Robert Lichter, and Neil Nevitte, found that "72 percent of those teaching at American universities and colleges describe themselves as liberal and 15 percent, conservative."[22] The second survey found "that among academics at the University of California and at Stanford, the ratio of Democrats to Republicans is 8 or 10 to 1. . . . The ratio of Democrats to Republicans was 28:1 among sociologists and 30:1 for anthropologists."[23] The second study dubbed this the "D to R ratio" and concluded that the American university is a "one-party state." It was these two rather small, noncomprehensive, nonrepresentative, but still relatively orthodox studies, bolstered by a penumbra of journalistic commentary and advocacy pieces not based on independent research, that disseminated ACTA's charge that American universities lacked and, worse, actively suppressed intellectual diversity.[24]

Though ACTA's argument hinged on the validity of these two studies, they were flawed in a number of ways. First, each of the two cited studies fell short of the standards of academic peer review. The Rothman et al. essay did not go through a standard peer review process at publication, and the authors had not as of 2007 released the data on which they relied, though it was originally gathered in 1999.[25] Various people have tried with no success to find this 1999 study, conducted by a firm that no longer exists in its original form.[26] Though the 1999 study's apparent professionalism and independence was used in news reports to validate Rothman et al.'s findings, this kind of professional, scholarly validation of their data could not as of this writing be conducted by other researchers.[27]

As for the second study, by Daniel B. Klein and Charlotta Stern, their work does not appear to have been peer reviewed either. One version circulated on the Internet in manuscript form (dated 2003), and an extended treatment of the same material later appeared in *The Critical Review* (2006), a journal of unknown procedures published by the Critical Review Foundation, which is funded in part by the conservative groups that also fund the Students for Academic Freedom, which in turn posted *The Critical Review*'s studies of faculty bias.[28] This process inflated the quantity of actual research to the casual or overworked eyes of, for example, journalists and congressional staffers.[29] But it did not enable the results of this already very small set of surveys to be reviewed or reproduced by the standards of professional, independent, and open science.

Second, neither of these surveys came from outside the Horowitz-ACTA conservative network.[30] Their authors appeared to receive funding from only those sources and to use personnel who we associated with those networks. While we cannot say that these funding sources dictated the research results, and we can say that scholars are free to collaborate with whomever they choose, and we can additionally say that similarities of outlook often enhance collaboration, it is also true that virtually all research on the impact of funding sources suggests that researchers are more likely than not to reach the conclusions desired by their sponsors. This is true even in work with "hard" data such as clinical trials of new pharmaceutical molecules, where various blind procedures and objective measurements do not prevent results that are up to 70 percent more favorable to a sponsor's product than results in studies without this type of sponsorship.[31] Social and cultural research generally requires complex interpretations of intricate, many-variable, nonlinear systems, making rigor in interpretation both more difficult and more important. The chances for this open and complex interpretation is lower when research, like that being discussed here, is funded by foundations whose explicit mission has not been the disinterested pursuit of truth, but the promotion of conservative principles and approaches.[32] These foundations—Olin, Safe, and Bradley, among others—and the think tanks they fund have a long and successful history of getting the answers that they are looking for.[33] Scholars who accept money from such sources have a clear professional obligation to resolve the questions of their professional peers by releasing their underlying data. This is an obligation that these two sets of authors did not meet.

Third, these studies were contradicted by a series of other surveys that show ratios much closer to the "balance" ACTA and Horowitz claim to desire. In addition to older surveys mentioned by both Rothman et al. and Klein and Stern, a more thorough study, "The American College Teacher" (2001), conducted by UCLA's well-known Higher Education Research Institute, "found that 5.3 percent of faculty members were far left, 42.3 percent were liberal, 34.3 percent were middle of the road, 17.7 percent were conservative, and 0.3 percent were far right."[34] A reasonable division of the category "middle of the road" could lead to the interpretation that liberals had a 60–40 advantage in university faculties, which is of course common enough in American congressional districts (as is the reverse). An equally reasonable interpretation would suggest that college campuses as a whole were split between liberals and conservatives. Finally, the most thorough reinvestigation of these claims concluded that the political orientation of a group of faculty varies greatly by discipline, with many having conservative pluralities, and further, that the most accurate description of the overall political tendency of the professoriate is a movement toward the center.[35] The surveys ACTA uses are anomalous in the literature and thus in special need of replication and corroboration.

ACTA's findings are also partially at odds with their own data. Once one gets past the sound bites and reads the full studies, the ACTA-cited research undermine ACTA's most prominent claims. For example, Rothman et al. cast doubt on the 72–15 number that was always cited in press reports[36] by noting that "liberals outnumber conservatives . . . by 51% to 19% among engineering faculty and 49% to 39% among business faculty," which are numbers that would allow much give-and-take between department "parties." Although they claim that the humanities and social sciences are four-fifths or three-quarters liberal, Rothman et al. elsewhere say that "62% of humanities faculty and 55% of social scientists are Democrats," which describes a fairly low D-to-R advantage. And again: "Business faculties contain equal proportions (26%) of Democrats and Republicans, and Republicans actually outnumber Democrats by 31% to 24% among agriculture professors." These fair-and-balanced ratios do not support Rothman et al.'s more alarmist numbers, making it all the more desirable that they release the underlying data. When the authors do find large D-to-R imbalances, they seem not so much scandalous as implausible: the statement that "Democrats outnumber Republicans by more than 4 to 1 among biologists and nearly 10 to 1 among physicists," especially in light of their claims about humanities disciplines, suggests errors in calculation.[37]

Fourth, the anomalies in the surveys may be partially explained by the fact that surveys did not examine the full range of academic and professional disciplines that comprise the modern research university. Rothman et al. did not identify the disciplines surveyed; Klein and Stern, however, explicitly omitted the natural sciences, engineering, law, business, and medicine.[38] These fields would most likely contribute quite a few Republicans to the mix, but in any case there is no obvious justification for omitting exactly those fields that teach the majority of students, spend the lion's share of university budgets, and have far greater impact than sociology or anthropology on the management and direction of society.

Fifth, if faculty did lack diversity, it could as easily be because they were timid centrists rather than liberals or leftists. One could argue that in the wake of Bill Clinton's takeover of the Democratic Party, the Democrats moved to the Right and overlapped with the economic conservatives of the Republican Party (though less so with the social and religious Right). The fact that fewer than 3 percent of faculty in the Klein and Stern study describe themselves as either Green or Libertarian could mean that faculty had become generally unimaginative moderates who would oppose any major social change that somehow escaped the notice of congressional Republicans. Though faculty did balk at hard-core culture-war positions (e.g., categorical rejections of all abortion, gay marriage, affirmative action, antiwar protest, and so on), key disciplines had largely accepted its economic components—free trade, business leadership of society and politics, the managerial role of technical economics, among others. Generations of commentators with experience of academia have noted its pronounced methodological conservatism, its preference for further study rather than major decision, its obsession with proof, its rigid merit hierarchies, its favoritism toward the aggressively smart, and its resistance to change. If faculty were ruining the youth of the nation, it was as likely to be through too little radicalism as through too much.

Finally, neither survey offered compelling reasons for equating preponderant "liberalism" or Democratic Party affiliation with the absence of intellectual diversity. In their piece, "Professors and Their Politics," Klein and Stern made the only attempt, but it was not successful. Their claim that "the Democratic tent is relatively narrow" rested on survey responses to terms that encoded the "ideal-type" definitions of the beliefs of the two parties and thus produced orthodox responses. The authors asked for stereotypes, and they got stereotypes in return. In addition, the proof that Democrats agree among themselves more than do Republicans was weakened by the fact that on the main terrain of agreement—the value of government intervention in many matters—Republican social scientists also scored high.[39] Within the standardized terminology, the authors' own numbers suggested quite a bit of diversity, and were the authors to have moved away from the simplistic, decades-old categories of American party politics in which they traded, even political thinking would have shown still greater diversity than the authors claimed.

There is a more important issue that comes up here. Were the questions to have moved out of the realm of party politics and onto professional subjects, the alleged "one-party system" and its static terminology would have disappeared. In the classroom, faculty may exploit politics for accessible examples of concepts, for (sometimes cheap) humor, or for occasional (and undesirable) target practice, but their research and teaching are structured and guided by professional topics and principles. Both surveys used catch-all terms that had no direct bearing on professional and institutional issues. The surveys simply did not ask questions about educational policy that would have enabled the authors to correlate policy with the stereotyped issues they equate with political thought. The surveys did not show that either party affiliation or views on "ideal-type" D or R issues affect attitudes about educational matters; instead, they asked only about political attitudes because they *assumed* that these would affect political behavior. In other words, the authors appear to have assumed that if they showed consensus on a political topic—say, that liberals tend to support abortion rights—then they had shown an isomorphic consensus on, say, the value of admitting more women to economics doctoral programs; they did not therefore actually have to ask questions about the proportion of women in doctoral programs. They thus assumed what they were trying to prove: the alleged causal link between party or "ideological" uniformity and uniformity in teaching and research. There was no basis for this conclusion in either the poll data or the argumentation.

Given the very small number of studies cited and the serious flaws in those studies, ACTA's and the ABOR's sponsors' claims of monolithic and coercive liberalism should have been fixed in the press somewhere between exaggerated and false. But both organizations also made a second claim, which was that students were actually experiencing the effects of this bias in the classroom. Horowitz's contribution to this argument was his book *The Professors*, which identified one hundred faculty members who were tainting scholarship and students' minds. In addition to having serious evidentiary flaws,[40] this book read much like a personal blacklist: the more statistical and less obviously politicized case was made by "Intellectual Diversity," which did not stop with stating the *presumption* of bias but also tried to establish the *fact* of bias. It did this by commissioning its own survey of students at *US News & World Report's* top fifty liberal arts colleges and research universities, and then reporting finding that these students experience bias and irrelevant politicized remarks on a regular basis.[41]

As stated, the findings were alarming: "29 percent of the respondents felt that they had to agree with the professor's political views to get a good grade." "48 percent reported campus panels and lecture series on political issues that seemed 'totally one-sided.' 46 percent said professors 'used the classroom to present their personal political views.' "[42] The report then recycled the claim found in "Defending Civilization" that this indoctrination was happening because "the notion of truth and objectivity is regarded by many professors as antiquated and an obstacle to social change. In this 'postmodern' view, all ideas are political, the classroom is an appropriate place for advocacy, and students should be molded into 'change agents' to promote a political agenda."[43] On the basis of their survey, combined with the authors' prior belief in a widespread faculty rejection of the notion of truth, the report concluded, "Faculty imbalance, combined with the idea that the 'politically correct' point of view has a right to dominate classroom and campus discussions, has had fearful consequences for university life."[44] The university, it said, generates lots of politicized liberal students, but it does not produce *knowledge* anymore.

The authors offered no evidence that one single professor, much less all of them, held the incorrectly described postmodernist epistemology that claims there is no truth. The claim was and is ridiculous, and having commented on an earlier version of it in chapter 15, "The Blame-Academia Crowd: Culture War After 9/11," I will pass over it here.

The only solid ground for the ACTA argument was their commissioned survey, but a close reading of the questions and responses suggests that ACTA presented the results incorrectly.

These were the survey's first two questions.[45]

Q1. On my campus, some panel discussions and presentations on political issues seem totally one-sided.

Strongly agree	15%
Somewhat agree	33%
Somewhat disagree	24%
Strongly disagree	23%
Don't know	5%
Refused	0%

Q2. On my campus, some professors use the classroom to present their personal political views.

Strongly agree	10%
Somewhat agree	36%
Somewhat disagree	24%

Strongly disagree	29%
Don't know	1%
Refused	0%

The survey repeated this wording and the response categories in most of its nineteen questions. Thus, respondents were repeatedly asked whether "some" discussions, "some" professors, or "some" courses involve politics, the names of politicians, political labels, and the like.[46] They were then invited to either "strongly" or "somewhat" agree or disagree.

Unfortunately, multiplying "some" professors by respondents who "somewhat" agreed that these professors "present their personal political views" (Q2) created a very large gray zone. "Some" is a word that catches all responses greater than zero, meaning that if the respondent had had one professor that commented on U.S. war policy in class, this would trigger a positive response. The "somewhat agree" response catches many degrees of *non*-certainty that would otherwise wind up in the "disagree" columns: the respondent may have heard a story about a politicized professor without having a direct experience, and would feel obligated to somewhat agree that some faculty talk politics in class.[47]

A survey that wanted an estimate of the real scope of the behavior in question would ask for precise size estimates and, to avoid the effects of rumor and multiplied citings, would specifically require firsthand experience. Q1 would then have read "On your campus, how many panel discussions and presentations on political issues that you have attended have you felt were totally one-sided"? "A" would be zero, "B" would be 1–2 per academic year, and so on. As written, however, the survey created a penumbra of possibility and speculation that ACTA then added to the positive cases to create an impression of a widespread trend.

This takes us to a second flaw in the survey, which was its method of reporting its findings. Q2 above found that only 10 percent of student respondents strongly agreed that some professors used the classroom to present their personal political views. If we required strong agreement with the statement in order to assume direct and clear experience of the phenomenon in question, Q2 could reasonably be taken as evidence that there was not really much of a problem with political grandstanding in college classrooms. But ACTA took 10 percent to close to 50 percent by adding the top two categories together, yielding the startling finding that 46 percent of students "said professors 'used the classroom to present their personal political views.'" This statement was misleading in two ways: it dropped the "some" used in the question—at best, 46 percent of students said *some* professors do this—and it treated responses of different strengths as though they were the same. Splitting the difference, perhaps we could say that about a quarter of college students thought that some professors brought politics into the classroom. What would this mean, exactly—that a quarter of students have taken courses with the 5 percent of professors who do this, or with the 25 percent who do this? It is hard to interpret these responses with all due caution and still think that a political epidemic had swamped regular administrative procedures and thus required committees of politicians to monitor college classrooms.

Similar misrepresentations dogged the crucial moments in ACTA's text. Sometimes this involved omitting responses that clearly failed to support ACTA's belief that students were being coerced by liberal faculty. For example:

Q14. On my campus, some courses present social and political issues in an unfair and one-sided manner.

Strongly agree	6%
Somewhat agree	23%
Somewhat disagree	34%
Strongly disagree	33%
Don't know	3%
Refused	0%

Even using their own suspect additive methods, 29 percent was not a very impressive proportion of students who felt that *some* courses were unfair and one-sided about material that was explicitly "social and political." If we include only those students who felt strongly and had perhaps been angered or offended, the number dropped to 6 percent. The same goes for ACTA's major claim that faculty had become one-sided and intolerant of other points of view. The survey showed the following results:

Q13. On my campus, some professors are intolerant of certain political and social viewpoints.

Strongly agree	5%
Somewhat agree	16%
Somewhat disagree	26%
Strongly disagree	51%
Don't know	2%

Remarkably, more than half of all students *strongly* disagreed with this statement, and only 5 percent strongly agreed: a fifth agreed at all with this statement. My interpretation of this question is that the university remained rather more tolerant than the other institutions that have shaped these students' lives, including their families, communities, churches, and television news.

The same problem arose for ACTA's strongest allegation of direct faculty misconduct:

Q11. On my campus, there are courses in which students feel they have to agree with the professor's political or social views in order to get a good grade.

Strongly agree	7%
Somewhat agree	22%
Somewhat disagree	22%
Strongly disagree	46%
Don't know	3%
Refused	0%

These numbers did not show a widespread pattern of abuse. Only 7 percent of students showed a meaningful level of certainty of that professors' political and social views affected their grading.

The response that came closest to showing a pedagogical problem was question 10.

Q10. On my campus, some professors frequently comment on politics in class even though it has nothing to do with the course.

Strongly agree	14%
Somewhat agree	35%
Somewhat disagree	26%
Strongly disagree	24%
Don't know	1%
Refused	1%

The report translated these results as meaning "that a shocking 49 percent of the students at the top 50 colleges and universities say that their professors *frequently* injected political comments into their courses, even if they had nothing to do with the subject." ACTA overstated its case in its usual way. Students were asked if *some* professors do this, and just 14 percent "strongly agreed." In addition, ACTA spun the question about "commenting" on politics into "injecting political comments." The sense of an epidemic of faculty indoctrination was again misleadingly overstated.

The claims made by the Horowitz operations and by ACTA received a great deal of media attention. They did not receive an equal amount of corroboration. Though large-scale reviews of Horowitz's charges have not substantiated his claims,[48] Horowitz's and ACTA's statements about faculty bias and faculty indoctrination were taken seriously enough to prompt the Pennsylvania investigation of faculty conduct I mentioned earlier, where ACTA's president offered testimony.[49] Horowitz continued to push his categorical claims in the face of open skepticism. Describing the questions about evidence for several of his anecdotes as "irrelevant, nitpicking attacks," Horowitz declared, " 'everybody who is familiar with universities knows that there is a widespread practice of professors venting about foreign policy even when their classes aren't about foreign policy' and that the lack of evidence on [the case in question at] Penn State doesn't mean there isn't a problem."[50] Nonetheless, the Pennsylvania Select Committee on Academic Freedom in Higher Education concluded its hearings having aired many complaints about the drift of academics but no evidence of faculty coercing students. "Rep. Dan A. Surra, a Democrat on the panel who was a vocal critic of its formation, called the hearings a fishing expedition. 'We haven't caught anything yet,' he said. 'I hope as we sit down as a committee, we'll come up with recommendations that accurately reflect the lack of a problem.' "[51] Meanwhile, the state representative who had convened the select committee lost his job in his party's primary.

It would have been nice to think these setbacks would restore a little intellectual diversity to the public discussion of education and society. But the main goals of the cultural campaign had already been achieved: it had systematically associated the university with reflexive divergence from American society. Just when we might think that this was a good thing, because we could not get a minute's sense from the staging of politics on TV, we were told that the university's difference was unthinking dissent, and not just dissent but opposition, and not reasoned opposition but dogmatic opposition based on arrogance and leading to the manipulation of student minds. The university turned out once again to be particularly suspect when it produced cultural knowledge—its culture fields harbored the most undiluted and conspiratorial pack of liberal-radicals one could find in America. As we have seen, the evidence for these claims was exaggerated, misleading, or nonexistent. But what difference should that make? The very concept of evidence came from academia, and it was being used by liberals to shield themselves from the truth.

Horowitz and other members of his network regularly lost interest in the evidence surrounding real cases, suggesting that the real goal of the "intellectual diversity" campaign was not better balance in actual university classrooms. The goal that was in fact achieved was to sustain the culture-wars attacks on the actual practices associated with these classrooms, particularly in discussion formats in which cultural knowledge came into play. In reality, the college seminar enacted dialogue and negotiation across intellectual and social differences, and did so on a daily basis. No seminar instructor could succeed unless he or she combined expert knowledge with decent diplomatic skills. Though professors generally had the power advantage, the good ones refrained from acting like the "sole superpower" in a room of students. The practice of strategic equality was the essence of good teaching. By recasting equitable interaction as tyranny, culture warriors could make the post-9/11 themes of unilateral force and executive decision appear normal and right, while relegating equality, mutual respect, power sharing, and other features associated with postwar academia to a shadow world of defunct and radical dreaming.

Notes

Introduction

1. Documents on the UCSB hunger strike are in the UCSB Ethnic Studies Protest Collection, 1989–1995, California Ethnic and Multicultural Archives, Department of Special Collections, Davidson Library, University of California, Santa Barbara, CEMA 93, box 1, folders 7–11.

2. Robert H. Frank and Philip J. Cook, *The Winner-Take-All Society: Why the Few at the Top Get So Much More than the Rest of Us* (New York: Free Press, 1995).

3. Ian Dew-Becker and Robert J. Gordon, "Where Did the Productivity Growth Go? Inflation Dynamics and the Distribution of Income" (National Bureau of Economic Research Working Paper 11842), pp. 58–59, http://www.nber.org/papers/w11842 (accessed April 2, 2006).

4. Edmund G. "Pat" Brown, "Inaugural Address" (speech presented at start of second term as governor of California, January 7, 1963), http://www.governor.ca.gov/govsite/govsgallery/h/documents/inaugural_32b.html (accessed September 20, 2006).

5. Daniel Bell, *The Coming of Post-Industrial Society: A Venture in Social Forecasting* (1973; New York: Basic Books, 1976), xiii.

6. For example, Robert Zemsky, Gregory R. Wegner, and William F. Massy, *Remaking the American University: Market-Smart and Mission-Centered* (New Brunswick, NJ: Rutgers University Press, 2005), 6–7.

7. Stanton A. Glantz, Department of Medicine, University of California, San Francisco, cited in Scott Jaschik, "Does Tobacco Money Taint Research?" *Inside Higher Ed* (September 21, 2006), http://www.insidehighered.com/news/2006/09/21/tobacco (accessed September 21, 2006).

1. The Three Crises and the Mass Middle Class

1. Secretary of Education's Commission on the Future of Higher Education, "Commission Report 6/22/06 Draft," http://www.ed.gov/about/bdscomm/list/ hiedfuture/reports/0622-draft.pdf (accessed June 29, 2006). This language was softened under protest but expressed the views of many of the commission's members.

2. See the American Association of University Professors, "Financial Inequality in Higher Education: The Annual Report on the Economic Status of the Profession, 2006–07," http://www.aaup.org/AAUP/pubsres/research/compensation.htm (accessed May 7, 2007).

3. See chapter 9.

4. Christopher Newfield, "Nano-Punk for Tomorrow's People," review of "Tomorrow's People: The Challenges of Technologies for Life Extension and Enhancement" (conference at the James Martin Institute, Said Business School, University of Oxford, March 2006), http://www.martininstitute.ox.ac.uk/NR/ rdonlyres/0B4E5B3A-7D58-45A6-A63E-4ABBA77DEDB5/506/OxfordNewfield Rpt0306JMI.pdf; and http://repositories.cdlib.org/isber/cns/22 (accessed May 7, 2007).

5. For two useful critical overviews, see Arturo Escobar, *Encountering Development: The Making and Unmaking of the Third World* (Princeton, NJ: Princeton University Press, 1995); and Michael E. Lantham, *Modernization as Ideology: American Social Science and "Nation Building" in the Kennedy Era* (Chapel Hill: University of North Carolina Press, 2000). For a more supportive appraisal, see Nils Gilman, *Mandarins of the Future: Modernization Theory in Cold War America* (Baltimore: Johns Hopkins University Press, 2003).

6. United Nations, Human Development Reports, "What Is HD," http://hdr.undp .org/hd/ (accessed August 31, 2006).

7. Lisa McGill, *Suburban Warriors: The Origins of the New American Right* (Princeton, NJ: Princeton University Press, 2001).

8. See Christopher Newfield, "Jurassic U: The State of University-Industry Relations," *Social Text* 22, no. 2 (2004): 63n27. The classic account of the American loss of economic dominance is David Harvey, *The Condition of Postmodernity: An Enquiry into the Origins of Cultural Change* (New York: Blackwell, 1991). This statistic that the American work year has increased by 19 percent per person (Nicholas Crafts "East Asian Growth Before and After the Crisis," *IMF Staff Papers* 46, no. 2 (June 1999), Table 7, http://www.imf.org/external/pubs/ ft/staffp/1999/pdf/crafts.pdf [accessed July 15, 2007]) is complicated by data from the International Labor Organization, http://laborsta.ilo.org/; see "Yearly Statistics," then "4A Hours of work, by economic activity" (accessed July 15, 2007).

9. On the increasing acceptability of layoffs as a means of improving profits, see Louis Uchitelle, *The Disposable American: Layoffs and Their Consequences* (New York: Knopf, 2006).

10. Sandra Braman, "Tactical Memory: The Politics of Openness in the Construction of Memory," *First Monday* 11, no. 7 (July 2006), http://firstmonday.org/issues/issue11_7/braman/index.html (accessed April 26, 2007).

11. See Elizabeth Borqwardt, *A New Deal for the World: America's Vision for Human Rights* (Cambridge, MA: Belknap Press, 2005).

12. George Lipsitz and Ira Katznelson have argued that these benefits were overwhelmingly designated for and enjoyed by whites: George Lipsitz, *The Possessive Investment in Whiteness: How White People Profit from Identity Politics* (Philadelphia: Temple University Press, 1998); Ira Katznelson, *When Affirmative Action Was White: An Untold History of Racial Inequality in Twentieth-Century America* (New York: W. W. Norton, 2005).

13. Paul Buhle, *Taking Care of Business: Samuel Gompers, George Meany, Lane Kirkland, and the Tragedy of American Labor* (New York: Monthly Review Press, 1999); Nelson Lichtenstein, *State of the Union: A Century of American Labor* (Princeton, NJ: Princeton University Press, 2002).

14. Brenda Gayle Plummer, *Rising Wind: Black Americans and U.S. Foreign Affairs, 1935–1960* (Chapel Hill: University of North Carolina Press, 1996); Penny M. Von Eschen, *Race Against Empire: Black Americans and Anticolonialism, 1937–1957* (Ithaca, NY: Cornell University Press, 1997); Mary Dudziak, *Cold War Civil Rights: Race and the Image of American Democracy* (Princeton, NJ: Princeton University Press, 2000); Thomas Borstelmann, *The Cold War and the Color Line: American Race Relations in the Global Arena* (Cambridge, MA: Harvard University Press, 2001); Carol Anderson, *Eyes Off the Prize: The United Nations and the African American Struggle for Human Rights, 1944–1955* (New York: Cambridge University Press, 2003).

15. Robert M. Collins, *More: The Politics of Economic Growth in Postwar America* (New York: Oxford University Press, 2000).

16. Lizabeth Cohen, *A Consumers' Republic: The Politics of Mass Consumption in Postwar America* (New York: Vintage, 2003). See also David M. Potter, *People of Plenty: Economic Abundance and the American Character* (Chicago: University of Chicago Press, 1954); John Kenneth Galbraith, *The Affluent Society* (New York: Houghton Mifflin, 1958); Daniel Horowitz, *The Anxieties of Affluence: Critiques of American Consumer Culture, 1939–1979* (Boston: University of Massachusetts Press, 2004).

17. Christopher Newfield, *Ivy and Industry: Business and the Making of the American University, 1880–1980* (Durham, NC: Duke University Press, 2003), 115–116.

18. Daniel Bell, *The Coming of Post-Industrial Society: A Venture in Social Forecasting* (New York: Basic Books, 1973).

19. Walter Lippmann, *Public Opinion* (New York: Harcourt, Brace, 1922), esp. chap. 25, "The Entering Wedge." For wider context, see Alan Dawley, *Changing the World: American Progressives in War and Revolution* (Princeton, NJ: Princeton University Press, 2003).

20. Clark Kerr, *The Uses of the University* (Cambridge, MA: Harvard University Press, 1963), v–vi.

21. The key text that defined the link between middle-class America and continuous growth was Galbraith, *The Affluent Society*.

22. Foucault famously wrote, "By subjugated knowledges I mean two things: on the one hand, I am referring to the historical contents that have been buried and disguised in a functionalist coherence or formal systemization. . . . On the other hand, I believe that by subjugated knowledges one should understand something else, something which in a sense is altogether different, namely, a whole set of knowledges that have been disqualified as inadequate to their task or insufficiently elaborated: naïve knowledges, located low down on the hierarchy, beneath the required level of cognition or scientificity." Michel Foucault, "Two Lectures," in *Power/Knowledge: Selected Interviews and Other Writings, 1972–1977* (New York: Pantheon, 1980), 81–82.

23. "Where mass opinion dominates the government, there is a morbid derangement of the true functions of power. The derangement brings about the enfeeblement, verging on paralysis, of the capacity to govern. This breakdown in the constitutional order is the cause of the precipitate and catastrophic decline of Western society. It may, if it cannot be arrested and reversed, bring about the fall of the West." Walter Lippmann, *The Public Philosophy* (New York: New American Library, 1955), 19.

24. Erik Olin Wright, *Classes* (New York: Verso, 1985), esp. chap. 2.

25. See Gramsci's well-known discussion of workers whose position can be likened to a middle class whose growing cultural and political capacity was tied to its pivotal work activity: "The active man-in-the-mass has a practical activity, but has no clear theoretical consciousness of his practical activity, which nonetheless involves understanding the world in so far as it transforms it. His theoretical consciousness can indeed be historically in opposition to his activity. One might almost say that he has two theoretical consciousnesses (or one contradictory consciousness); one which is implicit in his activity and which in reality unites him with all his fellow-workers in the practical transformation of the real world; and one, superficially explicit or verbal, which he has inherited from the past and uncritically absorbed." Antonio Gramsci, "The Study of Philosophy," in *Selections from Prison Notebooks* (New York: International Publishers, 1971), 333.

2. Declarations of Independence

1. James Baldwin, *The Fire Next Time* (New York: Vintage, 1962), 85.

2. Martin Luther King Jr., *Where Do We Go from Here: Chaos or Community?* (Boston: Beacon, 1967), 32–33.

3. E. Franklin Frazier, *Black Bourgeoisie: The Rise of a New Middle Class* (New York: Free Press, 1957), 84–85.

4. For example, this was one of Malcolm X's central themes and was the rationale behind the Student Nonviolent Coordinating Committee's (SNCC) expulsion of white members. And this sentiment was not limited to African Americans: see also Clyde Warrior, who wrote, "We are not free. We do not make choices. Our choices are made for us; we are the poor. For those of us who live on reservations these choices and decisions are made by federal administrators, bureaucrats, and their 'yes men,' euphemistically called tribal governments. Those of us who live in non-reservation areas have our lives controlled by local white power elites. We have many rulers. They are called social workers, 'cops,' school teachers, churches, etc., and now OEO [Office of Economic Opportunity] employees. . . . For the sake of our children, for the sake of the spiritual and material well-being of our total community we must be able to demonstrate competence to ourselves." "We Are Not Free" (1967), in *Red Power: The American Indians' Fight for Freedom*, 2nd ed., ed. Alvin M. Josephy Jr., Joane Nagel, and Troy Johnson (Lincoln: University of Nebraska Press, 1997), 17, 19.

5. John Kenneth Galbraith, *The New Industrial State* (New York, Houghton Mifflin, 1967), 32–33.

6. Ibid., 243.

7. Ibid., 161. As we will see, this is exactly the position denounced by the conservative "shareholder revolt" against the power of employees.

8. Ibid., 162.

9. Ibid., 199.

10. Ibid., 246–248.

11. Ibid., 262.

12. Ibid., 312, and chap. 30 passim.

13. Ibid., 341.

14. Alvin Toffler, *Future Shock* (New York: Random House, 1970), 134–135.

15. Robert B. Reich, *The Work of Nations: Preparing Ourselves for 21st-Century Capitalism* (1991; New York: Vintage, 1992), 88–89.

16. Peter F. Drucker, *Post-Capitalist Society* (New York: Basic Books, 1993), 8. For a contextual argument that situates Drucker's work on the corporation as oppositional to the Keynesianism with which Galbraith sympathized, see Nils Gilman, "The Prophet of Post-Fordism: Peter Drucker and the Legitimation of the

Corporation," in *American Capitalism: Social Thought and Political Economy in the Twentieth Century* (Philadelphia: University of Pennsylvania Press, 2006).

17. For example, compare Drucker to the notion of a "cognitive elite" promoted by Richard Herrnstein and Charles Murray's *The Bell Curve: Intelligence and Class Structure in American Life* (New York: Free Press, 1994).

18. See Peter F. Drucker, "Managing Oneself," *Harvard Business Review* (March–April 1998): 64–74.

19. Desmond Ryan, "The Thatcher Government's Attack on Higher Education in Historical Perspective," *New Left Review* I/227 (January–February 1998), 4.

20. Malcolm X, "The Leverett House Forum of March 18, 1964," in *Speeches at Harvard*, ed. Archie Epps (1964; New York: Paragon, 1991), 142.

21. Robert M. Pirsig, *Zen and the Art of Motorcycle Maintenance* (New York: Bantam, 1974), 9.

22. Ibid., 163.

23. Jean-François Lyotard, *The Postmodern Condition: A Report on Knowledge*, trans. Geoff Bennington and Brian Massumi (1979; Minneapolis: University of Minnesota Press, 1984).

24. John Guillory, "The Sokal Affair and the History of Criticism," *Critical Inquiry* 28 (Winter 2002): 470–508. Lyotard's objection to taking the physical and natural sciences as the standard of valid knowledge was forceful but not especially radical—his fellow travelers included his ostensibly anti-postmodernist antagonist, Jürgen Habermas, who also argued that science's preeminence wrongly undermines other kinds of knowledge. In his important *Knowledge and Human Interests* (trans. Jeremy J. Shapiro [1968; Boston: Beacon Press, 1971]), Habermas argued that the rich tradition of inquiry into the nature and conditions of knowledge was truncated by nineteenth-century positivism, which radically narrowed this inquiry to "methodological inquiry into the rules for the construction and corroboration of scientific theories" (67). The philosophy of science comes to monopolize epistemology just as science comes to monopolize knowledge. Habermas's book was the philosophical equivalent of a jailbreak film, in which he chronicled various inadequate attempts to flee this monopoly. He was especially concerned about the way breakout arguments had been repeatedly dismissed as symptoms of "mere" psychology. This last theme has special pertinence to the humanities.

25. Most commentary on this book has focused on its alleged epistemological skepticism. Lyotard did reject classical realism wholeheartedly, and he identified postmodernism with an "incredulity toward metanarratives" (*Postmodern Condition*, xxiv). He described knowledge systems as narratives that integrate and make sense of the data at hand. Following Wittgenstein, he called them "language games," where meaning is "the object of a contract, explicit or not, between players (which is not to say that the players invent the rules)" (10). The

concept here would be familiar to readers of Carnap, Quine, Kuhn, and others. The fact that science is correct about what makes planes fly does not make science less linguistic, institutional, contractual, that is, less in need of a narrative that legitimates it by bringing all its pieces together. Lyotard's sense of science as a language-game marked not a "postmodernist" break with modernist philosophy of science, but its continuation.

26. Though Lyotard made some dubious claims about "postmodern" science, he was quite right about the cultural and social context in which science operated. For a critique of Lyotard's use of science, see Alan Sokal and Jean Bricmont, *Fashionable Nonsense: Postmodern Intellectuals' Abuse of Science* (New York: Picador, 1998), 134–138. Sokal and Bricmont clearly trade on their book's value as a critique of postmodernism overall, but their project is more precise. "We make no claim to analyze postmodernist thought in general; rather, our aim is to draw attention to a relatively little-known aspect, namely the repeated abuse of concepts and terminology coming from mathematics and physics" (4). Their procedure calls for two comments. First, they repeatedly criticize the transportation of scientific concepts into cultural and philosophical fields; they object to the misuse of such terms as "complexity" as metaphors and so on (see also their description of their methodology on 4–5). In other words, they object to the context-free use of terminology, and in this way their book can be seen as a useful cultural studies–style critique. Second, they write as though their discrediting of postmodernist uses of science amounts to a discrediting of postmodern thought. They seem to assume that scientific terms have a determinate effect on the discourses in which they appear, or, in other words, that science remains the deciding factor even in nonscientific discourses. It is *this* universalizing move that Lyotard rejected. Sokal and Bricmont do not discuss any other aspect of Lyotard's work, and certainly not his larger historical argument.

27. Lyotard, *Postmodern Condition*, 35.

28. Ibid., 33.

29. Ibid., 34.

30. Emancipation and optimization are overlapping competitors, not opposites, and this competition does not require an untenable contrast between them. On this question in the tradition of European higher education to which Lyotard also refers, Jacques Derrida wrote that "we know better than ever before what must have been true for all time, that this opposition between the basic and the end-oriented is of real but limited relevance. . . . One can no longer distinguish between technology on the one hand and theory, science and rationality on the other." "The Principle of Reason: The University in the Eyes of Its Pupils," *Diacritics* 13, no. 3 (Fall 1983): 12.

31. Lyotard, *Postmodern Condition*, 76.

32. A later and more comprehensive exploration of the ties between postmodernism and the economy is Frederic Jameson, *Postmodernism, or the Logic of Late Capitalism* (Durham, NC: Duke University Press, 1991).

33. Lyotard, *Postmodern Condition*, 44.

34. For a simplified but fairly influential example, see Kevin Kelly, "New Rules for the New Economy: Twelve Dependable Principles for Thriving in a Turbulent World," *Wired* 5, no. 9 (September 1997), http://www.wired.com/wired/archive/5.09/newrules.html (accesed February 12, 2006).

35. Lyotard, *Postmodern Condition*, 45.

36. Although the topic is outside the scope of this work, it is worth remembering that Lyotard tied the rise of the economic narrative to extensive bullying and coercion. He called this *terror*. "By terror," he wrote, "I mean the efficiency gained by eliminating, or threatening to eliminate, a player from the language game one shares with him. He is silenced or consents, not because he has been refuted, but because his ability to participate has been threatened" (Lyotard, *Postmodern Condition*, 63–64). Obviously, criticizing a cultural-studies analysis of science does not make one a terrorist. Criticism is not in itself the rejection of one's right to play. But the science wars have sometimes had the terrorist undertone of denying the right of narrative, nonscientific knowledge to say anything about science's effects or direction. This is the juncture for which Lyotard saved his most negative criticism. It is the juncture where science insists on its immunity from *narrative* knowledge by ignoring its placement in the social bonds it says corrupts everybody else. It is the juncture where science tries to throw literary and cultural study (LCS) and other narrative-based analysts out of the game. As I see it, this move, when it occurs, does not originate in scientific practice as such but in a version of the optimization narrative that sees science as irresistible and inevitable.

37. The optimization narrative claims to synthesize freedom and truth precisely by keeping them separate: it serves its idea of human freedom by seeming to separate human interests from the pursuit of knowledge through various forms of theory and technique. This dichotomy depends on a classical realism that has lost its philosophical plausibility, though it is sustained by economic interests.

38. For one strong meditation on the meanings of criticism after the exhaustion of romantic narratives of linear historical progress toward freedom, see David Scott, *Conscripts of Modernity: The Tragedy of Colonial Enlightenment* (Durham, NC: Duke University Press, 2004).

3. The Discrediting of Social Equality

1. Seth Rosenfeld, "The FBI's Secret UC Files," *San Francisco Chronicle*, special report, June 9, 2002, http://sfgate.com/cgi-bin/article.cgi?f=/c/a/2002/06/09/

MNCF1.DTL (accessed September 1, 2006). Rosenfeld's multi-part report was the culmination of a seventeen-year effort to obtain FBI documents about its investigation of UC, then-president Clark Kerr, and other figures. My discussion of UC and the FBI derives from Rosenfeld's investigation.

2. Seth Rosenfeld, "The Governor's Race," *San Francisco Chronicle*, special report, June 9, 2002, http://sfgate.com/cgi-bin/article.cgi?f=/c/a/2002/06/09/MNCF3 .DTL (accessed September 1, 2006).

3. Ibid.

4. See, for example, Elizabeth A. Fones-Wolf, *Selling Free Enterprise: The Business Assault on Labor and Liberalism, 1945–1960* (Champaign: University of Illinois Press, 1994); Sanford M. Jacoby, *Modern Manors: Welfare Capitalism Since the New Deal* (Princeton, NJ: Princeton University Press, 1997); Jennifer Klein, *For All These Rights: Business, Labor, and the Shaping of America's Public-Private Welfare State* (Princeton, NJ: Princeton University Press, 2003).

5. For a criticism of the impact recently attributed to the Powell memo, see Mark Schmitt, "The Legend of the Powell Memo," *American Prospect On-Line*, April 27, 2005, http://www.prospect.org/web/page.ww?section=root&name=View Web&articleId=9606 (accessed September 1, 2006). See also David A. Hollinger, *Cosmopolitanism and Solidarity Studies in Ethnoracial, Religious, and Professional Affiliation in the United States* (Madison: University of Wisconsin Press, 2006), 80–90.

6. Lewis F. Powell, "Confidential Memorandum: Attack of American Free Enterprise System," memorandum to Eugene B. Sydnor Jr., Chairman, Education Committee, U.S. Chamber of Commerce, August 23, 1971, http://www .mediatransparency.org/story.php?storyID=22 (accessed September 1, 2006).

7. See, for example, Sidney Blumenthal, *The Rise of the Counter-Establishment: From Conservative Ideology to Political Power* (New York: Harper and Row, 1986), esp. chap. 6.

8. Irving Kristol, "Why Big Business Is Good for America" (1978), in *Conservatism in America since 1930*, ed. Gregory L. Schneider (New York: New York University Press, 2003), 318–335.

9. "The campuses from which much of the criticism emanates are supported by (i) tax funds generated largely from American business, and (ii) contributions from capital funds controlled or generated by American business" (Powell, "Confidential Memorandum: Attack of American Free Enterprise System").

10. Cited in Omkar Muralidharan, "Introduction to Humanities Needs New Aims," *Stanford Review* 34, no. 4 (April 15, 2005), http://www.stanfordreview.org/Archive/ volume–XXXIV/issue4/News/News1/.shtml/ (accessed February 4, 2006).

11. William J. Bennett, *To Reclaim a Legacy: A Report on the Humanities in Higher Education*, National Endowment for the Humanities (November 1984), http:// higher-ed.org/resources/legacy.htm (accessed November 17, 2006).

12. Roger Kimball, *Tenured Radicals: How Politics Has Corrupted Our Higher Education* (New York: HarperCollins, 1991), 74.

13. Arnold is absent from Allan Bloom, *Closing of the American Mind* (New York: Simon & Schuster, 1987), but his role is played by the idealized rule of Neoplatonism.

14. Matthew Arnold, *Culture and Anarchy: An Essay in Political and Social Criticism*, in *The Complete Prose Works of Matthew Arnold*, vol. 5 (Ann Arbor: University of Michigan Press, 1960), 113, 118–119.

15. I have analyzed in detail the similar but more complex role played by Ralph Waldo Emerson in Christopher Newfield, *The Emerson Effect: Individualism and Submission in America* (Chicago: University of Chicago Press, 1996). Bloom noted that "my great influence was Leo Strauss"; see Eugene Kennedy, "A Scholar Who Made Education a Best Seller," *New York Times*, August 2, 1987; on Strauss's remarkable influence on the ideas and people that later came to power as neoconservatives, see Anne Norton, *Leo Strauss and the Politics of American Empire* (New Haven, CT: Yale University Press, 2004).

16. Kennedy, "A Scholar."

17. Some accessible examples, such as "physically challenged" (for "disabled") can be found in "Political Correctness," *Wikipedia*, http://en.wikipedia.org/wiki/Political_correctness (accessed March 23, 2006).

18. Robert Hughes, *Culture of Complaint: The Fraying of America* (Oxford: Oxford University Press, 1994), 18–19.

19. I take up the economic dimension of these attacks in chapter 4, "The Market Substitute for Cultural Knowledge." In the early 1990s, Noam Chomsky tied PC to a "post-affluence class war": see his *Year 501: The Conquest Continues* (Montreal: Black Rose Press, 1993), 54.

20. "According to a report prepared for the *National Council for Research on Women*, print media coverage of the debates began with a slow but steady trickle of articles about 'political correctness' on college campuses in the 1988 to 1990 period, with 101 articles appearing in 1988, and increasing to 656 in 1990. Then, however, the number of articles skyrocketed, with 3,989 articles appearing in 1991, a 500 percent increase over the year before." Media Transparency Project, "Targeting the Academy," http://www.mediatransparency.org/conservativephilanthropy.php?conservativePhilanthropyPageID=11 (accessed July 31, 2006).

21. Jerry Adler, "Taking Offense," *Newsweek*, December 24, 1990, 54.

22. George F. Will, "Literary Politics," *Newsweek*, April 22, 1991, 72.

23. Charles Krauthammer, "An Insidious Rejuvenation of the Old Left," *Los Angeles Times*, December 24, 1990, B5. Conservatives frequently attacked women's studies programs in tandem with ethnic studies. Culturally conservative journalists, during 1990–1992, seemed more wary of the danger to national unity posed by multicultural programs, but this does not imply reconciliation with

women's studies in the least. For an interesting set of responses to the PC-bashing rejection of feminism, see *The Women's Review of Books* for February 1992.

24. Dinesh D'Souza, *Illiberal Education: The Politics of Race and Sex on Campus* (New York: Free Press, 1991), 175, 185.

25. Ibid., 13.

26. Ibid., 214.

27. Ibid., 182.

28. Ibid., 50, 55, 186. D'Souza's dislike for racial difference is particularly striking because he claims to revere differences of nearly every other kind. He complains—sincerely, in my view—that "most American students seem to display striking agreement on all the basic questions of life. Indeed, they appear to regard a true difference of opinion, based upon convictions that are firmly and intensely held, as dangerously dogmatic and an offense against the social etiquette of tolerance" (231).

29. Lyndon B. Johnson, "To Fulfill These Rights" (commencement address at Howard University, June 4, 1965), http://www.lbjlib.utexas.edu/johnson/archives.hom/speeches.hom/650604.asp (accessed July 30, 2006).

30. Schlesinger linked ethnic studies programs to a preference for "group rights" over "individual rights" and to "the decomposition of America." *The Disuniting of America* (Knoxville, TN: Whittle Direct Books, 1991), 78. What many feared to be the Right's vision of multiculturalism materialized in this first edition (cleaned up in the Norton reprint). Every eight pages, it inserted a two-page advertisement for Federal Express. Each ad featured a happy, service-minded employee of a difference race and national origin, each dressed in the Federal Express uniform. The ads conveyed a corporate alternative to a "disunited America," in which cultural differences had dwindled to a range of skin colors and stereotyped postures of solicitude, all united by a common corporate citizenship.

31. Schlesinger claims that Gunnar "Myrdal showed why the Creed held out hope even for those most brutally excluded by the white majority, the Creed acting as the spur forever goading white Americans to live up to their proclaimed principles, the Creed providing the legal structure that gives the wronged the means of fighting for their rights." "America," Myrdal said, "is continuously struggling for its soul"; see Arthur M. Schlesinger Jr., *The Disuniting of America: Reflections on a Multicultural Society*, rev. and enlarged ed. (New York: W. W. Norton, 1998), 33.

32. Henry Louis Gates Jr., "Pluralism and Its Discontents," *Contention* 2, no. 1 (Fall 1992): 71.

33. For an astute overview of the various racial agendas of the period, see Stephen Steinberg, *Turning Back: The Retreat from Racial Justice in American Thought and Policy* (Boston: Beacon Press, 1995).

34. Kimball, *Tenured Radicals*, 207. Kimball's text foundered when it stressed the presence of politics, relativism, nihilism, and so on, and found its focus in an epilogue on multiculturalism. In eight pages Kimball slid from rejecting politics (193) to decrying race-based attacks on the unifying powers of "common culture" (194–195) to tacit declarations of the "West's" superiority (198, 206–207).

35. This last phrase is Avery Gordon's.

36. Mickey Kaus, *The End of Equality* (New York: Basic Books, 1992).

37. National Postsecondary Education Cooperative and American Council on Education, "Reconceptualizing Access in Postsecondary Education: Report of the Policy Panel on Access," August 1998, http://nces.ed.gov/pubsearch/getpubcats .asp?sid=090 (accessed July 30, 2006).

38. William G. Bowen, Martin A. Kurzweil, Eugene M. Tobin, *Equity and Excellence in American Higher Education* (Charlottesville: University of Virginia Press, 2005), 158. The authors state that "if we focus on what has been happening over the past 15 years, rather than over the past 40, we see no basis for being optimistic about score convergence."

39. "College participation rates have been stagnant since the mid 1990s, low income and minority students are increasingly excluded from 4-year institutions and are increasingly concentrated in public 2-year and proprietary institutions, the United States usually ranks last among the 30 OECD countries in gains in college participation rates since about 1990, and the gains in bachelor's degree attainment since 1980 have gone overwhelmingly to students born into the top quartile of family income (about $96,000 per year)." Tom Mortgensen, "Social Inclusion in Tertiary Education," Postsecondary Opportunity, January 27, 2006, http://postsecondaryopportunity.blogspot.com/2006_01_01_archive.html (accessed March 30, 2006).

40. Doug Henwood, "2004: Income Down, Poverty Up," *Left Business Observer* 112 (December 2005): 4.

41. Bowen, Kurzweil, and Tobin, *Equity and Excellence*, 76.

42. Henwood, "2004: Income Down, Poverty Up."

43. Jeffrey Selingo and Jeffrey Brainard, "The Rich-Poor Gap Widens for Colleges and Students," *Chronicle of Higher Education* 7 (April 2006), http://chronicle .com/weekly/v52/i31/31a00101.htm (accessed March 30, 2006).

44. On this trajectory, see Christopher Newfield, "Corporate Culture Wars," in *Corporate Futures: The Diffusion of the Culturally Sensitive Corporate Form*, ed. George Marcus (Chicago: University of Chicago Press, 1998): 23–62; and Christopher Newfield, *Ivy and Industry: Business and the Making of American Culture, 1880–1980* (Durham, NC: Duke University Press, 2006), chap. 8.

4. The Market Substitute for Cultural Knowledge

1. See Christopher Newfield, *Ivy and Industry: Business and the Making of the American University, 1880–1980* (Durham, NC: Duke University Press, 2003), chap. 6, for a discussion of this work.

2. Dinesh D'Souza, *Illiberal Education: The Politics of Race and Sex on Campus* (New York: Free Press, 1991), 13.

3. Ibid., 72.

4. Cited in Jon Guiffo, "Judging Richard," *Columbia Journalism Review* (November 2005), http://www.law.uchicago.edu/news/posner-cjr.html (accessed July 21, 2006).

5. *Ward's Cove Packing Co. v. Atonio*, 490 U.S. 642 (1989), 645–646.

6. Ibid., 653.

7. See in particular *Griggs v. Duke Power Co.*, 401 U.S. 424, 431 (1971) (construing Title VII to proscribe "not only overt discrimination but also practices that are fair in form but discriminatory in practice").

8. *Ward's Cove Packing*, 661.

9. Justice Stevens wrote, "I am thus astonished to read that the 'touchstone of this inquiry is a reasoned review of the employer's justification for his use of the challenged practice.' This casual—almost summary—rejection of the statutory construction that developed in the wake of Griggs is most disturbing" (*Ward's Cove Packing*, 671).

10. Justice Stevens regretted that the "Court announces that our frequent statements that the employer shoulders the burden of proof respecting business necessity 'should have been understood to mean an employer's production—but not persuasion—burden' " (*Ward's Cove Packing*, 671).

11. Michael Denning, *Culture in the Age of Three Worlds* (New York: Verso, 2004), 5.

12. Clinton is quoted as saying, "You had a rap singer here last night named Sister Souljah. I defend her right to express herself through music, but her comments before and after Los Angeles were filled with a kind of hatred that you do not honor today and tonight. Just listen to this, what she said. She told the *Washington Post* about a month ago, and I quote, 'if black people kill black people every day, why not have a week and kill white people?' Last year she said, 'you can't call me or any black person anywhere in the world racist. We don't have the power to do to white people what white people have done to us. And even if we did, we don't have that lowdown, dirty nature. If there are any good white people, I haven't met them.' " "Bill Clinton 1992: Road to the White House," http://www.cnn.com/ALLPOLITICS/1996/candidates/democrat/clinton/campaign.92.shtml (accessed May 27, 2006).

13. For a far more critical assessment of Clinton's racial politics than was available in media coverage of the campaign, see Clyde Woods, *Development Arrested:*

The Blues and Plantation Power in the Mississippi Delta (New York: Verso, 1998). Woods describes Clinton in his role as head of the Lower Mississippi Delta Development Commission as seeking "to rebuild the alliance between the New South and the plantation bloc while continuing the long tradition of incorporating a small segment of the African American community" (255).

14. See especially Barbara Ehrenreich, *Fear of Falling: The Inner Life of the Middle Class* (New York: Pantheon, 1989).

15. The most widely cited evidence for this pattern was Bob Woodward, *The Agenda: Inside the Clinton White House* (New York: Simon and Schuster, 1994). Just before the 1996 elections, another observer summarized Clinton's civil rights achievements more positively: "Since he entered office in January 1993, Clinton has appointed more women and minority-group members to Cabinet and other high-level positions than any other president. He has appointed the highest percentage of minority-group members and women to the federal bench. He became the first president to back measures to end bias against homosexuals, he stepped up enforcement of fair housing laws, and he stoutly defended the government's affirmative action role, declaring in a speech in July 1995 that his goal would be to 'mend it, not end it.'" Stephen A. Holmes, "The Clinton Record: On Civil Rights, Clinton Steers a Bumpy Course," *New York Times*, October 20, 1996.

16. See René Redwood, "The Glass Ceiling: The Findings and Recommendations of the Federal Glass Ceiling Commission," *Motion*, October 2, 1996, http://www.inmotionmagazine.com/glass.html (accessed June 4, 2006); *Good for Business: Making Full Use of the Nation's Human Capital: The Environmental Scan: A Fact Finding Report of the Federal Glass Ceiling Commission* (Washington, DC: U.S. Department of Labor, 1995); *A Solid Investment: Making Full Use of the Nation's Human Capital, Recommendations of the Federal Glass Ceiling Commission, November 1995* (Washington, DC: Government Information Center, 1995).

17. "Transcript of President Clinton's Announcement," *New York Times*, June 4, 1993, http://select.nytimes.com/gst/abstract.html?res=F00611F739590C778CDDAF08 94DB494D81 (accessed May 29, 2006).

18. "President's Reading of Nominee's Work," *New York Times*, June 4, 1993, http://query.nytimes.com/gst/fullpage.html?res=9F0CE3DA123DF937A35755C0A96 5958260 (accessed May 29, 2006).

19. Guinier summarized the negative coverage after April 30 as follows:
The attack was on. Columnists describe me as "breathtakingly radical," a closet extremist with an "in your face" civil rights agenda. I had a "we-they view of race relations." I would impose "a complex racial spoils system that would further polarize an already divided nation." I was "race-obsessed" and "divisive," "undemocratic" and "anticonstitutional." I demanded "equal legislative outcomes, requiring abandonment not only of the one-person-one-vote principle, but majority rule itself." Finally, the public was informed,

I advocated quotas. I believed "blacks should have special rights," and I supported "racial vetoes of majority actions." (Lani Guinier, "Who's Afraid of Lani Guinier," *New York*, February 27, 1994, 41, http://www.law.harvard .edu/faculty/guinier/publications/afraid.pdf [accessed May 29, 2006]).

20. Lani Guinier, "Epilog," *The Tyranny of the Majority: Fundamental Fairness in Representative Democracy* (New York: Free Press, 1994), 189. The epilogue reproduces Guinier's speech of June 4, 1993, in which she responds to Clinton's withdrawal of her Justice Department nomination.

21. A supporter described one of her cases, that of Etowah County, Alabama, which had never elected a black county commissioner before a voting rights challenge in 1986. When the commission was all white, each commissioner exercised sole control over county roadwork for his district, deciding how to allocate resources and whom to hire. With the election of the first black commissioner, the four white commissioners voted to give control over the black district's roadwork to a white commissioner, successfully defeating black citizens' voting rights by eliminating the power of their representative. When Lani Guinier wrote about a "permanent majority" that "constitutes itself based on prejudice," she was addressing situations such as that in Etowah County, where the electorate is so racially polarized that the representative of the minority community is shut out of the political process. William T. Coleman, "Three's Company: Guinier, Reagan, Bush," *New York Times*, June 4, 1993, http://select.nytimes.com/gst/abstract.html?res= F0061EF6345B0C778CDDAF0894DB494D81&showabstract=1 (accessed June 4, 2006). Coleman added, "Consider this statement: 'Democracy is trivialized when reduced to simple majoritarianism.' Lani Guinier has been attacked for suggesting that the 'tyranny of the majority' poses a problem in a few localities such as Etowah County, where there is a permanent, racially constituted majority that eliminates any meaningful African-American participation. Yet the quotation is not Ms. Guinier's. It is a statement by the conservative columnist George Will, writing about the right of senators to filibuster."

22. In *Where Do We Go from Here: Chaos or Community?* (Boston: Beacon Press, 1967), King wrote, "Integration is . . . mutual sharing of power. . . . Justice cannot be achieved without changes in the structure of society. This is a multiracial nation where all groups are dependent on each other. . . . There is no white path to power, short of social disaster, that does not share power with black aspirations for freedom and human dignity" (61–62).

23. Guinier, "Who's Afraid," 54.

24. Jean-François Lyotard, *The Post Modern Condition: A Report on Knowledge*, trans. Geoff Bennington and Brian Massumi (Minneapolis: University of Minnesota Press, 1984); see also chap. 2, note 36.

25. Guinier explained the principle by telling a story about her then-four-year-old son:

While I was writing one of my law journal articles, Nikolas and I had a conversation about voting prompted by a *Sesame Street Magazine* exercise. The magazine pictured six children: four children had raised their hands because they wanted to play tag; two had their hands down because they wanted to play hide-and-seek. The magazine asked its readers to count the number of children whose hands were raised and then decide what game the children would play. Nikolas quite realistically replied, "They will play both. First they will play tag. Then they will play hide-and-seek." Despite the magazine's "rules," he was right. To children, it is natural to take turns. . . . His was a positive-sum solution that many adult rule-makers ignore. (Guinier, "Who's Afraid," 2)

5. From Affirmative Action to the New Economy

1. Census Bureau household income survey, analyzed by Doug Henwood, "2004: Income Down, Poverty Up," *Left Business Observer* 112 (December 2005): 4.

2. See, for example, Isaac Shapiro and Joel Friedman, "New CBO Data Indicate Growth in Long-Term Income Inequality Continues," Center on Budget and Policy Priorities, January 2006, http://www.cbpp.org/1-29-06tax.htm (accessed June 23, 2006); Henwood, "2004: Income Down, Poverty Up," 4–5. The leading Republican chronicler of middle-class decline is Kevin Phillips: see *The Politics of Rich and Poor: Wealth and the American Electorate in the Reagan Aftermath* (New York: Random House, 1989); *Boiling Point: Republicans, Democrats, and the Decline of Middle-Class Prosperity* (New York: Random House, 1993); and *Wealth and Democracy: A Political History of the American Rich* (New York: Broadway Books, 2003). For recent Internal Revenue Service findings, see Greg IP?, "Income-Inequality Gap Widens," *Wall Street Journal*, October 12, 2007: A2.

3. Public Policy Institute of California, "Employment and Job Growth in California," October 2004, 1–2, http://web.ppic.org/content/pubs/jtf/JTF_EmploymentJTF .pdf (accessed June 18, 2006).

4. Legislative Analyst's Office, "The California Economy," January 1995, http:// www.lao.ca.gov/1995/010195_calguide/cgep1.html (accessed June 18, 2006).

5. Median home values for California (adjusted for inflation) are as follows: 1990–$249,800; 2000–$211,500. U.S. Census Bureau, "Historical Census of Housing Tables: Home Values," shows a significant decline in housing prices beginning around 1993 (http://www.census.gov/hhes/www/housing/census /historic/values.html, 42–44 [accessed June 18, 2006]). Comparative national and regional data are available in Office of Federal Housing Enterprise Oversight, "House Price Increases Continue; Some Deceleration Evident," June 1, 2006, e.g., 42–44, http://www.ofheo.gov/media/pdf/1q06hpi.pdf (accessed June 4, 2006).

6. For the UC history, see Christopher Newfield, Henning Bohn, and Calvin Moore, "Current Budget Trends and the Future of the University of California," UC Academic Senate Report, May 2006, http://www.universityofcalifornia .edu/senate/committees/ucpb/futures.report0506.pdf (accessed June 18, 2006). For state general fund totals for California State University, see Legislative Analyst's Office expenditure statistics, http://www.lao.ca.gov/LAOMenus/ lao_menu_economics.aspx (accessed June 4, 2006). After cuts that began in 1989–90, Cal State exceeded its 1986–87 budget levels only in 1995–96 ($1,629,674,000), which then rose substantially through 2002–3, when they were cut again.

7. California Opinion Index, "Economic Well-Being," August 2004, http://field .com/fieldpollonline/subscribers/COI-04%20Aug-Wellbeing.pdf (accessed June 18, 2006).

8. Pete Wilson, "California: Forging America's Future," January 2, 1995, http: //www.californiagovernors.ca.gov/h/documents/inaugural_36b.html (accessed June 23, 2006).

9. The gross state product in current dollars was $75.9 billion in 1965 and $909 billion in 1995. See California Department of Finance, "Gross State Product, In-come, and Cost-of-Living," Table D-1, http://www.dof.ca.gov/html/fs_data/ STAT-ABS/sec_D.htm (accessed June 4, 2006).

10. The most significant legal advocacy groups involved in contesting affirmative ac-tion have been the Washington Legal Foundation (created in 1977) and its spin-off, the Center for Individual Rights (1989). A summary of CIR's history and of its strategic approach to public advocacy law is "A Brief History of CIR," http:// www.cir-usa.org/history.html (accessed June 12, 2006). CIR played an important role in the *Hopwood* cases in Texas, discussed in chapter 6, "The Battle for Meri-tocracy"; in the *Bollinger* affirmative action cases involving the University of Michigan, discussed in chapter 7, "Diversity in the Age of Pseudointegration"; and in defending Proposition 209 in California from legal challenges.

11.   Much of the recent questioning about affirmative action has been prompted by Jerry and Ellen Cook, a white San Diego couple who became interested in the subject two years ago when their son was rejected for ad-mission at the University of California Medical School at San Diego.

    The Cooks, whose son was later accepted at the Davis medical school, embarked on a quest to pry statistical information from the five medical schools in the California system. The Cooks say their figures show the uni-versities are going well beyond the limits set in the *Bakke* case.

    "I obtained a piece of paper that shows the application rate and the eth-nic makeup of U.C.-Davis" medical school, Mr. Cook said in an interview. "Chicano students, for example, were 5 percent of the applicants but 18 percent of the students offered admission. That's mathematically just not possible unless race was the overwhelming factor in deciding who gets in and who doesn't."

"Chicanos were offered admission at five times the rate of whites," Mr. Cook said, "and 19 times the rate of Japanese."

Since the Hispanic applicants on average have lower test scores and grades than whites or Asians, Mr. Cook said, their preferential treatment for admission under the Bakke requirements would have to depend on some special quality in addition to their ethnicity. "Whatever quality they have," he said, "is it possible that they have it 19 times more often than Japanese and 5 times more often than whites?" (Richard Bernstein, "Moves Under Way in California to Overturn Higher Education's Affirmative Action Policy," *New York Times*, January 25, 1995)

12. California Civil Rights Initiative, Clause A, http://www.acri.org/209/209text .html (accessed June 12, 2006). The authors of the initiative were Glynn Custred and Tom Wood, the former a professor at Cal State Hayward, the latter associated with the conservative advocacy group, the National Association of Scholars. The link between anti-affirmative action language and 1960s civil rights language was well understood by affirmative action critics at the time. See, for example, John Bunzel, senior fellow at the Hoover Institute to the Commonwealth Club, "The California Civil Rights Initiative: The Debate over Race, Equality and Affirmative Action" (address, March 24, 1995), *Vital Speeches* 61, no. 17 (June 15, 1995): 530. Bunzel said, "One reason the voters will find it difficult to vote against the ballot initiative is that some of its language is a paraphrase of the 1964 Civil Rights Act, which gave political sanction not to racially preferential treatment, or special privileges for some, but to the elimination of discrimination against anyone. Supporters of the initiative say they are simply seeking to restate the motives and purposes of Congress when it passed this 30-year-old landmark legislation."

13. J. W. Peltason, "Statement, Regents Meetings July 10, 1995," press release, UC Office of the President (author's copy).

14. I have not found official figures for 1960s admissions at UC Berkeley. The Karabel Report, "Freshman Admissions at Berkeley: A Policy for the 1990s and Beyond," suggests that only 15 percent of high school grads were eligible to apply before 1960 but that all within that category who applied got in (http: //academic-senate.berkeley.edu/archives/karabel.html [accessed July 12, 2006]).

15. Peter Schrag, *Paradise Lost: California's Experience, America's Future* (New York: New Press, 1998), Introduction.

16. Peter Applebome, "The Debate on Diversity in California Shifts," *New York Times*, June 4, 1995.

17. Pete Wilson, "Equal Rights, Not Special Privileges," *Los Angeles Times*, June 1, 1995.

18. UCLA admissions did appear, in its own self-study, to be violating *Bakke*.

19. Asian American students were relatively unaffected by the changed procedures, as they already qualified for admission at between two and three times the rate of whites as a proportion of their population. Ten years later, Asian Americans constituted the largest enrollment group among UC freshmen (36 percent), though they comprised 14 percent of the state's graduating high school seniors. Lisa M. Krieger and Lisa Fernandez, "White Admissions Fall to Second Place for the First Time," *San Jose Mercury-News*, April 20, 2006, http://www.modelminority.com/article1073 .html (accessed May 23, 2006). The situation for African Americans was nearly the opposite, as they were enrolling at UC in proportions well below their share of graduating seniors and also well below their rate of UC eligibility. Darnell Hunt, director of the Ralph J. Bunche Center for African American Studies at UCLA, noted that "the paucity of African American admit offers becomes even more troubling when one considers that African American UC-eligible students more than doubled over the last decade. Between 1996 and 2003, the percentage of UC-eligible African American students rose from 2.8% to 6.2% (California Postsecondary Education Commission, May 2004). Furthermore, African American UC applicants increased 24% system-wide between 1995 and 2004" (cited in Frank D. Russo, "UCLA Study Has Shocking Information on Discrimination in Admissions to University of California," *California Progress Report*, June 19, 2006, http://www .californiaprogressreport.com/2006/06/ucla_study_has.html [accessed August 23, 2006]). African American enrollment rates for 2006 were 3.4 percent, or a little more than half the African American eligibility rate.

20. Nina Robinson with assistance from Kyra Caspary, Veronica Santelices, Saul Geiser, Roger Studley, Charles Masten, and Neal Finkelstein, "Undergraduate Access to the University of California: After the Elimination of Race-Conscious Policies," University of California Office of the President, March 2003, http:// www.ucop.edu/sas/publish/aa_final2.pdf (accessed April 16, 2005). For discussion of UCLA, whose 2006 freshman class was 2.2 percent African American, see Larry Gordon, "UCLA to Get Twice As Many Black Freshmen in Fall: Incentives and a 'Holistic' Admissions Process Have Improved Numbers That Troubled the School," *Los Angeles Times*, May 12, 2007, http://www.latimes.com/ news/local/la-me-ucla12may12.1.4111434.story (accessed May 12, 2007).

21. Lujuana Treadwell, "Boalt Hall Increases Minority Enrollment," *Berkeleyan*, August 26, 1998, http://www.berkeley.edu/news/berkeleyan/1998/0826/boalt.html (accessed June 13, 2006).

22. Michelle Locke, "UC Dean, Professor Debate Merits of Affirmative Action," *San Francisco Chronicle*, January 19, 2005, http://www.sfgate.com/cgi-bin/article. cgi?file=/news/archive/2005/01/19/state2053EST0168.DTL&type=printable (accessed June 13, 2006).

23. Cited in John Balzar, "Perspectives on Prop. 209: Selling Equality's Higher Costs," *Los Angeles Times*, September 10, 1996, A3.

24. For a good treatment of the region's historical context, see Stephen J. Pitti, *The Devil in Silicon Valley: Northern California, Race, and Mexican Americans* (Princeton, NJ: Princeton University Press, 2003).

25. Connerly called "for a review of all UC ethnic studies programs, saying that he is not convinced of their 'educational value.'" "'All of the infrastructure created back in the 1970s and '80s as a result of black nationalism and the black power movement, I think we need to re-examine it now,'" said Connerly, who is black. "'I want to visit privately with a number of faculty members and have them make the case that this is sound academic curriculum rather than the political correctness mind set. . . . I'm not convinced.'" Edward W. Lempinen, "Connerly Calls for Review of UC Ethnic Studies," *San Francisco Chronicle*, June 17, 1998. In addition, "Connerly accused [UC Berkeley Chancellor Chang-Lin Tien] of being 'sneaky' for implementing the Berkeley Pledge, a program to promote future diversity on the campus by offering academic help to underprivileged high school students." Pamela Burdman, "2 UC Chiefs to Speak Out Against CCRI: Cal's Tien, UCLA's Young to Publicly Resist Regents' Stand," *San Francisco Chronicle*, October 19, 1996. Outside of university admissions, when an Urban Institute study found that companies owned by women and members of minority groups got less than their proportionate share of federal contracts, Connerly remarked that "it was no coincidence that the Urban Institute study appeared just a week before the election. 'In the last 60 days, you have virtually every government agency and research outfit coming up with these half-baked studies,' Connerly said." Louise Freedberg, "Minority Firms Don't Get Their Share, New Study Says: Too Few Contracts for the Number of Qualified Companies," *San Francisco Chronicle*, October 30, 1996, 3. There is substantial evidence that Connerly consistently assumed the deficiency of minority-based activities.

26. For a discussion of the link between the tech boom and growing inequality, see James K. Galbraith and Travis Hale, "Income Distribution and the Information Technology Bubble" (University of Texas Inequality Project, Working Paper 27, University of Texas at Austin, January 14, 2004), http://utip.gov.utexas.edu/papers/utip_27.pdf (accessed June 23, 2006). On a related issue, California's poverty rate exceeded that of the United States as a whole around 1990, and the gap widened throughout the dot-com boom. When the boom came to an end, California's poverty rate also began to subside toward the national average. Public Policy Institute of California, "Just the Facts: Poverty in California," November 2006, http://www.ppic.org/content/pubs/jtf/JTF_PovertyJTF.pdf (accessed June 23, 2006). Elias S. Lopez and Rosa Maria Moller's "The Distribution of Wealth in California, 2000" has lots of statistics on wealth and poverty. California Research Bureau, November 2003, http://www.library.ca.gov/crb/03/10/03-010.pdf (accessed June 23, 2006).

27. Michael Lewis, *The New New Thing* (New York: W. W. Norton, 1999).

28. Data compiled by Jonathan Polansky from California Legislative Analyst's Office, "State of California Expenditures, 1984–85 to 2007–08," Source Data, http://www.lao.ca.gov/laoapp/LAOMenus/lao-menu-economics.aspx (accessed August 27, 2007). For a comprehensive account of the rise of the California prison system, see Ruth Wilson Gilmore, *Golden Gulag: Prisons, Surplus, Crisis, and Opposition in Globalizing California.* (Berkeley: University of California Press, 2007), especially chapter 2; on p. 5 she cites two other scholars calling The California prison boom "the biggest . . . in the history of the world."

6. The Battle for Meritocracy

1. Kevin Starr, *Material Dreams: Southern California Through the 1920s* (New York: Oxford University Press, 1990), 67.

2. Walter Mosley, *Black Betty* (New York: W. W. Norton, 1994), 32.

3. This article, by Cathleen Decker, is mislabeled: "Most Back Anti-Bias Policies but Spurn Racial Preferences," *Los Angeles Times*, March 30, 1995, A1, A12. In fact, most accept racial preferences when they remain flexible.

4. Other polls of the period found less white support but suggested a similar structure of ambiguity. For example, "Nationwide, three out of four Americans say they oppose policies that give preferences to minorities to make up for past discrimination," according to a recent Washington Post/ABC News poll. But only 28 percent want to "do away . . . entirely" with affirmative action programs. In other words, "they want something 'fair' but not 'mean.'" John J. Miller and Abigail Thernstrom, "Losing Race: California vs. Affirmative Action," *New Republic* 212 (June 26, 1995):17. Most of these polls did not go beneath the surface of their respondents' sometimes complex racial views. Those that did, as in the White House's focus groups of the period, were also not so hard on affirmative action, and a more aggressive Democratic administration might have done much more with them: "People sympathized with arguments that the rules are often unfairly exploited—although they also expressed concern that the Republicans want to roll back much of the social progress of the past decades. From such exercises has emerged White House strategy. On affirmative action the approach is, You can defend the practice only if you concede there are problems. In general the message is, The Republicans are going too far." David Corn, "Coasting Sounding: Anti-Affirmative Action Politics in California," *Nation* 260, no. 12 (March 27, 1995): 405.

5. Michael Young, *The Rise of the Meritocracy, 1870–2033* (London: Thames and Hudson, 1958).

6. For a fuller discussion of the origins of U.S. meritocracy, see Christopher Newfield, *Ivy and Industry: Business and the Making of the American University, 1880–1980* (Durham, NC: Duke University Press, 2003), chap. 5.

7. See Nicholas Lemann, *The Big Test: The Secret History of the American Meritoc-racy* (New York: Farrar, Straus, and Giroux, 2000), particularly the discussion of James Conant Bryant and Henry Chauncey at Harvard.

8. The new term for SAT is clearly more accurate, and one might also assume more desirable: the SAT can most easily justify its power to allocate scarce resources like first-year places at Williams College or UCLA on the grounds that it quanti-fies what the subject has achieved and hence what the subject has earned. But there are many other ways to measure achieved performance, most of them more reliable than the SAT, which in the professional literature now looks in-creasingly like a self-referential measure of the ability to take tests like the SAT, which in turn correlates with socioeconomic status. Countries whose students do better than American students on international exams tend to have more rig-orous, difficult curricula and tend to test students on their knowledge of sub-stantive areas like ancient philosophy, Chinese history, or calculus. These other measures are more complex, laborious, expensive, and often necessarily subjec-tive; since they try to measure actual accomplishment, they are also more defen-sible politically.

This raises a further problem in the meritocratic pursuit of ability. Through-out the 1990s, academic leaders defended SAT-type scores as a rough measure of achievement while at the same time assuming that such scores also indi-cated, though perhaps with less certainty, aptitude and future potential. The fountainhead of U.S. meritocracy sponsored critical research that it only par-tially incorporated into its practices. Academic study has shown that SATs have not eliminated cultural bias against certain social and racial groups, and that SATs produce psychological reactions in the subjects that distort the findings. One of the most important of these reactions is what the psychologist Claude Steele has defined as "stereotype threat." By comparing the performance of var-ious groups on the same test taken under different labels, he and his associates have demonstrated empirically that scores are higher when a stereotype ap-plied against the group to which one belongs is not in play. If an exam is de-scribed as a test of mathematical ability, women do worse than if it is described as a trial of different psychological profiling formats in which the math content is not important; the explanation seems to be that the latter context neutralizes the stereotype that women are not good at math. Steele has found similar reac-tions for African American students told they are taking an "intelligence test," white men told they are competing against Asian Americans on a test of math-ematical ability, white men doing the high jump under the gaze of a black rather than a white coach, and so on. An accessible overview of this research is Claude M. Steele, "Thin Ice: 'Stereotype Threat' and Black College Students," *Atlantic Monthly*, August 1999, 44–54. See also "Expert Report of Claude M. Steele," *Gratz et al. v. Bollinger et al.*, 539 U.S. 244 (2003), No. 97-75321 (E.D.

Mich.); *Grutter v. Bollinger et al.*, 539 U.S. 306 (2003), No. 97-75928 (E.D. Mich.).

Academic research has also shown that the SAT I and ACT exams—the former "aptitude" tests that examine general verbal and mathematical skills—are downright bad at predicting the one thing that they were validated for—freshman grades. Even when combined with class rank or grades, the SAT I leaves "almost 90% of the variation in grades unexplained." See Christina Perez, *Reassessing College Admissions: Examining Tests & Admitting Alternatives*, National Center for Fair and Open Testing (FairTest), November 2001, citing J. Baron and M. F. Norman, "SATs, Achievement Tests, and High School Class Rank as Predictors of College Performance," *Educational and Psychology Measurement* 52 (1992): 1047–1055. Perez offers a useful—though critical—overview of testing issues. Other research suggests that the SAT is a "wealth test" rather than a test of either ability or achievement. See Rebecca Zwick, "Is the SAT a 'Wealth Test'?" *Phi Delta Kappan* 84, no. 4 (December 2002): 307–311.

These research findings were starting to be translated into policy in the wake of the affirmative action controversies, during which opponents of affirmative action had invoked the SAT as an objective measure of merit. In 2001, University of California president Richard C. Atkinson announced that he had asked UC's Academic Senate to approve dropping the SAT I, the former "aptitude" test, and proposed that UC instead "require only standardized tests that assess mastery of specific subject areas rather than undefined notions of 'aptitude' or 'intelligence.'" See Richard C. Atkinson, "2001 Robert H. Atwell Distinguished Lecture" (speech delivered at the Eighty-third Annual Meeting of the American Council on Education, Washington, DC, February 18, 2001). Atkinson was careful to emphasize that he respects standardized tests and the Educational Testing Service, and was criticizing only those tests that lack a clear and direct relation to the mastery of important subject matter. The relevant UC Academic Senate committee's discussions are available at the University of California Office of the President's Web site, "UC and the SAT: Questions and Answers," http://www .ucop.edu/news/sat/qa.html (accessed July 14 2006). UC admissions did eliminate required submission of scores from the SAT I—the requirements are only that students take two SAT II tests and the ACT. University of California, Admissions, "Examination Requirement," http://www.universityofcalifornia.edu/ admissions/undergrad_adm/paths_to_adm/freshman/examination_reqs.html (accessed September 30, 2006). In 2005, after learning that the National Merit Scholarship program used the PSAT score (administered in the junior year in high school) in an invalid way to eliminate most potential candidates (including virtually all members of underrepresented groups), UC discontinued participation in that program. For the public announcement, see University of California, "Six UC Campuses to Redirect National Merit Funding to Other

Merit-Based Scholarships," news release, July 13, 2005. For related UC Academic Senate materials, see "Resolution on the Failure of the National Merit Scholarship Program to Meet the Requirements of UC's Definition of Academic Merit," June 22, 2005, http://www.universityofcalifornia.edu/senate/reports/nmsp.resolution .062205..pdf (accessed September 30, 2006). A background paper by the UC Academic Senate, "University of California Participation in the National Merit Scholarship Program: A Report from the Education Financing Model Steering Committee," May 3, 2005, can be found at http://www.universityofcalifornia .edu/senate/reports/nmsp.efm.background.pdf (accessed September 30, 2006). UC action was prompted by the statements of a recently retired UC Berkeley admissions official who had also participated in the National Merit program:

> [Patrick] Hayashi, who was a top aide to Atkinson, set the current debate in motion with an eight-page letter to his fellow trustees of the College Board last August, *Crosstalk* reports. In it, Hayashi, who retired from the board's trustees [in fall 2004], said that in the decade he spent as UC Berkeley's assistant vice chancellor for admissions and enrollment, none of the hundreds of National Merit Scholars who attended the university was black or Hispanic, and few were from low-income families. Hayashi noted in the letter that he had been repeatedly rebuffed in his attempts to get national data on how many minority and low-income students received National Merit Scholarships. "I estimate that the percent of National Merit Scholars who are black, Hispanic and American Indian is close to zero and that the absolute number of poor students from these groups is also close to zero," Hayashi wrote. "If we ever learned the precise figures, then we would be forced to question the wisdom and morality of sponsoring a 'merit' scholarship program that effectively locks out Black, Hispanic, and American Indian students." (Doug Lederman, "A New Attack on Standardized Tests," *Inside Higher Ed*, March 21, 2005, http:// insidehighered.com/news/2005/03/21/psat [accessed September 30, 2006].)

Many public universities have been migrating slowly but surely toward the expensive but individualized comprehensive review already practiced at nearly all selective private universities. But academic leaders have not repudiated standardizing testing. As a result, standardized test scores remain the popular gold standard of measured academic "merit" in a stressful admissions process that universities have allowed to remain confusing.

9. The proposal is available online at Affirmative Action and Diversity Project, "Adoption of Resolution: Policy Ensuring Equal Treatment—Admissions," July 12, 1995, http://aad.english.ucsb.edu/docs/SP-1.html (accessed June 13, 2006). The companion resolution, "Adoption of Resolution: Policy Ensuring Equal Treatment—Employment and Contracting," July 12, 1995, http://aad.english .ucsb.edu/docs/SP-2.html (accessed June 13, 2006), can be found on the same site, along with other useful documents of the period.

10. In the following year, about two months before the November 1996 vote on Proposition 209, Connerly and Wilson had a roundtable discussion in which they sounded a strategically egalitarian note. One account stated that "Connerly and his inner circle argue that repeal of affirmative action for state and local government employment, contracting and education would not be the end of it. They say their goal remains true fairness in society, and this is not achieved by granting breaks to some groups but by improving the means so that everyone is equally prepared to seize opportunity." "It will cost a lot to do this right," Connerly was said to remark.

Pressed to explain what they would do, Connerly's circle referred to Wilson's plan to spend nearly a billion dollars to reduce class size by one-third in the first through third grades, and to Wilson's remarks in July 1996 that "schools needed upgrading, particularly inner-city schools for the benefit of the disadvantaged," that "California must assist needy children with childhood health care beginning with prenatal care," and that "the role of parental guidance was so important that 'we've got to find a surrogate parent, a mentor' for children left at home without adult supervision." John Balzar, "Perspectives on Prop. 209: Selling Equality's Higher Costs," *Los Angeles Times*, September 10, 1996, A3.

These remarks were read by many as political manipulation, that is, as an effort to get swing voters to persuade themselves that Proposition 209 would not be so bad for poor and minority kids. And to no one's surprise, Proposition 209's victory did not lead to a Wilson-Connerly New Deal, even in the rapidly expanding dot-com economy of the late 1990s. But even if Connerly and his allies did not care about creating economic opportunity for the whole population, which would have involved reducing poverty, slowing the growth of California's low-wage economy, and massively increasing poor people's access to high-quality education, they were aware that broader economic and social development remained a majority interest of California voters.

11. Christopher Lasch, *The Revolt of the Elites and the Betrayal of Democracy* (New York: W. W. Norton, 1995), 64.

12. Louis Menand, "Everybody Else's College Education," *New York Times Magazine*, April 20, 1997, 48. In subsequent years, other major industrialized countries caught up and passed U.S. participation rates and exceeded U.S. graduation rates.

13. *Regents of the Univ. of Calif. v. Bakke*, 438 U.S. 265 (1978), No. 7811, at 318, http://www.law.cornell.edu/supct/html/historics/USSC_CR_0438_0265_ZO.html (accessed September 30, 2006).

14. The U.S. District Court opinion is *Hopwood v. State of Tex.*, 861 F. Supp. 551 (W.D. Tex. 1994), or *Hopwood 1*; *Hopwood v. Texas*, 78 F.3d 932 (5th Cir. 1996), is the Court of Appeals case known as *Hopwood 2*.

15. *Hopwood v. Texas*, 78 F.3d 932 (5th Cir. 1996).

16. In the majority opinion, Judge Jerry E. Smith wrote, "In March 1992 . . . the presumptive TI admission score for resident whites and non-referred minorities

was 199. Mexican Americans and blacks needed a TI of only 189 to be presumptively admitted. The difference in the presumptive-deny ranges is even more striking. The presumptive denial score for 'nonminorities' was 192; the same score for blacks and Mexican Americans was 179" (www.ca5.uscourts.gov/opinions/pub/94/94-50569.CVO.wpd.pdf, [accessed June28,2006]).

17. The University of Texas law school was not alone. Similar violations helped get the Connerly ball rolling in California. Many large public universities used racially coded formulas as a way of cutting corners and costs with very large applicant pools.

18. For a discussion of the *Bakke* case and its legacy, see chapter 7, "Diversity in the the Age of Pseudointegration."

19. *Hopwood v. Texas*, 78 F.3d 932 (5th Cir. 1996), *Hopwood 2*, 60.

20. Judith A. Winston, General Counsel, Department of Education, Summary (arguing that the Supreme Court's refusal to hear the Hopwood appeal should not be construed as endorsement of the Fifth Circuit's ruling or as an overturning of *Bakke*), July 30, 1996, http://www.acenet.edu/bookstore/descriptions/making_the_case/legal/ED_96_07.cfm(accessed June 27, 2006). This Department of Education ruling was reversed in April 1997 for schools in the three states covered by the Fifth Circuit.

21. *Hopwood v. State of Tex.*, 861 F.Supp. 551 (W.D. Tex. 1994), 566 (http://tarlton.law.utexas.edu/hopwood/hoptxt.htm[accessed June 29, 2006]).

22. As this court pointed out, "although the [rejected] plaintiffs had higher TIs than [most] minority applicants offered admission, the evidence shows that 109 nonminority residents with TIs lower than Hopwood's were offered admission. Sixty-seven nonminority residents with TIs lower than the other three plaintiffs were admitted." Ibid., 581.

23. *Hopwood 2*, 31–32.

24. Professor Otis Madison, Department of Black Studies, University of California at Santa Barbara, private conversations, July 6, 1995, Santa Barbara.

7. Diversity in the Age of Pseudointegration

1. See chapter 6 of this book, note 8.

2. See for example, Shelby Steele, "A Victory for White Guilt," *Wall Street Journal*, June 26, 2003; Abigail Thernstrom, "College Rulings Add Insult to Injury," *Los Angeles Times*, June 29, 2003, M1, M6.

3. Nicholas Lemann, "A Decision That Universities Can Relate To," *New York Times*, June 29, 2003, sec. 4, p. 14.

4. David A. Hollinger, *Postethnic America: Beyond Multiculturalism* (New York: Basic Books, 1995), 3; cf. 85, 101, 116, 118. In that same year, two conceptually more sophisticated books on the same subject appeared in Canada, though they remain less known in the United States: Will Kymlicka, *Multicultural Citizen-*

ship: A Liberal Theory on Minority Rights (New York: Oxford University Press, 1995); and James Tully, *Strange Multiplicity: Constitutionalism in an Age of Diversity* (Cambridge: Cambridge University Press, 1995). Hollinger is the more representative figure of the majoritarian terms of the U.S. debate. In Canada, Tully avoided Kymlicka's tendency to cast indigenous peoples as background players in English-French conflicts.

5. A functional pluralism is usually a form of cosmopolitanism, and cosmopolitanism has borrowed many of its ideas from pluralism. Bruce Robbins and Pheng Cheah, for example, have insisted that cosmopolitanism continues rather than supersedes nationalist paradigms. See their edited collection *Cosmopolitics: Thinking and Feeling Beyond the Nation* (Minneapolis: University of Minnesota Press, 1998); and also Bruce Robbins, *Feeling Global: Internationalism in Distress* (New York: New York University Press, 1999): "Cosmopolitanism or internationalism does not take its primary meaning or desirability from an absolute and intrinsic opposition to nationalism. Rather, it is the extension outward of the same sorts of potent and dangerous solidarity" (6).

6. See Nikkil Singh, *Black Is a Country: Race and the Unfinished Struggle for Democracy* (Cambridge, MA: Harvard University Press, 2005).

7. My understanding of the *Bakke* case is indebted to Joel Dreyfus and Charles Laurence III, *The Bakke Case: The Politics of Inequality* (New York: Harcourt, Brace, Jovanovich, 1979), esp. chap. 10; as well as to Cheryl Harris, "Whiteness as Property," in *Critical Race Theory: The Key Writings That Formed the Movement*, ed. Kimberelé Crenshaw, Neil Gotanda, Gary Peller, and Kendall Thomas (New York: New Press, 1995), 276–291; and Gertrude Ezorsky, *Racism and Justice: The Case for Affirmative Action* (Ithaca, NY: Cornell University Press, 1991).

8. The Supreme Court had initially granted the validity of such initiatives to remedy past discrimination. In a 1968 decision based on *Brown v. Board of Education*, the Court held that school boards "operating state-compelled dual systems [at the time of *Brown*] were . . . clearly charged with the affirmative duty to take whatever steps might be necessary to convert to a unitary system in which racial discrimination would be eliminated root and branch." *Green v. New Kent County School Board*, 391 U.S. 430, 437–438 (1968), cited in Scott R. Palmer, "Diversity and Affirmative Action: Evolving Principles and Continuing Legal Battles," in *Diversity Challenged: Evidence on the Impact of Affirmative Action*, ed. Gary Orfield with Michal Kurlaender (Cambridge, MA: Harvard Education Publishing Group, 2001), 95n23. As late as its decision in *United States v. Fordice* (1992), the Court reiterated its requirement that states "do more to desegregate their universities than simply adopt facially race-neutral admissions policies. Rather, states must at a minimum seek to establish effective neutrality" (Palmer, "Diversity and Affirmative Action," 84).

9. In so doing, the UC Davis medical school was following a recommendation of the Association of American Medical Colleges (AAMC) that medical schools "admit increased numbers of students from geographical areas, economic backgrounds,

and ethnic groups that are now inadequately represented." For the AAMC position, see Dreyfuss and Lawrence, *The Bakke Case*, 19. For the parameters of the UC Davis medical school admissions process, see chaps. 1–2. For the UC diversity defense, see 43, passim.

10. Clare C. Swanger, "Perspectives on the History of Ameliorating Oppression and Supporting Diversity in United States Organizations," in *The Promise of Diversity: Over Forty Voices Discuss Strategies for Eliminating Discrimination in Organizations*, ed. Elsie Y. Cross, Judith H. Katz, Frederick A. Miller, and Edith W. Seashore (New York: McGraw-Hill, 1994), 10.

11. *Regents of the Univ. of Cal. v. Bakke*, 438 U.S. 265 (1978), at 319–320:

> It is evident that the Davis special admissions program involves the use of an explicit racial classification never before countenanced by this Court. It tells applicants who are not Negro, Asian, or Chicano that they are totally excluded from a specific percentage of the seats in an entering class. No matter how strong their qualifications, quantitative and extracurricular, including their own potential for contribution to educational diversity, they are never afforded the chance to compete with applicants from the preferred groups for the special admissions seats. At the same time, the preferred applicants have the opportunity to compete for every seat in the class. The fatal flaw in petitioner's preferential program is its disregard of individual rights as guaranteed by the Fourteenth Amendment. *Shelley v. Kraemer*, 334 U.S. at 22. Such rights are not absolute. But when a State's distribution of benefits or imposition of burdens hinges on ancestry or the color of a person's skin, that individual is entitled to a demonstration that the challenged classification is necessary to promote a substantial state interest. Petitioner has failed to carry this burden. For this reason, that portion of the California court's judgment holding petitioner's special admissions program invalid under the Fourteenth Amendment must be affirmed.

12. Ibid., at 306. "The fourth goal asserted by petitioner is the attainment of a diverse student body. This clearly is a constitutionally permissible goal for an institution of higher education. Academic freedom, though not a specifically enumerated constitutional right, long has been viewed as a special concern of the First Amendment. The freedom of a university to make its own judgments as to education includes the selection of its student body" (Ibid., at 311–312).

13. Powell went so far as to assert, incorrectly, that because the "white 'majority' itself is composed of various minority groups, most of which can lay claim to a history of prior discrimination," general patterns of racial inequality were not empirically detectable. Powell, *Regents of the Univ. of Calif. v. Bakke*, 438 U.S. 265 (1978), cited in John D. Skrentny, *The Minority Rights Revolution* (Cambridge, MA: Harvard University Press, 2002), 175.

14. On the first condition:

In such an admissions program, race or ethnic background may be deemed a plus in a particular applicant's file, yet it does not insulate the individual from comparison with all other candidates for the available seats. The file of a particular black applicant may be examined for his potential contribution to diversity without the factor of race being decisive when compared, for example, with that of an applicant identified as an Italian-American if the latter is thought to exhibit qualities more likely to promote beneficial educational pluralism. Such qualities could include exceptional personal talents, unique work or service experience, leadership potential, maturity, demonstrated compassion, a history of overcoming disadvantage, ability to communicate with the poor, or other qualifications deemed important. In short, an admissions program operated in this way is flexible enough to consider all pertinent elements of diversity in light of the particular qualifications of each applicant, and to place them on the same footing for consideration, although not necessarily according them the same weight. Indeed, the weight attributed to a particular quality may vary from year to year depending upon the "mix" both of the student body and the applicants for the incoming class. (Ibid., at 317–318)

On the second condition:

In Harvard College admissions, the Committee has not set target quotas for the number of blacks, or of musicians, football players, physicists or Californians to be admitted in a given year. . . . But that awareness [of the necessity of including more than a token number of black students] does not mean that the Committee sets a minimum number of blacks or of people from west of the Mississippi who are to be admitted. It means only that, in choosing among thousands of applicants who are not only "admissible" academically but have other strong qualities, the Committee, with a number of criteria in mind, pays some attention to distribution among many types and categories of students. (Ibid., at 316–317)

For a liberal's valid doubts about Powell's distinction between "flexible" and quota-based plans, doubts that now appear in conservative critiques, see Ronald Dworkin, "The *Bakke* Decision: Did It Decide Anything," *New York Review of Books*, August 17, 1978. Justice David H. Souter expressed similar liberal doubts in his dissent in *Gratz et al. v. Bollinger et al.* 539 U.S. 244 (2003); for a conservative concurrence, see Michael S. Greve, "The Court Decides Anything Goes," *Chronicle of Higher Education* (July 4, 2003): B11.

15. Palmer notes that "voluntary remedial affirmative action" has not been categorically eliminated by the Court, pointing to *Wygant v. Jackson Board of Education*, 476 U.S. 267 (1986) and *Richmond v. J. A. Croson*, 488 U.S. 469 (1989). These decisions suggest three general principles: "First, a university cannot take affirmative action to remedy the effects of general societal dis-

crimination. Second, a university can take affirmative action to remedy the present effects of its own past discrimination if it has a sufficient basis in evidence for the belief that such action is warranted. Third, a university or other state entity can take affirmative action to remedy prior discrimination by other actors to avoid serving as a 'passive participant' in a pattern of discrimination, specifically where affirmative action is taken by a government entity seeking to ameliorate the effects of discrimination within its jurisdiction" (Palmer, "Diversity and Affirmative Action," 85). Only the third of these suggests a gray area beyond *Bakke*, and it has been partially foreclosed by other Court decisions, including *Podberesky v. Kirwan*, 38 F.3d 147 (4th Cir. 1994), cert. denied, 514 U.S. 1128 (1995), *Hopwood v. Texas* 78 F.3d 932 (5th Cir. 1996). In primary and secondary education, the door to more flexible affirmative action was once again slammed shut, this time by the Roberts Court, in *Parents Involved in Community Schools, Petitioner v. Seattle School District* No. 1, et al. *Meredith v. Jefferson County Board of Education*, 551 U.S.—(2007).

16. *Grutter v. Bollinger et al.* 539 U.S. 306(2003), at 312–313.

17. Ibid., at 312.

18. Good recent studies are collected in Orfield with Kurlaender, *Diversity Challenged*. In his introduction, Orfield notes that educators assumed the obviousness of the benefits of diversity in education until the Fifth Circuit Court of Appeals' decision in *Hopwood v. Texas*, 78 F.3d 932 (5th Cir.), cert. denied, 518 U.S. 1033 (1996), which, as discussed in chapter 6, denied that diversity was a compelling state interest and inspired educational researchers to investigate the effects of diversity. Among representative findings: "[Mitchell] Chang shows that more diversity promotes more interaction and . . . socialization across racial lines, and is associated with more discussion of issues, better retention in college, and higher satisfaction with the college experience. [Jeffrey] Milem shows that faculty on campuses with more diversity are more likely to use different teaching styles and to deal with diversity in their teaching. [Sylvia] Hurtado finds evidence of benefits in terms of leadership, awareness of other cultures, and ability to work collaboratively. The basic results of these studies are that diversity does make a difference, but that the differences are neither automatic nor uniform" (7).

19. Palmer notes that, for Powell, "the type of educational diversity that constituted a compelling interest was not pluralistic diversity of certain racial groups, but more individualistic diversity in which race is 'but a single though important element' " (Palmer, "Diversity and Affirmative Action," 88).

20. The argument that civil rights legislation tracks white rather than black racial preferences has been most systematically advanced by Derrick Bell in, for example, his discussion of the *Bakke* case in *Race, Racism and American Law*, 3rd ed. (Boston: Little, Brown, 1992), 652–657. Bell also argues that black racial ac-

tivism has benefited whites more than blacks in such matters as the desegregation of public schools, which led to overall improvements in public education, and gerrymandered legislative districts, which led to improvements in the representation of urban and suburban areas (659).

21. For a discussion of the retreat that occurred in *Ward's Cove Packing Co. v. Atonio*, 490 U.S. 642 (1989), see chapter 4, "The Market Substitute for Cultural Knowledge." Justice Byron White, contesting disparate impact theory, summarized the concept's history: "*Griggs v. Duke Power Co.*, 401 US 424, 431 (1971), construed Title VII to proscribe 'not only overt discrimination but also practices that are fair in form but discriminatory in practice.' . . . a facially neutral employment practice may be deemed violative of Title VII without evidence of the employer's subjective intent to discriminate that is required in a 'disparate treatment' case" (*Ward's Cove Packing*, 645–646). See, more recently, *Alexander v. Sandoval*, No. 99-1908 (2001), which Ellen Messer-Davidow reads as one of the final nails in the coffin of disparate-impact lawsuits. See her "Democracy Will Be Hard to Do," *Social Text* 24, no. 1 (Spring 2006): 9–10.

22. For a critical reading of Wilson as the "intellectual reincarnation of Daniel Patrick Moynihan," see Steven Steinberg, *Turning Back: The Retreat from Racial Justice in American Thought and Policy* (Boston: Beacon Press, 1995), 123–126. See also Alice O'Connor, *Poverty Knowledge: Social Science, Social Policy, and the Poor in Twentieth-Century U.S. History* (Princeton, NJ: Princeton University Press, 2001).

23. Godkin wrote, "The great burden which weights the negroes in the race is one which neither Government nor philanthropists can remove, and that is the want of all the ordinary claims to social respectability. . . . The negro race must, in short, win a good social position in the way other races have won it; and when it has its roll of poets, orators, scholars, soldiers, and statesmen to show, people will greatly respect it; but not till then, no matter how many novels are composed in its honor or how many sermons are preached against 'the sin of caste'" (*The Nation*, November 12, 1868, 387). Saul Bellow is reputed to have said, sometime in the 1980s, "Show me the Proust of the Papuans, the Tolstoy of the Zulus, and I will read him" (cited in Dinesh D'Souza, *What's So Great About America* [Washington, DC: Regency Publishing, 2002], 39). Speaking to the National Urban League in 1985, Glenn Lowry claimed, "To win the equal regard of our fellows, black Americans cannot substitute judicial and legislative decree for what is to be won through the outstanding achievements of individual black persons" ("Beyond Civil Rights," in *State of Black America* [Washington, DC: National Urban League, 1986], 172; cited in Steinberg, *Turning Back*, 240n28).

24. The speaker was Will Marshall, president of the Public Policy Institute, the DLC's think tank. Quoted in Ronald Brownstein, "Nomination May Add Race Issue to Democrats' Schism," *Los Angeles Times*, May 26, 1993, A1, A21.

25. *Grutter v. Bollinger et al.* at 16.

26. Ibid., at 21–22.

27. Ibid., at 18–19.

28. Ibid., at 18.

29. O'Connor did also opine that "we have repeatedly acknowledged the overriding importance of preparing students for work and citizenship, describing education as pivotal to 'sustaining our political and cultural heritage' with a fundamental role in maintaining the fabric of society" (Ibid., at 19).

30. Ibid., at 20.

31. "In order to cultivate a set of leaders with legitimacy in the eyes of the citizenry, it is necessary that the path to leadership be visibly open to talented and qualified individuals of every race and ethnicity. All members of our heterogeneous society must have confidence in the openness and integrity of the educational institutions that provide this training. As we have recognized, law schools 'cannot be effective in isolation from the individuals and institutions with which the law interacts' " (Ibid., at 20).

32. "Where the Court has accepted only national security and rejected even the best interests of a child, as a justification for racial discrimination, I conclude that only those measures the state must take to provide a bulwark against anarchy, or to prevent violence, will constitute a 'pressing public necessity' " (*Grutter*, Opinion of J. Thomas at 5).

33. See, for example, in the *Grutter* and *Gratz* cases, Brief for Julius W. Beckton et al. as amici curiae 5–7; Brief for 3M et al. as amici curiae 2–3; and Brief for General Motors Corp. as amici curiae 2–3.

34. Josh Getlin, "Case Sparks Recruitment Debate over Race, *Los Angeles Times* (June 22, 2003): A 38.

35. "About 14 percent of U.S. faculty in colleges and universities were minorities in 1997 . . . Five percent of the faculty were black; 5 percent, Asian/Pacific Islanders; 3 percent, Hispanic; and 0.4 percent, American Indian/Alaskan Native" National Center for Education Statistics, *District of Education Statistics 2000* (U.S. Department of Education, 2001), 194.

36. California again offered an interesting illustration of the problem. "The proportion of women among faculty members hired by the University of California has fallen sharply since a 1996 ballot measure barred the use of racial and gender preferences by state agencies, new statistics show. The university's revelation prompted female professors to call for action to reverse the decline. According to data presented by the nine-campus system at a hearing of the State Senate's Select Committee on Government Oversight, women made up a record 37 percent of new hires by the university in 1994, but the numbers have fallen since then, to 27 percent as of 1998—a year when women made up 48 percent of American doctoral recipients" (Alex P. Kellogg, "U. of California Reports Hiring

a Smaller Proportion of Women Since Passage of Prop. 209," *Chronicle of Higher Education* [February 2, 2001], daily edition, http://chronicle.com/daily/2001/02/2001020201n.htm (accessed November 2, 2004).

37. National Center for Education Statistics, *Digest of Educational Statistics 2001*, Table 207, http://nces.ed.gov/pubs2001/digest/tables/PDF/table207.pdf (accessed November 2, 2004).

38. Christopher J. Lucas, *Crisis in the Academy: Rethinking Higher Education in America* (1996; New York: St. Martin's Press, 1998) 17–18; William G. Bowen and Derek Bok note that "in 1965, only 4.8 percent of all U.S. college students were African American" (*The Shape of the River: Long-Term Consequences of Considering Race in College and University Admissions* [Princeton, NJ: Princeton University Press, 1998], 4). Lucas's numbers are not exactly equivalent to those of Bowen and Bok, who use numbers for African Americans, but they are comparable before 1965. The situation was even more restrictive at the elite schools in the "College and Beyond" Mellon study on which Bowen and Bok base their conclusions. "In the fall of 1951, black students averaged 0.8 percent of the entering class at the nineteen College and Beyond schools for which adequate records are available." By the mid-1960s, "the numbers actually enrolled remained small, with blacks making up only 1 percent of the enrollments of selective New England colleges in 1965." Similarly, "in 1965, barely 1 percent of all law students in America were black, and over one-third of them were enrolled in all-black schools. Barely 2 percent of all medical students were African American, and more than three-fourths of them attended two all-black institutions, Howard University and Meharry Medical College" (5). Measurable change followed intensified political protest and civil rights legislation: "The percentage of blacks enrolled in Ivy League colleges rose from 2.3 percent in 1967 to 6.3 in 1976, while the percentages in other 'prestigious' colleges grew from 1.7 to 4.8. Meanwhile, the proportion of black medical students had climbed to 6.3 percent by 1975, and black law students had increased their share to 4.5 percent" (7).

39. Committee on Affirmative Action and Diversity, "Report on Exit Surveys and Faculty Diversity," fall 2001; a brief summary, "Faculty Diversity Reported Weak," *93106*, February 4, 2002, is available online at http://www.instadv.ucsb.edu/93106/2002/February4/faculty.html (accessed August 12, 2004).

40. Nellie McKay, "What Does Genuine Respect for African-American Literature Mean?" *Chronicle of Higher Education* (July 17, 1998).

41. "JBHE Completes Its Count of Black Students and Faculty at the Nation's 50 Flagship State Universities," *Journal of Blacks in Higher Education* (August 2006), http://www.jbhe.com/features/51_survey_stateuniversities.html (accessed August 31, 2006).

42. See University of California Office of the President, "UC Preliminary Data on Undergraduate Applications," Table C: University of California Freshman Ad-

mits from California by Campus, Fall 1997 through 2002, http://www.ucop
.edu/news/factsheets/2002/admissions_campus.pdf (accessed August 23, 2006).
The other campuses record declines smaller than those of Berkeley and UCLA.

43. Richard C. Atkinson, "Diversity: Not There Yet," *Washington Post*, April 20, 2003, http://www.ucop.edu/pres/speeches/postoped.htm (accessed August 23, 2006). See also University of California Long-Range Guidance Team, Display 2: Underrepresented Minorities as a Percentage of California Public High School Graduates and New UC Freshmen, 1989–2005, "UC 2028. The Power and Promise of Ten," (Oakland: University of California Office of the President, 2006), 12.

44. Anthony P. Carnevale and Stephen J. Rose, *Socioeconomic Status, Race/Ethnicity, and Selective College Admissions* (New York: Century Foundation, 2003), http://www.tcf.org/Publications/Education/carnevale_rose.pdf (accessed August 23, 2006).

45. For example, between 1970 and 1996, Latinos increased their school enrollment by more than 200 percent in California and Illinois, by somewhat under 200 percent in Arizona and New Jersey, by around 150 percent in Texas, and by 443 percent in Florida. Gary Orfield and John T. Yun, *Resegregation in America's Schools* (Cambridge, MA: Civil Rights Project–Harvard University, 1999), 11, Table 7, http://www.civilrightsproject.ucla.edu/research/deseg/Resegregation _American_Schools99.pdf (accessed October 1, 2007).

46. Ibid., emphasis added. Additional national demographic data is available: University of California Office of the President, "Student/Workforce Data," http://www.ucop.edu/news/studstaff.html (accessed August 23, 2006).

47. Martin Van Der Werf, "Minority Faculty Members Make Slight Gains in Representation on Campuses, Report Shows," *Chronicle of Higher Education* (March 11, 2002).

48. See Peter Schrag, *Paradise Lost: California's Experience, America's Future* (New York: New Press, 1998), 87–93; Mark Baldassare, *California in the New Millennium: The Changing Social and Political Landscape* (Berkeley: University of California Press, 2000), esp. chap. 3; and Schrag, *California: America's High-Stakes Experiment* (Berkeley: University of California Press, 2006).

49. "Of the 90,000 people in the city of Santa Barbara, 58 percent are white and 35 percent are Latino." Compare this to the public school population: "The Santa Barbara elementary district's nine main campuses contain 5,800 students. The district is 22 percent white and 72 percent Latino. Four of the district's campuses are 90 percent Latino or more. The district enrollment is 2 percent Asian and 2 percent black" (Camilla Cohee, "Our Segregated Schools: Part One: A Class Struggle," *Santa Barbara News-Press*, April 14, 2002, A1). See also other articles in this series, which continued throughout that week of April 2002.

50. For good interview data on the negative racial effects of decisions not motivated explicitly by race, see Thomas Shapiro, *The Hidden Cost of Being African American: How Wealth Perpetuates Inequality* (New York: Oxford University Press, 2004).

51. Maintaining a distance is compatible with lamenting the size of this distance. Some writers do grant a link between economic and racial inequality, as does Hollinger, *Postethnic America*, Epilogue. Some writers have begun to call for "economic affirmative action," with unclear aims and effects. See Richard D. Kahlenberg, *The Remedy: Class, Race, and Affirmative Action* (New York: Basic Books, 1997); and "Affirmative Action: There's a Third Way," *Washington Post*, March 31, 2003, A13; Walter Benn Michaels, *The Trouble with Diversity: How We Learned to Love Identity and Ignore Inequality* (New York: Metropolitan Books, 2006).

8. Facing the Knowledge Managers

1. The best history of downsizing and layoffs as a systematic and largely unchallenged business strategy is Louis Uchitelle, *The Disposable American: Layoffs and Their Consequences* (New York: Knopf, 2006).

2. Peter F. Drucker, *Post-Capitalist Society* (New York: HarperBusiness, 2003).

3. See Desmond Ryan, "The Thatcher Government's Attack on Higher Education in Historical Perspective," *New Left Review* 1, no. 227 (January–February 1998): 3–32. In September 1997, the government of New Zealand's Ministry of Education published a green paper called "A Future Tertiary Education Policy for New Zealand," where it suggested privatizing the country's university system, among other things. The paper claimed that private business forms of financial accounting would improve education's efficiency: "Ownership policies that require TEIs [tertiary education institutions] to meet the cost of capital, and reflect that cost in their resource allocation and pricing decisions, would promote competition in the tertiary education and research sectors." The paper is online at http://www.minedu.govt.nz/index.cfm?layout=document&documentid=4710&indexid=10815&indexparentid=1216 (accessed October 1, 2006).

4. See, for example, Business-Higher Education Forum, "Spanning the Chasm: A Blueprint for Action" (Washington, DC, 1999).

5. See, for example, California State University, "The Cornerstones Report," December 1997, Principle 9, http://www.calstate.edu/cornerstones/reports/cornerstones_report/ (accessed October 1, 2006).

6. This awareness received its first famous expression in Adolph Berle and Gardiner Means, *The Modern Corporation and Private Property* (New York: Macmillan, 1933). See Doug Henwood's useful summary in *Wall Street* (New York: Verso Press, 1997), 252–258.

7. Michael C. Jensen, "Eclipse of the Public Corporation," *Harvard Business Review* 89, no. 5 (September–October 1989): 61–74.

8. See Connie Bruck, *The Predators' Ball: The Inside Story of Drexel Burnham and the Rise of the Junk Bond Raiders* (New York: Simon and Schuster, 1988). The financial services industry was doing the same thing to itself—income from "relationship" banking, or long-term partnerships between firms and financial specialists, was being replaced by income from transactions, or percentages of the value of instruments bought and sold.

9. Henwood, *Wall Street*, 73.

10. For an accessible summary of research on the situation in the 1990s, see Edward N. Wolff, "The Rich Get Richer: And Why the Poor Don't," *American Prospect* 12, no. 3 (February 12, 2001), http://www.prospect.org/cs/articles?article-the _rich_get_richer (accessed October 11, 2002): "Despite the overall gains in stock ownership, fewer than half of all U.S. households had any stake in the stock market by 1998—and many of those had only a minor stake. In 1998, while 48 percent of households owned some stock, only 36 percent had total stock holdings worth $5,000 or more and only 32 percent owned stock worth $10,000 or more. Moreover, the top 1 percent of households accounted for 42 percent of the value of all stock owned in the United States; the top 5 percent accounted for about two-thirds; the top 10 percent for more than three-quarters; and the top 20 percent for almost 90 percent."

11. Neil Fligstein, *The Transformation of Corporate Control* (Cambridge, MA: Harvard University Press, 1990), 15.

12. For a description of empowerment in the new corporation that was influential at the time, see Sumantra Ghoshal and Christopher Bartlett, *The Individualized Corporation* (New York: HarperBusiness, 1997).

13. Thomas A. Stewart, *Intellectual Capital: The New Wealth of Organizations* (New York: Doubleday, 1997), 95.

14. Stewart, *Intellectual Capital*, 86. Other illustrative articles from the period are David J. Teece, "Capturing Value from Knowledge Assets: The New Economy, Markets for Know-How, and Intangible Assets," *California Management Review* 40, no. 3 (Spring 1998): 55–79; Liam Fahey and Laurence Prusak, "The Eleven Deadliest Sins of Knowledge Management," *California Management Review* 40, no. 3 (Spring 1998): 265–276; Verna Allee, "12 Principles of Knowledge Management," *Training and Development* 51, no. 11 (November 1997): 71–74; Peter Haapaniemi, "The Quiet Revolution," *Chief Executive* 120 (January–February 1997): 56–57; William C. Miller, "Fostering Intellectual Capital," *HR Focus* 75, no. 1 (January 1998): 9–10; and Janine Nahapiet and Sumantra Ghoshal, "Social Capital, Intellectual Capital, and the Organizational Advantage," *Academy of Management Review* 23, no. 2 (April 1998): 242–266.

15. Stewart, *Intellectual Capital*, 91.

16. Ibid., 89.

17. Ibid., 91.

18. Ibid., 90.

19. On "increasing returns," see W. Brian Arthur, "Increasing Returns and the New World of Business," *Harvard Business Review* (July–August 1996): 100ff. For an accessible, skeptical treatment of the idea from the period, see Paul Krugman, "Will Capitalism Go Hollywood?" *Slate*, January 22, 1998, http://web.mit.edu/krugman/www/values.html (accessed August 25, 2006).

20. Immanuel Wallerstein, "The Bourgeois(ie) as Concept and Reality," in Etienne Balibar and Immanuel Wallerstein, *Race, Nation, Class: Ambiguous Identities* (1988; London: Verso, 1991), 147. This essay was a good summary of Wallerstein's claims about the tendency of capitalism toward monopoly via its need for "markets that can both be utilized and circumvented at the same time" (144).

21. For a condensed outline of the decade-long series of actions against Microsoft, see "Timeline: Microsoft Legal Wrangles," BBC News, http://news.bbc.co.uk/2/hi/special_report/1998/04/98/microsoft/506492.stm (accessed August 26, 2006).

22. Some observers thought this triviality was not just economic. "Unemployment rates in 1997 reached 8.8% and 7%, respectively, for Ph.D.s in obviously useless subjects like English and political science. But they are surprisingly high as well for hard sciences like biochemistry and computer science (4% and 2.4%, respectively)." Peter Brimelow, "Educators' Bad Math," *Forbes*, May 21, 1999.

23. For a how-to book that described English as "a degree for all seasons," see Julie DeGalan and Stephen Lambert, *Great Jobs for English Majors* (Lincolnwood, IL: VGM Career Horizons, 1994).

24. Michael Bérubé rightly observed that " 'literature' may indeed have declined in cultural authority but 'English' remains a potentially valuable career asset." *The Employment of English: Theory, Jobs, and the Future* (New York: New York University Press, 1998), 22. Bérubé was disputing John Guillory's claim that the study of literature has declined in direct proportion to the decline in the market value of literature's "cultural capital." Guillory, *Cultural Capital: The Problem of Literary Canon Formation* (Chicago: University of Chicago Press, 1993). Bérubé and Guillory were both correct, but about different things—English as teaching marketable skills (stable value) and literature as cultural capital (decreased value).

25. One commentator has called "mediating across sectors of society" and "mediating across cultures" the "most venturesome" of "the functions of the humanities in our time." Alberta Arthurs, "The Humanities in the 1990s," in *Higher Learning in America: 1980–2000* (Baltimore: Johns Hopkins University Press, 1993), 265–267.

26. Stewart, *Intellectual Capital*, 98–99.

27. Valdis Krebs, cited in Stewart, *Intellectual Capital,* 100.

28. N. Munk, "The New Organization Man," *Fortune* 137, no. 5 (March 16, 1998): 62–66, 68, 72, 74.

29. Stewart, *Intellectual Capital*, 100.

30. Ibid., 108.

31. This statement is based on my interviews with Silicon Valley employees between 1996 and 2001, and discussions with area journalists about their often-blocked attempts to talk to employees directly.

32. For an ethnography of one representative of the New Economy's "humane work-place" and its eventual loss to financial agents, see Andrew Ross, *No-Collar: The Humane Workplace and Its Hidden Costs* (New York: Basic Books, 2003).

33. This was the core message of Thomas J. Peters and Robert H. Waterman Jr., *In Search of Excellence: Lessons from America's Best-Run Companies* (New York: Harper and Row, 1982), one of the most widely popular business books in U.S. history. For a detailed discussion of human relations theory, see Christopher Newfield, "Corporate Culture Wars," in *Corporate Futures: The Diffusion of the Culturally Sensitive Corporate Form*, ed. George Marcus (Chicago: University of Chicago Press, 1998), 23–62. For an international comparison of the growth rates of economies with different degrees of management-labor conflict, see David M. Gordon, *Fat and Mean: The Corporate Squeeze of Working Americans and the Myth of Managerial "Downsizing"* (New York: Free Press, 1996).

34. The reference to high-tech artisans is in Ross, *No-Collar*, chap. 9.

35. On the university, tradition of professionalized craft labor, see Christopher Newfield, *Ivy and Industry: Business and the Making of the American University, 1880–1980* (Durham, NC: Duke University Press, 2003).

9. English's Market Retreat

1. Modern Language Association, "The Worst of Times amid the Best of Times?" *Committee on Professional Employment: Final Report* (1998), http://www.mla .org/resources/documents/rep_employment/prof_employment/prof_employment2 (accessed August 28, 2006).

2. MLA Ad Hoc Committee on the Professionalization of PhDs, "Professionalization in Perspective," http://www.mla.org/resources/documents/professionalization (accessed August 26, 2006).

3. Philip Smith, Marcia Dalbey, David Laurence, Adalaide Morris, Stephen Olsen, James Papp, Barry V. Qualls, and Eric Sundquist, "Report of the ADE Ad Hoc Committee on Staffing," *ADE Bulletin* 122 (1999): 3–26, http://www.ade.org/ reports/staffing_rpt.pdf (accessed August 26, 2006).

4. Coalition on the Academic Workforce, "Summary of Data from Surveys by the Coalition on the Academic Workforce," Table 1, http://www.mla.org/survey _coalition (accessed August 26, 2006). See also Mark Bousquet, "The Waste Product of Graduate Education: Towards a Dictatorship of the Flexible," *Social Text* 20, no.1 (Spring 2002): 81–104. On the job market's impact on women, see

MLA Committee on the Status of Women in the Profession, "Women in the Profession, 2000," *Profession 2000*: 191–217.

5. Jack H. Schuster, "Speculating About the Labor Market for Academic Humanists: 'Once More unto the Breach,'" in *The MLA Guide to the Job Search: A Handbook for Departments and for PhDs and PhD Candidates in English and Foreign Languages*, ed. Elaine Showalter (New York: MLA, 1996), 117–118. Schuster and his coauthor Martin J. Finkelstein have called the shift away from full-time tenure-track hiring a silent academic revolution. Schuster and Finkelstein, *The American Faculty: The Restructuring of Academic Work and Careers* (Baltimore: Johns Hopkins University Press, 2006), especially chapter 7. For example, Finkelstein noted that in the year 2001, only about one-quarter of new faculty appointments went to full-time tenure-track positions. "The Morphing of the American Academic Profession," *Liberal Education* 89, no. 4 (Fall 2003), http://www.aacu.org/liberaleducation/le-fa03/le-sfa03feature.cfm (accessed August 12, 2006). Many science fields were much less affected: physics, for example, was still "only" 20 percent temporary and nontenure track in 2004. "2004 Physics and Astronomy Academic Workforce," *AIP Report* (College Park, MD: American Institute of Physics, 2005), http://www.aip.org/statistics/trends/reports/awf.pdf (accessed October 19, 2007).

6. MLA Committee on Professional Employment, "Some Conclusions," *Committee on Professional Employment: Final Report*, http://www.mla.org/resources/documents/rep_employment/prof_employment/prof_employment9 (accessed August 26, 2006).

7. For example, the "Final Report of the MLA Committee on Professional Employment" stated that "we recommend that departmental and campus administrators make every effort to convert an optimal number of part-time positions to full-time—preferably tenure-track—positions." Sandra M. Gilbert et al. "Final Report of the MLA Committee on Professional Employment," *PMLA* 113 (1998): 1172. The American Association of University Professors has performed several analyses of the subject. See *The Status of Non-Tenure-Track Faculty* (1993), in *Policy Documents and Reports*, 9th ed. (Washington, DC: AAUP, 2001), and its analogous report ten years later, "Contingent Appointments and the Academic Profession," http://www.aaup.org/AAUP/pubsres/policydocs/contents/conting-stmt.htm (accessed August 26, 2006).

8. David Orr, "The Job Market in English and Foreign Languages," *PMLA* 85 (1970): 1185–1198, cited in "The History of the Job Crisis in the Modern Languages," *Committee on Professional Employment: Final Report*, http://www.mla.org/resources/documents/rep_employment/prof_employment/prof_employment6. Orr was already writing that "the academic professions that serve higher education in the United States seem today to be edging into serious economic trouble. Should present trends continue, life in the professions, particularly in the humanities, could turn grim indeed, and, as a result, few future

college students could expect an education of a quality comparable to that which is presently thought to be their inalienable right" (1185). He also noted that "economic factors in Ph.D.-granting institutions have caused them to rely more heavily than before on Ph.D. candidates, i.e., teaching assistants, to handle their lower-level courses" (1191).

9. Modern Language Association, "Preface," *Committee on Professional Employment: Final Report* (1998), http://www.mla.org/resources/documents/rep_employment/prof_employment/prof_employment1 (accessed August 27, 2006; emphasis in original).

10. Ibid.

11. Robert Scholes, *The Rise and Fall of English: Reconstructing English as a Discipline* (New Haven, CT: Yale University Press, 1998), 18, 119–120.

12. See, for example, "The American Historical Profession in the 21st Century: An Exchange," *Historically Speaking: The Bulletin of the Historical Society* 6, no. 1 (September-October 2004), particularly Bruce Kuklick, "The Future of the Profession." Kuklick warned of the "growing helot class of non-standing faculty," which he traced to "too many people trained with a Ph.D. degree to be historians, so that even in the enormous system of higher education, there are too few jobs for these individuals. This may be an issue of under demand rather than oversupply, but the consequences are the same," http://www.bu.edu/historic/hs/septemberoctober04.html#profession (accessed August 28, 2006).

13. MLA Ad Hoc Committee on the Professionalization of PhDs, "Professionalization in Perspective," http://www.mla.org/resources/documents/professionalization (accessed August 28, 2006).

14. The *Final Report* stated that the demand for academic humanists arose from two nonmarket social goals in American public policy: "an imperative to enlarge the college-going segment of the population and an imperative to expand institutional capacities for basic research," http://www.mla.org/resources/documents/rep_employment/prof_employment/prof_employment6 (accessed August 28, 2006).

15. Patricia Meyer Spacks, "Presidential Address 1994: Reality—Our Subject and Discipline," *PMLA* 110, no. 3 (May 1995): 350–357; Elaine Showalter, "Presidential Address 1998: Regeneration," *PMLA* 114, no. 3 (May 1999): 318–328.

16. Ad Hoc Committee on the Future of Scholarly Publishing, *The Future of Scholarly Publishing* (New York: MLA, 2002), http://www.mla.org/resources/documents/rep_scholarly_pub/scholarly_pub (accessed May 12, 2004).

17. "A Special Letter from Stephen Greenblatt," May 28, 2002, http://www.mla.org/resources/documents/rep_scholarly_pub/scholarly_pub (accessed May 12, 2004).

18. Ad Hoc Committee on the Future of Scholarly Publishing, *The Future of Scholarly Publishing*, http://www.mla.org/resources/documents/issues_scholarly_pub/repview_future_pub (accessed August 28, 2006).

19. For an example of Christ's thinking about the liberal arts mission, see "Innovation and Tradition in American Liberal Education" (speech to faculty, administrators, and guests at the National University of Singapore, November 8, 2004), http://www.smith.edu/president/speeches/innovation.html (accessed August 28, 2006). The speech stayed close to the standard liberal arts contributions of speaking, reading, and writing well, critical thinking, cultural fluency, and various aspects of personal character. These are qualities for which there is indeed a quasi-permanent social demand.

20. Carol Christ, "Retaining Faculty Lines," *Profession 1997* (New York: Modern Language Association, 1997), 55.

21. Bill Readings links "excellence" to cost-benefit analysis in *The University in Ruins* (Cambridge, MA: Harvard University Press, 1996), 30–32.

22. Ibid.

23. Ibid., 31.

24. Cited by Ibid., 192.

25. Ibid.

26. Ibid., 30.

27. These movements covered the full political spectrum. The best source of the left-wing version for the noneconomist was the British journal *New Left Review*, where only the rare 1990s issue passed without at least one essay on a major planning and coordinating matter involving states, markets, firms, and/or financial networks.

28. For more on Readings's view of the parent-child/teacher-student bond, see *University in Ruins,* chap. 10 and p. 189.

29. Ibid., 184–185.

30. Ibid., 187, 189, 190, emphases in original.

31. See Christopher Newfield, *Ivy and Industry: Business and the Making of the American University, 1880–1980* (Durham, NC: Duke University Press, 2003), chap. 7. In my usage there, "mangerial criticism" controls individuals on behalf of systems, rather than controlling markets on behalf of individuals and institutions.

32. There were exceptions to this tendency, of course, notably outside of LCS, for example, the work of political scientists like William Connerly and Thomas Dumm. The literature on Foucault is vast, and a full discussion of Foucault's reception in the anglophone world is well beyond my scope.

33. Michel Foucault, *The History of Sexuality: An Introduction*, vol. 1 (1976), trans. Robert Hurley (1978; New York: Random House-Vintage, 1980), 92, 95.

34. At the time, various critics took Foucault to task for his model, but some of the most focused of these overstated their case in a way that reduced their ability to propel new research. For example, Terry Eagleton wrote, "Nobody has demonstrated more profoundly and relentlessly than Foucault how subjectivity is subjugation and incarceration; and nobody has more violently suppressed the paradoxical companion truth, that if emancipation is not from, through, and by

human subjects, then it is nothing." "Marxism, Structuralism, and Post Structuralism," *Diacritics* 15, no. 4 (Winter 1985): 8. Eagleton ignored Foucault's important claim that this dichotomy between structure and subject was untenable, and sidelined the related point that LCS needed better articulations of their relation.

35. Judith Butler, *Gender Trouble: Feminism and the Subversion of Identity* (New York: Routledge, 1990), 57.

36. Harvey Blume, "Stephen Greenblatt: The Wicked Son" (interview), *Bookwire* (June 2001), http://www.bookwire.com/bookwire/bbr/reviews/june2001/ GREENBLATTInterview.htm (accessed August 28, 2006).

37. As another example, see Catherine Gallagher's similar statement: "The insistence on finding a single unequivocal political meaning for this critical practice, indeed in some cases on reducing it to a politics or a relation to power, is puzzling and certainly runs counter to what seems to me to be new historicism's most valuable insights: that no cultural or critical practice is simply a politics in disguise, that such practices are seldom intrinsically either liberatory or oppressive, that they seldom contain their politics as an essence but rather occupy particular historical situations from which they enter into various exchanges, or negotiations, with practices designated 'political.' The search for the new historicism's political essence can be seen as a rejection of these insights." Catherine Gallagher, "Marxism and the New Historicism," in *The New Historicism*, ed. H. Aram Veeser (New York: Routledge, 1989), 37. Gallagher is right to reject a causal link between politics and culture but not to repartition them.

10. The Costs of Accounting

1. V. Wayne Kennedy, "Message from the Senior Vice President—Business and Finance," *Annual Financial Report, 1995–1996,* (removed from UC website: in author's files).

2. Financial authority was, of course, abetted by "big-machine" scientific research during and after World War II, when research and accounting became increasingly interdependent. For parts of the story, see Richard Rhodes, *The Making of the Atomic Bomb* (New York: Simon and Schuster, 1986); and Stanley Aronowitz and William DiFazio, *The Jobless Future: Sci-Tech and the Dogma of Work* (Minneapolis: University of Minnesota Press, 1994).

3. Charles Schwartz, "Looking into the UC Budget" (1992–1998), especially the series "Expenditures for Administration," http://socrates.berkeley.edu/~schwrtz/ budgets.html (accessed August 22, 2006).

4. Robert Zemsky, Gregory R. Wegner, and William F. Massy, *Remaking the American University: Market-Smart and Mission-Centered* (New Brunswick, NJ: Rutgers University Press, 2005), 20. Also see my discussion of Eric Gould in chapter 14 of this book.

5. Jack H. Schuster and Martin J. Finkelstein, *The American Faculty: The Restructuring of Academic Work and Careers* (Baltimore: Johns Hopkins University Press, 2006), 269.

6. Zemsky, Wegner, and Massy, *Remaking the American University*, 21.

7. Neil Fligstein, *The Transformation of Corporate Control* (Cambridge, MA: Harvard University Press, 1990), 15. See also chapter 8 of this book, note 11.

8. John L. Pulley, "The Rich Got Richer in 2000, Study of Endowments Shows," *Chronicle of Higher Education* (April 13, 2001), http://chronicle.com/weekly/v47/i31/31a03901.htm (accessed August 12, 2006). The *Chronicle* was able to use the same headline again and again, for example, Kit Lively and Scott Street, "The Rich Get Richer," *Chronicle of Higher Education* (October 13, 2000), http://chronicle.com/weekly/v47/i07/07a04901.htm (accessed August 12, 2006). Others used it too: "The Rich Get Richer," *Inside Higher Ed* (January 23, 2006), http://insidehighered.com/news/2006/01/23/nacubo (accessed August 12, 2006). By this point, endowment returns had rebounded from the early 2000s: FY 2004's average was up 15.1 percent, and in FY 2005 it was up 9.3 percent. On the question of inequality, the *Inside Higher Ed* author observed that "gaps between institutions in the endowment survey are substantial. Harvard University's $25 billion fund tops second place Yale University by more than $10 billion. The growth alone in Harvard's endowment during the last year exceeds the size of the entire endowment of the University of Southern California or the University of Virginia. If you added up the endowments of the 10 historically black colleges with the largest funds, they would not equal the endowment of Williams College. Add up the endowments of the 10 community colleges with the largest funds and they don't equal the endowment of the University of South Florida."

9. Edward Wyatt, "College Endowments Learn to Live With Risk," *New York Times*, November 19, 2000.

10. William C. Symonds, "Rich College, Poor College, "*Business Week,* December 20, 2004, http://www.businessweek.com./magazine/content/04_51163913116_mz021.htm (accessed August 19, 2005). For fuller data and analysis, see American Association of University Professors, *Financial Inequality in Higher Education: The Annual Report on the Economic Status of the Profession, 2006-07*, http:aaup.org/AAUP/comm/rep/z/ecstatreport 2006-07 (accessed October 19, 2007).

11. For example, "All of the top performers in the 2000 fiscal year attributed their high numbers to the exceptional performance of venture capital, with some institutions citing returns of more than 300 percent for the year on those investments. The venture capital gains have risen with the heightened popularity of initial public offerings of stocks" (Lively and Street, "The Rich Get Richer").

12. For example, Yale's endowment manager, David F. Swensen, became an investment adviser through books as well, including *Pioneering Portfolio Management:*

An Unconventional Approach to Investment (New York: Free Press, 2000). On Swensen's techniques, see John L. Pulley, "Big Bucks, Closed Books," *Chronicle of Higher Education* (September 2, 2005), http://chronicle.com/weekly/v52/i02/02a04901.htm (accessed September 25, 2005).

13. Some investment managers did emphasize their desire to serve an educational mission: see Geraldine Fabrikant, "For Yale's Money Man, a Higher Calling," *New York Times*, February 18, 2007, citing David F. Swensen saying, for example, "I feel privileged to be in a place where the resources that we generate are applied to the world's problems."

14. For one thoughtful dissent from the size complex, see Mark B. Schneider, "Endowments Can Become Too Much of a Good Thing," *Chronicle of Higher Education* (June 2, 2006), http://chronicle.com/weekly/v52/i39/39b01801.htm (accessed June 27, 2006).

15. For coverage of this situation in Pennsylvania, see John L. Pulley, "Public Universities' Ambitious Campaigns Vex Many Small Private Institutions," *Chronicle of Higher Education* (December 3, 1999).

16. Erin Stout, "Fund Raising: Private Support Will Remain Strong," *Chronicle of Higher Education* (January 6, 2006), http://chronicle.com/weekly/v52/i18/18a01301.htm#campaigns (accessed August 22, 2006). The National Association of College and University Business Officers publishes an annual endowment study. Some of its data for various years is available at http://www.nacubo.org/x2376.xml (accessed August 23, 2006).

17. Caroline Preston, "A Gift for Athletics from a Wealthy Oilman Triggers a Furor at Oklahoma State U.," *Chronicle of Higher Education* (February 20, 2006), http://chronicle.com/daily/2006/02/2006022005n.htm (accessed February 28, 2006).

18. Richard Colvin, "The New Philanthropists," *Education Next* (http://www.hoover.org/publications/ednext/3217636.html (accessed October 19, 2007).

19. Clark Kerr, *The Uses of the University* (Cambridge, MA: Harvard University Press, 1963), 67.

20. Ibid., 89.

21. Early variants of RCM are associated with the University of Pennsylvania, the University of Southern California, Indiana University, and Harvard's "Each Tub on Its Own Bottom" system.

22. I first encountered enthusiasm for "open-book management" during interviews with management consultants in Silicon Valley in 1996, particularly, Jim Kouzes. For an analysis, see Christopher Newfield, "Corporate Culture Wars," in *Corporate Futures: The Diffusion of the Culturally Sensitive Corporate Form*, ed. George Marcus (Chicago: University of Chicago Press, 1998), 23–62.

23. This summary relies in large part on the following works: John R. Curry and Jon C. Strauss, "Whither Decentralized Management? Responsibility Center Management

25 Years Later" (manuscript, 2001), http://www.unt.edu/president/features/RCMresources/Curry-Strauss%20RCM.pdf (accessed August 23, 2006); William F. Massey, *Resource Allocation in Higher Education* (Ann Arbor: University of Michigan Press, 1996); Robert Whelan, *Responsibility Center Budgeting: An Approach to Decentralized Management for Institutions of Higher Education* (Bloomington: Indiana University Press, 1991); Wellford W. Wilms, Cheryl Teruya, and Marybeth Walpole, "Fiscal Reform at UCLA: The Clash of Accountability and Academic Freedom," *Change* (October–November 1997), http://www.gseis.ucla.edu/gseisdoc/change.html (accessed August 19, 2006); and Robert Zemsky and William F. Massy, "Expanding Perimeters, Melting Cores, and Sticky Functions: Towards an Understanding of Current Predicaments," *Change* 27, no. 6 (November–December 1995).

24. In the words of two of its most senior, long-term practitioners, "Martin Meyerson, President of the University of Pennsylvania in the 1970s, championed the development of Responsibility Center Management. By bringing marketplace incentives to higher education, he hoped to involve faculty and others in considering financial as well as academic issues when making tradeoffs between competing claims for limited resources" (Curry and Strauss, "Whither Decentralized Management?").

25. Wilms, Teruya, and Walpole, "Fiscal Reform at UCLA."

26. Larry R. Faulkner, personal correspondence with the author, January 11, 1998.

27. Curry and Strauss, "Whither Decentralized Management?" 28.

28. Zemsky, Wegner, and Massy, *Remaking the American University*, 63.

29. Curry and Strauss, "Whither Decentralized Management?"

30. Analysts regularly acknowledged that RCM could support the educational mission only when upper administrators bent their own rules. One good overview of its use in a range of universities concluded that "Planning for the future to support the mission of the university can be supplemented with relationships to market forces, but only in moderation. A tool important to a top-level university administrator is a discretionary funds account . . . discretionary spending informed by university mission or values can mitigate the negativities of the market's treatment of important entities." Douglas M. Priest and Rachel Dykstra Boon, "Incentive-Based Budgeting Systems in the Emerging Environment," in *Privatization and Public Universities*, ed. Priest and Edward P. St. John (Bloomington: Indiana University Press, 2006), 185–186. Most observers acknowledged that RCM's market orientation distorted academic planning, but generally did not arrive at the more rigorous conclusion—that more systematic and nonincremental educational evaluation should drive budgeting.

11. The Problem with Privatization

1. Thomas J. Kane and Peter R. Orszag, "Use of State General Revenue for Higher Education Declines," Tax Policy Center and the Urban Institute, 2002, http://www.urban.org/UploadedPDF/1000462_education.pdf (accessed March 12, 2006); SHEEO, "State Higher Education Finance Executive Overview, FY2004," 7, http://www.sheeo.org/finance/exov_fy06.pdf (accessed October 20, 2007).

2. Robert Zemsky, Gregory R. Wegner, and William F. Massy, *Remaking the American University: Market-Smart and Mission-Centered* (New Brunswick, NJ: Rutgers University Press, 2005).

3. Ibid., 5.

4. Ibid., 8, 56.

5. Ibid., 8–9.

6. Though I requested the data underlying this claim from Robert Zemsky, I did not receive a reply.

7. Thanks to Calvin Moore for making this comparison. In 2005–6, UCSF's contracts and grants income was approximately $465 million, surprisingly close to the alleged $400-million gap between UC Berkeley and UM Ann Arbor.

8. See, for example, admissions rates for 2006: University of California, "Freshman Admission Profile—UC Berkeley—Fall 2007," http://www.universityofcalifornia.edu/admissions/undergrad_adm/selecting/camp_profiles/camp_profiles_ucb.html (accessed August 29, 2006); other campus rates can also be accessed from this page.

9. Education Commission of the States, "Closing the College Participation Gap: State Profiles: Michigan," April 2003, http://www.cherrycommission.org/docs/Resources/Participation/Closing%20the%20Participation%20Gap%20Michigan.pdf (accessed August 29, 2006).

10. U.S. Census Bureau, "The Black Population: 2000," August 2001, 4, http://www.census.gov/prod/2001pubs/c2kbr01-5.pdf (accessed August 29, 2006).

11. Pell Grants typically provide aid to students from families with incomes below about $20,000 per year; for proportions at leading universities, see Karen Fischer, "Elite Colleges Lag in Serving the Needy," *Chronicle of Higher Education* (May 12, 2006), http://chronicle.com/free/v52/i36/36a00101.htm (accessed August 29, 2006).

12. For vivid accounts of the interplay of improvisation and "standards" in the college classroom, see Jane Tompkins, *A Life in School: What the Teacher Learned* (New York: Perseus Books, 1996), and Michael Bérubé, *What's Liberal About the Liberal Arts: Classroom Politics and "Bias" in Higher Education* (New York: W. W. Norton, 2006).

13. Daniel Golden, *The Price of Admission: How America's Ruling Class Buys Its Way into Elite Colleges—and Who Gets Left Outside the Gates* (New York: Crown, 2006), 57.

14. This series included Dana Y. Takagi, *The Retreat from Race: Asian-American Admissions and Racial Politics* (New Brunswick, NJ: Rutgers University Press, 1993); William G. Bowen and Derek Bok, *The Shape of the River: Long-Term Consequences of Considering Race in College and University Admissions* (Princeton, NJ: Princeton University Press, 1998); Jacques Steinberg, *The Gatekeepers: Inside the Admissions Process of a Premier College* (New York: Viking, 2002); Jerome Karabel, *The Chosen: The Hidden History of Admission and Exclusion at Harvard, Yale, and Princeton* (New York: Houghton Mifflin, 2005).

15. Golden describes how he stumbled onto his story in *The Price of Admission*, 18–20.

16. The way legacy and development admits contradict true meritocracy is *not* one of these problems. Golden's indignation rests on his use of what I have called meritocracy I as his standard, and he does not do sufficient justice to the complexity of the admissions process in its attempts to factor in "background" and other dimensions of an applicant's individuality.

17. For the touchstone effort to combine academic standards with near-universal higher education, see *The Master Plan for Higher Education in California* (1960), http://www.ucop.edu/acainit/mastplan/MasterPlan1960.pdf (accessed October 21, 2007); for commentory, see Christopher Newfield, Henning Bohn, and Calvin Moore, *Current Budget Trends and the Future of the University of California*, Appendix B, http://universityofcalifornia.edu/senate/reports/AC .Futures.Report0107.pdf (accessed October 21, 2007).

18. Peter D. Hart Research Associates, "Messaging Direction for the University of California: Recommendations from an August 2005 Survey Among California Voters" (2005), 14; UC document in author's files.

19. SHEEO, "State Higher Education Finance FY2006," http://www.sheeo.org/ finance/shet_fy06.pdf (accessed October 21, 2007).

20. Newfield, Bohn, and Moore, *Current Budget Trends*.

21. "UC Core Funds" is defined in Appendix A of Newfield, Bohn and Moore, *Current Budget Trends*.

22. Newfield, Bohn, and Moore, *Current Budget Trends*, 29.

23. Ibid., 30.

24. While pubic university tuition and fees increased 51 percent in constant dollars between 1996–1997 and 2006–2007, grant aid per student rose 46 percent in the same period. College Board, *Trends in College Pricing 2006*, Figure 3, http://www.collegeboard.com/prod_downloads/press/cost06/trends_college _pricing_06.pdf (accessed October 21, 2007); College Board, *Trends in Student Aid* 2006, Figure 7, http://www.collegeboard.com/prod_downloads/press/ cost06/trends_aid_06.pdf (accessed October 21, 2007). These averages conceal greater hardship for lower-income students with the greatest need for financial aid. This thinking rests on the manifest differences in the recent fortunes of

workers with and without at least some college. Wages for high school graduates were about half those of college graduates in 1975, and that gap widened steadily thereafter. By some measures, however, the gap is much smaller, about 45 percent; see Lawrence Mishel, Jared Bernstein, and Sylvia Allegretto, *State of Working America 2006/07* (Ithaca, NY: Cornell University Press, 2007). Workers with some college or with an associate's degree have always rested about halfway between and have seen smaller wage declines than have those with high school diplomas only; see U.S. Census Bureau, "Mean Earnings of Workers 28 Years and Over, by Educational Attainment, Race, Hispanic Origin, and Sex: 1975 to 2003," http://www.census.gov/population/www/socdemo/educ-attn .html (accessed October 21, 2007).

25. See Katharine C. Lyall and Kathleen R. Sell, *The True Genius of America at Risk: Are We Losing Our Public Universities to de Facto Privatization?* (Westport, CT: ACE/Praeger, 2006), 5–6.

26. "A System for Reporting Faculty Instructional Effort," Report of the Task Force for the Implementation of Workload Reporting Policy (University of California, Office of the President, August 2005), http://www.ucop.edu/planning/itfreport .pdf (accessed October 20, 2006).

27. Ibid., 4.

28. David Wessel, "Why It Takes a Doctorate to Beat Inflation," *Wall Street Journal*, October 19, 2006, A2.

29. Ibid.

30. Lyall and Sell, *True Genius*, 151–152. Lyall and Sell borrow these categories from Steven Brint, "Creating the Future: The New University Directions," *Minerva* 43 (March 2005): 30–59.

31. Ibid.

32. James J. Duderstadt and Farris W. Womack, *The Future of the Pubic University in America* (Baltimore: Johns Hopkins University Press, 2003), 127.

33. In 2006, "13 percent [of full-time undergraduates were] enrolled in institutions with published tuition and fee changes of $24,000 or higher" (College Board, *Trends in College Pricing 2006*, 4).

34. Private sources are also *unwilling* to support core operations. The reason should by now be clear: donations, no matter how generous, will be swallowed in one gulp by mass higher education. An example is one of the most prominent individual gifts in recent years, film mogul George Lucas's pledge of $175 million to USC's renamed School of Cinematic Arts. This was the largest gift in USC's history, and in the upper reaches of gifts to any university (the largest ever was the Walton family's $300 million donation to the University of Arkansas). The gift will allow the film school to build an entirely new physical plant, and will give this already top-ranked operation financial access to any students and faculty it desires. And yet Lucas's gift comes to less than 5 percent of USC's annual oper-

ating budget, and would disappear in one year's average augmentation of every unit of USC's operation. Total USC revenue for the 2004–2005 year was $2,123,486,000, as reported in "University of Southern California Financial Report 2005," http://www.usc.edu/private/factbook/usc.fin.rpt.12.8.05.pdf (accessed October 2, 2006).

12. The Failure of Market Measures

1. In discussing how this issue unfolded, I separate two issues. The first is whether financial incentives alter research results and damage the university's distinctive status as the source of impartial, objective, disinterested, or unbought knowledge. I turn to the 2000s debate on this question in chapter 14, "Half-Suffocated Reforms." A second issue is the incompleteness and imperfection of financial incentives, which is my topic here.
2. I discuss these arguments in greater detail in Christopher Newfield, *Ivy and Industry: Business and the Making of the American University, 1880–1980* (Durham, NC: Duke University Press, 2003), chaps. 6 and 8.
3. Kenneth. J. Arrow, "Economic Welfare and the Allocation of Resources for Invention," in *The Rate and Direction of Inventive Activity: Economic and Social Factors* (Princeton, NJ: Princeton University Press, 1962), 619.
4. Suzanne Scotchmer, *Innovation and Incentives* (Cambridge: MIT Press, 2004), 282.
5. "Virtually all the critical technologies in the Internet and Web revolution were developed between 1967 and 1993 by government research agencies and/or in universities. During the same period, there arose in parallel a private, free market solution—a $10 billion commercial online services industry. The comparison between the two is extremely clear and extremely unflattering to private markets. The commercial industry's technology and structure were inferior to that of the nonprofit Internet in every conceivable way, which is the primary reason that they were so rapidly destroyed by the commercial Internet revolution." Charles H. Ferguson, *High Stakes, No Prisoners: A Winner's Tale of Greed and Glory in the Internet Wars* (New York: Random House-Times Business, 1999), 13.
6. Two influential works on the features of successful economic regions are AnnaLee Saxenien, *Regional Advantage: Culture and Competition in Silicon Valley and Route 128* (Cambridge, MA: Harvard University Press, 1994); and Richard Florida, *The Rise of the Creative Class: And How It's Transforming Work, Leisure, Community and Everyday Life* (New York: Basic Books, 2002). For a convincing appraisal of how "brain circulation" undermines the public expenditures on which "brain work" depends, see Annie Vinokur, "Brain Migration Revisited," *Globalization, Societies and Education* 4, no. 1 (March 2006): 7–24.

7. For one of the standard treatments of how complex knowledge is found in "networks of relationships," see Walter W. Powell and Laurel Smith-Doerr, "Networks and Economic Life," in *The Handbook of Economic Sociology*, ed. N.J. Smelser and R. Swedberg (Princeton, NJ: Princeton University Press and Russell Sage Foundation, 1994).

8. Scotchmer, *Innovation and Incentives*, 275.

9. Special thanks to Gerald Barnett, director of the Office of Intellectual Property, University of California at Santa Cruz, for his especially lucid thinking about the ties between tech-transfer policy and research relationships.

10. For a discussion of the emergence of the Bayh-Dole legislation in the wider context of the long trajectory of the history of humanism and the U.S. research university, see Newfield, *Ivy and Industry*, 180–183.

11. Association of University Technology Managers, "AUTM U.S. Licensing Survey: FY 2004" (public summary version), ii, http://www.autm.net/newsletter/userFiles/File/FY04LicensingSurvey/AUTM_SurvSum04.pdf (accessed August 18, 2006). The public value of inventions always has a central placement in the report. The 2004 survey reported University of Michigan president Mary Sue Coleman saying that "it is not about the money. . . . Technology transfer must serve our core mission: sharing ideas and innovations in the service of society's well-being." The survey reported the numbers but also described some of the beneficial innovations that had helped society that year. These included headlines like "Resistant Starch Technology Makes Low-Carb, High-Fiber Foods," at Kansas State University; "Saving Forests and Creating a New Cash Crop in the Middle East and Asia," at the University of Minnesota; and "Restasis—A New Treatment for Dry Eye," at the University of Georgia; among many others. The topics are meant to convey a sense both that major progress is being made in areas of vital importance to the environment, human health, agriculture, communications, computing, and many other areas, and that this progress is coming from a wide range of public and private universities and not just a handful of star performers.

12. See, in particular, David C. Mowery, Richard R. Nelson, Bhaven N. Sampat, and Arvids A. Ziedonis, *Ivory Tower and Industrial Innovation: University-Industry Technology Transfer Before and After the Bayh-Dole Act* (Stanford, CA: Stanford Business Books, 2004); and Rebecca S. Eisenberg, "Public Research and Private Development: Patents and Technology Transfer in Government-Sponsored Research," *Virginia Law Review* 82, no. 8 (November 1996): 1671–1679.

13. AUTM's president for 2005–2006 took a somewhat different tack: "Our work now includes education and community service so we are now involved with the creation and transfer of known and new knowledge to the current and next generation, not simply patent licensing." AUTM, AUTM U.S. Licensing Survey:

FY 2005, 5, http://www.autm.net/events/File/US-LS-OS Final(1).pdf (accessed October 22, 2007). Data changes are so far modest.

14. This table does not appear in the FY 2005 update of the public survey summary.

15. "Wake Forest, Tulane, Ohio Univ., Emory, Case Western, Utah, Rochester, Iowa—all are significant recipients" (Gerald Barnett, director of the Office of Intellectual Property Management, University of California, Santa Cruz, personal correspondence with the author, May 2006).

16. AUTM, "AUTM U.S. Licensing Survey: FY 2004," 26.

17. Jennifer Washburn, *University Inc.: The Corporate Corruption of Higher Education* (New York: Basic Books, 2005), 188. Crow also asserted, "At Columbia, the faculty that have been most successful commercially are the best scientists that we have. Not, you know, among the best, but *the* best—those who've made the most fundamental research breakthroughs" (186).

18. UC figures come from Suzanne Quick, Office of Technology Transfer, University of California, "Technology Transfer Statistical Highlights, FY03–04," and are published as *Office of Technology Transfer Annual Report*, http://www.ucop .edu/ott/ars/ann04/ar04.pdf (accessed October 2, 2006). The figures for number of inventions earning royalties appear only in Quick's unpublished presentation (in author's files).

19. These figures exclude patents issued to the Department of Energy laboratories associated with UC. FY 2006 figures are from *UC Technology Transfer Annual Report 2006* (2007), Exhibit 5, http://www.ucop.edu/ott/general resources /documents/OTTRptFY06.pdf (accessed October 22, 2007).

20. Reported licensing activity is higher (e.g., 473 in FY 2006). I have excluded plant licenses and letter agreements (see *UC Technology Transfer 2006*, 10).

21. *UC Technology Transfer 2006*, Exhibit 12 (excluding legal reimbursements).

22. *University of California 2003–2004 Budget for Current Operations* (UC Office of the President, 2002), 3, http://www.ucop.edu/budget/rbudget/200304/2003-04 budgetforcurrent operations.pdf (accessed October 22, 2007).

23. Income bounced around in the 2000s, showing no steady progression, and FY 2004 was relatively typical. In the better year FY 2006, about $93 million in gross licensing income came to nearly 2 percent of extramural funding.

24. The numbers for the other major players are also surprisingly small, given the size of the gross licensing income that can be calculated as a percentage of total research expenditures: MIT, 3.45 percent; Johns Hopkins, 0.74 percent; Harvard, 4.5 percent; UC, 3.2 percent; Michigan, 2.1 percent; Illinois-Urbana and Chicago, 0.9 percent; Cornell, 0.71 percent; Duke, 0.73 percent; Penn, 1.12 percent; Caltech, 2.6 percent; Rice, 1.0 percent. Outliers include Florida, 8.3 percent; Iowa, 5.6 percent; Wake Forest, 33 percent; Brigham Young, 13.3 percent; Emory, 169 percent. *Net* institutional income is likely around one-third of gross, and actual return to research even less, leaving the great majority of major licensers with net institutional

income of under 1 percent of total research expenditures ("AUTM FY 2005," Data Appendix, my calculations).

25. *UC Technology Transfer 2006*, Exhibit 14.

26. Jerry G. Thursby and Marie C. Thursby, "Buyer and Seller Views of University-Industry Licensing," in *Buying In or Selling Out: The Commercialization of the American Research University*, ed. Donald Stein (New Brunswick, NJ: Rutgers University Press, 2004), 105. Their general statement was "Fewer than half of all active licenses generate income, and only a few generate the bulk of licensing income."

13. Hiding Culture's Contribution

1. Clayton M. Christensen, *The Innovator's Dilemma: When New Technologies Cause Great Firms to Fail* (Boston: Harvard Business School Press, 1997); and Geoffrey Moore, *Inside the Tornado: Marketing Strategies from Silicon Valley's Cutting Edge* (New York: Harper Collins, 1995).

2. Robert C. Dynes, "Remarks to the Academic Business Officers Group on Preserving UC's Impact on California" (speech, Century City, California, April 27, 2004), http://www.universityofcalifornia.edu/president/speeches.html (accessed June 21, 2004).

3. ICF Consulting, "California's Future: It Starts Here. UC's Contributions to Economic Growth, Health, and Culture," March 2003, http://www.universityofcalifornia.edu/itstartshere/report/fullreport.pdf (accessed July 19, 2005).

4. Ibid., sec. 11, 1.

5. Ibid, "Executive Summary," 22.

6. Ibid., sec. 11, 5.

7. U.S. Office of Management and Budget, Circular A-21, sec. B-4.

8. Report of the University Committee on Planning and Budget and the University Committee on Research Policy (UCORP), on "Indirect Cost Recovery" (revised draft, May 16, 2003, unpublished), copy in author's files.

9. The calculation here is on $200 million including ICR at a 50 percent rate = $66,666,667 in ICR. If direct costs ($133,333,333) had been covered at a 55 percent rate, the university would have received $73,333,333. The 5 percent shortfall translated into an additional $6,666,667 that the university must obtain from somewhere else in its budget in order to support unreimbursed research costs (assuming a 50 percent recovery rate).

10. The late Richard Goodman, Vice-Chair, UC Senate Committee on Planning and Budget, Berkeley, California, October 22, 2002. The NSF found that "the university share of total expenditures for research is now 20% of total expenditures, or about $6.5 billion in FY 2001." National Science Foundation, "Academic Re-

search and Development Spending Maintains Growth from All Major Sources in FY 2001," NSF 03-327 (August 2003), cited in "Finances of Research Universities," *Council on Governmental Relations* (November 5, 2003), http://www.cogr .edu/docs/UniversityFinances.doc (accessed October 23, 2007). See also Robert M. Rosenzweig, "The Politics of Indirect Costs" (August 1998), http://www.cogr .edu/docs/Rosenzweigarticle.htm (accessed October 23, 2007) (noting that the lower ICR rates of public compared to private universities reflected the assumption that state taxpayers would subsidize some research costs indirectly); and Charles A. Goodman, Traci Williams, David Adamson, and Kathy Rosenblatt, *Paying for University Research Facilities and Administration* (Santa Monica, CA: Rand Corporation, 2000), http://www.rand.org/pubs/monograph_reports/ MR1135-1/ (concluding that in the late 1990s universities were short between $0.7 and $1.5 billion in facilities and administrative costs based on negotiated rates).

11. More research needs to be done on this topic: The most common response I have received from a limited number of administrators is that while these calculations can be made, and seem plausible as such, they do not themselves generally make them.

14. Half-Suffocated Reforms

1. A. Bartlett Giamatti, *A Free and Ordered Space: The Real World of the University* (New York: W. W. Norton, 1988), 41. As for entrepreneurial faculty, Giamatti wrote, "I doubt that a faculty member can ordinarily devote the time and energy the university requires and also pursue a substantial involvement in any such outside company. Such involvement necessarily demands great concentration and commitment, particularly at the outset or if business goes badly" (264–265). For a Bayh-Dole–era expression of similar concerns, see Derek C. Bok, *Beyond the Ivory Tower: Social Responsibilities of the Modern University* (Cambridge, MA: Harvard University Press, 1982).

2. Sheila Slaughter and Larry L. Leslie, *Academic Capitalism: Politics, Policies, and the Entrepreneurial University* (Baltimore: Johns Hopkins University Press, 1997), 7–8.

3. Clark Kerr, *The Uses of the University* (Cambridge, MA: Harvard University Press, 1963), 122. "The basic reality, for the university," he wrote, "is the widespread recognition that new knowledge is the most important factor in economic and social growth. We are just now perceiving that the university's invisible product, knowledge, may be the most powerful single element in our culture, affecting the rise and fall of professions and even of social classes, of regions and even of nations" (v–vi). Kerr claimed that liberal knowledge had been eclipsed by German industrial research even as John Henry Newman was re-

newing Humboldt's call for knowledge for its own sake in 1852. In other words, the entire run of the research university was devoted to society's technological improvement. Kerr was relying on the pioneering research of Princeton economist Fritz Machlup in *The Production and Distribution of Knowledge in the United States* (Princeton, NJ: Princeton University Press, 1962). Machlup estimated that by the late 1950s, "the production, distribution, and consumption of 'knowledge' in all its forms" accounted for "29 percent of gross national product . . . ; and 'knowledge production' is growing at about twice the rate of the rest of the economy" (*Uses of the University*, 88). As I noted in chapter 2, "Declarations of Independence," these arguments would become better known in such venues as Alvin Toffler's *Future Shock* (New York: Random House, 1970) and Daniel Bell's *The Coming of Post-Industrial Society: A Venture in Economic Forecasting* (New York: Basic Books, 1973).

4. Jean-François Lyotard, *The Postmodern Condition: A Report on Knowledge* (1979; Minneapolis: University of Minnesota Press, 1984).

5. See Alan P. Rudy, Dawn Coppin, Jason Konefal, Bradley T. Shaw, Toby Ten Eyck, Craig Harris, and Lawrence Busch, *Universities in the Age of Corporate Science: The UC Berkeley–Novartis Controversy* (Philadelphia: Temple University Press, 2007).

6. Complementary books appearing at the same time include Christopher Newfield, *Ivy and Industry: Business and the Making of the American University, 1880–1980* (Durham, NC: Duke University Press, 2003); and Sheldon Krimsky, *Science in the Private Interest* (Boulder, CO: Rowman and Littlefield, 2003).

7. David L. Kirp, *Shakespeare, Einstein, and the Bottom Line* (Cambridge, MA: Harvard University Press, 2003).

8. Kirp, *Shakespeare*, quoting Mark Yudof, 64–65.

9. Ibid., 70.

10. Ibid., 71.

11. Eric Gould, *The University in a Corporate Culture* (New Haven, CT: Yale University Press, 2003), 31.

12. Ibid., chap. 3.

13. Ibid., 54, 55.

14. Ibid., 54.

15. See, for example, Jonathan D. Glater, "Young Lawyers, Swamped by Student Debts, Flee Public Jobs," *International Herald-Tribune*, September 13, 2003: "Law students, the study found, are now leaving school with an average debt of $77,300—more than twice what they borrowed just 10 years ago. Since 1985, tuition at law schools has tripled and in some cases quadrupled; in the same period, public interest salaries have not even doubled. The story is harsher if inflation is taken into account. According to the National Association for Law Placement, the earnings of lawyers in private practice have risen by 70 percent

since 1985—starting lawyers at many big New York firms now make $125,000—while those of public interest lawyers have increased 12.5 percent and of government lawyers just 3.5 percent."

16. Alice Gomstyn, "Nation Faces a College-Access Crisis, Education-Policy Group Warns," *Chronicle of Higher Education* (October 2, 2003), http://chronicle.com/prm/daily/2003/10/2003100203n.htm (accessed August 8, 2006). On U.S. participation rates, see one of the reports that Gomstyn cites, Center for Community College Policy, "Closing the College Participation Gap," http://www.communitycollegepolicy.org/html/top.asp?page=/html/Issues/Issue.asp?issueID=1 (accessed August 8, 2006).

17. Gould, *University in a Corporate Culture*, 63.

18. Ibid.

19. These statistics (p. 62) do not square with those cited in note 17 from p. 63. The overall financial picture would be clearer were the various studies to use more stable terms of comparison.

20. Ibid., 69.

21. Ibid., 77.

22. Derek Bok, *Universities in the Marketplace: The Commercialization of Higher Education* (Princeton, NJ: Princeton University Press, 2003), 3.

23. Ibid., 60–62.

24. Bok added, "If this [example] seems far-fetched, consider the [Coca-Cola] company's effort to organize 'Coke in Education Day' at high schools, complete with a prize for the best plan for marketing Coke-sponsored discount cards, lecturers on economics by Coca-Cola officials, technical assistance to home economics students baking Coca-Cola cakes, not to mention help for chemistry classes analyzing Coca-Cola's sugar content, and even an aerial photograph of the entire student body holding up the letters COKE" (*Universities in the Marketplace*, 172). Bok's source is Alex Molnar, "Sponsored Schools and Commercialized Classrooms: Schoolhouse Commercializing Trends in the 1990s" (August 1998), http://epslu.edu/ceru/Annual%20reports/cace-98-01.htm (accessed October 23, 2007).

25. Bok, *Universities in the Marketplace*, 61.

26. Ibid., 74–75.

27. Ibid., 71.

28. Ibid., 68.

29. A sample of this large and consistent literature on the impact of financial interests on research outcomes and clinical behavior: M.M. Chren and C.S. Landefeld, "Physicians' Behavior and Their Interactions with Drug Companies: A Controlled Study of Physicians Who Requested Additions to a Hospital Drug Formulary," *JAMA* 271 (1994): 684–689; J.E. Bekelman, Y. Li, and C.P. Gross, "Scope and Impact of Financial Conflicts of Interest in Biomedical Research: A

Systemic Review," *JAMA* 289 (2003): 454–463; S. Lipton, E.A. Boyd, L. A. Bero, "Conflicts of Interest in Academic Research: Policies, Processes, and Attitudes" *Accounting Research* 17 (2004): 83–102; and David Blumenthal, "Doctors and Drug Companies," *New England Journal of Medicine* 351, no. 18 (October 28, 2004): 1885–1890.

30. The landmark report was The World Health Organization, "The World Health Report 2000—Health Systems: Improving Performance," http://www.who.int/whr/2000/en (accessed October 23, 2007). The United States was ranked 37th in the world in Annex Table 1.

31. Ibid., 68.

32. Ibid., 173.

33. Ibid., 173–174.

34. Ibid., 175.

35. Ibid.

36. Ibid., 147.

37. Ibid., 145.

38. Stanton A. Glantz, John Slade, Lisa A. Bero, Peter Hanauer, and Deborah E. Barnes, eds., *The Cigarette Papers* (Berkeley: University of California Press, 1996); documents are available at http://www.library.ucsf.edu/tobacco (accessed October 23, 2007).

39. *United States of America v. Philip Morris, Inc. et al.*, Civil Action No. 99-2496 (GK). The full ruling is available at http://www.usdoj.gov/civil/cases/tobacco2/amended%20opinion.pdf (accessed October 23, 2007).

40. Bok's anger toward faculty selfishness is pronounced:

When campus authorities let values erode, their moral authority shrinks. Faculty members become less mindful of their responsibilities, less collegial in their relationships, less inclined to take on tasks beyond the minimum required. Individual professors are emboldened to pursue private ventures at a cost to the common enterprise. Inequities and inequalities grow more pronounced, and weaker groups feel impelled to organize collectively to protect themselves. As internal norms give way, formal rules are required to ensure that the work of the institution gets done. If the university will not act, out of fear of offending the faculty, the government will eventually intervene to protect legitimate interests. Bit by bit, therefore, commercialization threatens to change the character of the university in ways that limit its freedom, sap its effectiveness, and lower its standing in the society. (*Universities in the Marketplace*, 207)

41. Cited in Kirp, *Shakespeare*, 47.

42. Ibid., 53.

43. Ibid.

15. The Blame-Academia Crowd

1. In 2005, public expenditures on faith-based initiatives included appropriations of $99,198,000 for the "Community-based Abstinence Education Program." See White House Office of Faith-Based Community Programs, http://www .whitehouse.gov/government/fbci/grants-catalog-index.html (accessed August 21, 2006).

2. In 2003–4, the national average for state cuts in higher education appropriations was 2.1 percent (to $60.3 billion overall). The average concealed great variations, from increases in twenty-seven states to decreases of nearly 20 percent at the University of Massachusetts, nearly 14 percent in Colorado, about 6 percent in California, 4.5 percent in New York, 8 percent in Wisconsin, and nearly 4 percent in Washington state. "*Grapevine* Survey of State Higher Education Tax Appropriations for Fiscal Year 2004," http://www.grapevineinstu.edu/historical/Appropri ations%202003–04.pdf (accessed October 24, 2007). Multiyear declines were considerably higher, as I described in chapter 11, "The Perils of Privatization."

3. The most thorough book-length treatment of the issue is Chris Mooney, *The Republican War on Science* (New York: Basic Books, 2005). For an illustrative example of a characteristic congressional inquiry, see Richard Monastersky, "In Heated Hearing, House Panel Debates Research Behind Global-Warming Theory," *Chronicle of Higher Education* (July 20, 2006), http://chronicle.com/daily/2006/07/2006072003n.htm (accessed July 27, 2006).

4. For an early study that correlates the scientific goals of principal investigators with the military objectives of their funders, see Stanton A. Glantz and Norm V. Albers, "Department of Defense R&D in the University," *Science* 186 (November 22, 1974): 706–711.

5. University of California Office of the President, "Report of the Energy Research Advisory Board on the Relationship Between the University of California and the Los Alamos Scientific and the Lawrence Livermore Laboratories, May 1979," (document in author's files).

6. Another example: even as the Department of Energy was deciding that UC's mismanagement of some elements of Los Alamos meant that a future contract should involve industrial partners, a report argued that "an important, little-noted benefit of the University is to foster a culture of scientific skepticism and peer review. This attitude, both within the Laboratory and between Los Alamos and Lawrence Livermore National Laboratories, is absolutely crucial to the success of the Stockpile Stewardship Program and to the ability to certify the stockpile. A senior laboratory official at Los Alamos has told us, for example, that the culture of peer review is the only thing that allowed the successful dual revalidation of the W76 warhead conducted a few years ago." "Report by the Deputy Secretary of Energy and the Acting Administrator of the NNSA on the Future

Relationship Between Los Alamos National Laboratory and the University of California," April 26, 2003. This document was published on the National Nuclear Security Administration's Web page at http://www.nnsa.doe.gov/docs/newsreleases/2003/2003-04-30-R-03-091-DOE%20To?20Compete.pdf, but as of August 22, 2006, had been removed.

7. See Robert Dynes, "Message from UC President Dynes," UC Office of the President, July 20, 2005, http://www.lanl.gov/news/index.php/fuseaction/nb.story/story_id/6936/nb_date/2005-07-20 (accessed August 22, 2006). Dynes was attempting to assure the UC community that as a partner in the LANS LLC, it would remain the lab's scientific manager: "Science will continue to be the cornerstone of the work of the laboratory. The UC-Bechtel-led team's proposal will foster an atmosphere that allows lab scientists to continue to do the great science that the laboratory is known for, without being hampered by unnecessary bureaucratic processes to the greatest extent possible. Our team believes that science and technology are critical to the LANL mission, and our proposal underscores this." The LLC governing board was chaired by a UC representative and had three UC members and three members from Bechtel. "Representative" is not the correct word, however, as no reporting relationship was formally established. My comments are based on testimony by a member of UC's office of General Counsel at two meetings of the University Committee on Planning and Budget, 2006–7.

8. This long note is for those who doubt that unilateral executive authority was a core principle of the Bush II administration. Observers, having explicated texts such as the "Statement of Principles," June 3, 1997, Project for the New American Century, http://newamericancentury.org/statementofprinciples.htm (accessed August 24, 2006) were well aware of the long-standing views of principal figures within the Bush I administration, but 9/11 enabled the Bush II administration to curtail the free, unmonitored circulation of information and people in ways that surpassed expectations. The administration attempted to create a new classification for research, called "sensitive but unclassified," that would allow it to monitor a wider range of university activities and personnel. It tightened student visa requirements and export controls in ways that affected university research. For overviews and positions on new classifications for research, export controls, and visa restrictions, see the American Association of Universities publications "Research Issues" and "Homeland Security Issues," http://www.aau.edu/research/research.cfm and http://www.aau.edu/homeland/homelandSecurityIssues.cfm (accessed August 24, 2006). These restrictions may seem to some like administrative technicalities, but they impeded the flow of graduate student researchers and scientific information. They were philosophically akin to new legal restrictions in other realms: the administration, as is well known, used its war on terrorism to suspend habeas corpus for suspects in terrorism investigations. It famously

evaded the protections the Geneva Conventions extend toward enemy combatants; it held suspects in some prisons without charges or access to counsel by claiming that these prisons were beyond the reach of U.S. law; it violated anti-torture conventions; it rendered some detainees to third-party nations for interrogations that involved torture in order to avoid domestic legal restrictions; it overruled the legal concerns of its own military; and it rejected the right of basic kinds of judicial review for domestic terror suspects. The administration lost several Supreme Court cases on these issues, and yet after one such reversal, in January 2006, the White House informed the Supreme Court that the latter would no longer have jurisdiction over detainee cases. This was the case of Salim Ahmed Hamdan, Osama Bin Laden's driver, who has been held at the military facility at Guantánamo Bay since June 2002. The Justice Department had claimed that because Hamdan's case fell within previously established provisions that disallow a habeas corpus petition "or any other action against the United States or its agents relating to any aspect of the detention by the Department of Defense," the Supreme Court had no jurisdiction. "Respondent's Motion to Dismiss for Lack of Jurisdiction," in *Salim Ahmed Hamdan v. Donald H. Rumsfeld, Secretary of Defense, et al.*, 9, http://www.usdoj.gov/osg/briefs/2005/3mer/2mer/2005-0184.resp .html (accessed August, 24, 2006). However, in its decision on June 29, 2006, the Supreme Court denied this motion and found that the state had overstepped its authority in setting up special military commissions that violated the Uniform Code of Military Justice and the Geneva Conventions. For the full ruling, see *Hamdan v. Rumsfeld, Secretary of Defense, et al.*: http://www.supremecourtus.gov/ opinions/05pdf/05-184.pdf (accessed August 24, 2006). It was then disclosed that the National Security Administration had been caught illegally intercepting large volumes of personal electronic communications inside the United States. President Bush responded, in effect, that he himself had the authority to legalize illegal spying. "In Address, Bush Says He Ordered Domestic Spying," *New York Times*, December 18, 2005; "Bush Admits He Authorised Spying," BBC News, December 18, 2005, http://news.bbc.co.uk/2/hi/americas/4538286.stm (accessed August 24, 2006). Meanwhile, the CIA appeared to be working with the New York City police to investigate peace groups, the FBI applied its TALON surveillance program to a Quaker group that protested military recruitment at a Florida high school, and antiwar students at UC Santa Cruz discovered that they were acquiring FBI records of their own. On the CIA and New York City police, see "F.B.I. Watched Activist Groups," *New York Times*, December 20, 2005; "New York Police Covertly Join In at Protest Rallies," *New York Times*, December 22, 2005. On TALON and Quakers, see Francis Grandy Taylor, "The Pacifist 'Threat': Disclosure of Recent Government Surveillance of Quaker Activities Doesn't Surprise Members," *Hartford Courant*, January 16, 2006, http://www.commondreams.org/headlines06/ 0116-09.htm (accessed August 24, 2006); "Is the Pentagon Spying on America?"

MSNBC Nightly News, December 14, 2005, http://msnbc.msn.com/id/10454316/ (accessed August 24, 2006). On UC Santa Cruz, see "Santa Cruz Journal: A Protest, a Spy Program and a Campus in an Uproar," *New York Times*, January 14, 2006. Even the *New York Times*, which had not probed the White House's claim about Iraq's alleged possession of weapons of mass destruction and which withheld the NSA spy story for a year, right through the 2004 election, began to describe Bush's second term as "the Imperial Presidency." Former vice president Al Gore chimed in by claiming that "America's Constitution is in grave danger." Al Gore, " 'We the People' Must Save Our Constitution" address at Constitution Hall, Martin Luther King Day, January 16, 2006, http://www.commondreams.org/views06/0116-34.htm (accessed August 24, 2006). It was at least arguable that the Bush II administration was using the "war on terror" to introduce into the federal government a classic Schmittian state of exception. Carl Schmitt, *The Crisis of Parliamentary Democracy* (1926; Cambridge, MA: MIT Press, 1985). The common theme of all these measures, whether they involve engineering graduate students or enemy combatants, was increased secrecy imposed by executive authority in the name of state security.

9. Jerry L. Martin and Anne D. Neal, "Defending Civilization: How Our Universities Are Failing America and What Can Be Done About It," rev. ed., American Council of Trustees and Alumni, February 2002, 12, http://www.goacta.org/publications/Reports/defciv.pdf, (accessed July 11, 2006).

10. I classified all the comments in the report as follows:

   A. Anti-Americanism: The United States and/or its leaders have been essentially or inherently wrong, generally by being racist, exploitative, genocidal, or terroristic themselves: 1, 10, 13, 88, 101, 105.

   B. Blowback: The United States has been militaristic and/or terroristic and/or exploitative of its allies, and is getting back what it dishes out: 2, 3, 7, 9, 17, 18, 21, 23, 25 (soft), 28 (harder), 54, 65, 93, 96, 97, 106, 107, 108.

   C. The "cycle of violence" is bad. War is not the answer to these attacks: 11, 12, 19, 22, 26, 27, 30, 33, 35, 37, 39, 42, 43, 44, 46, 47 (hard), 48, 49, 50, 55, 60, 63, 64, 67, 68, 69, 70, 71, 72, 74, 79, 82, 83, 84, 89, 94, 98, 103, 104, 110, 112, 113.

   D. Reflect and analyze: The attacks must be understood in their historical context (learn about root causes like racism, poverty, injustice, or foreign policy bias, and change the nation's course as necessary): 6, 8, 14, 15 (close to C), 24, 29, 32, 34 (close to C), 36, 38, 40, 45, 51, 52, 53, 56, 57, 58, 59, 61, 62, 75, 76, 77, 78 (mild B), 80, 81 (international court), 87, 90, 92, 95, 102 (anti-Bush), 109 (bring ourselves to justice), 111.

   E. The rest, including reports of others' activities, possibly misguided steps taken by administrators against pro-war personnel, calls for administrative action, and others: 4, 5, 16, 20, 31, 41, 66, 73, 85, 86, 91, 99, 100, 114, 115 (report of faculty not at memorial service).

11. Richard L. Berke and Janet Elder, "A Nation Challenged: The Poll; Poll Finds Support for War and Fear on Economy," *New York Times*, September 25, 2001:

> "I would like to see quick justice, but if you jump the gun and attack the wrong person, it's not going to accomplish anything," said Ryan Clark, 19, a forest firefighter in Lewiston, Idaho. "You have to be at least somewhat certain who it is before anything takes place."
>
> But Mr. Clark insisted that he was not squeamish about American casualties, saying, "It's never a good thing for lives to be lost in a conflict, but some casualties now would be better than a whole lot later on."
>
> Diane Stevens, 49, a real estate broker from Washington, Conn., also called for patience, saying, "We should wait and get as much data as we can before we plunge into World War III, because that's where it's going to go."

12. Martin and Neal, "Defending Civilization," 1.
13. Ibid., 3.
14. Even Ward Churchill's inaccurate comparison of World Trade Center (WTC) victims to "little Eichmanns" (not cited in "Defending Civilization") did not condone the taking of lives, but angrily objected to the claim that Americans, including those WTC workers involved in international finance, were innocent of any action that may have helped provoke the attacks. Churchill's essay belongs to the genre of diatribe, as it sought to express strong negative feelings in order to force readers to choose sides. In the typology I offer here, it is a mixture of categories A and B, with more B than A, for though it describes no redeeming features in U.S. history or policy, it is more interested in sketching the historical background for an attack that it sees as classic blowback from U.S. policies that include the first Gulf War and subsequent economic sanctions against Saddam Hussein's Iraq. The relevant section was rarely cited and reads as follows:

> A good case could be made that the war in which they were combatants has been waged more-or-less continuously by the "Christian West"—now proudly emblematized by the United States—against the "Islamic East" since the time of the First Crusade, about 1,000 years ago. More recently, one could argue that the war began when Lyndon Johnson first lent significant support to Israel's dispossession/displacement of Palestinians during the 1960s, or when George the Elder ordered "Desert Shield" in 1990, or at any of several points in between. Any way you slice it, however, if what the combat teams did to the WTC and the Pentagon can be understood as acts of war—and they can—then the same is true of every US "overflight" of Iraqi territory since day one. The first acts of war during the current millennium thus occurred on its very first day, and were carried out by U.S. aviators acting under orders from their then-commander-in-chief, Bill Clinton. The most that can honestly be said of those involved on September 11 is that they finally responded in kind to

some of what this country has dispensed to their people as a matter of course.

That they waited so long to do so is, notwithstanding the 1993 action at the WTC, more than anything a testament to their patience and restraint.

They did not license themselves to "target innocent civilians."

There is simply no argument to be made that the Pentagon personnel killed on September 11 fill that bill. The building and those inside comprised military targets, pure and simple. As to those in the World Trade Center . . .

Well, really. Let's get a grip here, shall we? True enough, they were civilians of a sort. But innocent? Gimme a break. They formed a technocratic corps at the very heart of America's global financial empire—the "mighty engine of profit" to which the military dimension of U.S. policy has always been enslaved—and they did so both willingly and knowingly. Recourse to "ignorance"—a derivative, after all, of the word "ignore"—counts as less than an excuse among this relatively well-educated elite. To the extent that any of them were unaware of the costs and consequences to others of what they were involved in—and in many cases excelling at—it was because of their absolute refusal to see. More likely, it was because they were too busy braying, incessantly and self-importantly, into their cell phones, arranging power lunches and stock transactions, each of which translated, conveniently out of sight, mind and smelling distance, into the starved and rotting flesh of infants. If there was a better, more effective, or in fact any other way of visiting some penalty befitting their participation upon the little Eichmanns inhabiting the sterile sanctuary of the twin towers, I'd really be interested in hearing about it. (Ward Churchill, "Some People Push Back: On the Justice of Roosting Chickens," September 12, 2001, http://www.ratical.org/ratville/CAH/WC091201.html [accessed July 27, 2006])

15. Martin and Neal, "Defending Civilization," 7.
16. For a brief summary of Ann Coulter's lifetime sponsors, see Media Transparency, "Person Profile: Anne Coulter," http://www.mediatransparency.org/personprofile.php?personID=106 (accessed July 29, 2006). For a condensed overview of the same sponsors in relation to ACTA and other organizations, see Alan Jones, "Connecting the Dots," *Inside Higher Ed* (June 16, 2006), http://insidehighered.com/views/2006/06/16/jones (accessed 21 July 2006).
17. Patrick Martin, "Conference of US Right-wingers Hears Call to Execute John Walker," World Socialist Web Site, February 27, 2002, http://www.wsws.org/articles/2002/feb2002/coul-f27.shtml (accessed August 5, 2006). For a somewhat maddened commentary, see Eric Alterman, "Devil in a Blue Dress," *Nation*, September 23, 2002, http://www.thenation.com/docprint.mhtml?i=20020923&s=alterman (accessed August 5, 2006). For an earlier, moderate Coulter statement on Walker, see Paula Zahn, "Sound Off: Fair Trial for Lindh," transcript of CNN

broadcast, January 25, 2002, http://transcripts.cnn.com/TRANSCRIPTS/0201/25/ltm.15.html (accessed August 5, 2006).

18. Lamar Alexander, "Remarks of Senator Alexander to Commission on the Future of Higher Education" (speech, Nashville, TN, December 9, 2005), http://alexander.senate.gov/index.cfm?FuseAction=Speeches.Detail&Speech_Id=88 (accessed February 20, 2006). As another bit of evidence of senatorial belief that higher education has an embedded liberal bias, see Stephen Burd and Paul Fain, "Senator Says Congressional Republicans Are 'Restrained' in Treatment of Colleges, Despite Left-Wing Bias," *Chronicle of Higher Education* (February 8, 2006), http://chronicle.com/daily/2006/02/2006020802n.htm (accessed February 12, 2006). Pennsylvania Republican Rick Santorum said, "Candidly, I think the Congress has been remarkably restrained in spite of what most of us see as a hostility toward conservatism and for Republicans. . . . We've been remarkably restrained, given that, in doing anything to sort of punish higher education for its ideology, we don't, and we haven't."

19. ACTA, "How Many Ward Churchills? A Study by the American Council of Trustees and Alumni," May 2006, i, 2, http://www.goacta.org/publications/reports.html (accessed July 12, 2006). For example,

> *Duke University's* "Third World/West" course "call[s] into question the dominant Eurocentric diffusionist model—what James Blaut calls the 'colonizer's model of the world' " by showing how "Europe built on powerful older civilizations, at least as advanced as and probably more so than Europe at that time." "In questioning the notion of a European miracle," explains the course description, "this course will also give those older Eurasian and original American cultures their place in the narrative of an alternative conception of the world, and bring to the fore the amnesia that has informed mainstream views of world history." Assigned texts include Ward Churchill's *A Little Matter of Genocide*—a book whose claims about the U.S. Army's treatment of Native Americans are implicated in the University of Colorado's investigation of whether Churchill has committed academic fraud.
>
> *Stanford University* offers a course that not only challenges students' assumptions, but explains to them why such a challenge is psychologically and socially necessary. (4)

And again:

> *Ohio State University* is training students to become feminist activists and role models for politically unformed adolescent girls. "The Theory and Practice of Peer Outreach in Women's Studies" "prepare[s] undergraduate students with the necessary skills to effectively participate in the Peer Power program," which "uses interactive and dynamic presentations to introduce Women's Studies topics at the middle and high school grade levels in the greater Columbus area." Those topics include "the construction of

privilege and difference in the US, and the significance of diversity (i.e., race, class, sexuality, gender) within the US educational system." (10)

20. For mainstream coverage of the Columbia University controversies, see N.R. Kleinfield, "Mideast Tensions Are Getting Personal on Campus at Columbia," *New York Times*, January 18, 2005. See also, Jonathan R. Cole:

While I was provost at Columbia there were many efforts by outside groups to influence university policy and to silence specific members of the faculty. Repeated efforts were made to defame and discredit the renowned literary critic and Palestinian advocate Edward Said. External groups tried, but failed, to have Columbia deny an appointment to an eminent Middle East historian, Rashid Khalidi. Sixty-two members of Congress wrote to Columbia calling on us to fire Nicholas de Geneva, a professor of anthropology, after he made inflammatory remarks at an antiwar teach-in prior to the most recent Iraq War—even though his remarks were immediately criticized at the same teach-in by other Columbia faculty members.

Even when nobody loses his or her job, these assaults take a toll. As Professor Massad explains on his website, "With this campaign against me going into its fourth year, I chose under the duress of coercion and intimidation not to teach my course ['Palestinian and Israeli Politics and Societies'] this year."

Most of the recent attacks on university professors have been leveled against social scientists and humanists. Many critics of the university seem to believe that sanctioning one group of professors will have no effect on those in other disciplines. This is dangerously naive, both in principle and in practice. The stakes are high. The destruction of university systems has historically been caused by the imposition of external political ideology on the conduct of scholarly and scientific research. Defense of faculty members in the humanities and social sciences from external political pressure protects all members of the university community. ("Academic Freedom Under Fire," *Daedelus* (Spring 2005), http://www.columbia.edu/cu/univprof/jcole/_pdf/2005AcademicFreedom .pdf [accessed August 5, 2006].)

21. A standard work here is Richard Rorty, *Philosophy and the Mirror of Nature* (Princeton, NJ: Princeton University Press, 1979).

22. Richard K. Lester and Michael J. Piore, *Innovation: The Missing Dimension* (Cambridge, MA: Harvard University Press, 2004), 53, 69.

23. University of California, *Academic Personnel Manual*, "010: General University Policy Regarding Academic Appointees", revised September 29, 2003, http:// www.ucop.edu/acadadv/acadpers/apm/apm-010.pdf (accessed August 5, 2006). The principal author of the new language and this footnote was the legal scholar Robert Post. For a broader theoretical analysis, see Robert Post, "The Structure

of Academic Freedom," in *Academic Freedom after September 11*, ed. Beshara Doumani (Boston: Zone Books-MIT Press, 2006), 61–106.

24. The ancients at ACTA have felt similarly aggrieved by another widespread change in the structure of academic knowledge. "Our review of college and university courses revealed a remarkable level of homogeneity. As individual disciplines increasingly orient themselves around a core set of political values, the differences between disciplines are beginning to disappear. Courses in such seemingly distinct fields as literature, sociology, and women's studies, for example, have become mirror images of one another—a fact that colleges and universities openly acknowledge in their practice of cross listing courses in multiple departments" (ACTA, "How Many Ward Churchills?" 4). ACTA is of course simply describing "interdisciplinarity," a practice driven by research problems and in fact more developed in engineering and in the biological and physical sciences than it is in the humanities and social sciences. The subsequent paragraph sounded the alarm against the decline of survey courses, for which Ward Churchill is also apparently a symbol.

25. John Tierney, "Why Righties Can't Teach," *New York Times*, October 15, 2005.

26. See, for example, Anthony Giddens, *The Third Way: The Renewal of Social Democracy* (Cambridge: Polity Press, 1998). At the same time, I have been unable to find major examples of critiques of the welfare state on the influential culture-war grounds that it hampers job creation and pampers the undeserving that do *not* emerge from conservative think-tank networks that include major publication and media operations like the American Enterprise Institute, and that do *not* owe their intellectual framework to citations of conservative icons Ludwig Von Mises, Friedrich Hayek, and Milton Friedman. The Right's success in inventing a congenial knowledge base on this topic is remarkable.

27. See Andrew Hoberek, *The Twilight of the Middle Class: Post-World War II American Fiction and White-Collar Work* (Princeton, NJ: Princeton University Press, 2005), chapter 1.

28. Stanley Fish, "Conspiracy Theories 101," *New York Times*, July 23, 2006. For criticism of Fish's description of the stakes and positions in this particular issue, see Sherman Dorn, "Spanking Stanley Fish," http://www.shermandorn.com/mt/archives/000591.html (accessed August 5, 2006).

29. An example of this principle was the Dartmouth College statement about academic freedom, which reads in part that the college "both fosters and protects the rights of individuals to express their dissent. Protest or demonstration shall not be discouraged so long as neither force nor the threat of force is used, and so long as the orderly processes of the College are not deliberately obstructed." *Handbook of the Faculty of the Arts and Sciences*, Dartmouth College, July 26, 2004, 20, http://www.dartmouth.edu/~dof/pdfs/faculty_handbook.pdf (accessed August 5, 2006).

30. As recently as the mid-1990s, another English professor could make the same point without obvious concern about being misunderstood: "Should professors attempt to put across their own point of view about the material they teach in the classroom? Of course we should. What else could we do? It is because we have views about our subject that we have been hired to teach them. Our ethical constraint is only that we teach what we honestly believe the significance of the material to be." Louis Menand, "Culture and Advocacy" (1996), cited by Michael Bérubé, "Embrace Your Urge," August 1, 2006, http://www.michaelberube.com/index.php/weblog/2006/08/p241 (accessed August 5, 2006).

31. Jean-François Lyotard, *The Postmodern Condition* (Minneapolis: University of Minnesota Press, 1984), 63–64. I discuss Lyotard in chapter 2 of this book.

Conclusion

1. See, for example, Bruce Western, Vincent Schiraldi, and Jason Ziedenberg, "Education and Incarceration" (Washington, DC: Justice Policy Institute, 2003), 4.

2. Isabel Sawhill and John E. Morton, "Economic Mobility: Is the American Dream Alive and Well?" (Washington, DC: Pew Charitable Trusts, 2007), Figures 3–6.

3. Most critiques of declining public support generally do not see it as a carefully engineered new paradigm, as I describe it here. For example, Robert Zemsky, Gregory R. Wegner, and William F. Massy, *Remaking the American University: Market-Smart and Mission-Centered* (New Brunswick, NJ: Rutgers University Press, 2005) omit any mention of cultural and political mechanisms. A few critiques come closer to something like my effort here: Katherine C. Lyall and Kathleen R. Sell, for example, trace "de facto privatization" in part to "a corrosive political message" that tells "Americans they can have both benefits and lower taxes simply by rooting out 'waste, fraud and abuse.'" They cite a 1992 speech by Senator John Danforth (R-Missouri) that claimed that "the basic message [politicians] have given to the American people [is] that you should feel sorry for yourselves. . . . This is the first generation in the history of this country that has wanted to take more out of it than it [has] given." *The True Genius of America at Risk: Are We Losing Our Public Universities to De Facto Privatization?* (Westport, CT: Praeger, 2006), 77–78. Such comments describe symptoms rather than sources.

Appendix

1. The Center's home page is http://www.horowitzfreedomcenter.org/FlexPage .aspx?area=aboutus/ (accessed October 31, 2007).

2. For examples of coordinated university positions, see the American Association of Universities statements on "Homeland Security Issues," http://www.aau.edu/

homeland/homelandSecurityIssues.cfm (accessed August 3, 2006); and the Council on Governmental Relations statements about export controls at http://www.cogr.edu/files/ExportControls.cfm (accessed August 3, 2006).

3. McCarthyism refers to Senator Joseph McCarthy (R-Wisconsin) and his celebrated and yet finally unfounded claims in the early 1950s to possess long lists identifying communist agents operating at the highest levels of the U.S. government.

4. Quoted in Gary Younge, "Silence in Class," *Guardian* (UK), April 4, 2006. See Ellen Schrecker, "Worse than McCarthy," *Chronicle of Higher Education* (February 10, 2006), http://chronicle.com/free/v52/i23/23b02001.htm (accessed February 21, 2006).

5. John Munro, describing a portion of dissertation research, personal communication with the author, October 17, 2005.

6. See, for example, "The Hollow Core: Failure of the General Education Curriculum: A Fifty College Study by the American Council of Trustees and Alumni" (2004); "Becoming an Educated Person: Toward a Core Curriculum for College Students" (n.d.); "Degraded Currency: The Problem of Grade Inflation" (n.d.); "Teachers Who Can: How Informed Trustees Can Ensure Teacher Quality" (n.d.); among others, http://www.goacta.org/publications/reports.html (accessed July 31, 2006).

7. Younge, "Silence in Class." A somewhat different breakdown of Horowitz's operations appeared in a memo by Trent Couthest, "Funding Sources for the Center for the Study of Popular Culture," April 6, 2005, http://aaupuc.org/horowitz.htm (accessed August 1, 2006). The Horowitz network has had many nodes, but they are also highly redundant. Funding for a number of groups, including Students for Academic Freedom (founded in 2001) appears to be funneled through what became the David Horowitz Freedom Center; see Media Transparency, "Recipient Grants: David Horowitz Freedom Center," http://www.mediatransparency.org/recipientgrants.php?recipientID=63 (accessed August 1, 2006). Campus Watch was founded in 2002. Its funding comes from the Middle East Forum; see Media Transparency, "Recipient Grants: Middle East Forum," http://www.mediatransparency.org/recipientgrants.php?recipientID=207 (accessed August 1, 2006). Jihad Watch (founding date unknown; http://jihadwatch.org/spencer/, accessed August 1, 2006) is run by Robert Spencer, who is an adjunct fellow with the group that publishes all his books, the Free Congress Foundation, http://www.freecongress.org/ (accessed August 1, 2006). Professors Watch and Media Watch appear to be pages on the Front Page Magazine Web site rather than actual organizations in their own right. The link for Professors Watch takes the reader to Horowitz's book *The Professors.* The organization Media Watch is neither conservative nor associated with Horowitz; see http://www.mediawatch.com/. Discover the Networks is a Web site run by Horowitz, John Perazzo (see "Columnists: John Perazzo," *Front Page Magazine,* http://www.frontpagemag.com/Articles/authors.asp?ID=8 [accessed

August 1, 2006]) and Richard Poe, a senior fellow at the David Horowitz Freedom Center (see http://www.richardpoe.com/bio.html [accessed August 1, 2006]).

8. "The New Class Monitors," *Inside Higher Ed* (January 18, 2006), http://insidehighered.com/news/2006/01/18/ucla (accessed January 19, 2006). See "Bruin Alumni Association Targets 'Radical' Faculty," *Capitol Weekly*, January 17, 2006, http://www.capitolweekly.net/news/article.html?article_id=434 (accessed February 20, 2006). The organization was called the Bruin Alumni Association, named after UCLA's well-known sports team mascot. Horowitz severed his association with Andrew Jones, the student and former SAF intern who led the attacks when the operation that paid students $100 to inform on their teachers attracted too much negative attention; see Students for Academic Freedom, "Bruin Alumni Association: How Not to Run an Academic Freedom Campaign," January 26, 2006, http://www.studentsforacademicfreedom.org/letters/LettersJan-May2006/letter-BruinAlumniAssn012606.htm (accessed February 26, 2008).

9. Students for Academic Freedom, "Academic Bill of Rights," http://www.studentsforacademicfreedom.org/documents/1925/abor.html (accessed February 20, 2006).

10. "Professors' Politics Drew Lawmakers into the Fray," *New York Times*, December 25, 2006. One of the most active Horowitz watchers, from his home base at Pennsylvania State University, was Michael Bérubé; see, among other entries, "Indoctrinate U," January 11, 2006, www.michaelberube.com/index.php/weblog/2006/01/p12 (accessed February 20, 2006).

11. General Assembly of Pennsylvania, House Resolution No. 177, June 30, 2005, http://www.aaup.org/NR/rdonlyres/EFIA2FFC-4356-42FB-BCF6-C9F5710BE3E5/0/StatelegPA.pdf (accessed February 10, 2008).

12. Scott Jaschik, "A Win for 'Academic Bill of Rights,' " *Inside Higher Ed* (July 7, 2005), http://www.insidehighered.com/news/2005/07/07/tabor (accessed February 20, 2006). Also see David Horowitz, "Victory in Pennsylvania," *Front Page Magazine*, July 6, 2005, http://www.frontpagemag.com/Articles/ReadArticle.asp?ID=18667 (accessed February 20, 2006).

13. For more anecdotes like these, see postings at the Students for Academic Freedom's Complaint Center, http://www.studentsforacademicfreedom.org/comp/default.asp (accessed February 20, 2006).

14. See David Brooks, "Lonely Campus Voices," *New York Times*, September 27, 2003; John Tierney, "Why Righties Can't Teach," *New York Times*, October 15, 2005.

15. Tierney, "Why Righties Can't Teach." For my discussion, see chapter 15 of this book.

16. Christopher F. Cardiff and Daniel B. Klein, "Faculty Partisan Affiliations in All Disciplines: A Voter-Registration Study," *Critical Review: An Interdisciplinary Journal of Politics and Society* 17, nos. 3–4 (2005): 237–255; parenthetical phrase in original.

17. American Council of Trustees and Alumni, "Intellectual Diversity: Time for Action," http://www.goacta.org/publications/reports.html (accessed February 20, 2006).

18. Center for Survey Research and Analysis, University of Connecticut, "Politics in the Classroom: A Survey of Students at the Top 50 Colleges & Universities" (survey commissioned by ACTA), http://www.goacta.org/publications/Reports/PoliticsInTheClassroom.htm (accessed July 31, 2006). Though described as an ACTA report, this is the survey that forms the basis of the report "Intellectual Diversity," discussed below.

19. ACTA, "Intellectual Diversity," 7.

20. Ibid., i.

21. The articles in the series cited by Klein and Stern in Daniel B. Klein and Charlota Stern, "Professors and Their Politics: The Policy View of Social Scientists," *Critical Review: An Interdisciplinary Journal of Politics and Society* 17, nos. 3–4 (2005): 257–303 are Seymour Martin Lipset, "The Politics of American Sociologist," *American Journal of Sociology* 78, no. 1 (June 1972): 67–104; Lipset, "The Academic Mind at the Top: The Political Behavior and Values of Faculty Elites," *Public Opinion Quarterly* 46, no. 2 (Summer 1982): 143–168; Lipset, "The State of American Sociology," *Sociological Forum* 9, no. 2 (June 1994): 199–220.

22. Stanley Rothman, S. Robert Lichter, and Neil Nevitte, "Politics and Professional Advancement Among College Faculty," *Forum* 3, no. 1 (2005), http://www.bepress.com/forum/vol3/iss1/art2 (accessed July 31, 2006); the cited language is ACTA's paraphrase.

23. Although not cited as such in "Intellectual Diversity," this appears to be a reference to Daniel B. Klein and Charlotta Stern, "How Politically Diverse Are the Social Sciences and Humanities? Survey Evidence from Six Fields," listed on Klein's vita as "Political Diversity in Six Disciplines," *Academic Questions* 18, no. 1 (Winter 2005): 40–52; the link embedded in Klein's vita takes readers to a Swedish think-tank called Ratio, which has posted a manuscript version at http:///www.ratio.se/pdf/wp/dk_ls_diverse.pdf (accessed October 31, 2007).

24. Michael Bérubé, in "Mistah Kurtz, He Dead Right," noted that his university (Penn State) has more faculty than does the entire national faculty in the sample used by Rothman et al., and that each university surveyed had an average of nine recipients of the survey (http://www.michaelberube.com/index.php/weblog/mistah_kurtz_he_dead_right/, accessed August 1, 2006). Klein and Stern, though sympathetic to the aims of claims made by Horowitz and others, wrote that the voter-registration studies conducted by "the Center for the Study of Popular Culture (CSPC) and The American Enterprise Magazine" were done by "forwardly conservative organizations" without "independent control or certification of the data collection process. Thus there are concerns about the accuracy of CSPC's research" (Klein and Stern, "How Politically Diverse," 3). Their

own study uses "randomly generated" lists of 1,000 members from the six disciplines they survey: 1,678 of the 5,484 mailings were returned; Bérubé's observation about sample size would be relevant here too.

25. Rothman, Lichter, and Nevitte, "Politics and Professional Advancement," appeared in the online journal *The Forum*. In keeping with its stated mission to fill the gap between *Atlantic Monthly* and standard social science journals, *The Forum* publishes material of interest to its editors and does not submit the articles to standard peer review (confirmed via correspondence with a *Forum* editor, August 2, 2006). As for the underlying survey data, Rothman et al. write, "The data come from the 1999 North American Academic Study Survey (NAASS) of students, faculty and administrators at colleges and universities in the United States and Canada. This survey was conducted in 1999 by Angus Reid (now Ipsos-Reid), a survey research firm." Elsewhere, however, Rothman claimed that the survey belongs to him and his coauthors. Thomas Bartlett, "New Paper Assails Report That Said Bias Against Conservative Professors Is Common in Academe," *Chronicle of Higher Education* (August 9, 2005), http://chronicle.com/daily/2005/08/2005080901n.htm (accessed February 19, 2006). In addition, at the start of the 2005 paper, the authors thank "Dr. Ivan Katchanovski, a statistical consultant to the NAASS project, for his assistance in providing the statistical analysis for this paper," suggesting an independent study but at least one shared researcher. On the withholding of the Rothman et al. data, see Bartlett, "New Paper Assails." The ambiguous information about the origins, sponsors, personnel, and current possession of the survey left the impression that the surgery was a joint production of different parts of a conservative network of scholars, and suggested that it would be next to impossible to examine the original data and methodology.

26. The private firm that conducted the survey no longer exists as such, and the survey does not appear to exist electronically. My search for it was similar to that of blogger Yoshie, at Critical Montages, who wrote, "The 1999 'North American Academic Study Survey' by Angus Reid? I have never heard of the study before. Has anyone? Can't find anything more about the 'North American Academic Study Survey' through Google Scholar, LexisNexis, JSTOR, Project Muse, Social Science Abstracts, Sociological Abstracts, and Worldwide Political Science Abstracts. Has anyone other than Rothman, Lichter, and Nevitte gained access to the survey's data and analyzed them? If not, why not? It's a survey presumably taken six years ago, and no one has made a peep about it till now?" (http://montages.blogspot.com/2005/04/conservatives-underrepresented-in.html, accessed August 1, 2006). Yoshie also offers a critique of the author's use of the survey as well as a reinterpretation of it.

27. Most notably Howard Kurtz, "College Faculties a Most Liberal Lot, Study Finds," *Washington Post*, March 29, 2005, C1, http://www.washingtonpost.com/wp-dyn/articles/A8427-2005Mar28.html (accessed July 31, 2006).

28. On the funding sources of the Critical Review Foundation, see Media Transparency, "Recipient Grants: Critical Review Foundation, Inc.," http://www.mediatransparency.org/recipientgrants.php?recipientID=1381 (accessed July 31, 2006).

29. Cardiff and Klein, "Faculty Partisan Affiliations"; Klein and Stern, "Professors and Their Politics," 257–303. Cardiff and Klein list the sources of their main table as follows:

Column A: 2003 survey data for academics through age 70 from Klein and Stern 2005a.

Column B: 1999 survey data obtained directly from Robert Lichter, used in Rothman et al. 2005, and detailed in "Lichter" worksheet of the Excel file available at http://www.gmu.edu/departments/econmics/klein/Voter/FinalApril106Redacted.xls.

Column C: 2001 survey data from Brookings 2001 and Light 2001.

Column D: 2004–2005 voter-registration data gathered for this paper from California records.

Column E: 2003–2005 voter registration data pooled from separate investigations at Capital University, Dartmouth College, Duke University, Ithaca College, and the University of Nevada–Las Vegas, detailed in "Other Schools" worksheet of the Excel file available at http://www.gmu.edu/departments/economics/klein/Voter/FinalApril106Redacted.xls.

Column F: 2001–2002 voter registration data for 32 elite schools reported in Horowitz and Lehrer 2002.

Column A is the sole Klein-Stern survey; column B references the one other study under discussion here (Lichter); column C refers to one study (Light 2001 is the write-up of Brookings 2001, the survey results themselves. Light does not study party affiliation or ideology but something different, "Government's Greatest Priorities for the Next Half-Century." "Liberals" are 58 percent and Democrats 77 percent of this sample, p. 3); columns D and E are new discrete data pools; column F is a study by David Horowitz that Klein and Stern, "How Politically Diverse?" had sought to supersede because of doubts about its validity.

30. On the funding background of the ACTA study, see Alan Jones, "Connecting the Dots," *Inside Higher Ed* (June 16, 2006), http://insidehighered.com/views/2006/06/16/jones (accessed July 21, 2006); and Barry Ames, David C. Barker, Chris W. Bonneau, and Christopher J. Carman, "Hide the Republicans, the Christians, and the Women: A Response to 'Politics and Professional Advancement Among College Faculty,'" *Forum* 3, no. 2 (2005). On the affiliations of the Rothman group, see Jones, "Connecting the Dots." On the background of one of Rothman's coauthors, Robert Lichter, see Fairness and Accuracy in Reporting (FAIR), "Study of Bias or Biased Study? The Lichter Method and the Attack on PBS Documentaries," press release, May 14, 1992, http://www.fair.org/index.php?page=2515

(accessed July 30, 2006). See above for the ties of the publication venue of Klein and his coauthors.

31. See, for example, J. D. Bekelman, Y. Li, and C. P. Gross, "Scope and Impact of Financial Conflicts of Interest in Biomedical Research: A Systematic Review," *Journal of the American Medical Association* 19 (May 2003): 2502–2503. For discussion, see chapter 14, "Half-Suffocated Reforms."

32. For example, "The Lynde and Harry Bradley Foundation is . . . devoted to strengthening American democratic capitalism and the institutions, principles and values that sustain and nurture it. Its programs support limited, competent government; a dynamic marketplace for economic, intellectual, and cultural activity; and a vigorous defense at home and abroad of American ideas and institutions. In addition, recognizing that responsible self-government depends on enlightened citizens and informed public opinion, the Foundation supports scholarly studies and academic achievement" ("The Bradley Foundation's Mission," http://www.bradleyfdn.org/foundations_mission.asp, accessed August 1, 2006). For a good overview of the targeted approach of the Olin Foundation, see John J. Miller, "Foundation's End," *National Review*, April 6, 2005, http://www.nationalreview.com/script/printpage.p?ref=/miller/miller200504060758.asp (accessed August 1, 2006). The Smith Richardson Charitable Trust, created in a complicated transaction involving the Randolph Foundation, shows more intellectual diversity in its mission and funded topics.

33. On the Randolph Foundation's tangled institutional affiliations, see Trent Douthett, "Funding Sources for the Center for the Study of Popular Culture," American Association of University Professors–University of Cincinnati, April 6, 2005, http://www.aaupuc.org/horowitz.htm (accessed August 1, 2006). Randolph has no Web site, and Source Watch describes its contact information as unknown, http://www.sourcewatch.org/index.php?title=Randolph_Foundation (accessed August 1, 2006). Both ACTA and CSPC have received funds from the Randolph Foundation.

34. Jennifer A. Lindholm, Alexander W. Astin, Linda J. Sax, and William S. Korn, *The American College Teacher: National Norms for the 2001–02 HERI Faculty Survey*, cited by Anne D. Neal, president of ACTA, before the Select Committee on Academic Freedom in Higher Education of the Pennsylvania House of Representatives Public Hearing (Philadelphia, PA, January 10, 2006). Neal acts as though these figures are both self-explicating and not at odds with the findings of the other surveys on which ACTA's reports are based.

35. John F. Zipp and Rudy Fenwick, "Is the Academy a Liberal Hegemony? The Political Orientations and Educational Values of Professors," *Public Opinion Quarterly* 70, no. 3 (Fall 2006): 314; Neil Gross and Solon Simmons, "The Social and Political views of American Professors," working paper, September 24, 2007, http://www.wjh.harvard.edu/~ngross/lounsbery_9-25.pdf (accessed October 31, 2007).

36. For example, see Scott Jaschik, "Leaning to the Left," *Inside Higher Ed* (March 30, 2005), http://www.insidehighered.com/news/2005/03/30/politics (accessed August 3, 2006). Jaschik later cites the different figures without suggesting a tension between them and the stronger claims.

37. All citations in this paragraph are from Rothman, Lichter, and Nevitte, "Politics and Professional Advancement," 5. I have elided Rothman et al.'s contextualizing frame, which attempts to mitigate the conflicts in the figures.

38. The authors note that they look at their data in order to "see what they say about the ideological composition of contemporary social science" (Klein and Stern, "Professors and Their Politics," 257).

39. The authors wrote, "Despite the differences in their relative views, the Democrats and Republicans whom we surveyed agree with each other enough to give us pause about the applicability of the ideological ideal types (at least when it comes to social-science professors). Both Republican and Democratic respondents in our sample are quite interventionist in absolute terms, even when the ideological type suggests that they should be somewhat laissez faire" (Klein and Stern, "Professors and Their Politics," 270).

40. The authors of the most thorough analysis of Horowitz's book *The Professors* (Washington, DC: Regnery, 2006) stated that though he claimed to be interested only in classroom conduct and "not with what professors teach or with their personal political beliefs," he failed to offer evidence for his claims. The authors focused on his claims of classroom indoctrination, and their overview of their conclusions is worth quoting at length. We assume, they wrote,

> that to be reasonably deemed as indoctrinating their students, professors would have to do two things: first, they must teach one side of an issue to the exclusion of all others, and second, they must treat students who disagree with their political views unfairly—by harassing them, or especially by giving them lower grades.
>
> Not once in Mr. Horowitz's book do we see proof that a single professor teaches his or her own political views to the exclusion of all others, and nowhere does Mr. Horowitz provide a single example of a student whose grade was lowered because of his or her political beliefs.
>
> Indeed, for a book that is ostensibly about students' rights, student voices are pointedly absent. Our analysis finds that student testimonials are absent from 87 of the 100 profiles (not 101, as the title and chapter heading indicate) in Mr. Horowitz's book.
>
> Of the 13 that do appear, all are problematic as far as Mr. Horowitz's indoctrination argument is concerned. Two are irrelevant to this charge; two come from a website where students post dozens (sometimes hundreds) of anonymous opinions about their professors and where researchers can cherry-pick from the wide array of viewpoints expressed on any given

professor. Three are allegations that were investigated and proven groundless by university officials well before *The Professors* was published; another was investigated and summarily dealt with by the university, and even this complaint did not allege that professors taught one side of an issue to the exclusion of all others or downgraded a student based on their political views. One statement that negatively characterizes students' opinions of their professor is not supported by the evidence Mr. Horowitz cites, and another is not supported with any evidence at all.

Of the three remaining testimonials, not a single one alleges that a professor taught one side of an issue to the exclusion of all others, or that professors downgraded a student based on their political views, and in none of these instances did students attempt to address their grievances through existing university channels. (Free Exchange on Campus, "Facts Count: An Analysis of David Horowitz's *The Professors: The 101 Most Dangerous Academics in America*," May 2006, iii–iv, http://www .freeexchangeoncampus.org/index.php?option=com_docman&Itemid= 25&task=view_category&catid=12&order=dmdate_published&ascdesc= DESC (accessed May 29, 2006).

For a rebuttal from Horowitz's publication, see Jacob Laskin, "Discounting the Facts," *Front Page*, June 15, 2006, http://www.frontpagemag.com/Articles/ ReadArticle.asp?ID=22870 (accessed August 3, 2006).

41. ACTA, "Intellectual Diversity," 5.

42. Ibid., 4.

43. Ibid., 2–3.

44. Ibid., 3.

45. Ibid., 15.

46. A less common alternative wording asks in effect for the existence of two instances of the category in question: "Q11. On my campus, there are courses in which students feel they have to agree with the professor's political or social views in order to get a good grade."

47. The "somewhat agree" response is a notorious catch basin for undecideds who will say they agree because they have heard someone somewhere refer to such an experience though they have not had it themselves. "Some" and "somewhat" catch, in other words, a wide range of agreeable yet only partially informed people. If you asked a group this question—"Has the American occupation of Iraq improved some aspects of life for average Iraqis?"—you will always get a third to a half of your pool to think to themselves, "Well some things probably have gotten somewhat better, so I guess the answer is I agree—somewhat." See, for example, "Measuring a Middle Position," in Howard Schuman and Stanley Presser, *Questions and Answers in Attitude Surveys: Experiments on Question Form, Wording, and Context*, reprint ed. (Thousand Oaks, CA: Sage, 1996).

48. Free Exchange on Campus, "Facts Count"; see also Media Matters, "David Horowitz Debunks David Horowitz: A Media Matters Analysis of *The Professors*," April 18, 2006, http://mediamatters.org/items/200604180011 (accessed August 3, 2006). Key Horowitz anecdotes were also not substantiated. See, for example, Scott Jaschik, "Tattered Poster Child," *Inside Higher Ed* (March 15, 2005), http://www.insidehighered.com/news/2005/03/15/horowitz3_15 (accessed August 3, 2006); Scott Jaschik, "Retractions from David Horowitz," *Inside Higher Ed* (January 11, 2006), http://insidehighered.com/news/2006/01/11/retract (accessed August 3, 2006); and Jennifer Jacobson, "Conservative Activist Admits Lack of Evidence for Some Allegations of Faculty Bias," *Chronicle of Higher Education* (January 20, 2006), http://chronicle.com/weekly/v52/i20/20a03301.htm (accessed July 29, 2006).

49. See Neal, testimony before the Select Committee on Academic Freedom in Higher Education of the Pennsylvania House of Representatives Public Hearing. For one overview of the proceedings, see Michael Janofsky, "Professors' Politics Draw Lawmakers into the Fray," *New York Times*, December 25, 2005.

50. Jaschik, "Retractions."

51. Jennifer Jacobson, "Pennsylvania Lawmakers Discuss Curricula in Final Hearing on Bias in Classrooms," *Chronicle of Higher Education* (June 2, 2006), http://chronicle.com/daily/2006/06/2006060203n.htm (accessed June 4, 2006).

Acknowledgments

My education was supported by parents who were the first college graduates in their immediate families. They got their chance through the public higher education system that Californians built after World War II. I am grateful to my parents for their persistent support of my higher education, even when it led from physics and biology to philosophy and literature, and when it meant footing most of the bill for the private colleges and universities that created my belief that their high quality should be made available to everyone through those institution's public counterparts.

My professional career has taken place on the terrain of budget cuts and culture wars, and this book has benefited from a great deal of practical help with the details and backstage labor that produced both dramas. Different phases of my budgetary education were advanced by Charles Schwartz of UC Berkeley and Joel Michaelson of UC Santa Barbara. I would like to thank the University of California's Senate Committee on Planning and Budget (UCPB) for the years 2003–2007, and I especially appreciate the insight and effort generated by Henning Bohn and Calvin Moore when we worked on UCPB's "Futures Report" together. It was in UC's Academic Senate that I met many faculty who were willing to do important institutional research and then to stand and fight. The most indomitable of this impressive group has been Stanton Glantz of UC San Francisco, who served as UCPB chair in 2005–2006. I am grateful to him for his shaping of our common budgetary work and for his example of unstoppable battling for higher education.

Various administrators and colleagues at UC Santa Barbara have assisted this project. I would like in particular to thank Executive Vice Chancellor Gene Lucas, who created the conditions that allowed me to remain at UCSB and to think through UC's underlying structures. This book's research and the university service that informed it has led me a long way from my home department, and two department chairs and the Dean of Humanities and Fine Arts offered support for my far-flung commitments. Important part of my understanding of technology transfer were provided by Sherylle Mills Englander and Carol Mimura, though they are certainly not responsible for my interpretations. I am especially appreciative of Gerald Barnett's illuminating interventions, from which I have learned more than I could capture here. I have received valuable feedback from colleagues in a range of places, and was glad to have that of Cathy Davidson, Eric Guthey, Andrew Hoberek, Randy Martin, Dana Nelson, Bruce Robbins, Andrew Ross, Jeff Williams, and Ken Wissoker at various stages in the project.

I have been equally lucky with research assistance. At Duke University, Kelly Lynn Mulvey and Jessica Blaustein conducted valuable early research; later stages were greatly helped by Michael Perry, Gina Valentino, and Julia Brock at UCSB. I am grateful to Jordan T. Camp for taking the lead on the last round of permission requests and getting such good results. I owe special thanks to John Munro of UCSB's Department of History, who filled gaps in my knowledge of the secondary literature and improved arguments with criticisms or extensions. Talking with and learning from John was one of the real pleasures of writing this book.

Portions of Part II of this book are based on articles published by *Critical Inquiry,* and on an article published in *REAL—Yearbook of Research in English and American Literature* in Tubingen, Germany. I am grateful to the University of Chicago Press and to the yearbook publishers for permission to use that material here. Chapter 14 is based on an article previously published in *Social Text,* and I thank Duke University Press for their permission as well. I would like to acknowledge the generosity of Jonathan Polansky, the Regents of the University of California, the American University Technology Managers, and the State Higher Education Executive Officers for permission to use graphic representation of their valuable financial data. Figure 1 is reprinted by permission of the Modern Language Association from Philip Smith et al., "Report of the ADE Ad Hoc Committee on Staffing," *ADE Bulletin* 122 (1999). Table 4 is reprinted by permission of Knopf from Thomas Stewart, *Intellectual Capital* (1997).

The present book took shape in 2005, and I am grateful to Gerald Graff, Cathy Birkenstein, and Greg Meyerson, who during one long lunch in Greensboro, North Carolina, in June of that year helped me yank it around to face the right direction. I am grateful to my editor Lindsay Waters for his enthusiasm for the project, an enthusiasm whose value was only enhanced by his insistence on manuscript cuts. In addition to the many colleagues that I have learned from through the years of this book's development, I would like to mention a few people by name: Laurie Shannon, kindred analyst of academia's bad group psychologies; Janice Radway, friend and great American Studies synthesizer; Ruthie and Craig Gilmore, theorists of a counter-California; and Wahneema Lubiano, luminous once and future assassin of the unjust everywhere.

I wrote the book in the midst of two wonderful groups of family and friends. The first group is in Paris, where the French Newfields—Brad, Emily, and Jessica—and friends Philip Golub, Manuela Burgi, and Virginia Picchi, made writing about American academia seem part of a wonderful everyday life during the 2005–2006 academic year. The second group is in Santa Barbara, where Lisa Hajjar, Richard Falk, and Hilal Elver made me happy and helped me put the concerns of this book in the context of war and international relations. I also want to thank Cedric and Elizabeth Robinson for their inspiration and support, and Ann Jensen Adams, who on a long series of walks in the mountains above town responded sympathetically and helpfully to an equally long series of tirades about university operations. I am especially grateful to Ricki Morse, whose encouragement and affection has been crucial at every stage.

And it is a special pleasure to express my endless appreciation for Avery, who has inspired me from beginning to end. She offered me an escape route, and then, when I didn't take it, made both this book and my life far better than they would otherwise have been.

Index

Abortion, 239, 242, 284, 285
Academic Bill of Rights, 256, 277, 278–279
Academic Capitalism (Slaughter and Leslie), 221
Academic freedom: conservative criticism of, 52; corporate seminars, 224; culture warrior opposition to, 244; Dartmouth College statement on, 357n29; defense research, 242–243; epistemological challenges, 259; essential to university's function, 10; federal government seen as threat to, 221–222; Fish's definition of, 261; hallmark of postwar university, 257; Horowitz on, 279; politics seen as threat to, 61–62; research regulation, 232–233; University of California's redefinition of, 258
Academic planning, financial incentives in, 165–168
Accountability, 127, 153, 159–160
Accounting, 160, 161, 163, 170, 172, 173, 225
Acquisitions, 128
ACTA. *See* American Council of Trustees and Alumni (ACTA)
ACT exams, 315n
ACT UP, 157
Adjunct faculty, 144, 225, 231, 234, 235, 273
Adler, Jerry, 59, 60
Administrative costs, 160–161, 164–165
Admissions: component of financial strategy, 226; development admissions, 178–180, 181–182; legacy admissions, 178–180, 181–182; reformers' concern with, 231; skew toward financial returns in, 177–180. *See also* Race-conscious policies
Advanced degrees: income correlated with, 191–192; PhDs, 117, 147, 191, 329n22
Advocacy, 262, 358n30
Aerospace, 1, 81
Affirmative action, 83–88; *Bakke* case, 111–113; California campaigns against, 1; Clinton defends, 74; Connerly's proposal for ending, 98–99; counterrevolution against, 268; D'Souza's attack on, 69–70; economic aspects of attacks on, 269, 270; faculty and culture wars position on, 284; *Hopwood* cases, 101–106; language of civil rights movement used by opponents of, 84, 310n12; legacy admissions compared with, 178–179; meritocracy, 94–95, 97, 101–106; New Economy and attack on, 88–90; policy makers' attacks on, 26; Proposition 209, 84, 85, 87, 88, 317n10; public support for, 93–94, 313n4; quotas, 75, 77, 86, 94; relied on for even rudimentary integration, 115–116; Right uses to polarize, 239; shrinking educational resources, 104–105; standardized tests, 315n; university reformers, 236. *See also* Race-conscious policies
"Affluent society," 27, 34, 40
Affluent Society, The (Galbraith), 34

373

Keynesian growth economics, 7–8, 27, 36, 54, 82

Khalidi, Rashid, 356n20

Kimball, Roger, 55–56, 65, 304n34

King, Martin Luther, Jr.: affirmative action, 84, 85; Black power and white power, 32–33; Lyotard and, 46; Poor People's Campaign of, 34; power sharing advocated by, 77, 307n22; race consciousness of, 64; racial identity, 109

Kirp, David L., 223–225, 227, 233–234

Klein, Daniel B., 281, 282, 283, 284, 361nn21, 23, 24, 363n29, 365n39

Knowledge: advocacy contrasted with, 262, 358n30; disseminating seen as nonmarket activity, 68–69; epistemology, 45, 258–259; finance's relationship to, 126, 129, 138, 139; Foucault on subjugated, 296n22; high-tech network economy requires, 126; interpretive, 257–258, 260, 263; New Economy requires, 8, 9, 126; Pirsig's antidualist view of, 42; proprietary, 133, 135, 228; qualitative versus quantitative, 25; Stewart's classification of, 130–131; university-based, 259. See also Basic research; Cultural knowledge; Knowledge economy

Knowledge economy: becomes "winner-take-all," 5; college-educated majority to provide knowledge workers, 6, 28–29; Drucker on, 37–38; finance and knowledge workers, 128, 129; Galbraith on, 34–37; higher education seen as foundation of, 38–39; independent agency in, 6; knowledge entrepreneurs, 20; management structure of, 136–137; public acceptance of, 125; real challenge of, 138; Reich on, 37, 126; scientific research as model of knowledge worker, 139–140; seen as replacing industrial economy, 8–9; shareholder's revolt, 126–129; Toffler on, 37. See also Knowledge management (KM)

Knowledge management (KM), 129–141; culture and finance, 130, 135; culture wars, 138, 141; human capital converted to structural capital in, 130, 136–138; humanities graduates in, 134–135; star quadrant, 132–134; stratification of knowledge workers in, 130–132; unique knowledge as essential in, 132–133; universities and, 139–141

Krauthammer, Charles, 61

Kristol, Irving, 53–54

Kuhn, Thomas, 259

Kuklick, Bruce, 332n12

Kunstler, William, 53

Kymlicka, Will, 318n4

Labor: academic labor policies, 20; academic two-tiered system of, 142, 273–274; capitalist labor-management split, 137; decline in conditions for, 241; education as labor-intensive, 192, 273; finance and academic, 126; labor relations at high-tech companies, 137–138; Marx's labor theory of value, 36; New Economy, 89–90; NYU law school, 234; Pirsig on, 40; stratification of market for, 118. See also Unions; Working class

Lacan, Jacques, 156

Laclau, Ernesto, 156–157

Lasch, Christopher, 34, 99

Latinos: affirmative action controversy, 83, 86–87, 309n11; Arnold's view of politics and, 57; Chicano Studies protests University of California, 1–2; democratization of higher education in 1970s, 100–101; economic stratification of, 118; educational integration and population growth in, 118; higher education, 324n35; Hopwood cases, 102, 317n16; integration in Santa Barbara, 120–121, 326n49; "Mexican gentrification," 120; National Merit Scholarship Program, 316n; poverty rates among, 66; promise of golden-age California for, 90–91; reduced presence at University of California, 87, 90; student-loan debt for, 226; university faculties, 117

"Law and Economics" movement, 70

Lawrence Livermore National Laboratories, 243, 349n6

Law schools, 85, 87, 234, 270, 283, 346n15

Layoffs, 4, 24, 37, 81, 125–126, 146

Legacy admissions, 178–180, 181–182

Okies, 92
Oklahoma State University, 164
Olin Foundation, 282
OPEC oil embargo, 54
Open-book management, 166, 336n22
Optimization narrative, 44–46, 300n37
Orfield, Gary, 322n18
Orr, David, 331n8
Other America, The (Harrington), 34
Outsourcing, 9, 131, 132, 134, 192
Oxford Student Union, 253–254

Palmer, Scott R., 321n15, 322n19
Palo Alto Research Center (Xerox), 129
Participation rates, 66, 226, 304n39
Partnership benefits for gay couples, 241
Part-time faculty, 142, 143, 225, 231
Patents: Bayh-Dole legislation, 199–200,
   228; blockbuster, 206; new patent filings
   and invention disclosures, 1991–2005,
   200; returns only at top, 202–207;
   universities attempt to extract royalties
   from faculty discoveries, 127; University
   of California in generation of, 209;
   utility in basic research, 198. *See also*
   Licensing
Peace, 61
Peer review, 259–260, 262
Pell Grants, 176, 338n11
Peltason, Jack, 84
Penn State, *213,* 290, 361n24
Pennsylvania: Pennsylvania Select
   Committee on Academic Freedom in
   Higher Education, 290; University of
   Pennsylvania, 201, *213,* 229, 336n21,
   337n24
"Permatemps," 37, 234, 273
Personal agency, 39–42
Personal attention, 193–194
Peters, Thomas J., 330n33
Pharmaceutical companies, 223, 228–229,
   230
PhD degrees, 117, 147, 191, 329n22
Pickens, T. Boone, 164
Pink, Daniel, 126
"Pink collar" skills, 130
Pirsig, Robert, 40–42, 43, 44, 46, 267
Pluralism, 109–110, 145, 274, 319n5

Political correctness: backlash against racial
   equality and attacks on, 66–67; Cheney
   criticizes, 253; Chicano Studies protests
   at University of California, 1; equality
   seen as part of mindset of, 89, 312n25;
   invention of, 58–61, 302n20; *Newsweek*
   article on, 55, 59–60; race consciousness
   associated with, 64–65
Political crisis of 1960s and 1970s, 23–24
Political dissent, 29, 253
Political reform movements, meritocracy
   appealed to by, 95
Political science, 209
Politics: Arnold on, 57; conservatives on
   polarity of culture and, 58; crisis of 1960s
   and 1970s, 23–24; dimension of culture
   wars, *241;* dissent, 29, 253; middle class as
   emerging nonconservative bloc, 46;
   middle class choices regarding, 31–32;
   middle class favors expert over mass, 29;
   nonquantitative educational goods seen
   as political, 170; post-9/11 culture war
   victory in, *255;* seen as threat to academic
   freedom, 61–62; self-organization in, 33.
   See also Conservatives; Democratic Party;
   Liberalism; Political correctness;
   Republican Party
"Politics and Professional Advancement
   Among College Faculty" (Rothman,
   Lichter, and Nevitte), 281, 282, 283,
   361n22, 362nn25, 26
Poor People's Campaign, 34
Posner, Richard, 70
Post, Robert, 356n23
Postcapitalism, 37–38, 127, 137, 139–141
Postcolonial studies, 158
Postethnic America: Beyond Multiculturalism
   (Hollinger), 108–110
Postethnic model: Hollinger on, 108–110;
   and Supreme Court's affirmative action
   decisions, 110–111
Postindustrial economy: college degree seen
   as key to success in, 4, 8; college-educated
   majority to provide knowledge workers
   for, 6, 28–29; conformity as concern in, 7;
   information technology boom of 1990s,
   9. *See also* New Economy
Postmodernism, 43–47, 299n26